I0796140

AMERICA'S
BALLPARKS

LEVI'S LANDING
State Farm
365

BALLPARKS

A TRIP ACROSS THE COUNTRY TO VISIT BASEBALL'S PLAYING FIELDS, OLD AND NEW

Nancy J. Hajeski

4880 Lower Valley Road • Atglen, PA 19310

Library of Congress Control Number: 2025930180

Edited by Ian Robertson
Production by Kate North
Cover design by Jack Chappell
Type set in Player Pro Black/Player Pro/Chaparral Pro
ISBN: 978-0-7643-7012-0
Ebook: 978-1-5073-0612-3
Printed in India

Published by Schiffer Publishing, Ltd.
4880 Lower Valley Road
Atglen, PA 19310
Phone: (610) 593-1777; Fax: (610) 593-2002
Email: info@schifferbooks.com
Web: www.schifferbooks.com

CONTENTS

INTRODUCTION

"THESE HALLOWED GROUNDS"

BASEBALL IS AN INTRINSIC PART OF THE AMERICAN FABRIC *and quickly became so after its introduction in the mid-19th century. Within 40 years, the game had evolved into less of a sport and more of an obsession. Team loyalty was so ingrained in the fans that a team's success would elevate their spirits in ways that few other entertainments could. As such, the club's ballparks have often taken on mythic proportions, frequently regarded by the fans with the awe tourists reserve for the great cathedrals of Europe. The strong attachment people feel for their team's home is evidenced by their keen desire for artifacts like seats and signage whenever an aging field is demolished or refurbished.*

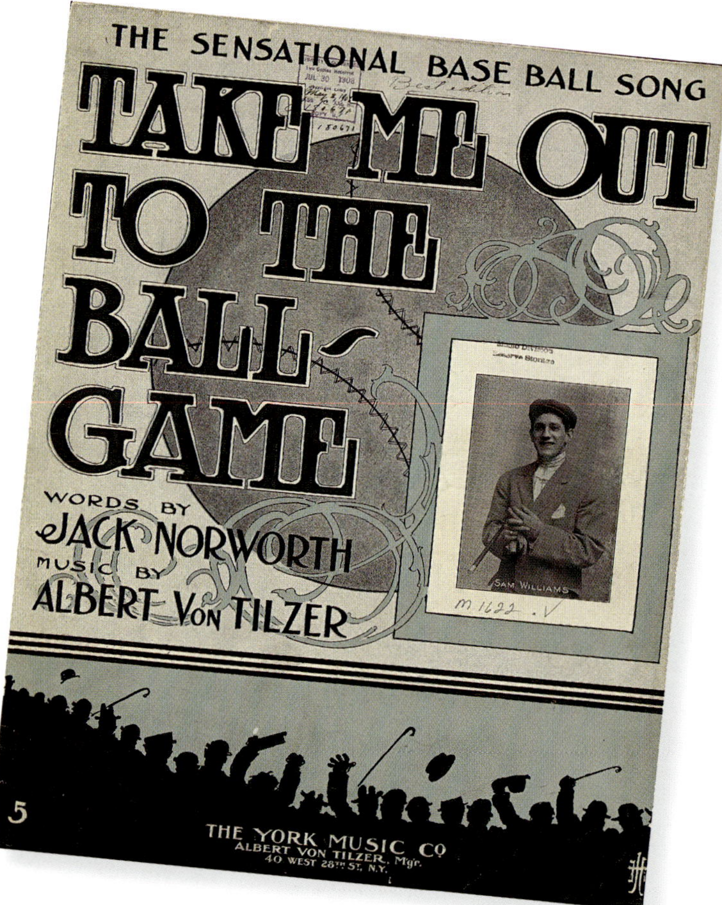

THE ORIGINS OF BASEBALL

For a sport referred to as America's "national pastime," it seems odd that the game's origins remain clouded—yet they do. The story of Abner Doubleday "inventing" the sport is no longer accepted as canon. What is known is that around 1835, a series of field games based on English sports like rounders, stoolball, and townball—that involved hitting a ball with a bat and running around the bases—began to gain in popularity. Because Doubleday became a Civil War general, perhaps invoking his name was an attempt to label the game as patriotic. At any rate, during the mid-1800s the sport was being enjoyed by a number of amateur clubs. In 1845, a prominent club called the New York Knickerbockers produced a set of rules created by founding member Alexander Cartwright. The "Knickerbocker Rules" included concepts like the diamond-shaped infield, foul lines, and three strikes making an out, critical elements that shaped the game as we know it today.

[ABOVE] Sheet music to "Take Me Out to the Ball Game," the 1908 Tin Pan Alley song by Jack Norworth and Albert Von Tilzer. This iconic ditty has become the unofficial anthem of North American baseball. It's traditionally played at ballparks as part of the seventh-inning stretch, and many fans lustily sing along, often replacing the words "home team" with their team's name.

[LEFT] Alexander Cartwright, dubbed the "father of modern baseball," crafted a set of rules for baseball that would evolve into the ones that govern today's game—a game Americans fully embraced as their favorite pastime. In 2022, Major League Baseball reported overall revenue of $10.32 billion, which corresponds to an average per-team revenue of $344 million.

[OPPOSITE PAGE] Dodger Stadium. Built in 1962, 50 years after the first MLB stadium—Boston's Fenway Park — this Los Angeles ballpark was the third-oldest stadium built for a Major League team that is still in operation.

“A baseball field must be the most beautiful thing in the world. It’s so honest and precise. And we play on it. Every star gets humbled. Every mediocre player has a great moment.”

—JIM LEFEBVRE, MLB PLAYER, COACH, AND MANAGER

Double play in a game between the 1886 New York Giants and the Boston Beaneaters at the original Polo Grounds in Upper Manhattan. As the popularity of the sport grew in North America, increasing numbers of dedicated ballparks were built. The word "field" or "park" was frequently attached to the names of early facilities, indicating a sort of bucolic informality. With the advent of pro baseball, the ballfield became part of a complex that included raised areas with fixed spectator seating, formal food services, and, perhaps most key, an enclosure that restricted access except to paying customers, similar to a fairgrounds.

INTO THE MODERN ERA

From these early roots a multibillion-dollar empire arose, with corporate naming rights now enriching the franchises, and some tickets prices reaching the upper decks. And yet, there is still a certain humility in baseball. One man stands with a bat; another faces him with a ball. It is simultaneously a coordinated team sport and an intense, focused cage match. Quality is showcased, fully on display, and possible humiliation is only a few pitches away. Nothing keeps an athlete humbler than the fear of losing that battle of wills. And few things feel better than a strikeout to a pitcher or a home run to a batter. This drama is played out countless times in any given game, and yet the tension in the stands never wanes; the expectations never flag.

Meanwhile, the stadium plays its role in this mock battle, providing clear sight lines, comfortable seating, and an ambiance of simmering excitement. Vendors carry tasty snacks right into the stands, crying out their wares like

MAJOR LEAGUE BALLPARKS, FROM OLDEST TO NEWEST

1912 Fenway Park (Boston Red Sox)
1914 Wrigley Field (Chicago Cubs)
1962 Dodger Stadium (Los Angeles Dodgers)
1966 Angel Stadium (Los Angeles Angels)
1966 Oakland-Alameda County Coliseum (Oakland Athletics)
1973 Kauffman Stadium (Kansas City Royals)
1989 Rogers Centre (Toronto Blue Jays)
1990 Tropicana Field (Tampa Bay Rays)
1991 Guaranteed Rate Field (Chicago White Sox)
1992 Oriole Park at Camden Yards (Baltimore Orioles)
1994 Progressive Field (Cleveland Guardians)
1995 Coors Field (Colorado Rockies)
1998 Chase Field (Arizona Diamondbacks)
1999 T-Mobile Park (Seattle Mariners)
2000 Comerica Park (Detroit Tigers)
2000 Minute Maid Park (Houston Astros)
2000 Oracle Park (San Francisco Giants)
2001 American Family Field (Milwaukee Brewers)
2001 PNC Park (Pittsburgh Pirates)
2003 Great American Ball Park (Cincinnati Reds)
2004 Citizens Bank Park (Philadelphia Phillies)
2004 Petco Park (San Diego Padres)
2006 Busch Stadium (St. Louis Cardinals)
2008 Nationals Park (Washington Nationals)
2009 Citi Field (New York Mets)
2009 Yankee Stadium (New York Yankees)
2010 Target Field (Minnesota Twins)
2012 loanDepot Park (Miami Marlins)
2017 Truist Park (Atlanta Braves)
2020 Globe Life Field (Texas Rangers)

pie makers in Olde London Town. Vocal fans of the home team sit amid raucous fans of the opposition, creating an atmosphere that can quickly become fraught—to the stifled amusement of fans of either persuasion seated nearby. Perhaps the sublime dichotomy of baseball is that for the most part, players act like gentlemen on the field, while their supporters behave like hooligans in the stands. But that's okay; friction is all part of the game . . . the hammer-blow contact of bat on ball, the thump of ball into glove, and the gritty, longitudinal slide of a player into home plate just seconds before being tagged out.

CASHLESS STADIUMS

Ballparks are always eager to incorporate new trends, and one of the most recent ones is improving the fans' experience by going "cashless." The speed and ease of making payments with this system, the safety of transacting, the reduction of fraud and theft, and the shorter concession lines are all big pluses. There is also evidence that a cashless system increases revenue for vendors—customers at cashless stadiums will spend up to 25 percent more than those dealing with cash transactions.

In January 2019, the first major North American sports team announced that its home stadium was going cashless—the MLB Tampa Bay Rays, who play at Tropicana Field. Of the 30 Major League teams, 27 were cashless as of 2022. The other three teams—the Blue Jays, Guardians, and Marlins—still accepted cash, but all strongly encourage cashless transactions.

Ball clubs across the MLB inspire fierce devotion from hometown spectators, and that loyalty extends to the fields the teams play on, with moves or changes often met with resistance. Here the "Bleacher Bums," faithful fans of the Chicago Cubs, occupy all the seats beyond the outfield wall in Wrigley Field. Although updated and renovated over the years, Wrigley, which opened in 1914, is the second-oldest ballpark in the Majors.

BASEBALL LINGO

ACE A baseball team's best and most consistent starting pitcher is the team's "ace."

AROUND THE HORN A play travels "around the horn" when the ball is hit to the third baseman, who then throws to second base for one out, and the ball is then thrown to first base for a second out.

BULLPEN The area in a ballpark where pitchers warm up during a game. Also refers to the relief pitchers on a team.

CAN OF CORN An easy catch made for an out.

CUTTER A fastball thrown with a slight curve, arriving at home plate away from the side of the plate from which it is thrown.

DINGER Home run.

DISH Home plate.

DUCKS ON THE POND When there are at least two runners on base, it is referred to as having "ducks on the pond."

5.5 HOLE This is the area of the infield between the third baseman and the shortstop.

FOUR BAGGER Another name for a home run.

FUNGO The long, narrow bat used to hit practice fly balls and grounders during warm-ups is known as a "fungo" bat.

HIT AND RUN This play happens when the batter is asked to swing at the pitch to try to hit the ball, while the base runner simultaneously attempts to steal a base.

HOT CORNER A term used when referring to third base.

KNUCKLER A pitch that is thrown by holding the baseball with the knuckles (or fingertips), causing the ball to move slowly and unpredictably.

PEPPER A warm-up game in which an infielder quickly tosses a ball to a batter at close range and the batter hits it back to the infielder.

PICKLE A play in which a base runner is trapped between bases and fielders are tossing the ball back and forth as the runner tries to reach either base safely.

SHOESTRING CATCH When a fielder makes a running catch just above his shoe tops.

SNOWCONE A catch made by a fielder when the ball is caught and is still showing at the top of the web of the fielder's glove.

SOUTHPAW Another name for a left-handed pitcher.

SQUEEZE PLAY This takes place when the runner on third base tries to score as the pitch is delivered, and the batter is expected to bunt.

WHEELHOUSE A hitter's power zone.

YARD This term refers to both a ballpark and a home run.

Citi Field • New York Mets

Citizens Bank Park • Philadelphia Phillies

Fenway Park • Boston Red Sox

loanDepot Park • Miami Marlins

Nationals Park • Washington Nationals

Oriole Park at Camden Yards • Baltimore Orioles

EAST DIVISION

NATIONAL LEAGUE EAST • Atlanta Braves • Miami Marlins • New York Mets • Philadelphia Phillies • Washington Nationals

AMERICAN LEAGUE EAST • Baltimore Orioles • Boston Red Sox • New York Yankees • Tampa Bay Rays • Toronto Blue Jays

Starting in 1969 the National and American Leagues were divided into East and West Divisions. A Central Division was then added to each league in 1994. This third division was created after the creation of expansion teams made two divisions unwieldy, but it also meant team owners could extend the lucrative playoff season. Prior to the divisions, the postseason consisted only of the World Series. Now each League Division Series would provide a champion that would then compete in the League Championship Series. The two ultimate winners would then meet in the World Series. Wild card berths were added in 1994 for the top non-division winners, who could potentially end up in the LDS.

Throughout the season, fans eagerly watch the American League East standings to see where the highly competitive New York Yankees and the Boston Red Sox place. Both teams have a long history of reaching the top of the division, and thus making it into the postseason, but the Tampa Bay Rays have challenged them in recent years. The National League East, meanwhile, keeps fans guessing, and champions can show up unexpectedly.

Rogers Centre • Toronto Blue Jays

Tropicana Field • Tampa Bay Rays

Truist Park • Atlanta Braves

Yankee Stadium • New York Yankees

HOME OF THE NEW YORK METS

NATIONAL LEAGUE (1962–PRESENT)

ONE OF BASEBALL'S FIRST EXPANSION TEAMS, *the New York Mets, was founded in 1962 to replace the city's two departed NL teams—the Brooklyn Dodgers and New York Giants. (Their team colors actually combined Dodgers' blue and Giants' orange.) After two seasons at the Polo Grounds, the Mets moved to their new home park, Shea Stadium in Queens. In 2009, replacement ballpark Citi Field arose on the site beside Shea, becoming the third home of the Amazin's.*

The Mets started out in New York a bit behind the eight-ball—upstarts in the fabled land of the Yankees, the Dodgers, and the Giants, teams all massively bolstered by fan support. But there was also a lot of public resentment against the latter two ball clubs for deserting the Big Apple and heading to California. Dodgers fans were particularly steamed.

At first it seemed as if the Mets could hardly fill the cleats of their predecessors. During their inaugural season, the team posted a record of 40–120, the worst regular-season record since MLB changed to a 162-game schedule. Yet, surprisingly, there turned out to be something endearing about the Mets, with their fumbling plays and inability to score in the early days. Before long they too had a healthy fan base. A World Series win in 1969—when the "Miracle Mets" trounced the Baltimore Orioles in one of the biggest upsets in baseball history—helped cement their place alongside the juggernaut Yankees.

By the 1990s, the Mets had begun looking for a new ballpark. Shea Stadium, for all its sleek, Tomorrowland promise, had been built as a multipurpose sports venue. Although it had been retrofitted as a baseball-only stadium after the departure of the football Jets for

Giants Stadium in New Jersey, it remained a problematic space. Fan seating was farther away from the action on the field than in any other MLB park. The team even went so far in 1998 as to unveil a preliminary model of a new ballpark; it featured a retractable roof and a movable grass field. The latter feature would allow the venue to host large events like conventions, and sports like college basketball. Possible locations the team considered included Mitchel Field or Belmont Park in Nassau County on Long Island, Sunnyside Yard in Queens, or the West Side Yard in Manhattan.

In December 2001, just before leaving office, New York mayor Rudy Giuliani announced the city had reached "tentative" agreements with the Mets and Yankees to help them fund new stadiums. Of the estimated costs of $1.6 billion, city and state taxpayers would pony up half the tab. The next mayor, Michael Bloomberg, used an escape clause to back out of both deals. He was leery of allocating such a large sum of taxpayer money for sports facilities, considering them a poor investment and labeling Giuliani's plan "corporate welfare."

Plans for a Mets field on Manhattan's West Side began to take shape as part of the city's bid for the 2012 Summer Olympics. When the Olympic prospect fell through, so did the West Side stadium, but plans for Shea's replacement continued to move forward. Finally, in 2006, the ball club and the city announced their plans to build a new stadium in Flushing at a cost of $610 million, with the Mets' portion coming to $420 million (the actual cost of construction was closer to $900 million). To sweeten the deal, Citigroup Inc. agreed to pay $20 million per year for 40 years for the naming rights of the stadium.

The Mets themselves own the stadium through a subsidiary called Queens Ballpark Company. Ultimately, Citi Field has been a moneymaker for the franchise: in 2022, it earned a record-breaking $244.3 million in revenue and a net income of $127 million, another record.

DESIGN AND ARCHITECTURE

The new venue was designed by Populous Holdings, Inc., a global architectural and design practice that specializes in sports facilities, arenas, and convention centers. The interior was heavily influenced by the Pittsburgh Pirates' PNC Park, a favorite ball field of then

BALLPARK STATS

ADDRESS
41 Seaver Way, Flushing, Queens, NY 11368

OWNER/OPERATOR
New York Mets

ARCHITECT
Populous (formerly HOK Sport)

CAPACITY
41,922

RECORD BASEBALL ATTENDANCE
45,186 on 7/16/2013 (2013 All-Star Game)

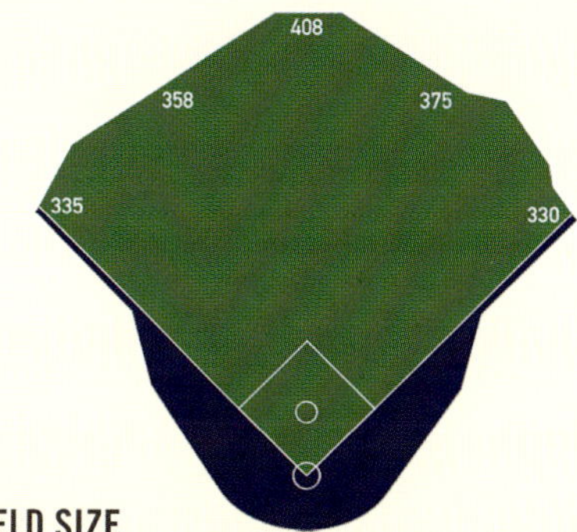

FIELD SIZE

Left field line 335 feet (102 m)
Left center 358 feet (109 m)
Deep left center 385 feet (117 m)
Center field 408 feet (124 m)
Deep right center 398 feet (121 m)
Right center 375 feet (114 m)
Right field line 330 feet (101 m)
Backstop 46–48 feet (14.0–14.6 m)

SURFACE
Kentucky bluegrass

TEAM MASCOT
Mr. Met

Mets owner Jeff Wilpon. There are also elements borrowed from Great American Ball Park, Coors Field, and Citizens Bank Park. The new stadium also contained unique orange foul poles (as opposed to traditional yellow), a concept carried over from Shea Stadium.

As an homage to New York City's more than 2,000 bridges, the stadium featured an overarching bridge motif, which also relates to the team logo, offering a symbolic bridge between the Mets and New York's former NL teams. There is even a pedestrian bridge in the outfield, Shea Bridge, that is modeled after the Hell Gate Bridge, a railroad bridge that connects Queens with the Bronx.

CRITICAL REACTIONS

Reviews of the new stadium were generally positive. Ballparks.com labeled it "perfect" and singled out the Jackie Robinson Rotunda, food critics raved over the numerous and varied dining options at the concessions, and *Business Insider* praised the structure's aesthetics, naming it one of America's top ten sports venues.

CITI FIELD FIRSTS

FIRST MLB GAME: 4/13/2009, San Diego Padres over Mets, 6–5

FIRST HOME RUN: 4/13/2009, Jody Gerut (San Diego Padres)

FIRST NO-HITTER: 6/1/2012, Johan Santana vs. St. Louis Cardinals

FIRST ALL-STAR GAME: 7/16/2013, AL over NL, 3–0

FIRST PLAYOFF GAME: 10/12/2015, Mets over LA Dodgers, 13–7

FIRST WORLD SERIES GAME: 10/30/2015, Mets over Kansas City Royals, 9–3 in Game 3

Yet, the stadium inevitably had its critics, especially among Mets fans. They complained about obstructed views and resented the omnipresent reminders of the Brooklyn Dodgers' legacy, at the cost of ignoring the Mets' nearly 50-year history. Owner Fred Wilpon, a Brooklyn native, soon conceded that his childhood love of the departed "Bums"—who had left for the West Coast in 1957—had caused him to overdo the hero worship. "All the Dodger stuff—that was an error of judgment on my part," he admitted. The team compensated by installing photographic images of famous Mets players and historic events on both the Field and Promenade levels. A hall of fame and museum that acknowledged the current team's achievements was also added before the 2010 season, and in 2012 the outfield wall was changed from black to a more fitting Mets blue.

Among the players, batters complained that Citi Field's large dimensions created a nearly utopian pitcher's park—and, as a result, home runs in the stadium were among the rarest in the Major Leagues. But by the 2012 season, general manager Sandy Alderson had changed the field's dimensions, making it less punitive to hitters.

FEATURES AND AMENITIES

Fans will find plenty to occupy them at the stadium before games or during the inning breaks.

JACKIE ROBINSON ROTUNDA Located at the front entrance of Citi Field and named after the Brooklyn Dodgers' legendary outfielder, the Jackie Robinson Rotunda honors both the baseball career and trailblazing life accomplishments of the first Black player in Major

Citi Field, constructed of a mixture of brick, limestone, granite, and cast stone, gives off a historical vibe but still offers fans all the modern-day amenities.

An aerial view of the stadium shows its proximity to Flushing Bay.

League Baseball. Engraved into its 160-foot-diameter (49 m) floor and etched into the archways are words and scaled-up images that defined Robinson's nine values: Courage, Excellence, Persistence, Justice, Teamwork, Commitment, Citizenship, Determination, and Integrity. The formal dedication took place during MLB's celebration of Jackie Robinson Day—April 15, 2009.

METS HALL OF FAME & MUSEUM The Mets Hall of Fame & Museum, which opened April 5, 2010, is adjacent to the Jackie Robinson Rotunda. It includes plaques honoring the inductees of the Mets Hall of Fame, the team's World Series trophies from 1969 and 1986, and artifacts on loan from noted collectors, former players, and the National Baseball Hall of Fame and Museum. There are autographed memorabilia, original scouting reports on players such as Darryl Strawberry, and handwritten notes from the team's first manager, Casey Stengel. Fans can enjoy interactive touchscreens, television screens, and timelines that guide them through the franchise's colorful history.

HOME RUN APPLE A favored tradition carried over from Shea Stadium is the Home Run Apple. When a Mets player hits a home run, a giant apple with a Mets logo lights up and rises from its housing in center field. This new apple is more than four times the size of the previous one, which is now outside the park in Mets Plaza. Beside the apple is a statue of Mets Hall of Fame pitcher Tom Seaver. Created by sculptor William Behrends, it was unveiled on April 15, 2022, during the season home opener.

METS ACHIEVEMENTS

WORLD SERIES CHAMPIONSHIPS: 2 (1969, 1986)

NL PENNANTS: 5 (1969, 1973, 1986, 2000, 2015)

NL EAST DIVISION TITLES: 6 (1969, 1973, 1986, 1988, 2006, 2015)

WILD CARD BERTHS: 4 (1999, 2000, 2016, 2022)

PLAYOFF APPEARANCES: 10 (1969, 1973, 1986, 1988, 1999, 2000, 2006, 2015, 2016, 2022)

WORST SEASON RECORD: 1962, 40–120 (.250)

BEST SEASON RECORD: 1986, 108–54 (.667)

With soaring archways and an elegant terrazzo floor, the Jackie Robinson Rotunda is a fitting tribute to one of the greatest trailblazers in baseball history.

[LEFT] Rising above the brick-and-concrete exterior of the left-field entrance are photos of illustrious Mets alumni. Farther down the concourse are banners of famous players.

[BELOW] At the start of 2022 season, Citi Field unveiled its statue of Mets Hall of Fame pitcher Tom Seaver. It stands beside the Home Run Apple outside the stadium and shows Seaver is his signature drop-and-drive delivery stance and is two times life-size to scale.

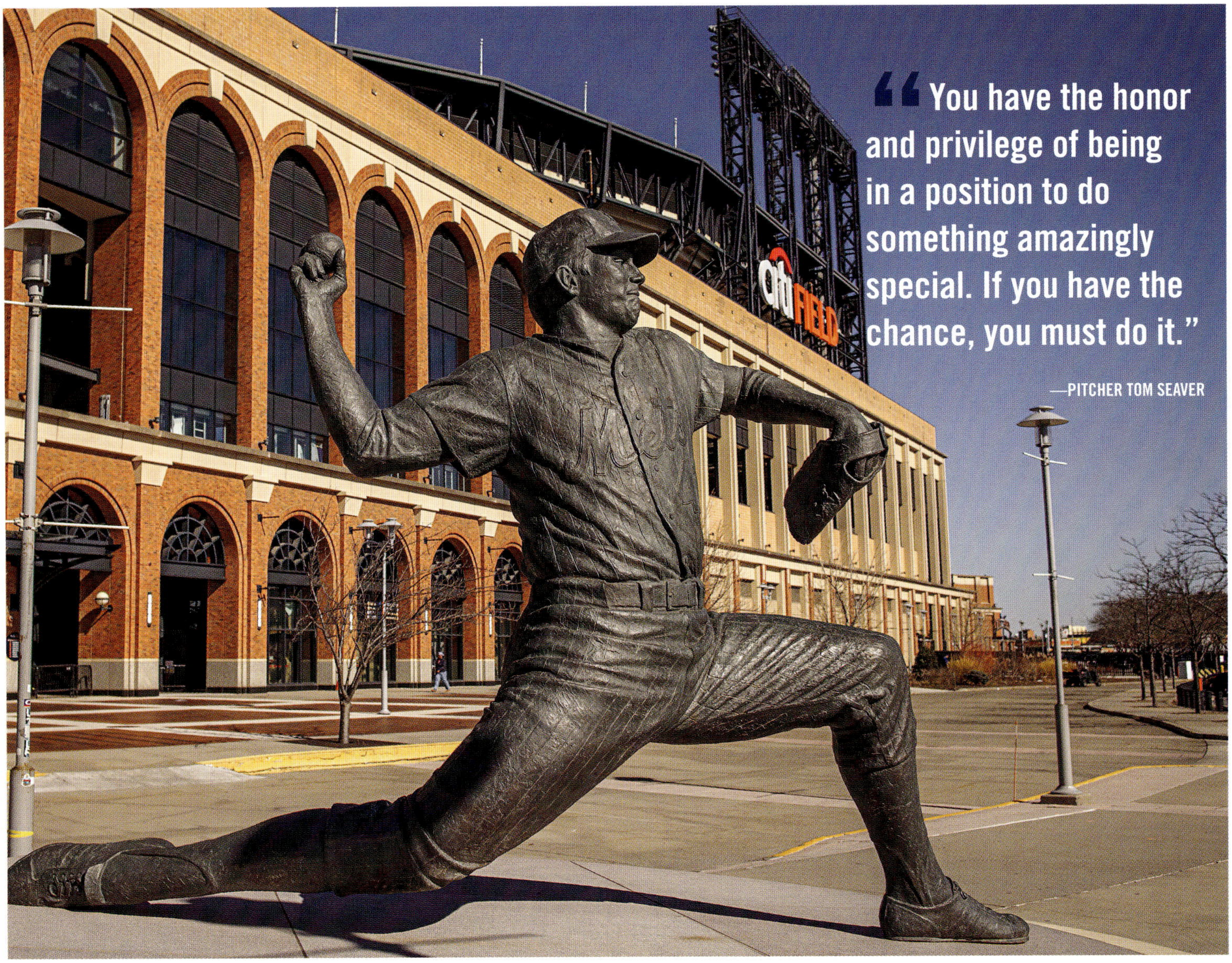

> **"You have the honor and privilege of being in a position to do something amazingly special. If you have the chance, you must do it."**
>
> —PITCHER TOM SEAVER

Shea Stadium's Home Run Apple now sits outside Citi Field. It is adorned with the Mets' familiar logo, which is full of symbolism: At left is a church spire, representing Brooklyn, the "borough of churches"; next is Williamsburg Savings Bank, Brooklyn's tallest building; farther to the right are the Woolworth Building, the Empire State Building, and the United Nations, all in Manhattan. The bridge in the foreground symbolizes that the Mets are a "bridge" to New York's National League teams of the past.

SEATING CHART

FANFEST AREA Behind the center field scoreboard lies the FanFest area. This expanded family entertainment area includes a miniature wiffleball field replica of Citi Field called Mr. Met's Kiddie Field, a batting cage, a dunk tank, video game kiosks, and other attractions.

FOOD AND DRINK The ballpark also offers a wide range of eateries, with restaurants and clubs available on every level. Sit-down dining options include the Clover Home Plate Club, Pat LaFrieda's Chop House, and Caesars Sportsbook at the Metropolitan Grille. The Taste of the City food court is behind center field and features the Union Square Hospitality Group, while the World's Fare Market is in right field. For snacks, food, and drinks on the go, various concessions sell burgers, cheesesteaks, hot dogs, fries, shakes, barbecue, pulled pork, pizza, porchetta sandwiches, deli sandwiches, lobster rolls, kosher food, empanadas, arancini balls, Mexican dishes, sushi, Korean and Chinese cuisine, and gluten-free options. Visitors can also enjoy wine, beer, hard lemonade, and cocktails.

The team's official mascot, baseball-headed Mr. Met, was first introduced in 1963 as a cartoon drawing in the programs. A year later, with the Mets now in Shea Stadium, a live, costumed version appeared on the field. The team later brought in his female counterpart, formerly Lady Met, then known as Mrs. Met. Mr. Met fell out of favor in the late 1970s but was revived in 1994, to fan acclaim. Mr. Met is now in the Mascot Hall of Fame, and in 2012 *Forbes* magazine voted him "the number one mascot in all of sports."

OTHER HOMES OF THE METS

SHEA STADIUM

1964–2008

Mets fans remember Shea Stadium as a gleaming symbol of the future that now lay ahead for New York baseball . . . they recall it fondly as a center of stellar entertainment . . . and, less fondly, as one of the noisiest sports venues in America due to the steady stream of jets taking off from nearby LaGuardia Airport. Once completed, it quickly became a sort of beau ideal of what a stadium should be, and it set the tone for designers for the next few decades.

"Nobody has ever called Shea Stadium a cathedral. In style, it was more like the old warehouse or outdated movie theater that Korean worshippers have transformed into a church in the borough of Queens. Not a cathedral—but a place where people go to be fulfilled, nonetheless."

— *NEW YORK TIMES* SPORTS COLUMNIST GEORGE VECSEY

The rosters for the Mets and Yankees are introduced before the start of Game 3 at Shea Stadium. Dubbed the "Subway Series," the 2000 World Series between the New York teams saw the Yankees win four games, celebrating their 26th championship in front of Mets fans at Shea.

A new stadium that would be located in Flushing, Queens, was originally offered to the Brooklyn Dodgers in the mid-1950s to replace aging Ebbets Field, but owner Walter O'Malley balked at the out-of-borough location . . . and then infuriatingly moved the beloved team to Los Angeles. Ditto the New York Giants, who were offered the same site and also headed west to San Francisco. Mayor Robert Wagner established a committee to bring a National League franchise back to New York, a group headed by prominent lawyer William A. Shea. The powerful and effective Shea tried to entice other teams to move to the Big Apple, including the Cincinnati Reds, Pittsburgh Pirates, and Philadelphia Phillies. With expansion not an option, Shea actually started a third league, the Continental League. Then, when his ally, Branch Rickey—the legendary baseball innovator—began chatting up congressmen in Washington about an antitrust action, MLB agreed to allow expansion teams. But the National League warned Shea, New York needed a new ballpark.

"At Shea Stadium, I saw the top of the mountain."

—JOHN LENNON

MAKING MUSIC AT SHEA

The stadium gained world renown as the venue for a 1965 outdoor concert by the Beatles, the British supergroup responsible for the worldwide Beatlemania that would soon spearhead the upcoming "British Invasion." In spite of the constant and deafening screaming of the 60,000 fans drowning out their music, the Fab Four gamely put on a terrific show, later released on film. Master songsmith Billy Joel was the final artist to perform at legendary Shea Stadium—performing for 110,000 people at the historic The Last Play at Shea on July 16 and 18, 2008. The two shows sold out in a record-breaking 45 minutes.

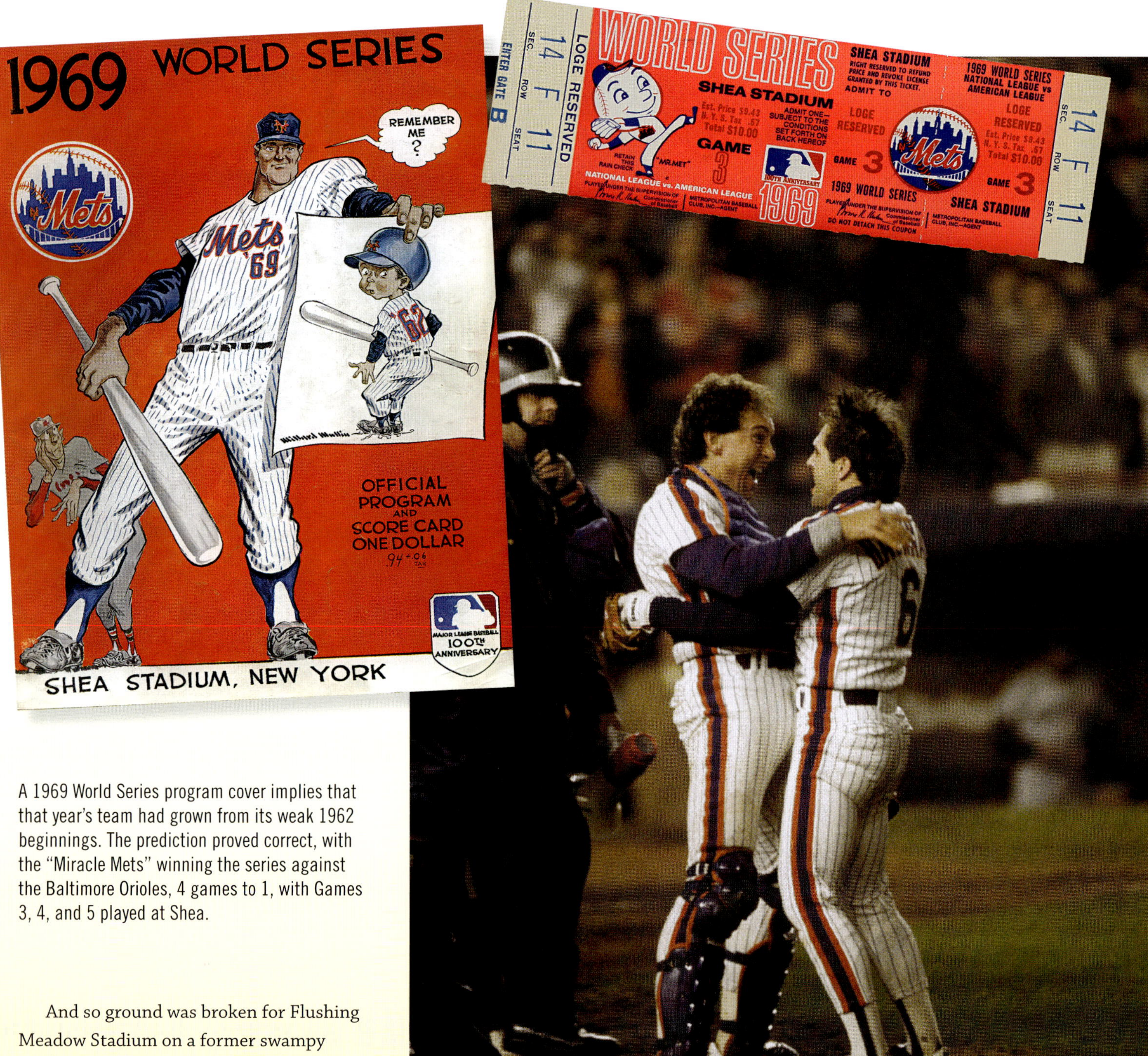

A 1969 World Series program cover implies that that year's team had grown from its weak 1962 beginnings. The prediction proved correct, with the "Miracle Mets" winning the series against the Baltimore Orioles, 4 games to 1, with Games 3, 4, and 5 played at Shea.

Gary Carter and Wally Backman at Shea Stadium, celebrating the Mets' 1986 World Series victory. They beat the Boston Red Sox to win their second championship in the franchise's history.

And so ground was broken for Flushing Meadow Stadium on a former swampy marshland that was now a stable landfill. Still, some critics dubbed it the "Valley of the Ashes." This construction zone lay next to the site of the 1939 World's Fair, "Dawn of a New Day," and around the time Shea was being designed, another world's fair, "Peace Through Understanding," was being planned to open there in 1964.

The final design was for a partially open ballpark—as opposed to a circular coliseum—with soaring switchback ramps, five tiers, innovative escalators speeding fans to their seats, and effective mercury vapor lighting. On the structure's exterior, colorful decorative panels formed an airy montage of Mets blue and orange. As the home of both the baseball Mets and the football Jets, the park was able to convert from a football gridiron to a baseball diamond by two motor-operated stands. Also, as a nod to the Jets, every seat was directed at the center of the field. The new stadium, one of the largest in baseball, was also highly accessible at most times of day—easily reachable by car, bus, or subway.

SHEA OPENS WITH A BANG

After two seasons at Manhattan's Polo Grounds, the Mets played their first game at Shea Stadium on April 17, 1964, with William Shea throwing out the first pitch. The Mets ended up losing to the Pittsburgh Pirates, whose Willie Stargell scored the first run in the new stadium, a solo homer to right field to lead off the second inning. (Shea's scoreboard, like Citi Field's, was inaugurated by a home run.) Beyond some seats being replaced, few changes occurred to the venue over the years. Just before the 1987 season, large blue panels with neon images of baseball players were installed, and then 50 club suites were added to the press level. The scoreboard was updated from 86 feet (36 m) to 175 feet (53 m) in 1988.

The New York Yankees even played at Shea Stadium from 1974 to 1975 while Yankee Stadium underwent renovations. Other tenants included the NFL New York Jets from 1964 to 1983, when they moved across the Hudson to Giants Stadium, and the NFL New York Giants in 1975. Gaining the stadium another place in history, during the dark days following the attacks on the World Trade Center on September 11, 2001, Shea was used as a relief center.

Once plans for Citi Field were underway, Shea—the "once and future" stadium—was no longer needed. On September 28, 2008, the Mets played their final regular season game there against the Florida Marlins. At the close of the season, Shea fell under the wrecking ball. Its Home Run Apple and orange foul poles are now part of the Citi Field tradition. The former site is currently used for parking at the new stadium.

[ABOVE] Prior to the 1988 season, as part of its retro-fitting as a baseball-only venue, Shea's exterior was painted Mets blue, and neon silhouettes of baseball players were added to the windscreens.

[BELOW] A doomed Shea Stadium was dismantled in 2009.

2004–PRESENT

CITIZENS BANK PARK

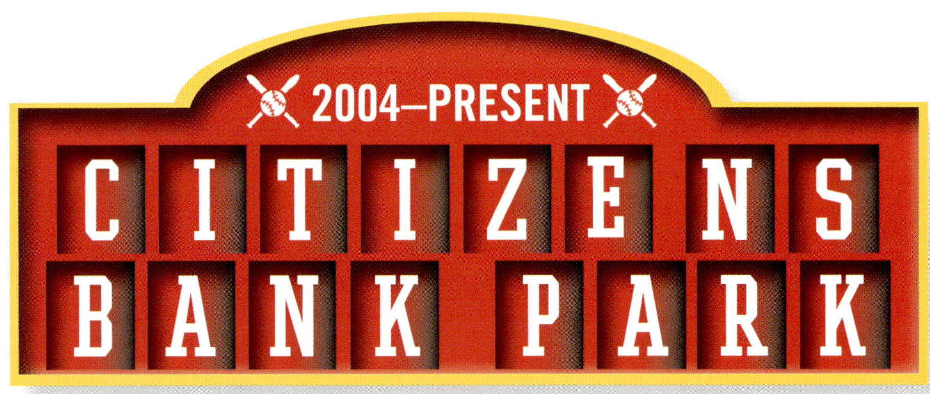

HOME OF THE PHILADELPHIA PHILLIES

NATIONAL LEAGUE (1883–PRESENT)

THE PHILADELPHIA PHILLIES *were formed in 1883 and originally played in three other stadiums before moving to Citizens Bank Park in April 2004. The 43,500-seat stadium offers fans lush natural grass and a stunning view of the Philadelphia skyline. In addition to memorable baseball, the park offers an in-stadium entertainment complex named in honor of Phillies' great Richie Ashburn and a Memory Lane of Phillies lore, along with batting and throwing games. The venue regularly earns a place in lists of Best Ballpark Eats.*

Truth be told, in spite of their occasional moments of glory or triumph, the Phillies have a patchy record in the Majors. The first American sports franchise to amass more than 10,000 loses, they hold the world record for the most losses by any single team in professional sports. Still, due to their long history, they are also only one of nine teams to have won more than 10,000 games. Their Hall of Fame third baseman, Mike Schmidt, is considered by many the Phillies' greatest player of all time. And, like other teams that

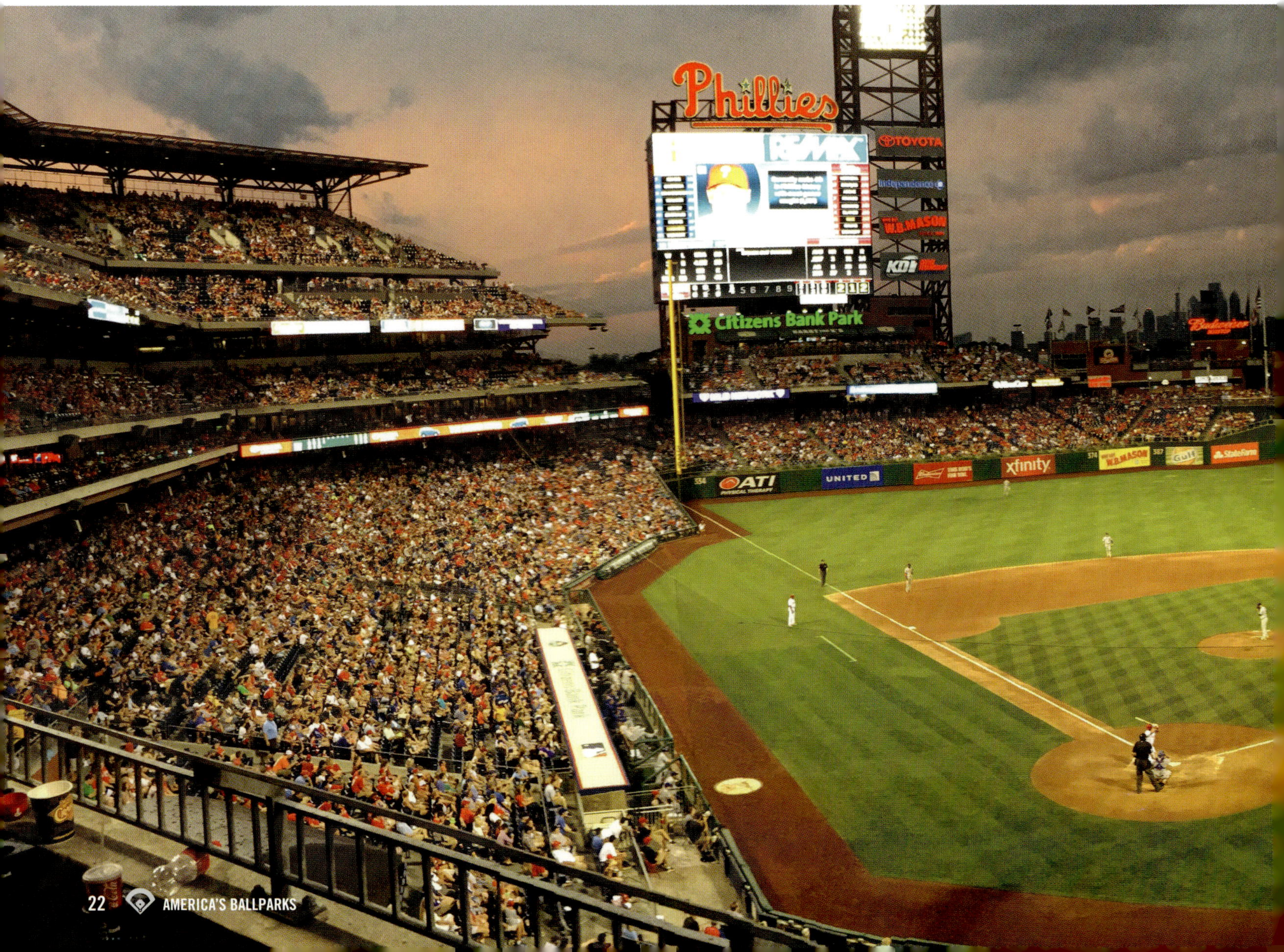

sometimes stumble their way through a season, their fans cannot be faulted for loyalty. The adjective "rabid" is often invoked.

The Phillies had already outgrown four parks when, in 1999, they joined the Philadelphia Eagles and their western Pennsylvania counterparts the Pittsburgh Pirates and the Pittsburgh Steelers with requests to replace their two aging stadiums—Veterans Field and Three Rivers Stadium, respectively. This necessity was brought home to the Phillies teams when a railing collapsed in Veterans' Stadium during the 1998 Army-Navy game, injuring eight cadets. The Pirates even threatened to leave the state altogether. The Pennsylvania legislature ended up approving a basic funding package for four new stadiums for the Steelers, Pirates, Eagles, and Phillies in 1998. In Pittsburgh, with architectural plans already in place, the city and county quickly began construction on two new venues, but talks continued to drag on in Philadelphia.

The Eagles finally agreed to a location at the site of an abandoned food warehouse, just southeast of "the Vet" in the South Philadelphia Sports Complex. Called Lincoln Financial Field, it saw its first football game in August 2003. Many Phillies fans and local businesses desired a downtown ballpark for their beloved team, but when that proved problematic, management settled on the site of another food warehouse beside Lincoln Field. The new stadium, Citizens Bank Park, was officially completed on August 12, 2003, and opened in April 2004. (The Phillies organization had sold the naming rights to Citizens Bank for $95 million over 25 years.) In terms of transportation, deliveries, and other logistics, it certainly made sense to locate the city's major teams in a central location, but many Phillies advocates—players, staff members, and fans—still express regret at the lack of a Center City ballpark.

BALLPARK STATS

ADDRESS
1 Citizens Bank Way, Philadelphia, PA 19148

OWNER
City of Philadelphia

OPERATOR
Global Spectrum

DESIGNER/CHIEF ARCHITECT
EwingCole's Stanley Cole

CAPACITY
42,901

RECORD BASEBALL ATTENDANCE
46,575 on 10/2/2011 (2011 NLDS vs. St. Louis Cardinals)

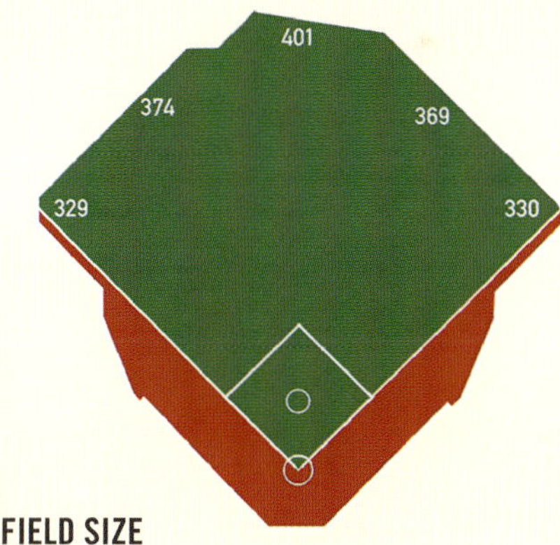

FIELD SIZE

Left field foul pole 329 feet (100 m)

Left field power alley 374 feet (114 m)

The "Angle" (left of CF to LCF) 409 feet (125 m) – 381 feet (116 m) – 387 feet (118 m)

Center field, straightaway 401 feet (122 m)

Right field power alley 369 feet (112 m)

Right field foul pole 330 feet (101 m)

SURFACE
Kentucky bluegrass

TEAM MASCOT
Phillie Phanatic

DESIGN AND CONSTRUCTION

The Phillies new home was designed to incorporate the best features of America's great prewar ballparks along with providing up-to-date amenities and the latest technological advances in sports entertainment. It was also intended to create a relatively intimate feel, similar to the beloved Connie Mack Stadium, last used by the Phillies in 1970. According to its architects, EwingCole, "The design, inspired by Philadelphia's rich tradition of architecture and baseball, transforms an industrial site into an inviting streetscape."

The exterior of the structure, meant to blend in with an adjoining neighborhood of mainly brick homes, was composed primarily of multiple shades of red brick, precast concrete, and granite, all complemented by a green roof with a copper patina finish. The finished park successfully combined the aesthetic of Philadelphia's traditional sports architecture with a modern, 21st-century sensibility.

Public response to the new park was positive, if not overwhelming. Opinions like "a fine ballpark" and "a nice stadium overall" found their way into print. Alas, the stadium's rather bleak location—"sitting in a sea of asphalt"—made critics scowl; meanwhile, many players appreciated that it was a hitter-friendly park. Most people heartily agreed that the venue had the best, most fan-friendly concourse in MLB, starting with the temptations of Ashburn Alley, chockfull of local eateries, historical mementos, and kids' gaming areas. In fact, the venue prides itself on being one of the most kid-friendly ballparks in America.

> **"I think the ballpark is a big part of why we're drawing the fans we are, and clearly we've had on-field success since we've been in the ballpark . . . we always thought that if we could get into a baseball-only facility our whole picture would change, and the reality has borne that out."**
>
> —DAVID MONTGOMERY, CHAIRMAN, PHILADELPHIA PHILLIES, CITIZENS BANK PARK

The Populous design for Citizens Bank Park features 97,000 square feet (9,012 m^2) of architectural precast panels, embedded with more than 475,000 bricks.

An overhead shot of Citizens Bank Park, which is in the city's South Philadelphia Sports Complex, home to Philly's four major sports franchises.

FEATURES AND AMENITIES

Citizen's Bank Park is no slacker when it comes to keeping fans entertained and well fed.

ASHBURN ALLEY Located behind center field, this food-and-entertainment concourse is named after Phillies Hall of Fame center fielder Richie Ashburn. It honors the man who played for the city from 1948 to 1959 and was a broadcaster for the team from 1963 until his death in 1997 . . . and whose name many fans wanted on the stadium itself. The welcoming walkway features restaurants, games, artifacts from Phillies' history, a memorabilia shop, and a large bronze statue of Ashburn directly behind center field, as well as the Stars and Stripes, the flags of the Commonwealth of Pennsylvania and the City of Philadelphia, a POW/MIA flag, and flags from Phillies championships.

ALL-STAR WALK The All-Star Walk runs the length of Ashburn Alley. Here, granite markers pay tribute to Phillies players who have appeared in the MLB All-Star Game since its inception in 1933.

A street sign directs stadiumgoers to Ashburn Alley. It gets its name from a patch of grass that bordered the third base line at Shibe Park, where Richie Ashburn was known to lay down bunts that were somehow called fair. Today, the name refers to the ballpark's food-and-entertainment concourse.

BILEVEL BULLPENS Located in right-center field, the exposed bilevel bullpens allow the fans to get very close to the players, especially the opposing team seated on the upper level. Fans are allowed to heckle players but must keep their comments clean.

MEMORY LANE AND TOYOTA WALL OF FAME Located behind the brick batting eye in center field, Memory Lane includes an illustrated history of baseball in Philadelphia, while the Toyota Wall of Fame in Left Field Plaza commemorates those who contributed to the franchise's history. It was into this area that Ryan Howard hit the park's longest home run, 505 feet (154 m), against Aaron Harang of the Reds on June 27, 2007.

ROOFTOP BLEACHERS This seating area takes its design cues from the 1920s and 1930s stands outside Shibe Park. Located in center field underneath the Liberty Bell, these bleachers are similar to the seating outside Chicago's Wrigley Field.

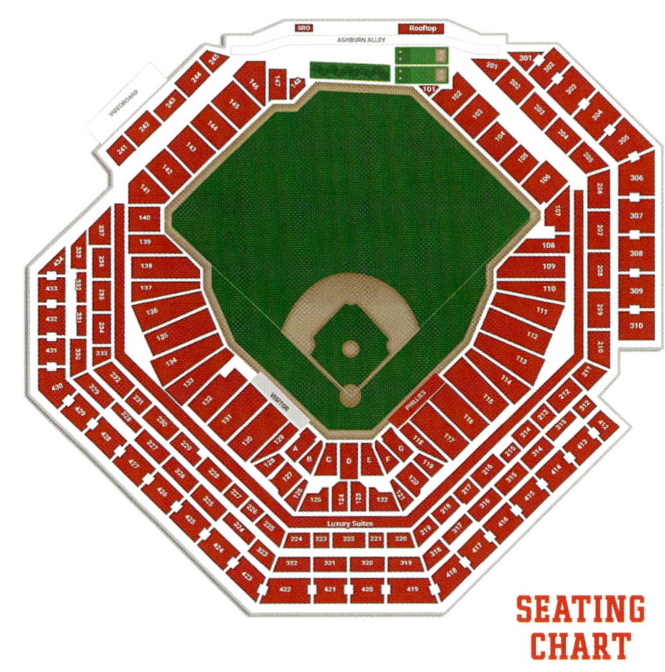

SEATING CHART

PHILLIES ACHIEVEMENTS

WORLD SERIES CHAMPIONSHIPS: 2 (1980, 2008)

NL PENNANTS: 8 (1915, 1950, 1980, 1983, 1993, 2008, 2009, 2022)

NL EAST DIVISION TITLES: 10 (1976, 1978, 1980, 1983, 1993, 2007, 2008, 2009, 2010, 2011)

WILD CARD BERTHS: 2 (2022, 2023)

PLAYOFF APPEARANCES: 16 (1915, 1950, 1976, 1977, 1978, 1980, 1981, 1983, 1993, 2007, 2008, 2009, 2010, 2011, 2022, 2023)

WORST SEASON RECORD: 1941, 42–111 (.279)

BEST SEASON RECORD: 1976, 101–61 (.623)

[BELOW] One of the most recognizable mascots in Major League Baseball, the big green Phillie Phanatic is well loved by fans. As well as entertaining the crowd during games, the fuzzy Phanatic ventures out of the ballpark to make public relation and goodwill appearances for the Phillies.

> "Ya gotta believe!"
>
> —PHILLIES SLUGGER TUG MCGRAW

LIBERTY BELL Rising 102 feet (31 m) above street level, this 52-foot tall (16 m) by 35-foot wide (11 m) tower houses a mechanical, lighted replica of the Liberty Bell that "rings" and lights up after every Phillies home run and win.

GAMES OF BASEBALL This interactive area features a video trivia game, a run-the-bases game with the Phillie Phanatic, and a "Ring 'Em Up" game where fans throw at targets of a catcher. Players earn coupons and exchange them for prizes at a kiosk such as hats, shirts, and other ballpark-imprinted memorabilia.

[OPPOSITE PAGE] Spectators begin to fill the tiered bleachers or get some snacks from one of the many ballpark options in preparation for a game.

[RIGHT] Fans crowd the rooftop bleachers below the Liberty Bell. The victory cry of the Phillies fans is "Ring the bell!"—referring to the giant version of the iconic Philadelphia landmark at Citizens Bank Park, which lights up and swings back and forth after every Phillies home run and win.

PLAYER COMMEMORATIONS Scattered throughout the park, visitors will find tile mosaics, murals, and terrazzo floors with silhouettes of famous Phillies. Of note are the statues outside the building: Richie Ashburn stands in Ashburn Alley, Robin Roberts at the first base gate, Mike Schmidt at the third base gate, and Steve Carlton at the left field gate. Local sculptor Zenos Frudakis created each of the 10-foot-high (3.0 m) statues. The 7.5-foot-tall (2.3 m) bronze statue created by Lawrence Nowlan, another local Philly sculptor, of legendary broadcaster Harry Kalas stands behind Section 141, near the restaurant that bears his name.

FOOD AND DRINK AMENITIES These include Budweiser Batter's Eye, offering a full lineup of Anheuser-Busch products; Bull's BBQ to the left side of the scoreboard in the new "Boardwalk Eats" section featuring ribs, turkey legs, pork, beef and chicken sandwiches and "Bulldogs" (kielbasa); Chickie's & Pete's, famous

[LEFT] This work of art honors Mike Schmidt, the Phillies titanic third basemen, who posed for it live in midswing. It is now a fan favorite for taking selfies. Alas, the iconic Schmidter cheesesteak sandwich, named in Schmidt's honor and once a staple for fans, is no longer available at the park.

[BELOW] The Robin Roberts statue is unique for its painted finish.

for their crinkly Crab Fries with a cheese dipping sauce; Campo's Philadelphia cheesesteaks; Tony Luke's famous cheesesteaks and roast pork; P.J. Whelihan's pub and restaurant, specializing in wings; Harry The K's Bar and Grille, built into the base of the scoreboard, serves finger food and sandwiches; Jim Beam Bourbon Bar with cocktails and local, craft, domestic, and imported beers; and Manco & Manco, a New Jersey pizza franchise.

PREMIUM CLUBS There are two premium seating areas in the park—the air-conditioned Diamond Club is located behind home plate, has 1,164 seats, and offers exclusive food and souvenir shopping, and a place to watch batting practice. A second level, called the Hall of Fame Club, is also air-conditioned, contains 6,600 seats, and features the same amenities. It houses team memorabilia going back to the 1880s, along with memorabilia from the Philadelphia Athletics. The Hall of Fame level also houses the A/V crew on the first-base side, which controls the scoreboard and all other monitors throughout the park, as well as the press box, television, and radio booths.

SOUTH PHILADELPHIA SPORTS COMPLEX

The South Philadelphia Sports Complex currently houses Philadelphia's four major sports teams—Citizens Bank Park is home to the MLB Phillies; Lincoln Financial Field is home to the NFL Eagles; and the Wells Fargo Center is home to both the NBA 76ers and NHL Flyers. The latter also hosts the NLL Philadelphia Wings and the NCAA Temple Owls. This site was once home to three iconic—and since demolished—stadiums: John F. Kennedy Stadium, formerly called Philadelphia Municipal Stadium (1926–1992), Veterans Stadium (1971–2004), and the multisport and entertainment Spectrum (1967–2011). Before urban development, the region was a shanty town called "the Neck," part of the undeveloped League Island area formerly known as Passyunk Township.

CITIZENS BANK PARK FIRSTS

FIRST MLB GAME: 4/12/2004, Cincinnati Reds over Phillies, 4–1

FIRST HOME RUN: 6/20/2004, Jimmy Rollins (Kansas City Royals)

FIRST NO-HITTER: 10/6/2010, Roy Halladay vs. Cincinnati Reds

FIRST ALL-STAR GAME: Scheduled for 2026

FIRST PLAYOFF GAME: 10/3/2007, Colorado Rockies over Phillies, 4–2

FIRST WORLD SERIES GAME: 10/25/2008, Phillies over Tampa Bay Rays, 5–4 in Game 3

OTHER HOMES OF THE PHILLIES

RECREATION PARK
1883–1886

This rough-hewn ballpark served as the Phillies first home prior to the opening of the Baker Bowl. It was also reputedly home to the first baseball game ever played in Pennsylvania, when Equity defeated Pennsylvania 65–52 (!) on June 16, 1860. First used by the Philadelphia Centennials in 1875, then as a horse market, the field was leased by Alfred J. Reach of the National Association. He cleared out the debris, resodded it, built a grandstand, renamed it Recreation Field, and recruited an independent team called the Fillies. As the Phillies they played their first game there on April 2, 1883, defeating the amateur Manayunk Ashlands 11–0.

BAKER BOWL
1887–1938

Philadelphia Ball Park, with a seating capacity of 12,500, was built for the Phillies in time for the 1887 season. The field was encircled by a quarter-mile (400 m) bicycle track that was 15 feet (4.6 m) wide, and fans were encouraged to ride to the games, then circle the field after the games. Destroyed by fire in 1894, the venue, now called National League Park, was rebuilt the following year—becoming the first of the primarily brick-and-steel parks and the first with a cantilevered upper deck. The name was coined by the *Philadelphia Inquirer* newspaper in July 1923 in honor of Phillies owner William F. Baker. He bought the club in 1913 and would own it until his death in 1930. The park was also referred to in the press as the "Cigar Box" and the "Band Box" due to its small outfield. These terms were later used on similarly diminutive fields, such as Fenway Park or Ebbets Field, that favored home run hitters. Baker Bowl was also called the "Hump" because a partially submerged railroad tunnel outside the park extended into the outfield. Fielders claimed they could actually feel passing trains rumbling under their feet.

A 1917 postcard of a game at the Baker Bowl shows an announcer with a megaphone.

Baker Bowl
National League Park
The Phillies' baseball park from its opening in 1887 until 1938. Rebuilt 1895; hailed as nation's finest stadium. Site of first World Series attended by U.S. President, 1915; Negro League World Series, 1924-26; Babe Ruth's last major league game, 1935. Razed 1950.
PENNSYLVANIA HISTORICAL AND MUSEUM COMMISSION 2000

[ABOVE] Early baseball card for "Red" Dooin. Charles Sebastian Dooin (1879 –1952) was an MLB catcher during the first two decades of the 20th century, playing 1,219 of his 1,290 games as a Phillie. He then managed the team during its Baker Bowl days, from 1910 through 1914.

[LEFT] An historical marker noting its former site is the only thing that remains of the Baker Bowl.

SHIBE PARK / CONNIE MACK STADIUM

1909–1970

Fans enter Connie Mack Stadium, circa 1950s.

First home to the American League Athletics during the early 20th century, this beautiful stadium welcomed the National League Phillies starting in 1938. When it opened in 1909, Shibe was baseball's first steel-and-concrete ballpark. Constructed five blocks west of the Baker Bowl and straddling the rural neighborhoods known as Swampoodle and Goosetown, it was named after team president Ben Shibe. The design and execution were by William Steele and Sons, who had worked with the new steel-reinforced concrete technology on Philadelphia's first skyscraper, the Witherspoon Building. Here they created a facade in an ornate French Renaissance style that included arches, vaulting, and Ionic pilasters, plus a signature tower and cupola. The grandstands were of red brick and terra-cotta, with friezes displaying baseball motifs. A pleased Ben Shibe boasted that the design was "for the masses as well as the classes."

"I remember going to Shibe Park, Connie Mack, when I was a kid with my dad and my mom. It felt more neighborhood-esque. . . . I love the new downtown ballparks. I love when the venue is situated in a vibrant part of the urban setting."

—BASEBALL MANAGER JOE MADDON

The park hosted eight World Series (seven with the Athletics, one with the Phillies in 1950) and two All-Star Games in 1943 and 1952. The latter event was the only All-Star Game called for rain after five innings. In 1939, the first American League night game also took place there. It was perhaps the most fondly remembered of the Phillies' several homes. As Phillies Hall-of-Fame center fielder and broadcaster Richie Ashburn recalled about the place, "It looked like a ballpark. It smelled like a ballpark. It had a feeling and a heartbeat, a personality that was all baseball." The *Philadelphia Public Ledger* declared it "a palace for fans, the most beautiful and capacious baseball structure in the world." American League president Ban Johnson stated that "Shibe Park is the greatest place of its character in the world."

A crowd waiting to enter lines up outside while traffic whizzes by Connie Mack Stadium, June 1957.

In 1953 the stadium was renamed Connie Mack Stadium for the Athletics' longtime manager—and the longest-serving manager in baseball history. As the team's controlling partner, he sold the debt-ridden ballpark to the Phillies and sold the Athletics to industrialist Arnold Johnson. Johnson immediately moved the team to Kansas City . . . and Mack nearly expired after hearing the news.

A player slides safe into third base during a 1926 Cleveland vs. Athletics game at Shibe Park.

VETERANS STADIUM
1971–2003

When Connie Mack Stadium began showing its age, Phillies owner R. R. M. Carpenter Jr. initially proposed a stadium on land adjacent to the Garden State Park Racetrack in Camden, New Jersey. But Philly fans had already lost their MLB Athletics to Kansas City and their NBA Warriors to San Francisco. They refused to give up another franchise, so in 1964 city voters approved a $25 million bond for a combined baseball and football venue. (Construction eventually totaled $63 million, making it one of the costliest sports venues of its time.) Veterans Stadium opened in 1971 as home to both the Phillies and the NFL Eagles. Similar to the multipurpose San Diego Stadium, its design—known as an "octorad"—was nearly circular and meant to accommodate fans of both sports. Critics grumbled that it served neither.

Sadly, the stadium deteriorated noticeably as it aged; it was overrun with mice, and there was even a peephole into the cheerleaders' dressing room. Veterans Stadium closed on September 28, 2003, and on March 21, 2004, it was imploded in 62 seconds. The Eagles moved to Lincoln Financial Field and the Phillies moved to the adjacent Citizens Bank Park. In its heyday, "the Vet" hosted three World Series (1980, 1983, 1993), two MLB All-Star Games (1976, 1996) and 17 Army-Navy football games.

[OPPOSITE PAGE] A vintage postcard shows Veterans Stadium in its heyday.

[RIGHT] A crowd gathers to watch as "the Vet" comes tumbling down in a series of explosions as a demolition crew levels the hulking skeleton on March 21, 2004.

[BELOW] An overhead shot of the field as the Phillies took on the Houston Astros, circa 1980s.

[INSET, BELOW] Red Sox manager Darrell Johnson, Cincinnati Reds manager George "Sparky" Anderson, Yankee catcher Thurman Munson,and Cincinnati Reds catcher Johnny Bench greet President Gerald R. Ford before the Major League Baseball All-Star Game at Veterans Stadium on July 13, 1976. Philadelphia had hosted the All Stars in 1943 and 1952, but this was the first at Veterans Stadium. The game would return in 1996.

CLOSE-UP

ANATOMY OF A BALLPARK

Stadiums and arenas often have configurations that can be converted for a variety of sports—football, soccer, basketball, track and field, even ice hockey. And while pro baseball teams have played in these multi-use facilities, the classic ballpark is their optimal setting. Fans agree that for the best spectator experience, for seating that brings them closest to the action on the field, the specialized geometry of a dedicated ballpark remains the ideal.

The features of a classic ballpark include, but are not limited to, the playing field, dugouts, bullpens, clubhouses, training areas, different tiers of grandstand seating, bleachers, concourses, and recreational areas.

THE FIELD

A baseball field is traditionally referred to as a diamond. It has two main sections—the infield and the outfield. The infield is a square that measures 90 feet on each side, with three bases and home plate at each corner of the square, plus the pitcher's mound with a plate that is 60 feet, 6 inches from the rear point of home plate. The outfield is the grassy, fan-shaped area within the two foul lines, formed by extending two sides of the square. Foul territory, where a hit ball is no longer in play, lies beyond that line and behind home plate. In the outfield there is often a narrow warning track to alert fielders they are approaching a fence or wall.

"Infield mix" is the official term for the dirt found on a baseball field. Fans may call it baseball dirt or baseball clay, while brand names like DuraEdge®, Turface®, Beam Clay®, and AMP® refer to different commercial products.

MAKING AN ENTRANCE

The tunnel leading to the ball field is sometimes referred to as a vomitorium. The word comes from the Latin root *vomere*, meaning "to vomit" or "to spew forth." Yet, it does not refer to the contents of one's stomach—a vomitorium is a passage or opening below or behind a tier of seats in a theater, amphitheater, or stadium. It leads to or from the seating area, allowing audience members to pass in large numbers.

DEFINITIONS

BALLPARK / BASEBALL PARK A type of sports venue where baseball is played. A larger ballpark may also be called a baseball stadium because it shares characteristics of other outdoor stadiums.

STADIUM A place or venue for (mostly) outdoor sports, concerts, or other events that consists of a field or stage either partly or completely surrounded by a tiered structure designed to allow spectators to stand or sit and view the event.

> "I'm seven years old and my dad takes me to Yankee Stadium, my first game . . . you come up out of the tunnel and into the light. It was huge. How green the grass was, the brown dirt . . . my dad taught me to keep score. Mickey hit one out."
>
> —BILLY CRYSTAL, *CITY SLICKERS*

THE DUGOUT

The team benches are in a low shelter with a roof that is open to the field in front. There is a dugout for the home team and one for the visiting team, located in foul territory between home plate and either first or third base. It is occupied by all players not prescribed to be on the field, as well as managers, coaches, and other authorized personnel. Equipment like gloves, bats, helmets, and the catcher's gear may be stored here.

THE BULLPEN

This is the area where relief pitchers warm up during a game and then wait there to be called in. In most Major League parks, the bullpen is located out of play, behind the outfield fence. The term first appeared shortly after the turn of the 20th century; it refers to latecomers to a game being cordoned off in standing room areas "like cattle," which then became "bullpens."

THE CLUBHOUSE

This facility typically contains the locker rooms, showers, whirlpools, and perhaps a massage table. The clubhouse is the players' private space, where they can eat, sleep, shower, shave, play cards, listen to music, roughhouse with teammates, or just relax. It is also a place for players to prepare themselves mentally and physically for the game. It is often the site of an inspirational pep talk—or a tongue lashing—from managers and coaches. Naturally there are clubhouses for both the home team and the visitors.

A Florida Marlins pitcher warms up in the visitors' bullpen, which is on the field in foul territory at Wrigley Field, home of the Chicago Cubs.

TRAINING FACILITIES

Most ballplayers are diligent about maintaining their strength training and field skills during the off season, but coaches understand that it's important for them to continue these training exercises during the season. This is why certain ballparks offer batting cages, weight rooms, and gyms. Some teams are now training off-site at state-of-the-art player development complexes. These facilities allow pro athletes to focus on specific areas that need improvement.

SEATING

Stadium seating can make or break a ballpark. Fans require comfort, easy access, proper orientation to the field, and clear sight lines. If one of these elements is missing from a new ballpark, attendance may flag. The hierarchy of grandstand seats begins with upper-tier "nosebleed" seating, which offers great panoramas but distance from the field. Midtier seats mix affordable seating with decent views of the field. Lower-bowl seats place spectators closest to the field and offer a thrilling atmosphere and possible interaction with players. Top-of-the-line premium seating includes luxury boxes, club chairs, and VIP areas . . . and furnish extra amenities, comforts, and perks. Bleachers, open seats once called "bleaching boards," are separate from the grandstand, often beyond the outfield fence. Although they are usually the cheap seats, many fans prefer their atmosphere of rowdy enthusiasm.

CONCOURSES

"Buy me some peanuts and Cracker Jack . . ." Snacks have clearly been a big part of the ballpark experience since baseball's earliest days. Vendors still wander the stands during games hawking hot dogs and beer. Yet, fans apparently needed more sustenance (or distractions), so eventually ballparks included concourses—wide, level walkways circling behind the grandstand—that contained food and drink concessions, food courts, team stores, retail shops, historical displays, kiosks, and pushcarts, but with enough openings out to the field that fans could still view the game. Many ballparks boast multilevel concourses, some with so many retail shops the venues become known as "mallparks."

Lucky fans get a close-up view of Washington Nationals right fielder Nate McLouth hitting the grandstand after catching a fly ball in foul territory at Nationals Park.

RECREATIONAL AREAS

Ballparks that have extended their footprint beyond their immediate structure now offer fans gardens, monument parks, memorial plazas, meditation areas, and landscaped walkways. Within many ballparks there are also picnic areas, children's play zones, some with mini ball fields, and other spaces where fans can bring blankets and lounge on the grass.

Sign outside the Busch Stadium dining and entertainment complex. These days, baseball fans have a wider choice of food and drink options, as well as extras like family-friendly amusements.

THE BASEBALL DIAMOND

SF Giants Javier Lopez winds up to throw. The pitcher's mound, also known as the "hill," is the raised dirt area in the center of the infield in an 18-foot diameter (5.5 m) circle.

> "Great views of the game from all vantage points make a ballpark great. It needs to have an open feeling, combining the wide-open swaths of grass on the field and a community in the stands."
>
> —C. TRENT ROSECRANS, CINCINNATI REDS CORRESPONDENT

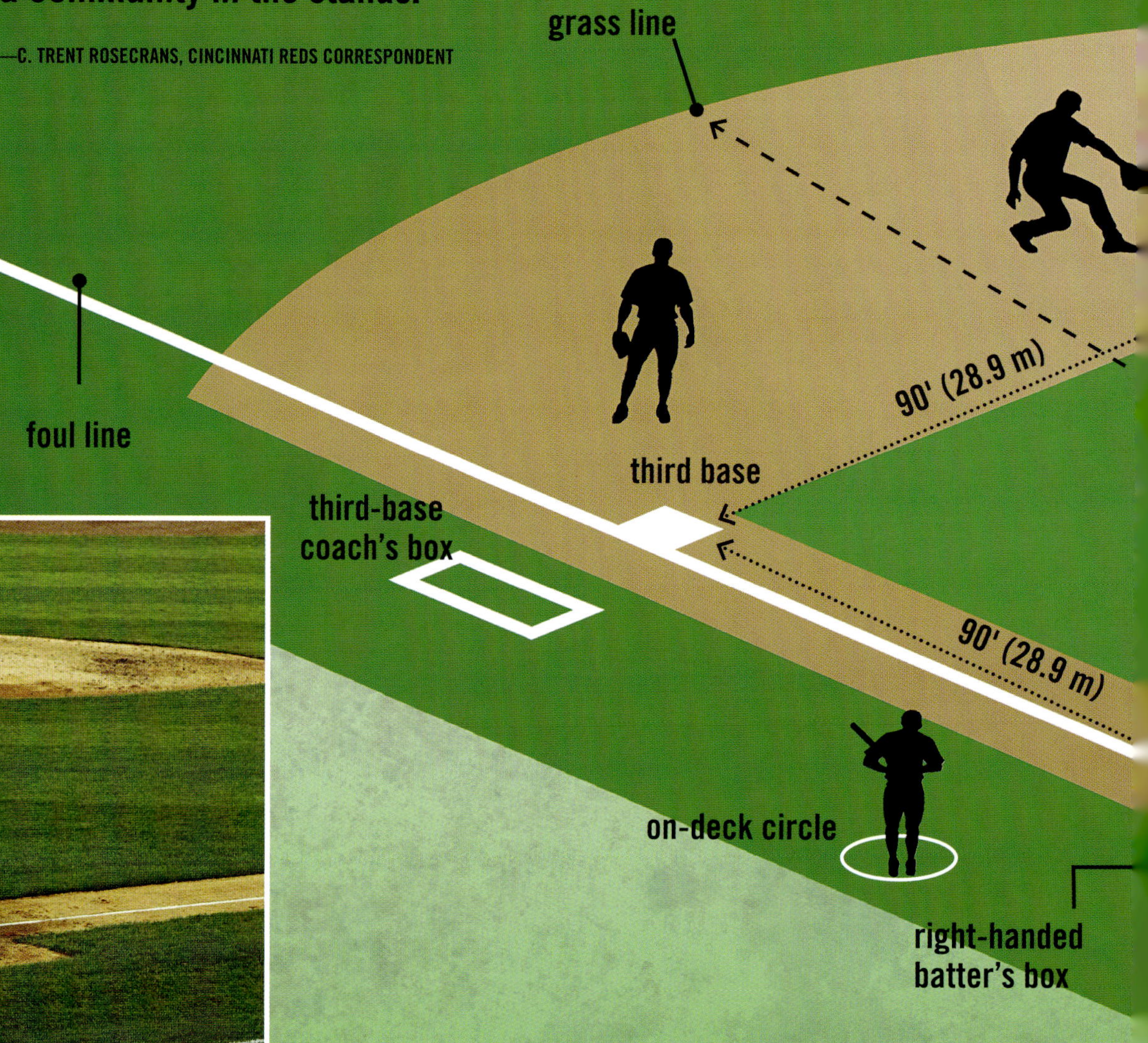

grass line

foul line

90' (28.9 m)

third base

third-base coach's box

90' (28.9 m)

on-deck circle

right-handed batter's box

Oakland A's coach Mike Gallego looks on as center fielder Rajai Davis takes a lead off third base.

A Texas Rangers player makes contact with the ball. This batter swings from the left-handed batter's box, while the catcher crouches in his box behind home plate.

In the on-deck circle, LA Dodger Jason Heyward works on his swing before his turn at bat.

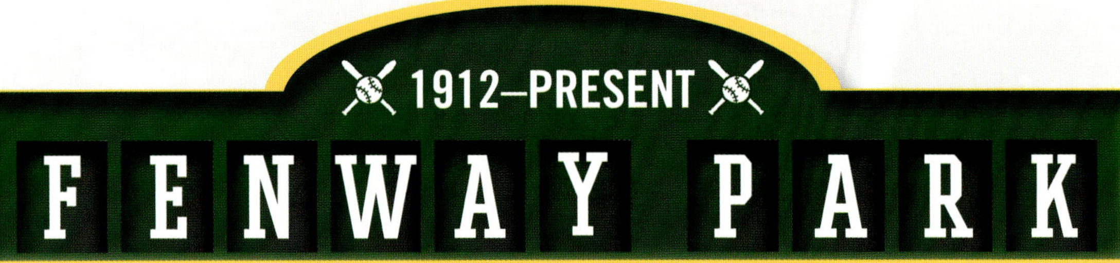

HOME OF THE BOSTON RED SOX

AMERICAN LEAGUE (1901–PRESENT)

IT MAKES SENSE THAT ONE OF THE OLDEST, *most revered teams in pro ball plays in the oldest venue in the Major Leagues. Both the team and the ballpark have had plenty of seasoning, including scandals, curses, and hoaxes. But beyond all the lore and legends, there is the team's performance—which has always been competitive and, quite often, entertaining.*

The Red Sox ball club was founded in 1901 as one of the American League's eight charter franchises. Unofficially known as the Americans at the time, the team would later get a new name. "Red Sox" was chosen by team owner John I. Taylor around 1908 to acknowledge a series of local teams that had been known as the "Boston Red Stockings." This roster of clubs included the Boston Braves, who played in Bean Town for 81 seasons before becoming the Atlanta Braves.

THE CURSE OF THE BAMBINO

By 1919, the Red Sox were a juggernaut on the field—the best team in baseball, winning five of the first 15 World Series. The team's greatest asset was George Herman "Babe" Ruth, a terrific pitcher and powerful hitter. But the Red Sox owner and theatrical producer, Harry Frazee, needed funds to invest in a musical called *My Lady Friends* (later the Broadway hit *No, No, Nanette*), so he agreed to sell Ruth to the Yankees for an astronomical $100,000. The rest, as they say, is history. The Babe made the Yankees a top team, and his ability to attract masses of fans actually helped the team's owners finance the first Yankee Stadium. As for the Red Sox . . . well, they did not win a World Series for another 86 years.

Now, few professional athletes are as superstitious as baseball players. They see omens and hexes around every corner. And the Red Sox were no exception. But sometimes it might seem as if an uncanny string of bad luck really might have a supernatural cause. Many of their followers believed the team was being punished for making that foolhardy deal, and they called it the "Curse of the Bambino." Desperate fans tried spray-painting a street sign that said, "Reverse Curve" to read "Reverse the Curse" and staging an exorcism outside Fenway Park. Finally in 2004, after beating their nemesis, the Yankees, for the AL pennant, the Sox swept the Cardinals for the World Series title. One final spooky thrill—the player who made the final out that won the game for Boston—Cards shortstop Edgar Renteria—wore No. 3, Ruth's number. When the dust settled, Boston erupted into a celebration that shook the staid old port city from the North End to Southie.

Overall, the Red Sox have won a total of nine World Series titles, tied for the third-most wins in the Majors, after competing in 13 championship series. Their most recent crown was in 2018. It also should be noted that they won the first-ever World Series in 1903, but after they earned the pennant again in 1904, the National League champion New York Giants refused to play them in the Series. Looks like Boston and New York were mixing it up even back then.

THE PARK ALONG FENS

In 1911, while the Red Sox were still playing on Huntington Avenue Grounds, owner John I. Taylor purchased a parcel of land bordered by Brookline Avenue, Jersey Street, Van Ness Street, and Lansdowne Street. The site was near a green belt of reclaimed marshland known as the Fenway. After Taylor developed the land into a modern baseball stadium and called it Fenway Park, he insisted the name came from the venue's location. But it needs to be noted that Taylor's family also owned the Fenway Realty Company, which gave the ballpark's name a lot of promotional currency.

The first game at the new venue was played April 20, 1912, with Boston mayor John F. Fitzgerald throwing out the ceremonial first pitch. The Rex Sox defeated the New York Highlanders—their soon-to-be archrivals the Yankees—7 to 6 in 11 innings. Newspaper coverage of the ballpark's opening was overshadowed by continuing reports on the disastrous sinking of the *Titanic* several days earlier. In 1919, nearly 50,000 supporters turned

BALLPARK STATS

ADDRESS
4 Jersey Street, Boston, MA 02215

OWNER
Fenway Sports

OPERATOR
Fenway Sports Group / Boston Red Sox

ARCHITECT
James E. McLaughlin

CAPACITY
37,305 (day); 37,755 (night)

RECORD BASEBALL ATTENDANCE
47,627 on 9/22/1935 (doubleheader vs. New York Yankees)

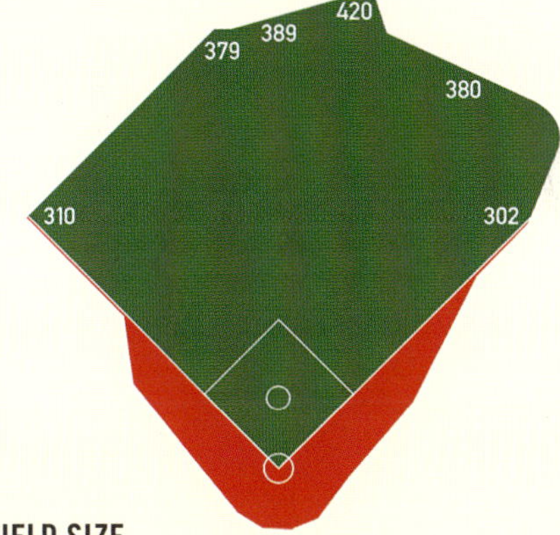

FIELD SIZE

- **Left Field** 310 feet (94.5 m)
- **Deep Left-Center** 379 feet (115.5 m)
- **Center Field** 389 feet, 9 inches (118.8 m)
- **Deep Right-Center** 420 feet (128 m)
- **Right Center** 380 feet (115.8 m)
- **Right Field** 302 feet (92 m)
- **Backstop** 60 feet (18.3 m)

SURFACE
Kentucky bluegrass

TEAM MASCOT
Wally the Green Monster

[LEFT] Banners commemorate winning seasons outside Fenway Park, Gate A, in the stadium's northwest corner, on the third-base side.

out for a rally for Irish independence and to see Éamon de Valera, president of the Irish Republic. This was purportedly the largest crowd ever gathered in Fenway.

DESIGN AND CONSTRUCTION

Fenway Park was constructed on an asymmetrical block, which resulted in asymmetrical field dimensions—a common hazard with ballparks from that era. The structure was designed by architect James E. McLaughlin, and the general contractor was the Charles Logue Building Company. The facade's crisp exterior was achieved through the use of "tapestry brickwork" running throughout the park walls. Tapestry brick incorporates differing shades of red brick laid in decorative patterns. It a was a popular architectural style in the early 1900s and is seen in many of the buildings and apartments around the Fenway-Kenmore neighborhood. This helped the ballpark blend in well with its surroundings.

UNIQUE FEATURES

Fenway Park soon became known for its many unusual or odd attributes. Best known is the "Green Monster," the daunting left-field wall, which is the tallest wall in any Major League Baseball park at 37 feet (11.27 m). It's such a signature of the ballpark that the team's mascot, "Wally the Green Monster," was named after it. Today there are even seats atop the wall, offering a different perspective on the

> **"A little lyrical bandbox of a ballpark, a compromise between man's Euclidean determinations and nature's beguiling irregularities."**
>
> —JOHN UPDIKE, AUTHOR

THE WAREHOUSE INCIDENT

Fenway Park was built among many similar-looking buildings in the Kenmore Square section of Boston. As a result, it blends in neatly with its neighborhood. Perhaps too neatly. When pitcher Roger Clemons first came to Boston in 1984, he took a taxi from Logan Airport and told the driver "Fenway Park." Clemons was confused when the driver announced their arrival. "No, Fenway Park," the pitcher protested. "It's a baseball stadium. This is a warehouse." When Clemons was directed to look up at the light towers, he realized his mistake. He was at his new home. The taxi driver probably dined out on this story for years.

The street-facing exterior of Fenway Park before changes were made after 2003. This urban ballpark has never been known for its architectural beauty.

field. “The Triangle” is the section of center field where the walls form a triangle, and where the far corner is 420 feet (130 m) from home plate. Pesky’s Pole is what fans call Fenway’s right-field foul pole. Johnny Pesky was a beloved midcentury player, but he hit only six home runs in his 539 games at Fenway. According to teammate Mel Parnell, who named the pole, Pesky benefited from the right-field foul pole which was—and still is—only 302 feet (92 m) from home plate. Today the pole bears thousands of fan and player signatures.

Fenway Park and Wrigley Field are the only two MLB stadiums that still display manual scoreboards. Although Fenway now has a digital scoreboard, it also uses the manually operated scoreboard under the Green Monster. Dating to 1934, the scoreboard is run by three interior operators during the game.

The Rooftop Garden is where the team grows their own fruits and vegetables. Green City Grocers helped the Sox build the 5,000-square-foot (464.5 m^2) plot, called Fenway Farms, on the third-base side of the EMC level. The produce they gather is used in the food sold at the restaurant and concession stands.

Another beloved feature of Fenway Park is the singing of Neil Diamond’s “Sweet Caroline,” which became the unofficial song not long after it was first played there in 1997. One explanation says that it was broadcast in honor of a newborn baby named Caroline, but whatever its genesis, the song’s contagious, upbeat vibe was

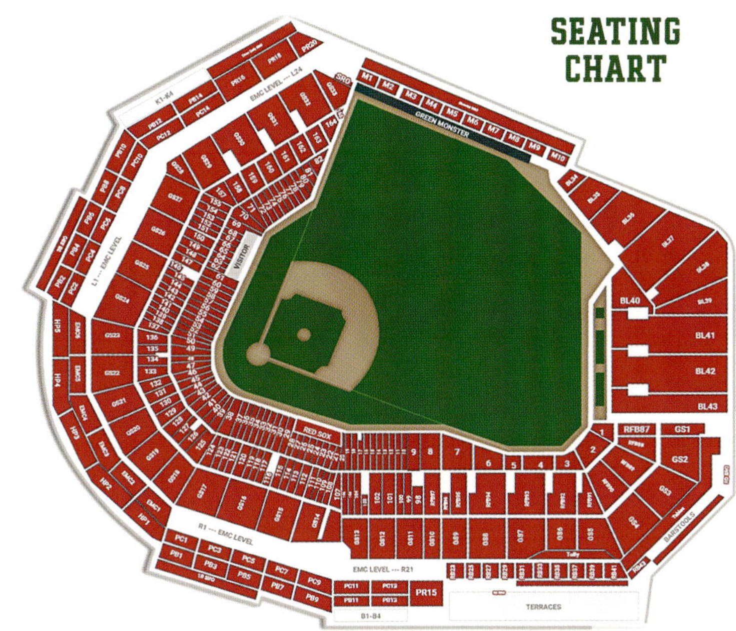

[ABOVE] A night game at Fenway. The reason Fenway Park’s seating capacity is greater during night games is because during day games, the seats in center field (Section 35) are covered with a black tarp to provide a batter’s eye.

[TOP] A ticket to the 1912 World Series. Considered one of the most exciting matchups of the era, it pitted Red Sox fireballer Smoky Joe Wood against NY Giants star pitcher Christy Mathewson. The Series went to eight games, due to a tie game being called on account of darkness. The Sox took the championship in Game 8.

[LEFT] Fenway’s most famous quirk is, of course, the 37-foot-2-inch-high (11.33 m) left-field wall, known as the Green Monster—or “the Monstah” in Boston parlance. From its towering height to its manual scoreboard, the massive left field wall is unique in MLB. It is said that a fly ball hit towards it favors a pitcher, while being a left fielder’s nemesis.

clear. The stadium replayed the song often, and it was eventually played for luck after the seventh inning if the Sox were leading. It is now heard during the eighth inning at all home games.

A NEW FENWAY?

On May 15, 1999—a day that went down in infamy for Red Sox fans—CEO John Harrington announced plans for a new Fenway Park to be built near the existing structure. This modernized replica of the venerable ballpark would have seated 44,130, with identical field dimensions except for a shorter right field and reduced foul territory. Special sections of the existing ballpark were to be preserved, mainly the original Green Monster and the third-base

[ABOVE] Sculptor David Halberstam immortalized the decades-long friendship of Red Sox legends Ted Williams, Bobby Doerr, Dom DiMaggio, and Johnny Pesky in *The Teammates: Portrait of a Friendship*, which stands outside Gate B. The teammates played seven seasons together, as well as serving in World War II.

[ABOVE] Boston brought its fair share of baseball greats to the city's ballpark. Sitting in a low wall of the home team's dugout is George Herman "Babe" Ruth, Ernest G. "Ernie" Shore, George "Rube" Foster, and Dellos "Del" Gainer, wearing the Red Sox uniform, sometime between 1915 and 1917.

[LEFT] A statue of Hall of Famer Carl "Yaz" Yastrzemski, the top performer in pennant race history, stands outside Gate B. Yaz played his entire 23-year Major League career with Boston.

RED SOX ACHIEVEMENTS

WORLD SERIES CHAMPIONSHIPS: 9 (1903, 1912, 1915, 1916, 1918, 2004, 2007, 2013, 2018)

AL PENNANTS: 14 (1903, 1904, 1912, 1915, 1916, 1918, 1946, 1967, 1975, 1986, 2004, 2007, 2013, 2018)

AL EAST DIVISION TITLES: 10 (1975, 1986, 1988, 1990, 1995, 2007, 2013, 2016, 2017, 2018)

WILD CARD BERTHS: 8 (1998, 1999, 2003, 2004, 2005, 2008, 2009, 2021)

PLAYOFF APPEARANCES: 8 (1903, 1912, 1915, 1916, 1918, 1946, 1967, 1975, 1986, 1988, 1998, 1990, 1995, 1998, 1999, 2003, 2004, 2005, 2007, 2008, 2009, 2013, 20146, 2017, 2018, 2021)

WORST SEASON RECORD: 1932, 43–111 (.279)

BEST SEASON RECORD: 2018, 108–54 (.667)

side of the park, as part of the new layout. Most of the current stadium would be demolished to make room for new development, with one section of the structure remaining to house a baseball museum and public park. The proposal was highly controversial, projecting that the park had less than 15 years of usable life left and would require hundreds of millions of dollars of public investment to restore. This proposal was later revealed to be part of a scheme by then-current ownership to increase the market value of the team, which they were anxious to sell. Several protest groups—such as "Save Fenway Park"—were formed in an attempt to block the move.

The result of this conflict was a significant renovation of Fenway Park, one that stretched over a 10-year period beginning around 2002. It was headed by Janet Marie Smith, then vice president of planning and development for the Sox, whom the *Boston Globe* described as "the architect credited with saving Fenway Park." At the completion of the renovations, it was estimated that Fenway Park will remain usable until as late as 2062. And there was great rejoicing among the fans.

FEATURES AND AMENITIES

Always placing its fans foremost, Fenway Park offers its loyal supporters a number of historic displays and entertainment opportunities, along with many concessions both inside and outside the stadium.

[ABOVE] Fenway Farms. Utilizing a milk crate container growing system, the park shows it commitment to helping protect and preserve the Boston environment.

[RIGHT] Wally the Green Monster entertains fans during a game.

[BELOW] The lone red seat in the green expanse of the right field bleachers—Section 42, Row 37, Seat 21—indicates the distance of the longest home run ever hit at Fenway. The date was June 9, 1946, when legendary Ted Williams connected on a pitch from Fred Hutchinson of Detroit with a fierce blast that sent the ball soaring up and up . . . until it found the straw hat of Joe Boucher from Albany, New York, who was seated 502 feet (153 m) from home plate.

THE SELLOUT STREAK

On May 15, 2003, a Red Sox game against the Texas Rangers sold out. This was the beginning of a sellout streak that would last until 2013. On September 8, 2008, when the Red Sox hosted the Tampa Bay Rays, Fenway Park broke the all-time Major League record for consecutive sellouts with 456, surpassing the record previously held by Cleveland's Jacob's Field. Then on June 17, 2009, the venue celebrated its 500th consecutive Red Sox sellout. The streak came to an end on April 10, 2013—with an attendance of 30,862—but only after the Red Sox had sold out an astonishing 794 regular season games and an additional 26 postseason games.

HALL OF FAME The stadium celebrates its baseball traditions inside the park with the Boston Red Sox Hall of Fame. Opened in 1995, it honors players who spent at least three years with the club and have been out of uniform as active players at least three years. Nonuniformed honorees and memorable moments are also included. Outside the venue stand statues of team greats Ted Williams, Carl Yastrzemski, and "The Teammates." Retired number banners, World Series banners, and American League pennants line the exterior along Van Ness and Jersey Streets.

FAVORITE SEATING Among the many places to sit at the stadium, the Field Boxes, or "lower bowl," offer excellent views for those who don't mind spending the money. The Loge Box, to the right of home plate, is also a favorite with season ticket holders. Really devout fans are known to congregate close to center field in Section 40. Naturally, the bleachers are always popular with the more demonstrative fans, as are the new seats on the top of the Green Monster.

FOOD AND DRINK The ballpark's widest selection of food and drink is at the Big Concourse. Here visitors can dine at family-size picnic tables, take in pregame entertainment, and visit the Kid Nation booth. This is the ideal place to share the excitement before or during a game. New food items for 2023 included avocado fries,

[BACKGROUND] Fenway Park has often been referred to as "America's Most Beloved Ballpark," not just for its impressive age, but also due to its rare sense of intimacy, its endearing quirks, and its old-school charm. It is also called "Friendly Fenway" and "the Cathedral of Baseball."

[BELOW] A painting on the brick interior wall salutes the ballpark's early years of 1912 to 1934, when a rebuild of the ballpark began.

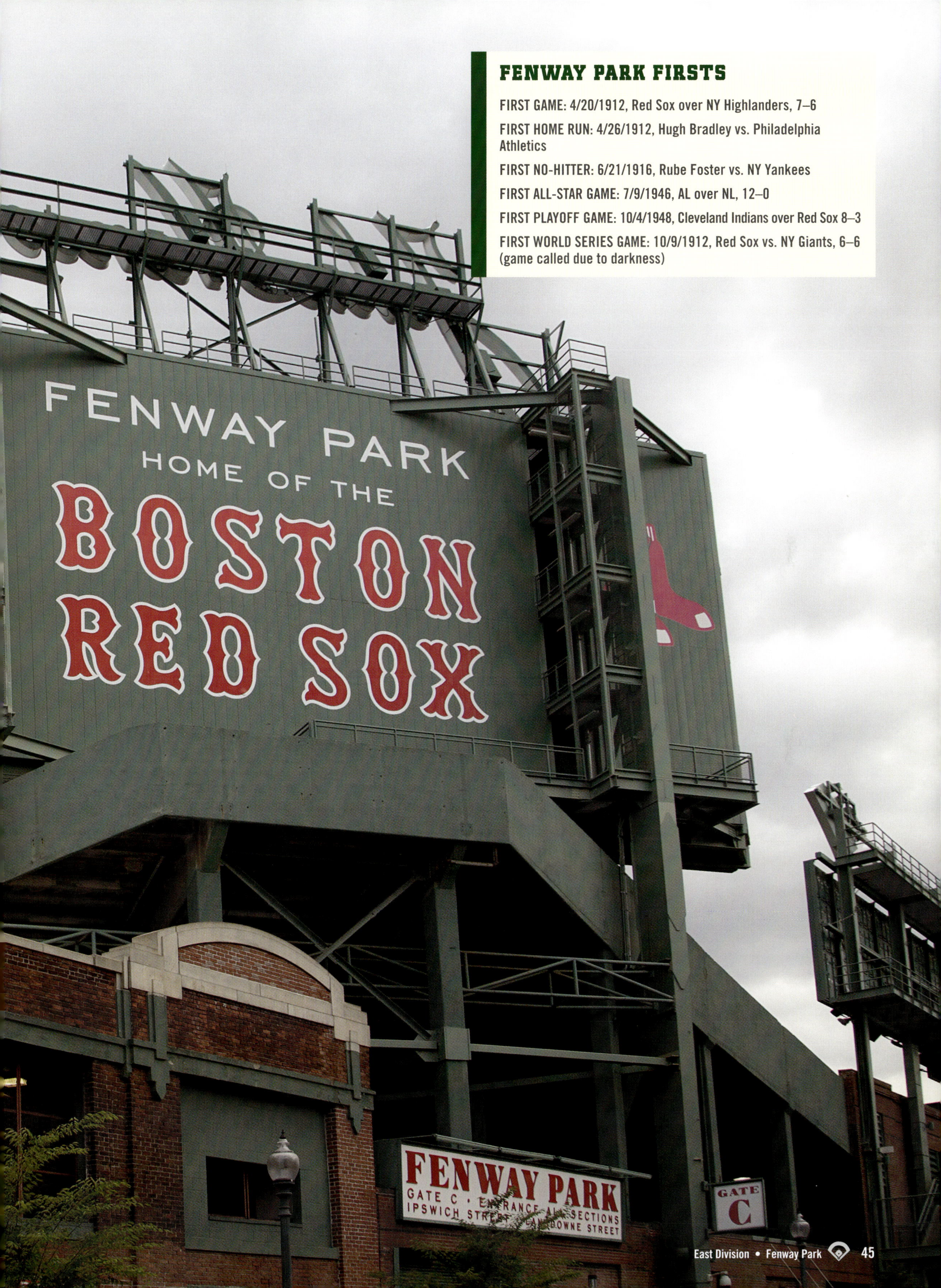

FENWAY PARK FIRSTS

FIRST GAME: 4/20/1912, Red Sox over NY Highlanders, 7–6

FIRST HOME RUN: 4/26/1912, Hugh Bradley vs. Philadelphia Athletics

FIRST NO-HITTER: 6/21/1916, Rube Foster vs. NY Yankees

FIRST ALL-STAR GAME: 7/9/1946, AL over NL, 12–0

FIRST PLAYOFF GAME: 10/4/1948, Cleveland Indians over Red Sox 8–3

FIRST WORLD SERIES GAME: 10/9/1912, Red Sox vs. NY Giants, 6–6 (game called due to darkness)

crab cake sandwiches, maple bacon burgers, and spicy watermelon margaritas. Although Sam Adams is the ballpark's official beer, people in search of national brands or microbrewed specialties will not be disappointed with their choices.

NEIGHBORHOOD ATTRACTIONS On game days, Lansdowne Street and Jersey Street are mobbed with visitors hours before the first pitch. At this time, Jersey Street becomes a pedestrian mall, alive with concession stands, live bands, and the team store. Popular food concessions include El Tiante's Grille, Fenway Fish Shack, and A Taste of Boston, which features a rotating selection of local vendors. The old ticket booths are now exhibits containing memorabilia from each of the Red Sox World Series championship teams. There is even the old bullpen buggy, a popular spot for photos and selfies. Adjacent to the stadium, at the intersection of Lansdowne and Ipswich Streets, is the MGM Music Hall at Fenway, a state-of-the-art, multipurpose live-performance venue. It occupies four levels and can accommodate up to 5,005 patrons.

[ABOVE] View of the concourse from the Royal Rooters Club. This second-level venue takes its name from an early-20th-century fan club for Boston's baseball team and is filled with Red Sox memorabilia, featuring artifacts like Dave Roberts's stolen base from the 2004 ALCS and the baseball used by Roger Clemens during his 20-strikeout game in 1986.

[RIGHT] An aerial shot of Fenway Park shows just how embedded it is in the Fenway-Kenmore neighborhoods of Boston. Its crowded-in location has meant that changes to its configuration or any expansions have been limited, which has resulted in many of the park's famous quirks.

[BELOW] Fenway shortly after it was built. The park's address was originally 24 Jersey Street. In 1977, the section of Jersey Street nearest the park was renamed Yawkey Way in honor of longtime Red Sox owner Tom Yawkey. The street name has since reverted to Jersey.

[ABOVE] Plaques commemorating winning seasons decorate Fenway's walls. The year 1918 would see the last of Red Sox World Series domination before the Curse of the Bambino took hold, not to be broken until 2004.

Boston policemen pose in the dugout during the 1903 World Series.

OTHER HOMES OF THE RED SOX

HUNTINGTON AVENUE GROUNDS
1901–1911

The baseball field that was the first home of the Boston Red Sox—the Boston Americans until 1908—was the Huntington Avenue American League Baseball Grounds. The team played there from 1901 to 1911, before moving to their permanent home near Kenmore Square. The stadium, which was built for $35,000, was located on what is now the site of Northeastern University. At the time, it lay across the New York, New Haven, and Hartford railroad tracks from South End Park, where the MLB Boston Braves played. Beyond the outfield could be seen the massive Boston Storage Warehouse building—from which a famous 1903 "bird's-eye view" photo of the ballpark was taken—and Boston Opera House, which opened in 1909.

In 1903, the stadium was the site of the first World Series game between the modern American and National Leagues. The following year, it saw history made with the first perfect game in the modern era, thrown by Cy Young on May 5. Built on a former circus lot, the field was extremely large by current standards—530 feet (160 m) to center field, later expanded to 635 feet (194 m) in 1908. The field also had some oddities not seen in modern venues—patches of sand in the outfield where grass refused to grow, and a tool shed in deep center field that often ended up in play.

The Huntington Avenue Grounds was demolished in 1912 after the Sox departed. Since 1954 the site has been home to the Cabot Center, an indoor athletic venue for Northeastern. To commemorate the ballpark, a plaque and a statue of Cy Young were erected in 1993 where the pitcher's mound used to be, now called World Series Way. Meanwhile, a plaque from 1956 on the side of the Cabot Center marks the former location of the left field foul pole.

A two-section panorama that appeared in the *Boston Globe* gives a view of the infield and grandstands during a game between the Red Sox and Detroit Tigers held on August 6, 1911. Visible in the background center is the grandstand of the South End Grounds, where the Boston Braves played.

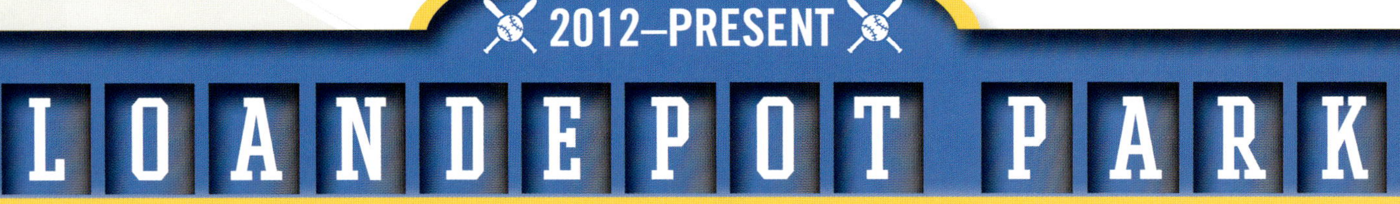

HOME OF THE MIAMI MARLINS

NATIONAL LEAGUE (1993–PRESENT)

THE MIAMI MARLINS *currently play in loanDepot Park, which is conveniently located minutes from downtown Miami in Little Havana. It inhabits 17 acres (6.9 ha) on the site of the former Miami Orange Bowl and is notable for its retractable roof, only the sixth example found in Major League Baseball. It is the third-smallest baseball stadium both in official capacity and in actual capacity.*

On March 7, 1990, Wayne Huizenga, CEO of Blockbuster Entertainment Corporation, announced that he had purchased 15 percent of the NFL's Miami Dolphins and 50 percent of the Dolphins' home, Joe Robbie Stadium, for an estimated $30 million. Huizenga stated his intention was to aggressively pursue a baseball expansion franchise.

Major League Baseball had earlier announced its decision to add two teams to the National League, with one definitely slated for the state of Florida, but Huizenga would need to beat out competition from the cities of Orlando and Tampa Bay. Ultimately a Miami-based franchise was offered to Huizenga for a $95 million expansion fee. For a time, the name Florida Flamingo was considered for the new team, but Marlins was ultimately adopted on the basis of its usage by a number of Miami-based minor league teams. The Florida State League minor league Marlins changed their name to the Miracle and headed to Fort Myers in 1992. Founded in 1991 as the Florida Marlins, the new ML team first played in 1993 at Joe Robbie Stadium in suburban Miami Gardens.

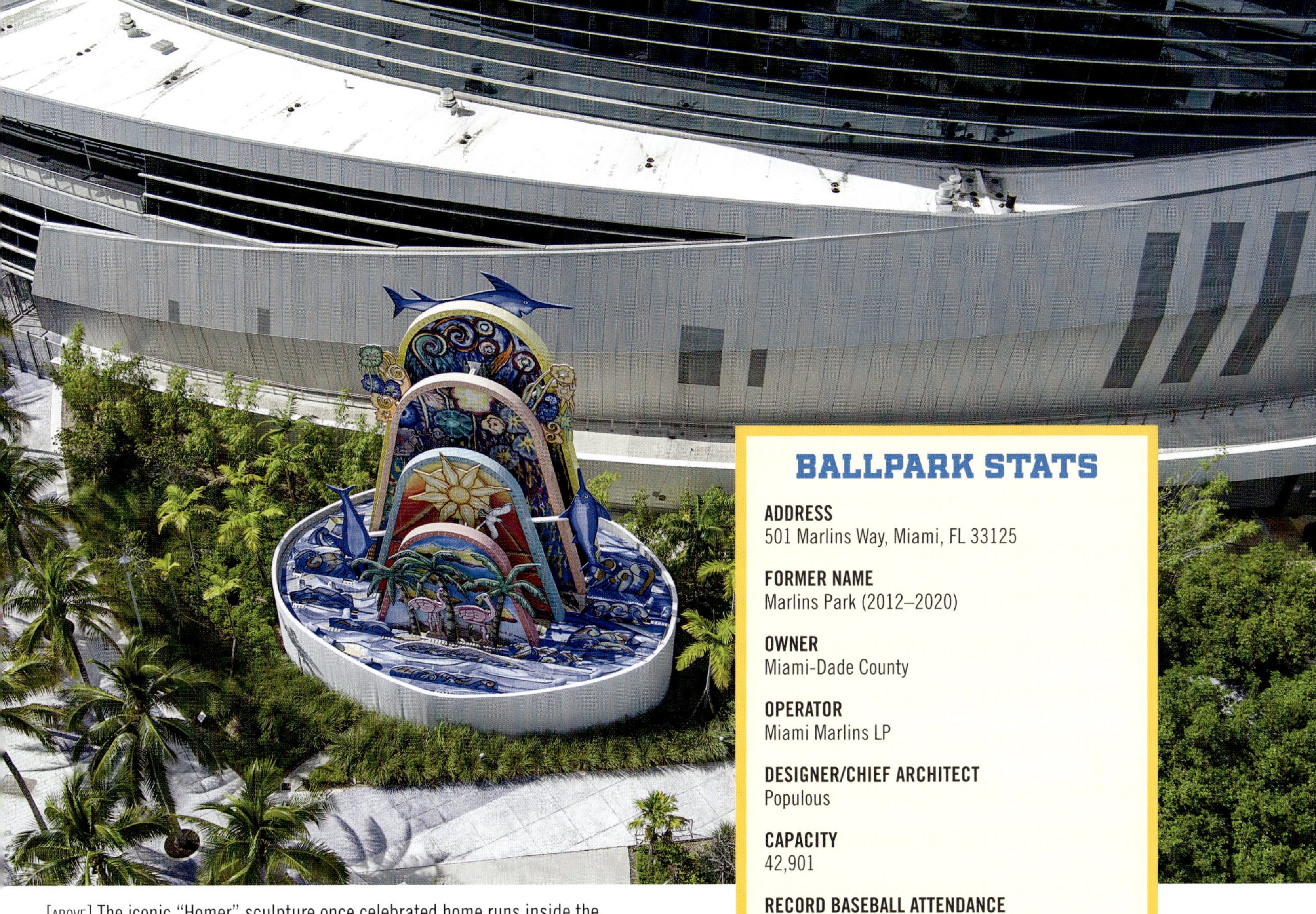

[ABOVE] The iconic "Homer" sculpture once celebrated home runs inside the park, but since the 2018-2019 offseason it has resided outdoors.

[OPPOSITE PAGE} The soaring columns of the retractable roof's support structure lend this ballpark its unique silhouette.

BALLPARK STATS

ADDRESS
501 Marlins Way, Miami, FL 33125

FORMER NAME
Marlins Park (2012–2020)

OWNER
Miami-Dade County

OPERATOR
Miami Marlins LP

DESIGNER/CHIEF ARCHITECT
Populous

CAPACITY
42,901

RECORD BASEBALL ATTENDANCE
72,000 on 3/11/2023 (World Baseball Classic: USA vs. Japan)

407
386
392
344
335

FIELD SIZE

- **Left field line** 344 feet (105 m)
- **Left-center power alley** 386 feet (118 m)
- **Center field** 400 feet (120 m)
- **Right-center power alley** 387 feet (118 m)
- **Right field line** 335 feet (102 m)
- **Backstop** 47 feet (14.3 m)

SURFACE
BK1: Batting A Thousand by Shaw Sports Turf

TEAM MASCOT
Billy the Marlin

Miami

Multiple issues were soon apparent regarding the unsuitability of Joe Robbie for the Marlins—poor seat and sight-line configuration for watching baseball, visual references to Miami's NFL team, such as logos and color schemes, and the distance of the action in relation to the seats. Miami's tropical climate during baseball season included temperatures of 95°F (35°C) or higher, while games would often be rained out by storms. The climate impacted both fan attendance and player performance at home. And by 2004, the Florida Marlins were the only MLB team playing in an NFL-configured stadium.

In 1999, Huizenga, claiming a loss of more than $30 million, sold the Marlins to John W. Henry. The new owner quickly strove for a baseball-only venue, one with a retractable roof and air-conditioning. Then, during an MLB-engineered ownership swap, Henry became owner of the Red Sox and Expos owner Jeffrey Loria took over the Marlins. Loria continued the search for a new home, with local enthusiasm growing after the Marlins won the World Series in 2003. By 2005 the Marlins had begun exploring relocation options in Las Vegas, Portland, and San Antonio. This threat prodded Governor Charlie Crist and local mayors to support public funding for the stadium.

The ballpark's minimalist design elements include sculptural letters spelling out "M A R L I N S" that lead guests along the stairs and walkways.

The Marlins were still viewing other options, including the former site of the Miami Arena, when in August 2007 the University of Miami Hurricanes announced they were leaving the Orange Bowl, creating a very attractive local vacancy. In February 2008 the city and county commissions finally agreed to fund the new stadium. The Orange Bowl was demolished in March 2008 and construction on the new ballpark began in July 2009. Marlins Park began operations on April 4, 2012, at which time the team became known as the Miami Marlins.

NEW OWNERS AND SPONSORSHIP ISSUES

In 2017, the Loria ownership sold the Miami Marlins to a group of investors led by Derek Jeter and Bruce Sherman. Subsequent changes to the stadium included offering stadium-naming rights to mortgage company loanDepot in 2021—a decision reported to bring a yearly $10 million—which renamed the facility loanDepot Park. Many critics felt the name—minus proper capitalization and spacing—was MLB's most ridiculous instance of corporate branding. Yet, when he announced the new name, the ball club's then CEO, Derek Jeter, maintained that the loanDepot connection would be "beneficial to our organization" and would help make a positive impact on the local community.

On November 16, 2018, the team unveiled a new logo, colors, and uniforms for the 2019 season, replacing the former "rainbow" M with a logo in red, blue, gray, and black.

DESIGN AND CONSTRUCTION

Bucking the recent trend for retro-inspired ballparks, the architects of loanDepot Park jettisoned the nostalgia and opted for an emphasis on the future with a sleek, minimalist design and plenty of new technology. This stadium represents what is considered the "neomodern" style of baseball architecture, which utilizes simpler forms than postmodernism and neo-eclecticism and rejects classical ornamentation or decorative elements.

THE RETRACTABLE ROOF

The ballpark's remarkable roof is composed of three operable panels, one upper and two lower panels. The lower panels sit on the east and west ends of the upper panel, which rises 216 feet (66 m) above second base. Moving along two 750-foot (228 m) tracks and spanning 566 feet (172.5 m), the roof creates an opening that is wider than any NFL retractable roof stadium.

As a LEED Gold Certified building, it was paramount for the stadium to maintain the energy efficiency of the retractable roof. The solution is its regenerative drive system, which reduce the power consumption during braking at times when the moving panel is being pushed by the wind, while opening and closing the roof costs only an estimated $15 or less in electricity.

“We had a vision five years ago to turn the Marlins franchise around, and as CEO, I have been proud to put my name and reputation on the line to make our plan a reality.”

—DEREK JETER, FORMER CEO

But that simplicity doesn't mean the ballpark is boring. While the focus is meant to be on utility and economy, the aesthetic provides plenty of uncluttered beauty. The park was inspired by Spanish artist Joan Miró and contains many colorful "only in Miami" features, such as brightly tiled walkways by kinetic-op artist Carlos Cruz-Diaz, pastel Miami deco-influenced wall tiles on the parking garages, and a vivid aquarium with live fish set into the home plate backstop. The city's famous beachfront topography is also reflected in the strata of colorways: the cobalt-blue glass at eye level represents "ocean," stucco and concrete stands in for "sand" or "buildings," and the paler, blue-gray glass at the upper levels represents "sky." Unique cobalt blue seats make a vivid impact against the green turf in the field, again representing sky and earth.

The exterior features deep-blue glass, white stucco, metal panels, and a glass curtain wall. The sweeping circular facade of fluid glass has a graceful aluminum veneer draping around it. Two distinctive white super columns support the ballpark's retractable roof when it's open. To facilitate the movement of fans, there are eight passenger elevators and ten escalators, plus two vertical circulation ramps that can be used to travel from level to level, or to exit the ballpark.

PUBLIC REACTION

The general consensus when the park debuted was positive, with certain reviewers gushing over the sleek design, a departure from the steel-and-concrete ballparks, the unrestricted views of the playing field, and the range of amenities.

Many critics pointed out that although some ballfields attempt to meld visually with their neighborhoods—Coors Field in Denver with its red-brick exterior and Progressive Field's industrial aesthetic recalling Cleveland's bridges, for example—loanDepot displays a jarring disconnect between the ultra-modern park and its intimate Little Havana neighborhood. The stadium and its super columns loom so large they visually overpower their surroundings. Problems getting to the venue in game-day traffic were also often mentioned.

With its sleek lines in stark white, the ballpark stands out against the deep-blue skies of twilight. Some say this architectural marvel is quintessentially Miami.

FEATURES AND AMENITIES

The state-of-the-art technology found throughout the venue includes electronic mixed-media artwork, and many digital menu boards on the concession stands continuously switch from English to Spanish and back as a way to market the space to Latino fans, and there are no hand-operated advertisement signs—ads are all computerized. There is even an LED show at night that illuminates the super columns that support the roof. The stadium's total of 46 suites includes 12 Founders Suites, 10 Legends Suites, 12 MVP Suites, 6 Fiesta Suites, 2 Championship Suites, and 2 Hall of Fame Suites.

BILLY'S KID ZONE This children's play area is in Section 34. It includes arcade games, while guests 12 years of age and older can test their skills taking a virtual swing right from home plate. Billy the Marlin even appears at the kid zone during the fifth inning for a photo opportunity.

BOBBLEHEAD MUSEUM The entertaining Bobblehead Museum features a collection of current and former Marlins player bobbleheads, as well as current and past baseball players, mascots, and broadcasters from all MLB teams. While displaying more than 600 bobbleheads at any given time, the entire structure moves slightly, causing the heads to constantly bobble.

SEATING CHART

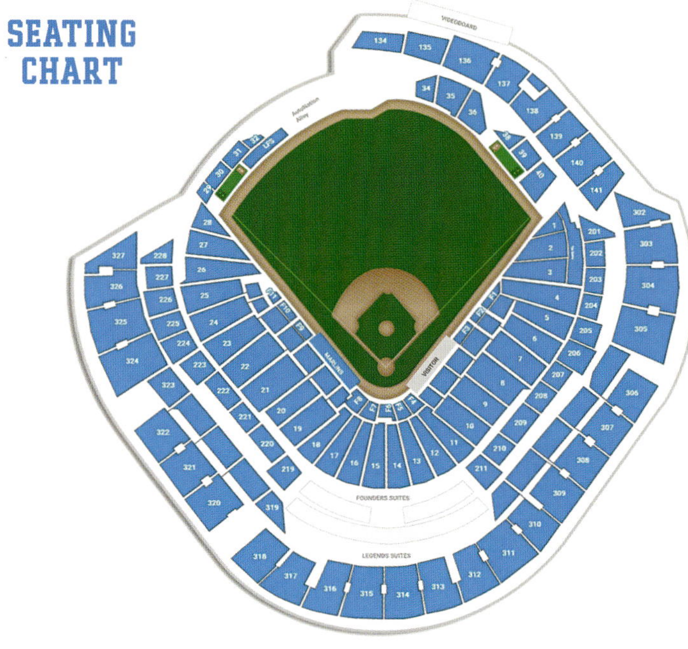

SPECIAL EVENTS The ballpark has proven a popular venue for hosting sporting, corporate, and entertainment events. Since opening day, it has been the site of banquets and awards dinners, bar/bat mitzvahs, birthday and holiday parties, weddings, receptions, social events, concerts, conferences, family shows, fundraisers, trade showcases, press conferences, product launches, public consumer shows, and nonbaseball sports like soccer, football, boxing, etc.

LOANDEPOT/MARLINS PARK FIRSTS

FIRST MLB GAME: 4/4/2012, St. Louis Cardinals over Marlins, 4–1

FIRST HOME RUN: 4/13/2012, J. D. Martinez (Houston Astros)

FIRST NO-HITTER: 9/2013, Henderson Álvarez vs. Detroit Tigers

FIRST ALL-STAR GAME: 7/11/2017, AL over NL, 2–1

MARLINS ACHIEVEMENTS

WORLD SERIES CHAMPIONSHIPS: 2 (1997, 2003)

AL PENNANTS: 2 (1997, 2003)

AL EAST DIVISION TITLES: 0

WILD CARD BERTHS: 4 (1997, 2003, 2020, 2023)

PLAYOFF APPEARANCES: 4 (1997, 2003, 2020, 2023)

ALL-STAR GAMES: 1 (2017)

WORST SEASON RECORD: 1998, 54–108 (.333)

BEST SEASON RECORD: 1997, 92–70 (.568)

[ABOVE] The park lit up at night. The sweltering heat and humidity of a Florida summer means that most games are played in the evening.

[RIGHT] Sited for seven seasons beyond the park's left-center-field wall, Marlin's Home Run sculpture is adorned with flamingos, seagulls, clouds, and palm trees. During its time indoors, when activated by a home run, marlins would jump out of the water and lights would shine. Designed by pop artist Red Grooms, it cost $2.5 million. Often labeled "hideous" or "tacky," its critics need to bear in mind that the sculpture is an intentionally kitschy piece of legitimate art and not merely a gimmick promoting the team.

[OPPOSITE PAGE] Fans watch a game against the Atlanta Braves in 2014.

JOE ROBBIE STADIUM

1993–2011

Before the construction of Marlins Park, the ball club played at the home of the NFL Dolphins, Joe Robbie Stadium in suburban Miami Gardens. Built in 1987—and named for the founder of the Dolphins—the venue was designed to accommodate baseball and soccer, in addition to football. Robbie himself firmly believed pro baseball would come to southern Florida, and he wanted his stadium to be ready.

The Dolphins originally played 21 seasons in Miami's venerable Orange Bowl, but when the city threatened to quadruple their rent, Robbie began considering a new home for his team. The resulting stadium, built in then-unincorporated Miami-Dade County, was unique—the first multipurpose stadium ever built in the United States that was entirely privately financed. Designed by HOK, it cost a total of $115 million.

The Marlins arrived in 1993, and during their first year they drew more than three million fans. They also won the World Series in 1997 and 2003. Yet, for all its beauty and versatility, the stadium was not meant for summertime sports—and the soaring South Florida temperatures made it the hottest stadium in the Major Leagues. As a result, the Marlins played most of their home games at night before their departure in 2011. Since 2008, the stadium has also been home to the University of Miami's football team, the Hurricanes.

A POPULAR VENUE

Under its various names, Joe Robbie Stadium has hosted two World Series (1997, 2003), six Super Bowls (XXIII, XXIX, XXXIII, XLI, XLIV, and LIV), the 2010 Pro Bowl, four BCS National Championship games (2001, 2005, 2009, 2013), one CFP Championship in 2021, the second round of the World Baseball Classic, and Wrestlemania XXVII. It also hosts the annual college football mainstay, the Orange Bowl, and the Miami Open tennis tournament.

[ABOVE] Interior of Dolphin Stadium in its football configuration, with the baseball diamond dirt

[MIDDLE RIGHT] The stadium in its Sun Life incarnation, from 2010 to 2016

[BOTTOM RIGHT] No longer a baseball park, the stadium is now home to the NFL Dolphins. In August 2016, naming rights were sold to the Hard Rock Cafe Inc. for $250 million over 18 years.

[OPPOSITE PAGE, TOP RIGHT] A postcard showing the stadium. Opened in 1987 as Joe Robbie Stadium, the venue has subsequently been known as Pro Player Park, Pro Player Stadium, Dolphins Stadium, Dolphin Stadium, Land Shark Stadium, and Sun Life Stadium.

[OPPOSITE PAGE, BOTTOM] The stadium during a Florida Marlins game, August 2008

HOME OF THE WASHINGTON NATIONALS

NATIONAL LEAGUE (1969–PRESENT)

THE NATIONAL LEAGUE'S WASHINGTON NATIONALS, *formerly the Montreal Expos, play at scenic Nationals Park, which is located along the Anacostia River in the Navy Yard region of Washington, DC. Affectionately known as the Diamond of the District, the stadium is part of the newly developed Capital Riverfront neighborhood, reclaiming land that was once an industrial complex. Completed in 2008, the park was the first professional sports venue in the US to be LEED-certified green.*

In 2004, the Montreal Expos officially announced they would be leaving their home city, where their luster as the first Canadian MLB team had dimmed considerably. The movers and shakers in Washington, DC—a city without a Major League team since 1971—immediately began searching for a site for a new stadium, something that would attract the team to America's capital. Several options were considered, including land near Robert F. Kennedy Stadium, but the final choice was a site in southeast DC near the Anacostia River waterfront. That same year, MLB chose Washington as the franchise's new home. Renamed the Nationals, they relocated in time for the 2005 season, playing at Robert F. Kennedy Stadium until their new home was completed in 2008. When it was broadcast, the team's first game at the new Nationals Park was the most-watched MLB opening night in the history of ESPN.

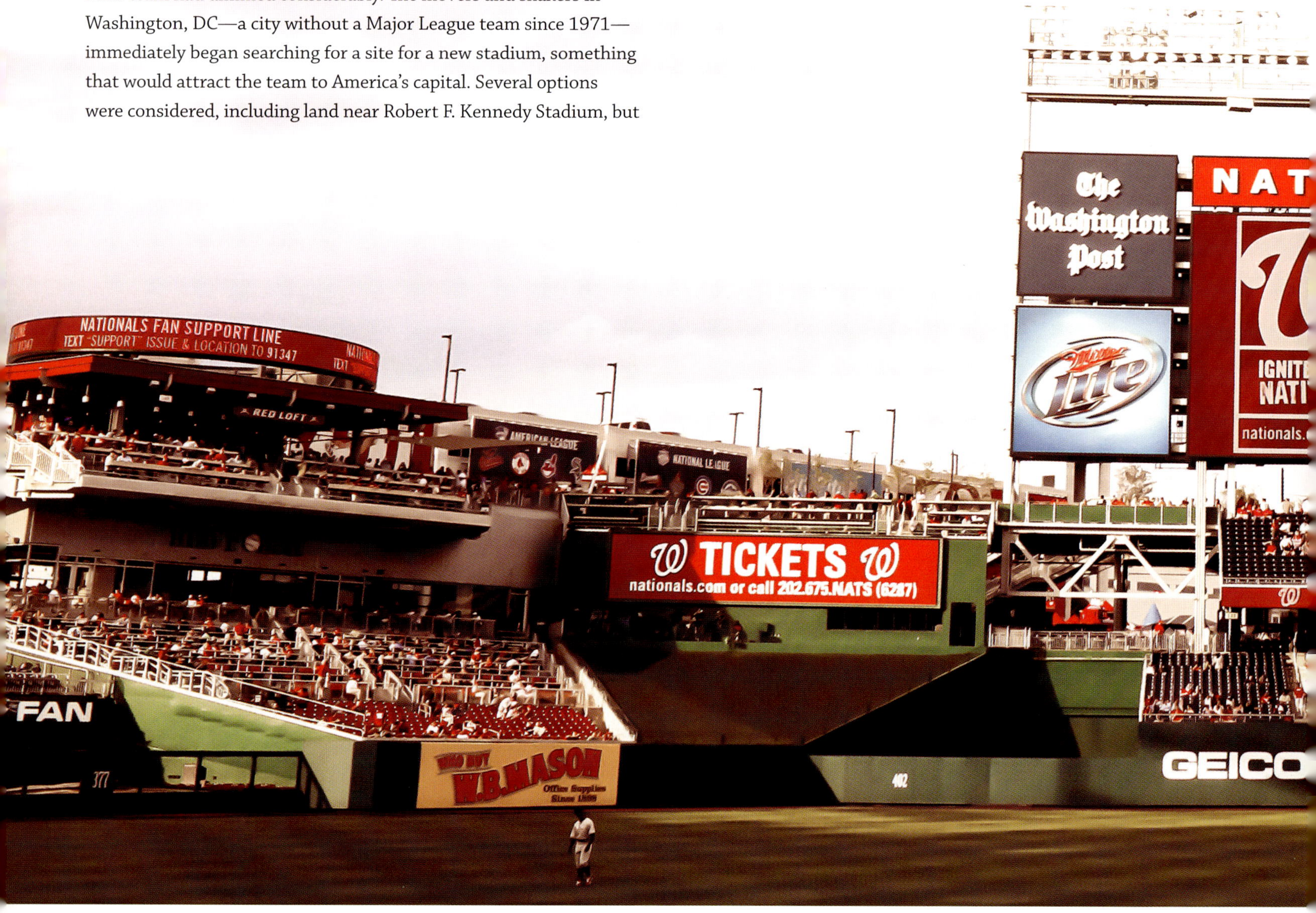

DESIGN AND CONSTRUCTION

With a design based on I. M. Pei's East Wing of the National Gallery of Art, Nationals Park was intended to redefine the architecture of a modern sports facility. The exterior elements of steel, glass, and precast concrete were meant to complement the existing architecture of Washington, while the concourse and seating decks created distinct "neighborhoods," each of them providing a unique identity and viewing experience. The vertical circulation ramps connecting the multiple levels of the venue provide panoramic vistas of the river, the Navy Yard, the Capitol, the Washington Monument, and the surrounding city.

The main concourse is the same height as the sidewalk, and because the field is over 24 feet below street level, more than half the crowd can walk straight off the street into their seats without ever using elevators, escalators, ramps, or stairs. HOK Sport even placed an odd right-angled jog into the right-center-field fence, "borrowed" from the now-demolished Griffith Stadium, former home to the Washington Senators.

BALLPARK STATS

ADDRESS
1500 South Capitol Street SE, Washington, DC 20003

OWNER
Events DC

OPERATOR
Washington Nationals

ARCHITECT
HOK Sport (now Populous); Devrouax & Purnell Architects - Planners

CAPACITY
41,339[

RECORD BASEBALL ATTENDANCE
45,966 on 10/12/2012 (vs. St. Louis Cardinals)

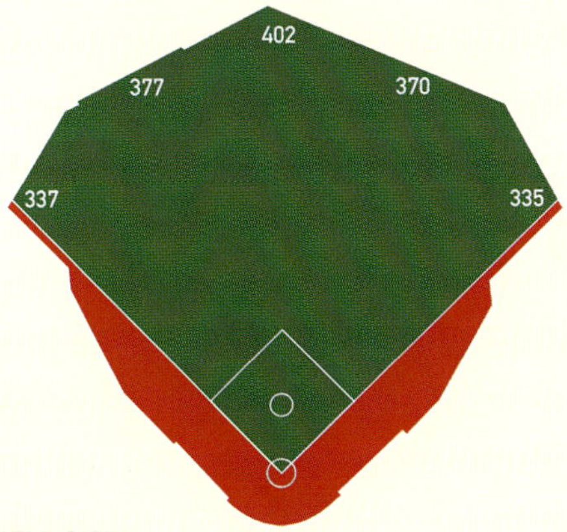

402
377
370
337
335

FIELD SIZE

- **Left Field** 337 feet (103 m)
- **Left-Center** 377 feet (115 m)
- **Center Field** 402 feet (123 m)
- **Right Center** 370 feet (113 m)
- **Right Field** 335 feet (102 m)

SURFACE
Kentucky bluegrass blend

TEAM MASCOT
Screech the Bald Eagle

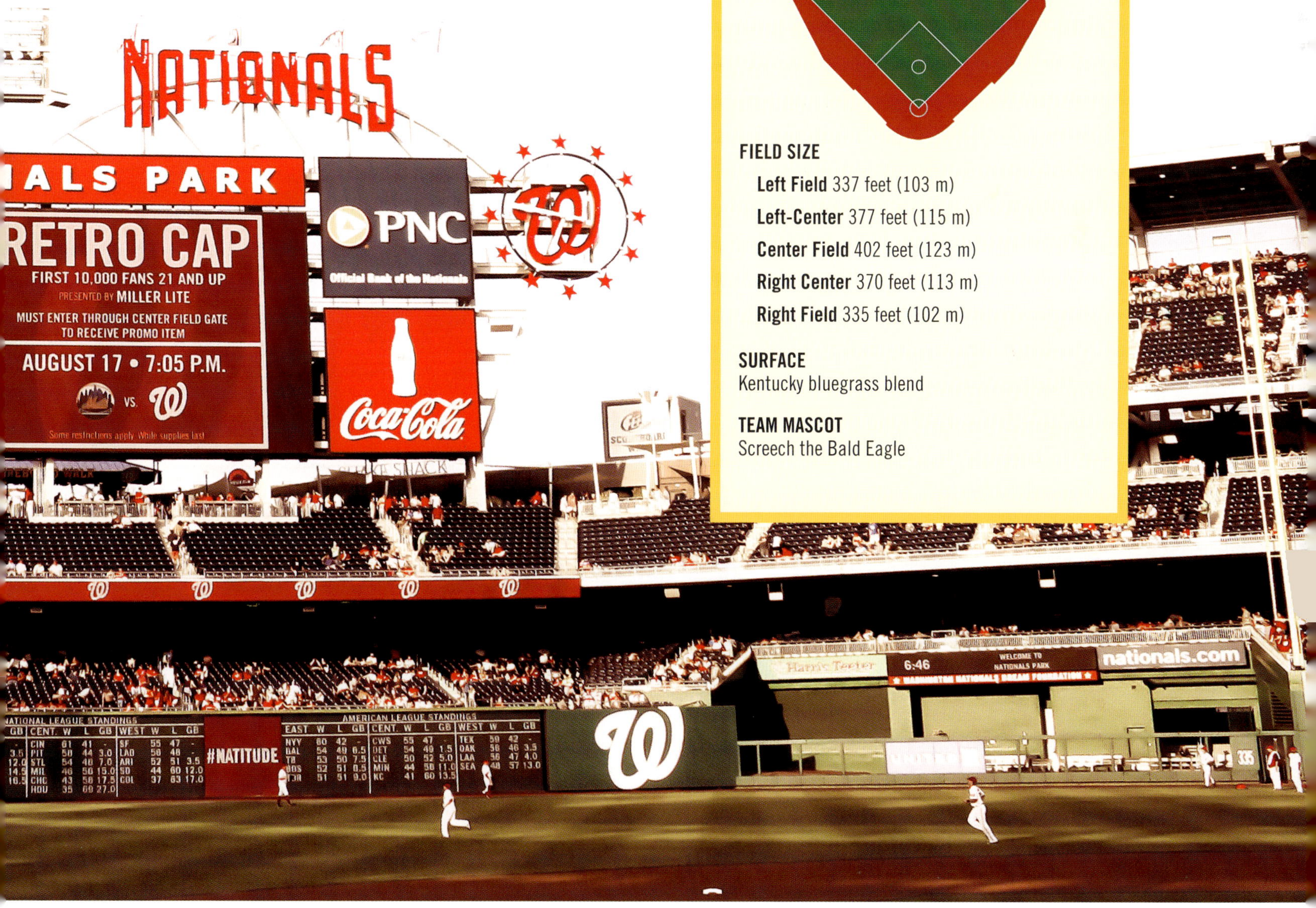

The ballpark features a variety of entertainment options and interactive experiences for fans, as well as state-of-the-art video and audio technology, including a 4,500-square-foot high-definition scoreboard and more than 600 linear feet of LED ribbon board along the inner bowl fascia.

The site also achieved its "green" goal of becoming the first major stadium in the country accredited as a Leadership in Energy and Environment Design structure, as well as receiving the United States Green Building Council's coveted "Silver Status."

PUBLIC REACTION

The new ballpark, with its intentionally old-fashioned ambiance, certainly pleased the fans. The internet was flooded with comments like "one of the best stadiums in baseball right now," "outstanding food and beverage options," "wide-open spaces and plenty of room to walk around," "hardly a bad seat in the house," and "beautiful stadium, great atmosphere!" The venue received four stars on Yelp! from nearly a thousand patrons, it has an A rating from Ballparksofbaseball online, and it is also cited as "good for kids."

NATIONALS PARK FIRSTS

FIRST MLB GAME: 3/30/2008, Nationals over Atlanta Braves, 3–2

FIRST HOME RUN: 3/30/2008, Chipper Jones (Atlanta Braves)

FIRST NO-HITTER: 9/28/2014, Jordan Zimmermann vs. Miami Marlins

FIRST ALL-STAR GAME: Scheduled for 2026

FIRST PLAYOFF GAME: 10/9/2012, Baltimore Orioles over Nationals, 8-0

FIRST WORLD SERIES GAME: 10/25/2019, Houston Astros over Nationals, 4–1 in Game 3

Negative comments point out the cramped feeling of the relatively small field and the so-so sight lines, leaving some attendees with the sense that the field doesn't reflect the high design standards of the rest of the stadium.

UPDATED FEATURES

In 2009, during the off-season, several ballpark improvement projects were completed, including expansion of the Red Porch Restaurant in center field, the addition of an outdoor deck to the Center Field Lounge, and new signage for the concourse.

HONORED PLAYERS In 2009, three statues of honored players were installed—Walter Johnson of the original Senators, Frank Howard of the expansion Senators, and Josh Gibson of the Negro League's Washington Homestead Grays. On a more whimsical note, an oversized Washington Nationals hat was placed above the entrance to the team store. The next year the Ring of Honor was added. This is a display of players' names atop the Lexus President's Club seats behind home plate, celebrating Hall of Famers from all eras: Joe Cronin, Rick Ferrell, Goose Goslin, Clark Griffith, Bucky Harris, Walter Johnson, Harmon Killebrew, Heinie Manush, Sam Rice, and Early Wynn of the Washington Senators; Cool Papa Bell, Ray Brown, Josh Gibson, Buck Leonard, Cumberland Posey, and Jud Wilson of the Negro League Washington Homestead Grays; and Gary Carter and Andre Dawson from the Montreal Expos (the Nationals' previous incarnation). New names are regularly added to the ring.

THE WALL OF DREAMS This display commemorates fans who own a little piece of Nationals Park by having purchased personalized baseballs. These baseballs show that they have donated between $250 and $5,000 to support the Dream Foundation, which was the charitable arm of the Washington Nationals. It had since been replaced by Nationals Philanthropies.

[OPPOSITE PAGE AND ABOVE] The ballpark's bright, old-timey interior color scheme contrasts with the austere monotone exterior. It sits against the backdrop of DC's Capitol Riverfront district. Its reviews are mostly positive, but some have complained that views of the Capitol and Washington Monument are limited.

SEATING CHART

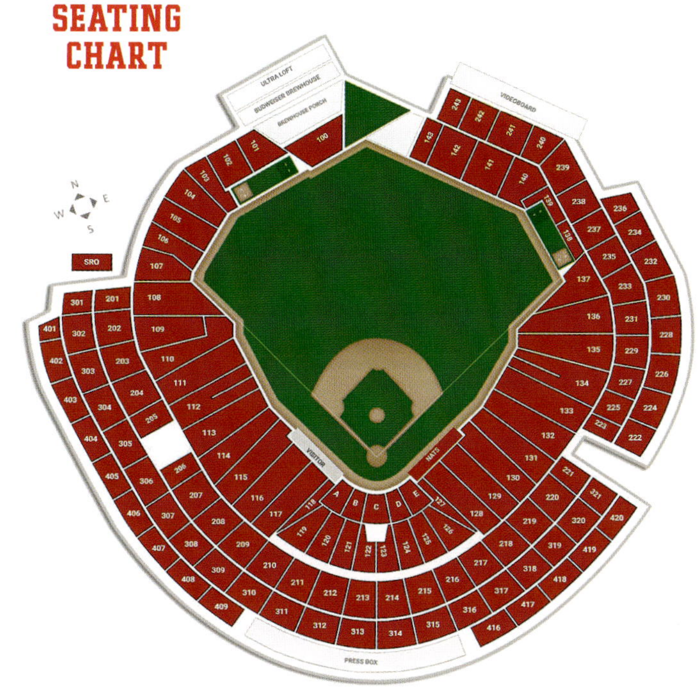

[ABOVE] Teddy Roosevelt rallies the fans prior to the start of a game. He is one of the characters that run the Presidents Race, along with "George," "Abe," "Tom," "Bill," "Calvin," and "Herbie." This promotional event is held at every home game at Nationals Park in the middle of the fourth inning. Their Nationals jerseys' numbers reflect their terms as president. Teddy is notorious for having failed to win a single race for almost seven seasons, even when given head starts or other advantages. He shocked fans on October 3, 2012, with his first win, an achievement that came during the first game played after the Nationals reached the postseason for the first time.

SPORTS HALL OF FAME In 2011, Nationals Park became home to the Washington DC Sports Hall of Fame, formerly found in RFK Stadium. Nominees for the honor are determined by a selection committee and "must have gained prominence in the Washington area through their achievements in sports as an athlete, coach, owner, executive, member of the media or contributor."

STADIUM CONCERTS For the massive crowds that many concerts bring in, ballparks are the answer to seat so many music fans. Nationals Park has therefore become a popular entertainment venue, having hosted concerts by top recording artists like Bad Bunny, Elton John, Billy Joel, Bruce Springsteen, Paul McCartney, Motley Crue, One Direction, Green Day, Pink, Taylor Swift, and Lady Gaga.

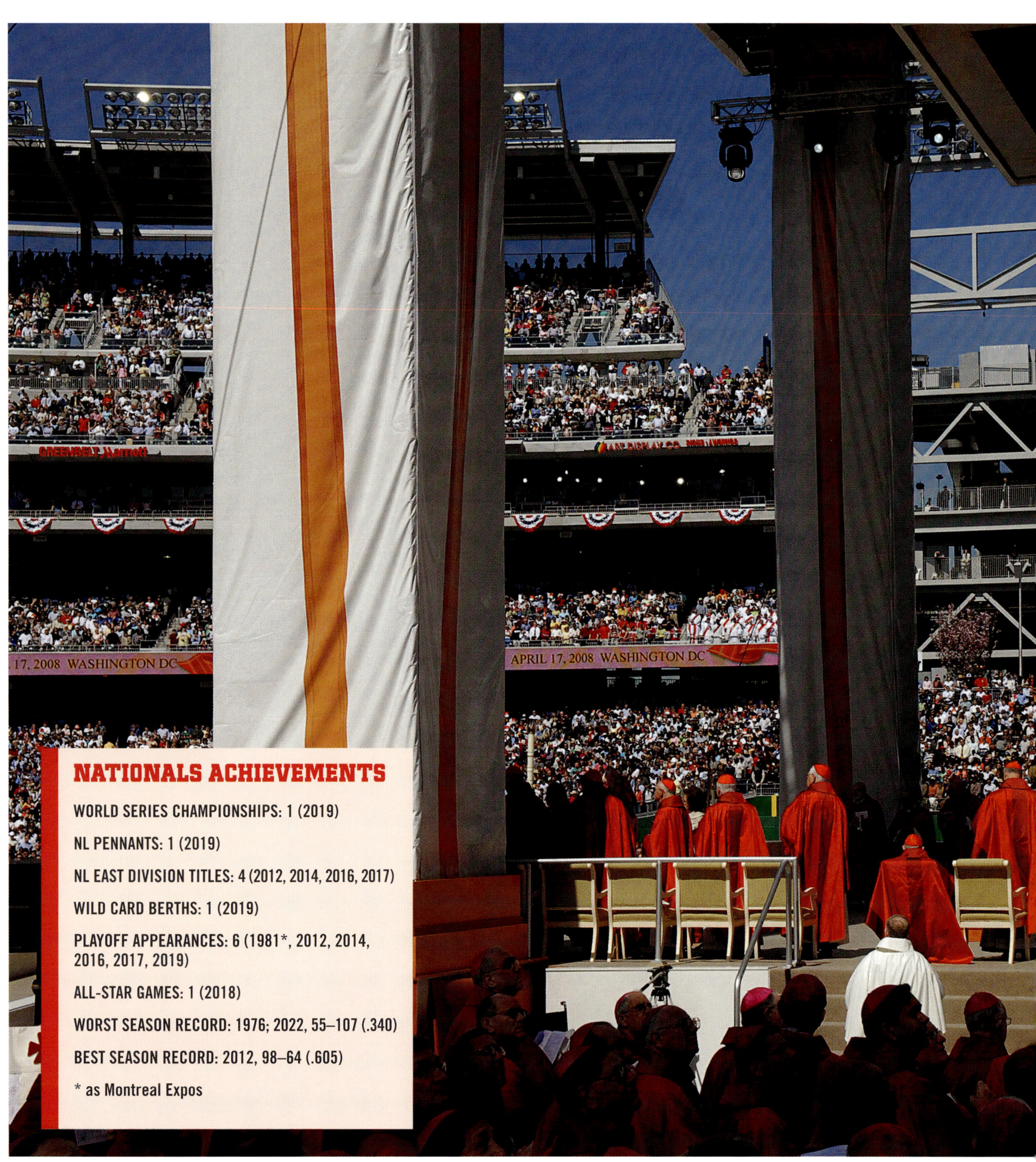

NATIONALS ACHIEVEMENTS

WORLD SERIES CHAMPIONSHIPS: 1 (2019)

NL PENNANTS: 1 (2019)

NL EAST DIVISION TITLES: 4 (2012, 2014, 2016, 2017)

WILD CARD BERTHS: 1 (2019)

PLAYOFF APPEARANCES: 6 (1981*, 2012, 2014, 2016, 2017, 2019)

ALL-STAR GAMES: 1 (2018)

WORST SEASON RECORD: 1976; 2022, 55–107 (.340)

BEST SEASON RECORD: 2012, 98–64 (.605)

* as Montreal Expos

[RIGHT] Three bronze sculptures by Omri Amrany greet fans as they walk to the center-field gate, *top to bottom*: Walter Johnson, Frank Howard, and Josh Gibson.

[BELOW] On April 17, 2008, Pope Benedict XVI visited the newly built Nationals Park and celebrated Mass with nearly 46,000 of the faithful, people who had been chosen from among 200,000 applicants. This religious spectacle was the first nonbaseball event held at the park.

OTHER WASHINGTON, DC, BALLPARKS

GRIFFITH STADIUM
1911–1965

Griffith Stadium was a familiar venue in Washington from 1911 to 1965. The site was originally a wooden ballpark constructed in 1891, first called Boundary Field or National Park. The team that played there was the Washington Senators/Nationals. The ballpark burned down in 1911 and in its place rose a concrete-and-steel stadium first called National Park, then American League Park. In 1923 it was named after Senators' owner Clark Griffith, and it housed his team from that year until 1960, when they headed to Minneapolis. In 1961, the expansion franchise Senators played one season in Griffith Park before moving to District of Columbia Stadium in 1962. By 1972 they were in Texas, playing as the Rangers.

Griffith Stadium hosted the All-Star Game in 1937 and the World Series in 1924, 1925, and 1933. It was home to the Negro League Homestead Grays in the 1940s, hosting the Negro World Series in 1943 and 1944. For 24 seasons, from 1937 to 1960, it housed the NFL Washington Redskins.

The venerable old stadium was demolished in 1965, and the site is now part of Howard University Hospital.

The start of an American tradition: On April 14, 1910, President William Howard Taft throws the ceremonial first pitch to Washington Senators ace Walter Johnson at the Senators' Opening Day at Griffith Stadium.

> "The game was interrupted by the cheering, which spread in a great wave from the grandstand to the bleachers as the crowd recognized the president."
>
> —*WASHINGTON POST* ON WILLIAM HOWARD TAFT, FIRST PRESIDENT PHOTOGRAPHED AT A BASEBALL GAME

[LEFT] In October 1924, the Washington Senators took on the New York Giants in a World Series contest at Griffith Stadium. This incarnation of the Senators went on to win the championship.

A TOWN OF MANY TEAMS

The nation's capital has had quite a varied history with its numerous baseball teams. The current Nationals are the eighth major league franchise to be based in Washington, DC, and the first since 1971. Teams from the later part of the 19th century included the Washington Olympics, the Nationals, Blue Legs, four more iterations of the Nationals, and the Senators. Teams of the 20th century include the Senators/Nationals (1901–60), which in 1961 became the Minnesota Twins, and the Senators (1961–71), which in 1972 became the Texas Rangers.

ROBERT F. KENNEDY STADIUM

2005–2007

Robert F. Kennedy Stadium was home to the Nationals for their first three seasons in Washington (2005 to 2007) while they awaited construction of Nationals Stadium. Originally called District of Columbia Stadium—or D.C. Stadium—when it opened in 1961, it was about 2 miles (3 km) east of the Capitol Building.

Robert F. Kennedy was one of the earliest major stadiums designed to feature both baseball and football. While other stadiums already hosted both sports—Cleveland Stadium from 1931 and Memorial Stadium in Baltimore from 1950—RFK was the first to utilize what was called the circular "cookie-cutter" design. Rarely was a stadium so greatly utilized; it was home to an NFL team—the Redskins, two MLB teams—the Senators and Nationals, five professional soccer teams, two college football teams, a bowl game, and a USFL team. It hosted five NFC Championship games, two MLB All-Star Games, men's and women's World Cup matches, nine men's and women's first-round soccer games in the 1996 Olympics, three MLS Cup matches, and two MLS All-Star Games, along with American friendlies and World Cup qualifying matches. It also hosted college football, college soccer, baseball exhibitions, boxing matches, a cycling race, an American Le Mans Series auto race, marathons, and numerous concerts and other events.

The venue was renamed in honor of Senator—and presidential candidate—Robert F. Kennedy in January 1969 after his assassination seven months earlier. After the Redskins moved out in 1997 and the Nationals relocated in 2007, the venue was left without a big draw. The stadium closed in 2019, and demolition was begun in 2023.

[BELOW] Workers prepare RFK Stadium for the Nationals' first baseball season on March 24, 2005. The team played three seasons at the stadium.

OLYMPIC STADIUM

In the Nationals' earlier incarnation as the Montreal Expos, the team played in their own designated ballpark from 1977 to 2004. Known as Olympic Stadium, it was constructed as the main venue for the 1976 Summer Olympics and then was meant to house the city's new MLB team. It was the first stadium to have a retractable roof, but the construction of the inclined tower that was to power the roof was not completed in time for the Olympics. The games proceeded anyway and the stadium hosted the opening and closing ceremonies and several sporting events.

The roof assembly was finally completed, but never functioned properly, and was eventually dismantled. In 1999 it was replaced by a permanent roof. These issues seemed to foretell future problems—and the stadium eventually became known as one of the worst in the sport. It has suffered exterior, structural, and financial problems and has not had a permanent tenant since the Expos left in 2004. A remnant of the failed roof is the Montreal Tower, which stands at the north base of the stadium and now contains an observatory. Inclined at 45 degrees and at a height of 541 feet (165 meters), it is the world's tallest inclined tower.

1992–PRESENT

ORIOLE PARK AT CAMDEN YARDS

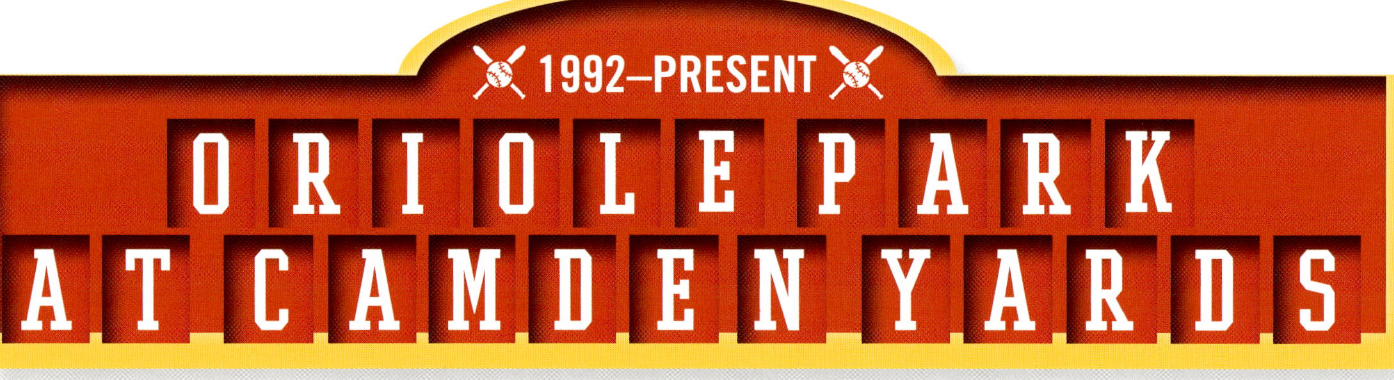

HOME OF THE BALTIMORE ORIOLES

AMERICAN LEAGUE (1901–PRESENT)

THE BALTIMORE ORIOLES HOME PARK, *known as Camden Yards, lies near that city's Inner Harbor on land that was once the site of Babe Ruth's father's saloon. A treasured feature of the Baltimore landscape for decades, the ballpark would set a new standard for "modern-yet-retro" stadium design that influenced a number of builds, as well as providing many ways for the franchise to generate income.*

The Baltimore Orioles, a charter member American League team, originated in Wisconsin as the Milwaukee Brewers. Renamed the Browns, they moved to St. Louis in 1901, where their attendance record was often the lowest in the league. In 1954 the embattled franchise moved to Maryland, where they adopted the name of the official state bird, the striking black-and-orange Baltimore oriole.

For 38 seasons the Orioles played at Memorial Stadium, part of Baltimore's Waverly neighborhood. A stadium rebuild was completed just before their arrival, when it also became home to the NFL Baltimore Colts. The facility drew criticism due to its oblong shape, creating a feeling of "pushing" baseball spectators back from the field. After years of fan complaints, in the 1980s a plan was developed by the Orioles and city officials to construct a dedicated ballpark on the edge of downtown Baltimore, near the acclaimed Inner Harbor urban renewal project. Construction of the stadium began on June 29, 1989, and on April 6, 1992, the Orioles played the Cleveland Indians on their new home field. The total cost came to $225 million—$100 million for land acquisition, $125 million for the stadium.

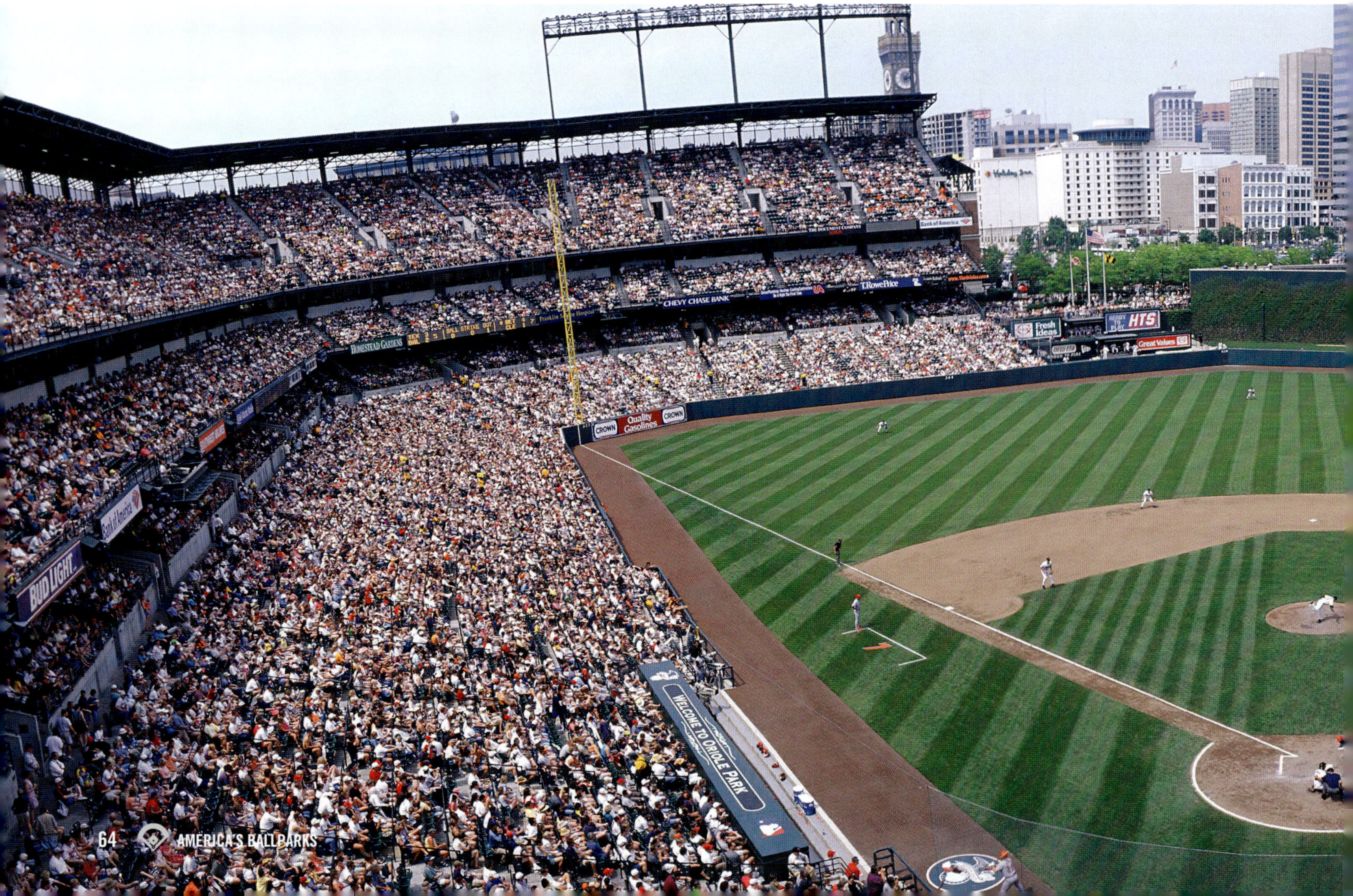

DESIGN AND CONSTRUCTION

Camden Yards was designed by Joseph Spear of HOK Sport following an edict from the club to create a stadium similar to the classic ballparks of the early 1900s—like Shibe Park and Forbes Field—"constructed of steel trusses with a brick facade, an asymmetrical playing field, small foul territory [and] green slatted chairs." Spear outdid himself, using the same time-honored construction methods, including steel columns, beams, and trusses to support the facility instead of concrete. Meanwhile, with its brick facade and repeating arch motif, Camden Yards looked like it had been part of the cityscape for many years. Another concession to the surrounding neighborhood was the low-raked upper deck, which kept the ballpark at a comfortable height. Because the field was below street level, patrons were able to walk down to seats in the lower deck. Large, open-air concourses allowed fans to navigate around the ballpark, while escalators, elevators, and ramps gave speedy access to the upper deck. The new ballpark became such an icon that it went on to influence the design and structure of almost every baseball stadium built since 1992, more than 20 in number.

Visible behind the right field wall stands the eight-story B&O Warehouse, built in 1899 as a storage facility for the B&O Railroad. It instantly reinforced the aged aspect of the new stadium and is now used by the franchise for a variety of purposes.

Although it is more than 30 years old, Camden Yards is consistently rated one of America's top ballparks, in part the basis of its influential retro design, harborside neighborhood, and intimate ambiance.

PUBLIC REACTION

Public reaction to the stadium was overwhelmingly positive. Critics applauded its nearly mythic sweep, its relatively uncluttered interiors, and its decision to be contextual, rather than following a template. The ballpark might not have been so remarked upon if it had been one of several of the "retro" brick-and-steel stadiums offering modern amenities along with that nod to tradition, and not the first. But the fact remains that it was the first. Even 30 years after its construction, it is still praised by critics and the public alike. George Will even referred to it as "one of the three most important developments of post World War II baseball, along with breaking the color barrier and free agency." Current fans insist, meanwhile, that the interior aesthetics still cannot be improved upon.

BALLPARK STATS

ADDRESS
333 West Camden Street, Baltimore, MD 21201

OPERATOR
Maryland Stadium Authority

ARCHITECT
HOK Sport (now Populous)

CAPACITY
45,971

RECORD BASEBALL ATTENDANCE
49,828 on 7/9/2005 (vs. Boston Red Sox)

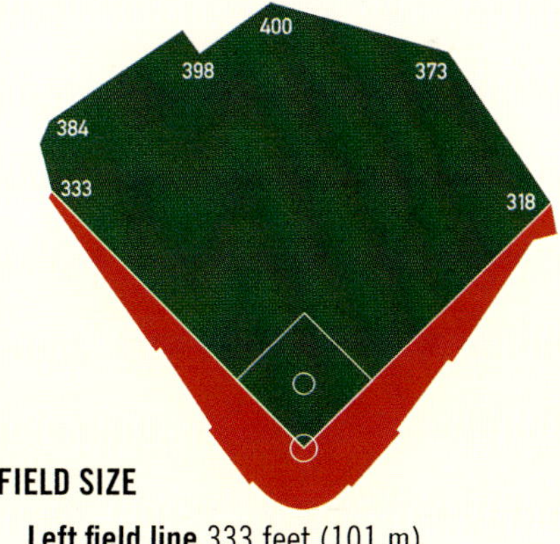

FIELD SIZE

- **Left field line** 333 feet (101 m)
- **Straight away left** 384 feet (117 m)
- **Left center** 398 feet (121 m)
- **Deep left center** 410 feet (125 m)
- **Center field** 400 feet (122 m) (Not posted)
- **Right center** 373 feet (114 m)
- **Right field line** 318 feet (97 m)

SURFACE
Bluegrass (Tuckahoe Turf Farms, New Jersey)

TEAM MASCOT
The Oriole Bird

BALLPARK FEATURES

Camden Yards consists of a three-tier grandstand that extends from behind home plate down the first baseline and down the third base line around the left field foul pole. Prior to the start of the 2022 season, the Orioles completed a $3.5 million project to change the outfield dimensions in an effort to curb the number of home runs at the ballpark. A thousand seats were removed from left field, the left field wall was pushed back nearly 27 feet (8.23 m), and its height was raised to 13 feet (4 m) from the original 7 feet 4 inches (2.2 m).

RETRO SEATING All the seats are green, intentionally replicating those in bygone ballparks, except for two orange seats that honor home runs by Orioles Hall of Famers. The seat in right center field marks the location of Eddie Murray's 500th home run, and the seat in left field marks the spot of Cal Ripken Jr.'s 278th home run, breaking Ernie Banks's record for home runs by a shortstop.

FIELD HISTORY Both foul poles at Camden Yards are the same ones used at Memorial Stadium for over three decades.

HONORED PLAYERS Beyond center field lies a welcoming grassy picnic and park area filled with colorful flower gardens and shady trees. In 2012, statues of six Orioles members of the Baseball Hall of Fame—Frank Robinson, Earl Weaver, Jim Palmer, Eddie Murray, Cal Ripken, and Brooks Robinson—were added here.

FOOD AND DRINK AMENITIES The ballpark offers numerous restaurants, pubs, and concessions for fans to enjoy. Among the most popular tasty treats are the Triple Crown Sandwich, which combines a hot dog, bacon on a stick, and pulled pork, and the Walk Off, a sausage in a pretzel roll served with crab dip.

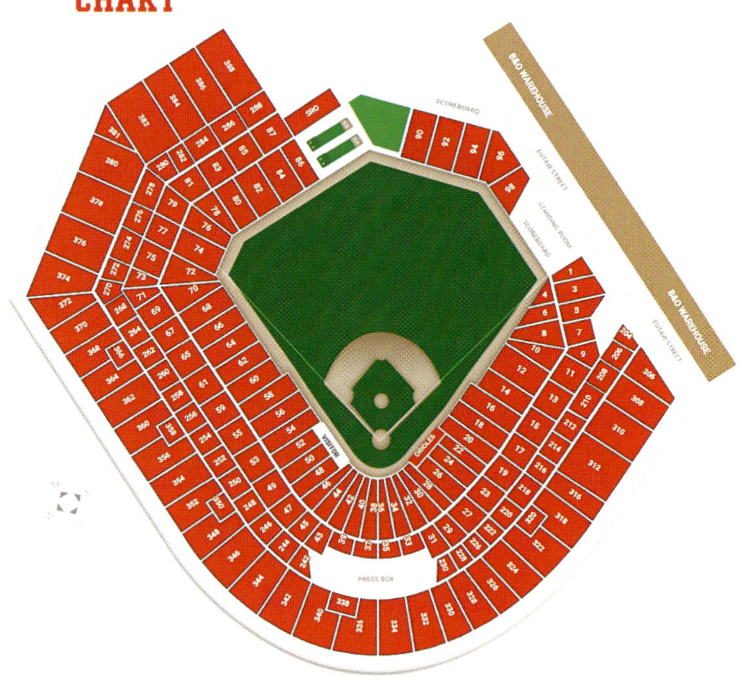

[ABOVE] In keeping with the team's name and mascot, International Migratory Bird Day was recognized at an Orioles game, featuring an honorary first pitch thrown by Fish and Wildlife Service Director H. Dale Hall and also showcasing FWS personnel on hand to operate a community information booth.

[RIGHT] On the street, in the plaza of Camden Yards, stands a statue of Baltimore native Babe Ruth by Susan Luery entitled *Babe's Dream*. Ruth's father's saloon, which he ran from 1906 to 1912, was located in what is now center field.

> **"The Ballpark That Forever Changed Baseball."**
>
> —ORIOLES' TRADEMARKED PHRASE MARKING CAMDEN YARD'S 20TH ANNIVERSARY

[ABOVE] A view of Eutaw Street between the B&O Warehouse and Oriole Park at Camden Yards. Camden Yards was the first of the "retro"-style MLB ballparks. A number of cities with Major League teams constructed old-style, fan-friendly facilities similar to Camden Yards: Arlington, Texas (Ameriquest Field, 1994); Atlanta, Georgia (Turner Field, 1997); Cincinnati, Ohio (Great American Ballpark, 2003); Cleveland, Ohio (Jacobs Field, 1994); Detroit, Michigan (Comerica Park, 2000); Milwaukee, Wisconsin (Miller Park, 2001); and Pittsburgh, Pennsylvania (PNC Park, 2001).

[RIGHT] The Chicago White Sox bullpen watches the game with empty stands behind them as the White Sox play at Camden Yards on April 29, 2015. For the first time in MLB history, fans were not allowed to the game because of the ongoing civil unrest and protest in Baltimore in the wake of Freddie Gray's death. The 25-year-old had died earlier that month from a spinal injury while in police custody. Camden Yards—and all other MLB ballparks—again banned fans during a shortened 60-game 2020 season due to the COVID-19 pandemic.

ORIOLES ACHIEVEMENTS

WORLD SERIES CHAMPIONSHIPS: 3 (1966, 1970, 1983)

AL PENNANTS: 7 (1944, 1966, 1969, 1970, 1971, 1979, 1983)

AL EAST DIVISION TITLES: 10 (1969, 1970, 1971, 1973, 1974, 1979, 1983, 1997, 2014, 2023)

WILD CARD BERTHS: 3 (1996, 2012, 2016)

PLAYOFF APPEARANCES: 14 (1966, 1969, 1970, 1971, 1973, 1974, 1979, 1983, 1997, 2012, 2014, 2016, 2023)

ALL-STAR GAMES: 1 (1993)

WORST SEASON RECORD: 1988, 54–107 (.335)

BEST SEASON RECORD: 1969, 109–53 (.335)

[ABOVE] The entrance to Camden Yards gives a first glimpse of its traditional style. Other elements continue the vintage theme, such as an outfield wall made up entirely of straight wall segments—the first MLB park to feature this since Brooklyn's Ebbets Field.

[BELOW] The ballpark got its name because it was constructed on the former site of the rail yard for the B&O Railroad's Camden Station. It is the longest field name in MLB, consisting of five words.

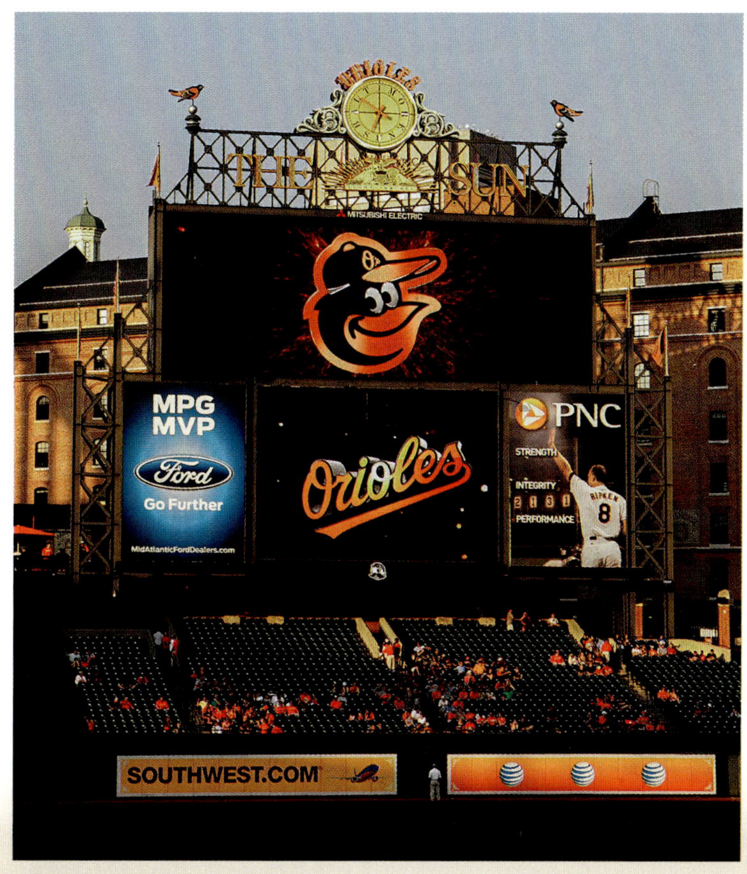

[ABOVE] The iconic ironwork Orioles clock and *Baltimore Sun* logo sat above the scoreboard until they were removed in 2023.

[LEFT] The scoreboard lights up with the Oriole's logo. The team's name gave rise to avian-themed nicknames, including, "the O's," "the Birds," "Why Not? Orioles," "the Buckle-Up Birds," and "the Birdland Power Co."

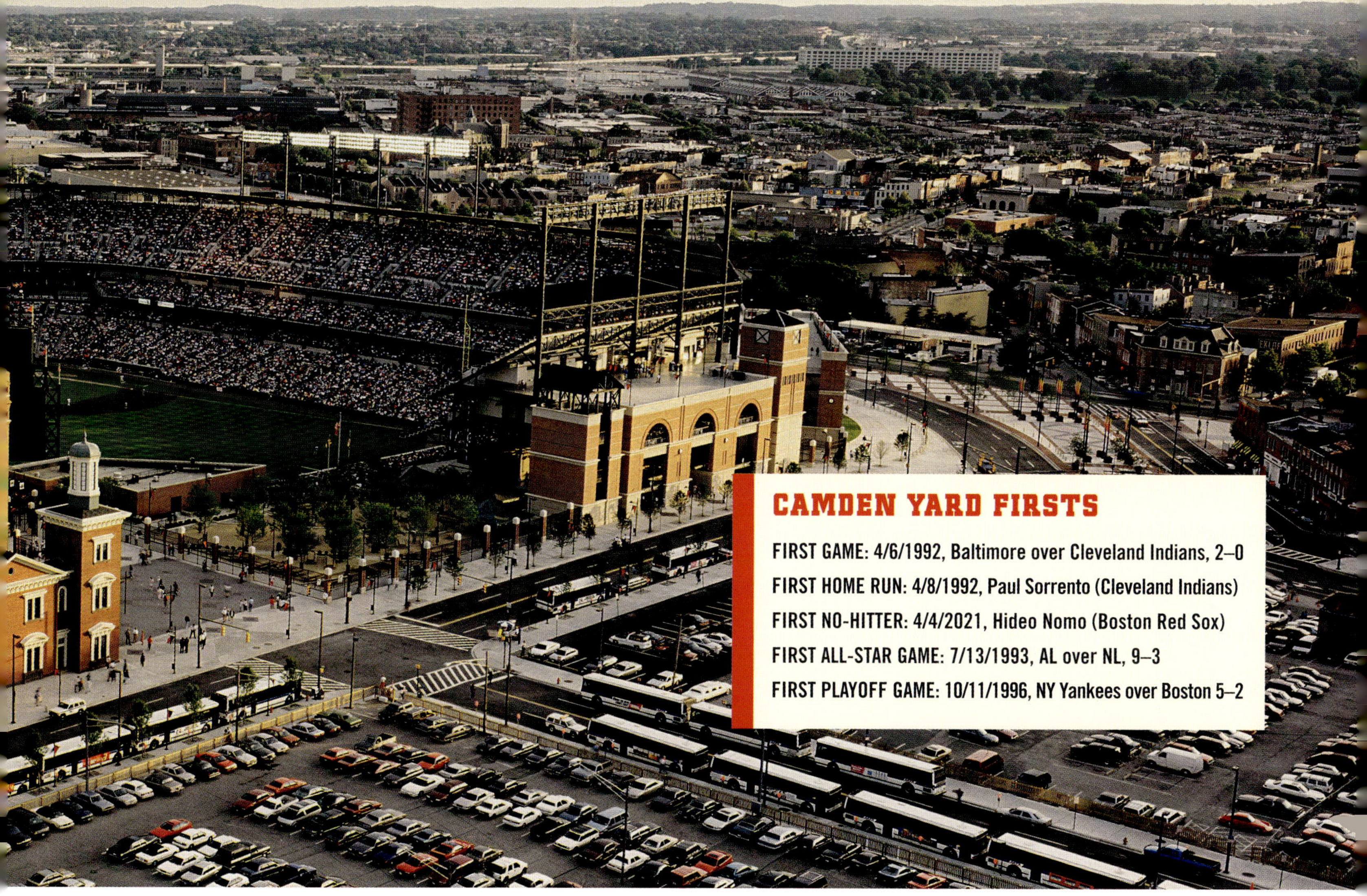

CAMDEN YARD FIRSTS

FIRST GAME: 4/6/1992, Baltimore over Cleveland Indians, 2–0

FIRST HOME RUN: 4/8/1992, Paul Sorrento (Cleveland Indians)

FIRST NO-HITTER: 4/4/2021, Hideo Nomo (Boston Red Sox)

FIRST ALL-STAR GAME: 7/13/1993, AL over NL, 9–3

FIRST PLAYOFF GAME: 10/11/1996, NY Yankees over Boston 5–2

OTHER HOMES OF THE ORIOLES

MEMORIAL STADIUM

1954–1991

When Major League Baseball returned to Baltimore in 1954, it was to a city with a long history as a baseball hub. In 1882, the Orioles club became a member of the American Association, then joined the National League in 1892 and became charter members of the American League in 1901. A year later they moved to New York as the Highlanders, which morphed into a powerhouse team called the Yankees.

In 1903, the Minor League Orioles debuted in Baltimore and, during their tenure, played in four different venues, all known as Oriole Park. Municipal Stadium, located in Baltimore's northeast Waverly Park, had been built in 1922 as a football stadium, and in 1944 it became the official new home of the Orioles. The team drew large crowds and actually won the International League championship that same year. The public supported the idea of an improved home for their heroes, and in 1947 they voted in a $2.5 million measure to rebuild Municipal Stadium. Alterations included relocating the main grandstand to the south side of the site.

On April 20, 1950, the Orioles played their first game at Memorial Stadium, which was named to honor soldiers who had died in both world wars. Originally the venue had a single-tier grandstand with a seating capacity of 31,000, but the city decided to add an upper deck to increase the capacity to 47,700, hoping the change would attract an MLB franchise.

THE RETURN OF MLB

The city got its wish in 1954, when the Browns franchise left St. Louis for Baltimore, and the team played their first game as the Orioles on April 15, 1954. The stadium now featured two seating decks that stretched from home plate in a horseshoe shape along the first and third baselines, with the lower deck running into the outfield. The electrical scoreboard, the largest in the world at that time, was sponsored by a local business, the Gunther Brewing Company. The stadium's facade was a reddish brick, and the entrance to

Memorial Stadium was affectionately known as the Old Gray Lady of 33rd Street. The stadium stood on an oversized block officially called Venable Park on 33rd Street.

home plate featured a tall concrete wall that honored Baltimore's fallen servicemen and servicewomen.

Subsequent changes to the venue included the construction of 2,600 field box seats, new dugouts, lengthening of the upper deck, and increasing seating capacity for both baseball and football. NFL fans found the stadium less than ideal for watching the hometown Colts due to the horseshoe shape of the grandstand, which distanced spectators from the 50-yard line. The Colts played there from 1953 to 1983, then moved to Indianapolis, leaving the Orioles as the stadium's sole tenant. Then in 1988 the Oriole's broke the news—they were building a new ballpark in downtown Baltimore. Their final game, to a sellout crowd at Memorial Stadium, was a loss to the Detroit Tigers on October 6, 1991. In 1996–1997 the stadium hosted the former NFL Cleveland Browns, now the expansion Baltimore Ravens, as they awaited construction of their new football stadium near Camden Yards. Memorial Stadium was demolished in 2001, doubtless saddening the many Orioles and Colts fans who'd grown up watching their teams play there, but the site gained new life as Cal Ripkin Senior Youth Development Field, which was designed for both baseball and football.

> **"The plane banked and climbed, clearing the upper deck railing by a few feet, began to turn right, and then fell into the chair-back seats of Section 1 of the upper deck, behind where home plate would be located for baseball."**
>
> —*BALTIMORE EVENING SUN*

[ABOVE] On December 19, 1976, watching the Pittsburgh Steelers trounce the Baltimore Colts proved too much for fans, who luckily left the stadium early. Few were left to see a plane buzz the stadium multiple times before crashing into the upper deck about 10 minutes after the 40-14 game ended. Nobody was seriously injured.

[LEFT] The Orioles play one of the final Major League Baseball games at Memorial Stadium, September 14, 1991.

[ABOVE] Cal Ripken Sr. (*left*) got to coach and manage his sons, Cal Jr. and Billy. Cal Jr. (*right*), nicknamed "the Iron Man," played his entire 21-season career for the Orioles and was the last Oriole to bat at Memorial Stadium, hitting into a double play against Detroit's Frank Tanana on October 6, 1991.

[RIGHT] These words were removed before the destruction of Memorial Stadium. A permanent home was found for them outside Camden Yards, at the end of the B&O Warehouse.

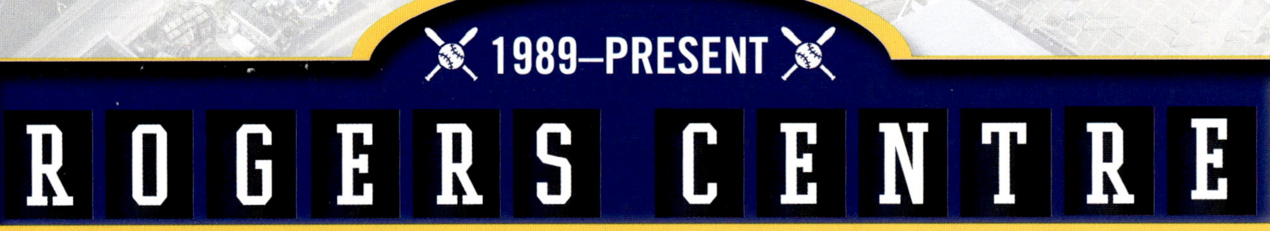

HOME OF THE TORONTO BLUE JAYS

AMERICAN LEAGUE (1977–PRESENT)

THE TORONTO BLUE JAYS, *Canada's lone Major League Baseball team, play in Rogers Centre. This domed, multipurpose stadium is in the downtown area of Ontario's capital, near the northern shore of Lake Ontario, and among other amenities, it even boasts a Marriott Hotel in center field.*

Located on the shoreline of Lake Ontario, one of the Great Lakes, the city of Toronto is understandably prone to extreme weather. In November 1982, the Canadian Football League's Grey Cup championship—featuring the hometown Argonauts' first appearance since 1971—was held at the open-air Exhibition Stadium in a pelting rainstorm. Most of the players and spectators got soaked, including Bill Davis, the premier of Ontario . . . and even the bathrooms overflowed. The press gleefully dubbed the debacle the "Rain Bowl."

Meanwhile, a Major League expansion franchise, the Blue Jays, had been founded in Toronto in 1977, and was still playing in Exhibition Stadium, awaiting a new ballpark.

Toronto clearly needed a covered sports venue. This idea was not new; it began when the city bid on the 1976 Summer Olympics and proposed building a domed stadium for the event at the Harbour City development. Alas, the games that year were awarded to Montreal. Still, the notion of a protected sports arena went forward, and the drenching during the Grey Cup only cemented the city's determination to get it done. In June 1983, seven months after that memorable storm, Bill Davis announced that a three-person committee would look into the feasibility of constructing a domed stadium at Exhibition Place.

The committee examined various options. In 1985, an international design competition was launched to create the new stadium. Proposed sites included Exhibition Place, Downsview Airport, and York University. Finally a site was chosen on railway lands at the base of the CN Tower, in the region of Union Station. The land had previously been a Canadian National Railway switching yard. It was a desolate location, but part of a master plan to reinvigorate the area, which included CityPlace. The design submitted by Robbie/Allen eventually won—in part because it provided the largest roof opening of all the finalists and appeared the most technically sound.

DESIGN AND CONSTRUCTION

The stadium design was put together by architect Rod Robbie and structural engineer Michael Allen, while the actual stadium was constructed by the EllisDon Construction company of London, Ontario, and the Dominion Bridge Company of Lachine, Quebec. Ground was broken on October 3, 1986, and construction took about two and a half years, ending in May 1989. The opening ceremony took place on June 3, 1989, with the first game on June 5. The approximate cost of construction was CA$570 million, which was paid by the federal government, the Ontario provincial government, the City of Toronto, and a consortium of corporations.

Initially the build was complicated by several factors: A functioning water pumping station that had to be relocated, the soil was contaminated from decades of industrial use, railway buildings needed to be torn down or relocated, and the site was full of archaeological finds. Some 1,500 artifacts were unearthed, including a 200-year-old French cannon and a telescope.

Built during the era of the "cookie cutter" stadium, Rogers Centre features outfield walls that are equidistant from home plate, which means hitting a home run has the same odds for lefty and righty batters. Tenants have included the Toronto Blue Jays (1989–present), CFL Toronto Argonauts (1989–2015), NBA Toronto Raptors (1995–1999), and the NCAA International Bowl (2007–2010). SkyDome was the first stadium to have a fully retractable roof. Unlike other covered fields, the roof separates into pieces and disappears from sight in less than 20 minutes, completely revealing the playing field and nearly all the seats. The hydro cost for opening or closing the roof is roughly an economical $10. The stadium is also air-conditioned for relief on hot summer days. When the stadium's roof is open, the soaring CN tower can be seen beyond left field.

BALLPARK STATS

ADDRESS
1 Blue Jays Way, Toronto, ON M5V 1J1, Canada

FORMER NAME
SkyDome (1989–2005)

OWNER
Rogers Communications

OPERATOR
Rogers Stadium Limited Partnership

DESIGNER/CHIEF ARCHITECT
Rod Robbie, Robbie Adjeleian NORR Consortium

CAPACITY
41,500

RECORD BASEBALL ATTENDANCE
52,383 on 7/9/1991 (1991 All-Star Game)

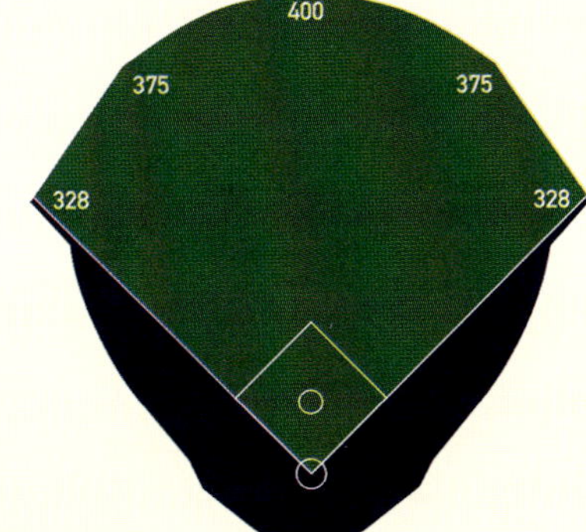

FIELD SIZE

Left field line 328 feet (100 m)
Left center 368 feet (112 m)
Left-center power alley 381 feet (116 m)
Center field 400 feet (120 m)
Right-center power alley 372 feet (113 m)
Right-center 359 feet (109 m)
Right field line 328 feet (100 m)
Backstop 60 feet (18 m)

SURFACE
AstroTurf 3D Xtreme with dirt infield

TEAM MASCOT
Ace and Junior

“The sky is a huge part of the whole roof process. The name [SkyDome] has a sense of the infinite, and that’s what this is all about.”

—CHUCK MAGWOOD, PRESIDENT OF THE STADIUM CORPORATION OF ONTARIO

The structure’s official name during early construction was “Ontario Stadium Project,” but locals already referred to it as “the Dome,” as did local media. The *Toronto Sun* held a “Name the Stadium” contest, with the winner receiving lifetime seating behind home plate for all events. More than 150,000 entries flooded in, suggesting 12,897 different names. The four finalists were Towerdome, Harbourdome, SkyDome, and the Dome. After SkyDome was chosen, a drawing was held for every fan who had suggested it. Kellie Watson’s name was drawn from the more than 2,000 entries.

NEW OWNERS, NEW NAME

In November 2004, the parent company of the Blue Jays, Rogers Communications, purchased the stadium (except for the attached hotel), and in February 2005, company president and CEO Ted Rogers announced the SkyDome would now be called Rogers Centre. The change was not popular with many fans, who still call their stadium the SkyDome.

RECENT RENOVATIONS

In 2004, Rogers refurbished the stadium by replacing the Jumbotron with a Daktronics video display and erecting other new monitors, including several built into the outfield wall. He also installed a new FieldTurf artificial playing surface. Other improvements made over the next decade or so included a roof upgrade with new sliding technology, an expansion of Jay’s Shop, an upgrade to Astroturf Gameday Grass 3D, and the addition of a center-field porch.

During the years after Rogers took over, there was talk of replacing the venue with a smaller, baseball-only stadium that

BLUE JAYS ACHIEVEMENTS

WORLD SERIES CHAMPIONSHIPS: 2 (1992, 1993)

AL PENNANTS: 2 (1992, 1993)

AL EAST DIVISION TITLES: 6 (1985, 1989, 1991, 1992, 1993, 2015)

WILD CARD BERTHS: 4 (2016, 2020, 2022, 2023)

PLAYOFF APPEARANCES: 10 (1985, 1989, 1991, 1992, 1993, 2015, 2016, 2020, 2022, 2023)

WORST SEASON RECORD: 1979, 53–109 (.327)

BEST SEASON RECORD: 1985, 99–62 (.615)

[LEFT] The illuminated dome of Rogers Centre colors the Toronto skyline.

[BELOW] A view from the CN Tower. Opened in 1989 as the home of the Blue Jays, Rogers Centre was the first ballpark to have a retractable, motorized roof.

{BOTTOM] More than 40,000 spectators packed the stadium to watch the Blue Jays take on the New York Yankees on June 1, 2016. The retractable dome was down for this open-air contest, which began in twilight and ended hours later under a dark night sky.

included residential towers, retails shops, and public spaces. Then in 2022 the organization announced a two-phase renovation of the existing stadium to extend its life. This multiyear CA$300 million privately funded renovation is scheduled to be completed between 2024 and 2025, and it is the largest-scale infrastructure project at Rogers Centre since it opened in 1989. There are still plans afoot to pursue a new stadium in 10 or 12 years.

The Phase 1 renovations began after the 2022 season. The multipurpose venue that once hosted the Argonauts Canadian football and Raptors basketball teams would now be baseball specific. To create the new Outfield District, all the 500-level seats were replaced with new patios and gathering spots. Amenities included the spacious Corona Rooftop Patio, which showcases Toronto's skyline, and the colorful, family-oriented Park Social over left field. Upcoming Phase 2 plans include demolishing the current 100-level seating bowl and structure at the end of the 2023 season. New seats will be installed from foul pole to foul pole, oriented toward the infield and with less obstruction, and, with the remodeled bowl structure, they will be closer to the field. These new 100-level seats will have additional leg room, back slats for better airflow, cupholders, adjustable armrests, and handrails in every aisle.

FEATURES AND AMENITIES

The stadium's offerings to fans include historical exhibits, fun activities for families or children, team shops, and an assortment of snacks and culinary treats. One food specialty that visitors are sure to find at Rogers Centre is poutine, Canada's national dish, which is a combination of deep-fried french fries, poutine gravy, and white cheddar cheese curds. Variations include buffalo chicken, pulled pork, and lobster.

THE JAYS SHOP This store sells authentic team merchandise and the latest fashion apparel and offers a large selection of merchandise to tempt shoppers.

OUTFIELD DISTRICT The new Outfield District, part of the recent renovation, features a number of fan-friendly amenities. These include The Stop, with its easy-to-grab eats, WestJet Flight Deck, which offers food, arcade games, and themed activities, and Schneiders Porch, a top hot dog stop with elevated views of the park. Another popular spot is the Corona Rooftop Patio, a spacious gathering area that allows fans to take in Toronto's impressive skyline and enjoy a drink while watching the game. For families there is Park Social over left field, a colorful and childlike area designed to replicate sitting in one of the city's many parks.

ORIGINAL ARTWORK Found throughout the complex are works of art, including *The Audience*, a depiction of fans by Michael Snow; *A Tribute to Baseball* by Lutz Haufschild; *The Art of the Possible* sculpture by Mimi Gellman, which honors the stadium's builders; *Salmon Run,* a fountain with steel cutouts by Susan Schelle; and *Spiral Fountain* by Judith Schwartz. A number of the historic artifacts unearthed when the Skydome was excavated are also on display inside the stadium.

TORONTO MARRIOTT CITY CENTRE HOTEL Another notable destination is the Toronto Marriott City Centre Hotel, which is right in center field. This hotel gives fans the ability to book a hotel room directly in the ballpark.

The Audience is a sculpture by Michael Snow on display outside the Rogers Centre.

ROGERS CENTRE/SKYDOME FIRSTS

FIRST MLB GAME: 6/5/1989, Milwaukee Brewers over Blue Jays, 5–3

FIRST HOME RUN: 6/5/1989, Fred McGriff vs. Milwaukee Brewers

FIRST NO-HITTER: 6/29/1990, Dave Stewart (Oakland Athletics)

FIRST ALL-STAR GAME: 7/9/1991, AL over NL, 4–2

FIRST PLAYOFF GAME: 10/7/1992, Oakland Athletics over Blue Jays, 4-3

FIRST WORLD SERIES GAME: 10/20/1992, Blue Jays over Atlanta Braves, 3–2 in Game 3

[ABOVE] An aerial image looking down at Rogers Centre from the CN Tower

[BELOW] Blue Jays mascot Ace the Blue Jay riles up fans during a game against the Tampa Bay Rays, May 19, 2011, in Toronto. Blue Jays won 3–2. Ace wears jersey No. 00. In 2002 he and his female counterpart, Diamond, replaced former mascot BJ Birdy. Diamond was retired in 2004.

SEATING CHART

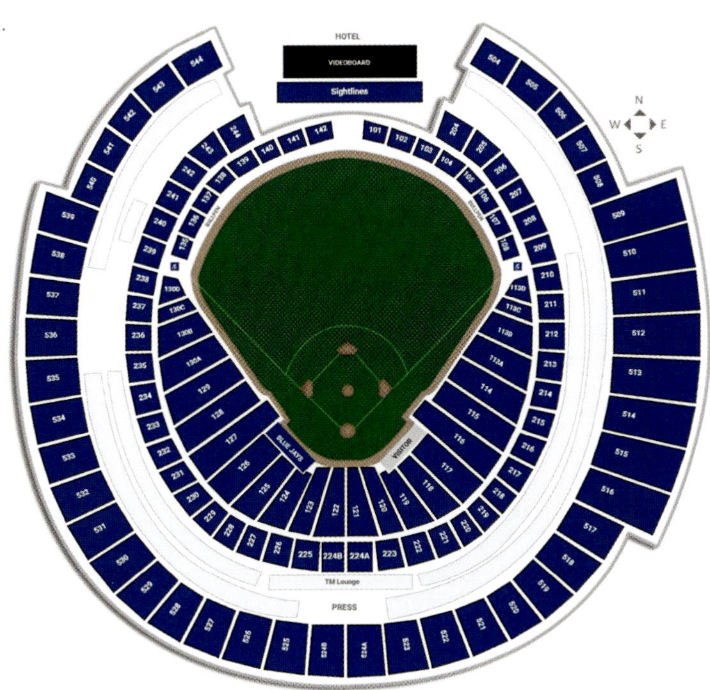

OTHER HOMES OF THE BLUE JAYS

EXHIBITION STADIUM

1959–1989

This multipurpose stadium that opened in August 1959 was on Lake Shore Boulevard West and Ontario Drive. Originally meant to host Canadian National Exhibition events, it served as the home of the CFL Toronto Argonauts from 1959 to 1988, the MLB Blue Jays from 1977 to 1989, and the NASL Toronto Blizzard from 1979 to 1983. The venue also hosted the Canadian Football League Grey Cup 12 times over the course of 24 years.

It was the fourth stadium to be built at that location since 1879. Although the original grandstand was lost due to a fire in 1906, it was quickly rebuilt. In 1947 a second fire destroyed the stadium, which led to the city constructing a covered north-side grandstand known as CNE Grandstand for CA$3 million in 1948. This part of the stadium's structure stayed even as the stadium underwent various changes to its configuration over the years until its closure in 1999.

In 1959, when the Toronto Argonauts moved from Varsity Stadium for the season, a smaller CA$650,000 bleacher section was constructed along the south sideline, allowing the stadium to seat 33,150. In 1970 the grass in the field was publicly labeled "a disgrace," so the metropolitan council voted to replace it with artificial turf. A reconfiguration was needed in 1974 to make the venue compatible for baseball, when the expansion Blue Jays finally brought the Major League to Toronto, after the city failed to acquire the San Francisco Giants.

With its proximity to Lake Ontario, Exhibition Stadium was frequently cold at the start and end of baseball season and at the end of football season. The first time the Jays played there, on April 7, 1977, it became the only MLB game in history played with the field covered in snow. The Maple Leaf's Zamboni had to be requisitioned to clear it off. One time in 1986, fog so thickly covered the interior of the stadium that Kelly Gruber managed an inside-the-park home run when his routine pop-up was obscured to the outfielders. High winds were also a problem—in April 1984 a game against the Texas Rangers was postponed because of 60-mile-an-hour (97 km/h) winds. Starting pitcher Jim Clancy was even blown off balance several times. Last, the ball park's food concessions drew large numbers of seagulls from the lake, and they often swooped low over the players. Yankee slugger Dave Winfield was vilified—and then arrested—for accidentally killing a seagull with a thrown baseball, but he later

[TOP] A first and only in MLB game history: April 7, 1977, the Jays' groundskeeping crew prepares a snow-covered field for a baseball game.

[LEFT] The second MLB game for the Toronto Blue Jays. Unlike the first game, played in a snowstorm, this day was bright and sunny, with the temperature well below freezing.

A view of Exhibition Stadium taken on May 27, 1988, shows the field being prepared before the Chicago White Sox faced the Toronto Blue Jays.

BASEBALL IN CANADA

As part of the British Commonwealth, Canadians naturally have an affinity for cricket, but baseball quickly became a popular pastime once it was introduced. According to the Canadian Baseball Hall of Fame, the first baseball game in Canada was played on June 4, 1838, in Beachville, Ontario, between teams from Oxford and Zorra. The field configuration included five bases, and the players used a hand-hewn stick as a bat and a ball created from twisted yarn and covered with calfskin.

In addition to Major League play, there are many independent professional and summer collegiate baseball leagues in Canada. The largest is the Western Canadian Baseball League, with 11 teams scattered throughout Alberta and Saskatchewan. The Swift Current 57s and Okotoks Dawgs are tied— six each—for the most championships. The winner of the league is awarded the Harry Hallis Memorial Trophy. Canada has also appeared in the WBC and the Olympics; the country won two gold medals in the Pan American Games in 2011 and 2015—both in wins against the United States.

redeemed himself when he won a World Series with the Blue Jays in 1992.

In spite of its problems, the stadium and the grandstand were favored locations for pop music concerts, including performances by the Who, Pink Floyd, Chicago, U2, David Bowie, Elton John, Rush, Iron Maiden, Van Halen, AC/DC, Bruce Springsteen, Janis Joplin, Whitney Houston, and New Kids on the Block.

THE END OF AN ERA

It was the aforementioned "Rain Bowl" that finally spelled the downfall of Exhibition Stadium. The wretched conditions at the game had been seen by over 7.862 million television viewers in Canada. The next day, there was a rally at Toronto City Hall where tens of thousands of Argonauts fans chanted, "We want a dome! We want a dome!" A committee was formed to look into a site for a covered stadium, and in April 1984, Canadian National agreed to donate 7 acres (2.8 ha) of former railway land near their CN Tower; groundbreaking began in October 1986.

Except for an occasional wrestling match or concert and a series of CASCAR races in the 1990s, Exhibition Hall remained inactive during the decade after SkyDome opened. The facility was demolished on January 31, 1999. BMO Field, named for rights holder the Bank of Montreal, was constructed on its former site and opened in 2007.

[BELOW] The walls come tumbling down. The "Mistake by the Lake" was demolished in January 1999.

HOME OF THE TAMPA BAY RAYS

AMERICAN LEAGUE (1998–PRESENT)

THE SCRAPPY FLORIDA EXPANSION TEAM *called the Tampa Bay Rays plays their brand of baseball at St. Petersburg's Tropicana Field, which is a multipurpose domed stadium. The air-conditioned venue, the only indoor professional baseball facility in Florida, helps fans and players keep their cool on even the hottest days.*

Originally named the Florida Suncoast Dome, Tropicana Field is located near downtown St. Petersburg. The 1.1-million-square-foot (102,193 m^2) venue opened to the public on March 3, 1990, at a cost of $138 million. With the 1993 arrival of the region's National Hockey League expansion franchise, the Tampa Bay Lightning, the venue was rechristened the ThunderDome. Ultimately the venue had been built with the intention of attracting a Major League Baseball franchise to the Bay area.

Plans for a stadium began after Tampa was awarded the NFL Tampa Bay Buccaneers and the professional soccer Tampa Bay Rowdies in the 1970s, when sister city St. Petersburg decided it wanted a share of the local professional sports scene—specifically an MLB team. Both cities already had a deep connection to baseball, since they were among the first homes of MLB spring training in the 1910s.

Due to Florida's semi-tropic temperatures and frequent thunderstorms, St. Pete city officials agreed on the need for a domed stadium, and construction started in 1986. The Chicago White Sox, in need of a replacement for aging Comiskey Park, were targeted as tenants, but Chicago and Illinois officials came through with a new park for them in 1989. The Suncoast Dome was completed in 1990 without a tenant, and subsequent rumors involving the acquisition of the Seattle Mariners and the San Francisco Giants proved groundless. The arena football Tampa Bay Storm finally debuted there, and in 1993 the NHL Tampa Bay Lightning moved in, skating there for three seasons.

The Gulf Coast's desired baseball franchise finally materialized in the form of the Tampa Bay Rays, which were awarded to investor Vince Naimoli's ownership group on March 9, 1995, the same day that the Arizona Diamondbacks were awarded to Phoenix. Originally called the Devil Rays, at the end of the 2007 season the name was changed to Rays, standing for both a manta ray and a ray of sunshine. On October 4 the stadium was rebranded Tropicana Field in accordance with a naming rights agreement between the new team and Bradenton's Tropicana Dole Beverages North America.

The Rays actually played their first game there in 1998, and over time the Trop became an integral part of the ball club's journey and, for many, an oasis of comfort, with its protective dome and air-conditioned seating. Meanwhile, the Lightning and the Storm moved to the new Amalie Arena in downtown Tampa. During their first decade at the Trop, the Devil Rays struggled to find their footing. They never had a winning record, nearly always ending up fifth in their division. But since their 2008 season, the team has shown great promise, advancing to the postseason nine times and making it to the World Series twice.

Though originally configured for baseball, Tropicana Field has hosted 14 other sports and competitive events. These include hockey, basketball, football, sprint car racing, gymnastics, soccer, tennis, weight lifting, table tennis, karate, motorcycle racing, equestrian events, track-and-field competitions, and figure skating. As an entertainment venue it has featured pop, alternative, R&B, and country acts like ZZ Top, Earth, Wind, & Fire, Goo Goo Dolls, REO Speedwagon, Nelly, Miranda Lambert, the Beach Boys, Big & Rich, the B-52s, Flo Rida, Pat Benetar, and Ozzfest.

DESIGN AND CONSTRUCTION

The stadium's original designers in 1990 were HOK Sport, Lescher & Mahoney Sports, and Criswell, Blizzard & Blouin Architects. In a case of monumentally poor timing, the Trop debuted on the eve of the retro ballpark craze inspired by Camden Yards. As a result, the facility was deemed unfashionable almost immediately. With its pale, monochromatic exterior and white "beach umbrella" roof,

BALLPARK STATS

ADDRESS
1 Tropicana Drive, St. Petersburg, FL 33705

FORMER NAMES
Florida Suncoast Dome (1990–1993)
ThunderDome (1993–1996)

OWNER
City of St. Petersburg

OPERATOR
Tampa Bay Rays Ltd.

DESIGNER/CHIEF ARCHITECT
HOK Sport; Lescher & Mahoney Sports; Criswell, Blizzard & Blouin Architects

CAPACITY
25,000 (42,735, including tarp-covered seats)

RECORD BASEBALL ATTENDANCE
43,373 on 7/12/ 1998 (vs. NY Yankees)

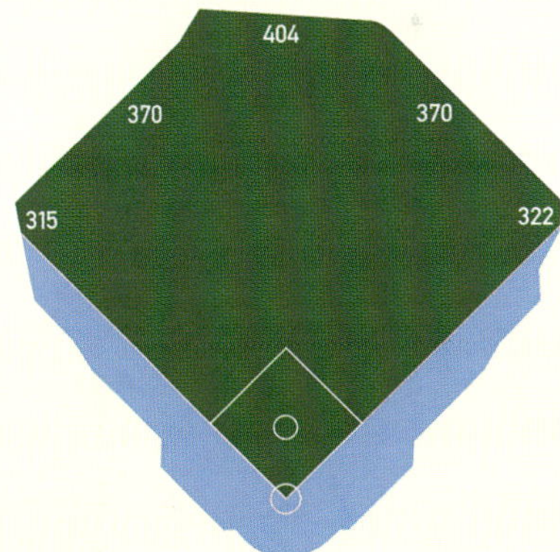

FIELD SIZE

- **Left field** 315 feet (96 m)
- **Left-center** 370 feet (110 m)
- **Center field** 404 feet (123 m)
- **Right-center** 370 feet (110 m)
- **Right field** 322 feet (98 m)
- **Backstop** 50 feet (15 m)

SURFACE
Shaw Sports Turf

TEAM MASCOTS
Raymond the Seadog, DJ Kitty, and Stinger

it hardly beckoned to visitors in search of that famous Florida Deco style. The interior aesthetics fared little better in reviews, often rated near or at the bottom of polls. On the plus side, the friendliness and helpful attitude of the staff were frequently noted.

After the Rays were awarded to Tampa Bay, the stadium required a facelift, so in October 1996 it underwent a 17-month, $85 million transformation into a baseball-specific park. The architects used the legendary Ebbets Field as their model, including a replica of the famous Dodger's rotunda. This renovation added 319,000 square feet (29,636 m^2) of space, creating room for modern amenities and incorporating baseball traditions throughout the facility. Updates included all-dirt base paths and AstroTurf, making Tropicana Field the first Major League ballpark in more than 20 years to feature these elements (the current field surface is Shaw's Sports Turf). The renovations also introduced a number of dining, shopping, and entertainment options to the complex.

The first regular season game took place on March 31, 1998, when the Devil Rays lost to the Detroit Tigers 11–6. Tiger Luis Gonzalez hit the revamped stadium's first home run, countered by the Rays' Wade Boggs, who got a dinger later in the game. In 1999 Boggs also achieved his 3,000th hit, a home run, at the Trop.

With regular seating for only 25,000 fans, Tropicana Field is the smallest MLB stadium on the basis of capacity, although several tarp-covered sections on the 300 level bring that number to close to 43,000 (these seats are rarely used beyond playoff games). "The Trop" is also the only venue in the Majors with a non-retractable dome.

SEATING CHART

In 1995, when MLB finally expanded to the Tampa Bay area, naming rights for the ThunderDome sold to Tropicana Products, who renamed it Tropicana Field.

PUBLIC OPINION

The updated version of the stadium generated a decent amount of positive feedback. Naturally, the presence of the dome and air-conditioning was applauded—watching a summer baseball game at 72°F (22.2°C) was ideal, especially when it hit 90°F (32.2°C) outside. Some reviewers appreciated the numerous standing room sections, which allowed fans to view the field from different angles. Many enjoyed how the interior of the dome changed colors and after a Rays victory turned a celebratory red.

Unfortunately, the ballpark is still consistently voted one of MLB's three worst stadiums, along with the Oakland Coliseum and Angel Stadium. From the start, criticisms of the design included the ceiling catwalks and the cramped restrooms and concourse. The structure's setting, surrounded by a massive parking lot, was problematic, as was the tough travel logistics for drivers. For fans who live in Tampa or Orlando, or the suburbs surrounding St. Petersburg, getting to the games and then out of the parking lots is often very challenging. The lack of access bridges and decent public transport makes it one of the most difficult MLB stadiums to reach. During play, the light-gray roof obscures pop-ups for players and spectators alike. Problems with the ballpark are often cited for the steady decline in fan attendance. Observers also remark on a curious lack of team presence in the neighborhood—no Rays banners, posters, or other promotional items displayed in the bars and restaurants directly adjacent to the stadium.

FEATURES AND AMENITIES

Tropicana Field's advertising spots proclaim that it offers something for everyone, from pre-game activities for families to historical features for purists. Art lovers will be pleased to note that the stadium is less than a mile from the exquisite Chihuly Collection of unique art glass.

TROPICANA FIELD FIRSTS

FIRST MLB GAME: 3/31/1998, Detroit Tigers over Rays, 11–6

FIRST HOME RUN: 3/31/1998, Luis Gonzalez (Detroit Tigers)

FIRST NO-HITTER: 6/25/2010, Edwin Jackson (Arizona Diamondbacks)

FIRST PLAYOFF GAME: 10/2/2008, Rays over Chicago White Sox, 6-4

FIRST WORLD SERIES GAME: 10/22/2008, Philadelphia Phillies over Rays 3–2 in Game 1

SEATING OPTIONS Fans have the choice of several seating options, ranging from the economically priced Upper Deck to the luxurious premium Home Plate Club, which comes with food and beverage service. The ballpark also offers wheelchair-accessible seating and assistive listening devices for fans with disabilities.

PLAYER HISTORY The Ted Williams Museum and the Hitters Hall of Fame further add to the fan experience. Inside the museum, visitors view the Tampa Bay Rays' history, Ted Williams's career highlights, pictures of past players, and more.

[ABOVE] Play on the field distracts fans who have stopped to visit the aquatic denizens of the Ray's Touch Tank.

[BELOW] The main entry rotunda, with baseball diamond flooring, is said to be structurally similar to the one that used to welcome fans to Ebbets Field.

[BELOW] DJ Kitty on Star Wars Day during a game against the Milwaukee Brewers in 2023. The Tampa Bay Rays currently have three mascots. The original mascot, Raymond the Seadog, is a furry blue creature that wears a large pair of sneakers, a backward ball cap, and a Rays jersey. DJ Kitty, a black-and-white cat, wears a Rays ring, chains, and a backward Rays hat. Stinger, a cownosed ray, is mainly seen on Sundays and is the designated greeter for the Touch Tank.

[OPPOSITE PAGE] Directly on the other side of the concourse from the Ted Williams Museum, a king-sized No. 10 leaps out to catch a fly ball.

THE TOUCH TANK A highlight of Tropicana Field for visitors young and old is the Touch Tank, home to several cownose stingrays, a species also found in the waters of Tampa Bay. Thanks to a partnership between the ball club and a dedicated team of biologists from the Florida Aquarium, visitors are able to gently touch and interact with the stingrays throughout the game. The 35-foot (10.7 m), 10,000-gallon (37, 854 L) exhibit is just beyond the right-center field fence. Home runs hit into the tank by the Rays earn a charitable donation—$2,500 to the Aquarium and $2,500 to the player's charity of choice.

FOOD AND DRINK The park offers more than 50 concession stands where visitors will find a variety of traditional ballpark fare, like hot dogs and nachos, along with unique local menu items. Fan favorites include Ducky's, a sports lounge offering sliders, wings, and sandwiches; RumFish Grill, serving fresh-caught seafood; and Papa John's, for classic pizza and garlic knots.

RAYS ACHIEVEMENTS

AL PENNANTS: 2 (2008, 2020)

AL EAST DIVISION TITLES: 4 (2008, 2010, 2020, 2021)

WILD CARD BERTHS: 6 (2011, 2013, 2019, 2022, 2023)

PLAYOFF APPEARANCES: 9 (2008, 2010, 2011, 2013, 2019, 2020, 2021, 2022, 2023)

WORST SEASON RECORD: 2002*, 55–106 (.342)

BEST SEASON RECORD: 2020, 40–20 (.667)

* as Devil Rays

LOOKING TOWARD THE FUTURE

In the late 1980s, the construction of Tropicana Field had forced some residents of St. Petersburg's historic Gas Plant community to relocate. Promises were made regarding new opportunities for displaced people and businesses, but nothing ever materialized. Finally, on September 19, 2023, an historic agreement was announced. The City of St. Petersburg, Pinellas County, Tampa Bay Rays, and Hines Development would be moving forward with a new state-of-the-art ballpark and a transformational development of the Historic Gas Plant District. This project would include attainable housing, equitable business opportunities, office spaces, meeting spaces, and open areas—an impactful economic development that would benefit everyone. The project would accomplish several goals for the city: Keep the Rays in town and away from Tampa's tempting plans for Ybor Stadium; ease the affordable housing crisis; and bring Black families back to the neighborhood from which they were relocated.

> "Baseball has the power to connect people, connect communities, and inspire us."
>
> —STUART STERNBERG, RAYS OWNER

St. Petersburg mayor Ken Welch announced that the team's proposal had been chosen over three other finalists. The Rays and their Houston-based partner Hines placed the highest bid for the rights and also guaranteed a new stadium by the 2028 season. Their proposal included a 7-million-square-foot (650,321 m2), mixed-use venue with Rays stadium at its center, as well as 5,700 multifamily units, 600 senior residences, and more than 850 affordable workforce housing units. Cultural features would be a key addition—including the Woodson African American Museum, honoring the local Black community, and the Booker Music Hall, which will seat up to 3,000 people. The "Gameday Street Experience" would convert the streets surrounding the ballpark into a pedestrian mall centered on food vendors and family-friendly entertainment.

HOME OF THE ATLANTA BRAVES

NATIONAL LEAGUE (1876–PRESENT)

IN 2017, TRUIST PARK *became the home of the venerable Atlanta Braves baseball franchise. The property also features a mixed-use development that includes an entertainment district, apartments, offices, restaurants, and more. Their new ballpark must have agreed with the Braves; they continued to be one of the best teams in the National League, winning the pennant and hosting—and winning—the World Series against the Houston Astros in 2021.*

The Braves have the honor to be the oldest continuously operating pro sports franchise in North America. Founded in Boston in 1871 as the Red Stockings, they played under a number of names until the team selected "Braves" in 1912. In 1953, after 81 seasons in Boston, the team moved to Milwaukee, where their roster included Hank Aaron, Eddie Mathews, and Warren Spahn. In spite of winning the World Series in 1957, fan attendance lagged. The owners relocated the team to Georgia in 1966. Success eluded them in Atlanta until 1991, when they became one of baseball's most outstanding teams, nailing down a record 14 consecutive division titles and playing in eight consecutive National League Championship Series. After 14 years in the National League West Division, Atlanta was moved to the East Division in 1994 during an MLB realignment.

As of 2023, the Braves franchise has played for an astonishing total of 139 seasons. In 2013, after nearly 50 years in downtown Atlanta, the franchise announced that the team would be relocating into adjacent Cobb County—roughly 10 miles (16 km) from the city center—where they planned to construct a new ballpark. Although their current home, Turner Field, was not even 20 years old, it needed expensive infrastructure upgrades and also lacked the space to develop the property around the stadium in the manner the team desired.

A 60-acre (24 ha) parcel of land was purchased near the Galleria/Cumberland Mall, and ground was broken on the site on September 16, 2014. The Braves played their first game at their new home

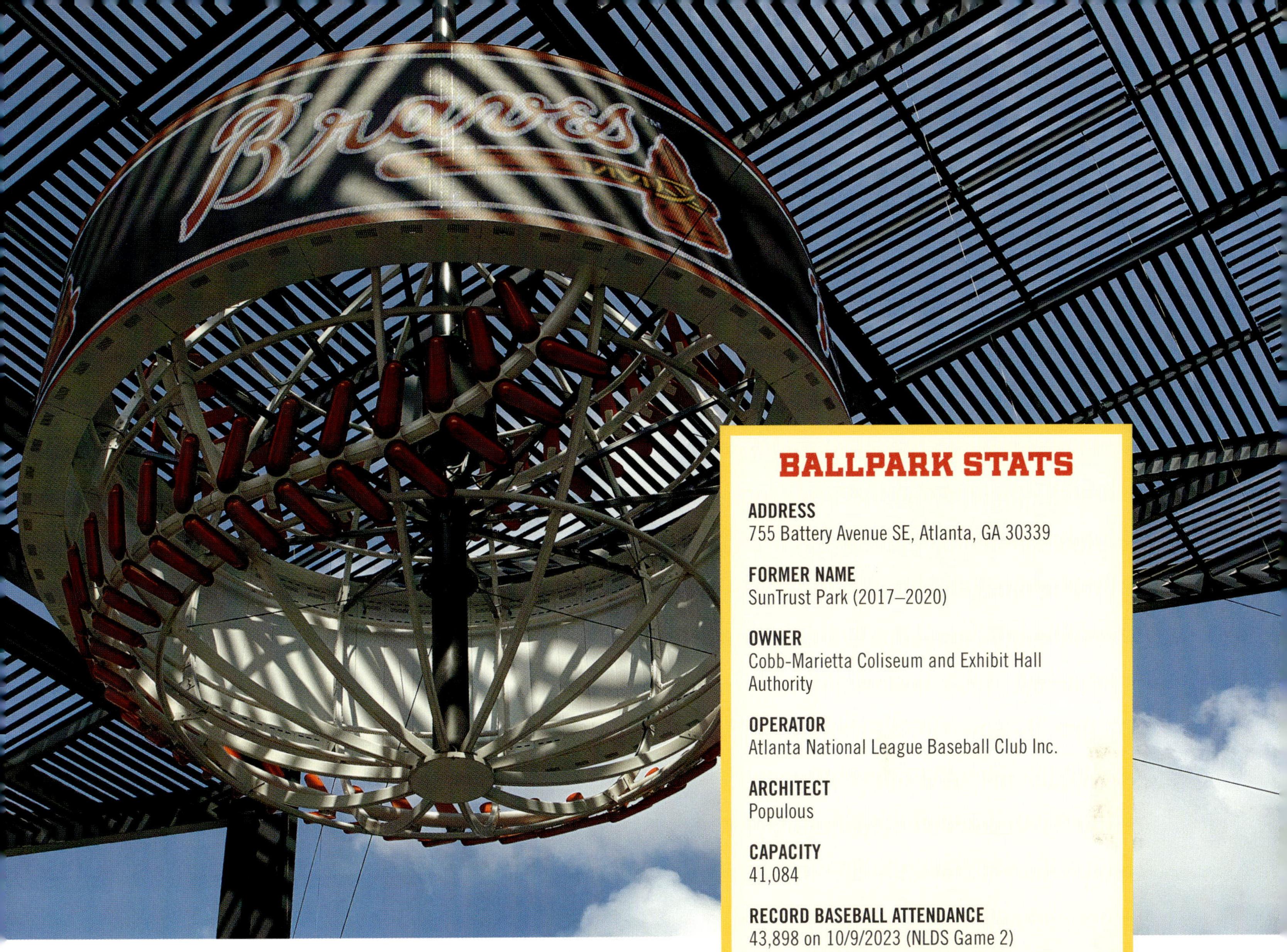

[ABOVE] Visitors to the ballpark are greeted by a stunning 7-foot-tall-by-69-foot-long (2.1 x 21 m) curved LED display wrapped 360 degrees around a giant metal baseball suspended over a water fountain in the main plaza.

[OPPOSITE PAGE] An aerial view of the Truist Park baseball stadium shows the adjoining Battery Atlanta neighborhood.

on April 13, 2017, a victory against the San Diego Padres. Called SunTrust Park, the new venue reflected a 25-year naming rights deal with SunTrust Bank. In January 2020, a merger between SunTrust and BB&T Corporation (Branch Banking and Trust Company) resulted in a new name, Truist Park.

ARCHITECTURE AND DESIGN

The team owners requested a number of special features from the design firm Populous. Encouraging fans to enjoy the venue both before and after games was one requirement. Creating a vibrant environment around the ballpark for the community to enjoy outside the regular baseball season was another.

To this end, Populous combined an authentically Southern experience with enough attractions to give visitors reasons to come early and linger late. They provided high-quality amenities and modern technology throughout a welcoming, comfortable concourse and came up with draws like the Xfinity Lounge's rooftop patio along with the first zip line and climbing tower in an MLB park. Just beyond the stadium, they created the Battery Atlanta,

BALLPARK STATS

ADDRESS
755 Battery Avenue SE, Atlanta, GA 30339

FORMER NAME
SunTrust Park (2017–2020)

OWNER
Cobb-Marietta Coliseum and Exhibit Hall Authority

OPERATOR
Atlanta National League Baseball Club Inc.

ARCHITECT
Populous

CAPACITY
41,084

RECORD BASEBALL ATTENDANCE
43,898 on 10/9/2023 (NLDS Game 2)

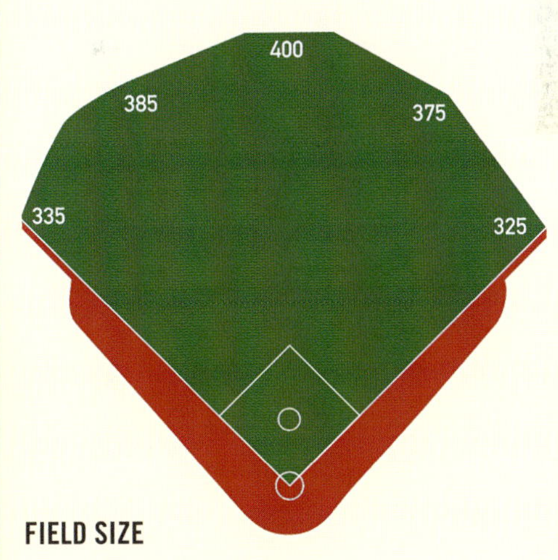

FIELD SIZE

Left Field 335 feet (102 m)

Left-center 385 feet (117 m)

Center field 400 feet (122 m)

Right-center 375 feet (114 m)

Right field 325 feet (99 m)

SURFACE
Seashore Paspalum, Platinum TE

TEAM MASCOT
Blooper

a large entertainment district—with entrances to the park's outfield—which also included apartment buildings, office buildings, restaurants, and more. The result was a sports destination with the ambiance of a theme park, one that had something to offer visitors of all ages—from family groups, to couples, to work friends—seeking a fun day away from the office. The stadium, constructed for a total of $672 million, officially opened on April 8, 2017, and became the anchoring centerpiece of the surrounding development

The classical red-brick and pre-cast concrete facade of Truist Park makes the facility visually pleasing and lends it a throwback appeal, in spite of it being one of the newest parks in the Majors. Upon entering the stands proper, fans are met with a sea of green seats encircling the pristine playing field. The seats in the lower level even feature mesh bottoms and backs to increase airflow, keeping fans cool and comfortable during the game. The three overlapping decks create the sensation of being right on top of the action while also offering superior sight lines of the field.

The ballpark's seating capacity is 41,500, with the main grandstand stretching from the right-field foul pole to home plate and down and around the left-field foul pole.

PUBLIC RESPONSE

Reviewers of the new ballpark lauded its many positive features—the beauty of the stadium, the range of amenities, the friendly, welcoming ambiance, the unobstructed sight lines, the ease of access outside congested downtown Atlanta, the on-site parking, a sense of safety, the history presented along Monument Garden, and the helpful assistance for the disabled.

Complaints included high prices at concessions (*er,* what else is new?), the orientation of some seats, which spectators claimed faced in the wrong direction to follow action at home plate, and a lack of information about where to board shuttles.

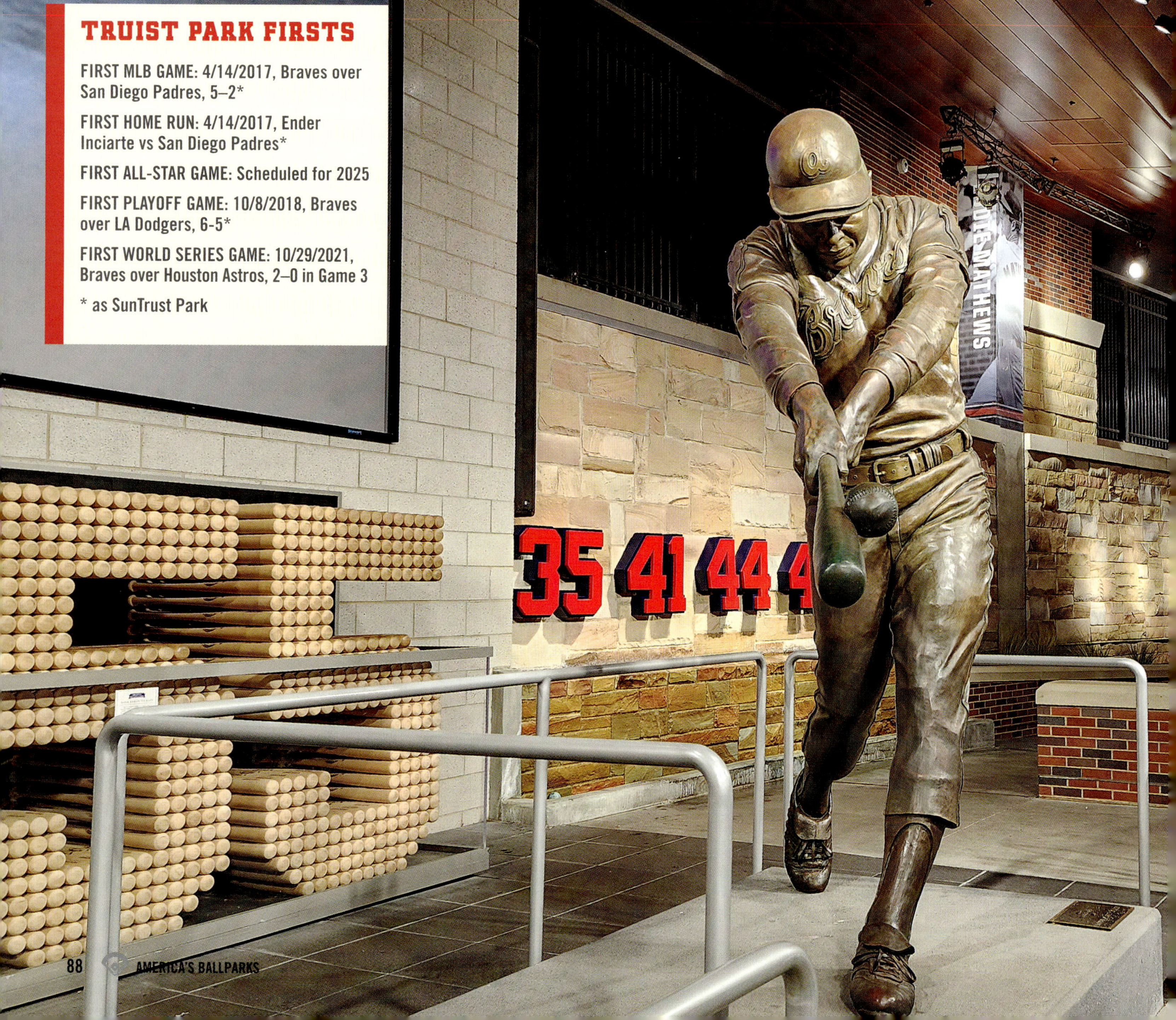

TRUIST PARK FIRSTS

FIRST MLB GAME: 4/14/2017, Braves over San Diego Padres, 5–2*

FIRST HOME RUN: 4/14/2017, Ender Inciarte vs San Diego Padres*

FIRST ALL-STAR GAME: Scheduled for 2025

FIRST PLAYOFF GAME: 10/8/2018, Braves over LA Dodgers, 6-5*

FIRST WORLD SERIES GAME: 10/29/2021, Braves over Houston Astros, 2–0 in Game 3

* as SunTrust Park

SEATING CHART

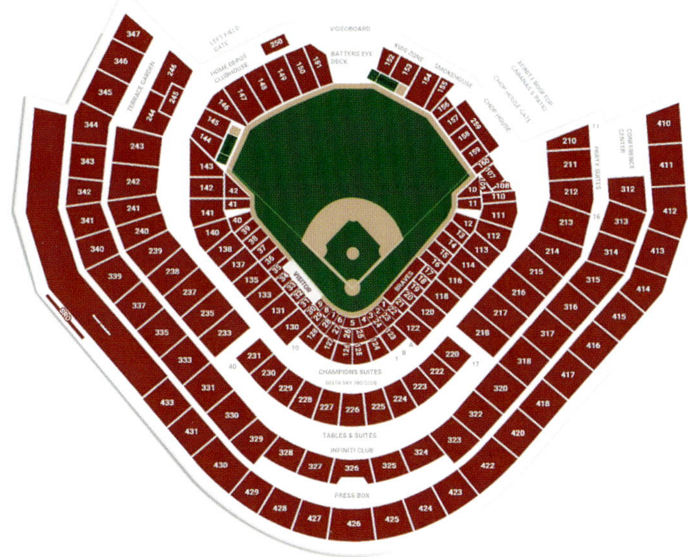

[ABOVE] In its short existence, this park has already experienced a name change, having opened in 2017 as SunTrust Park.

[LEFT] Monument Garden features a statue of baseball legend Hank Aaron among its many striking tributes to the Braves and their long, storied history.

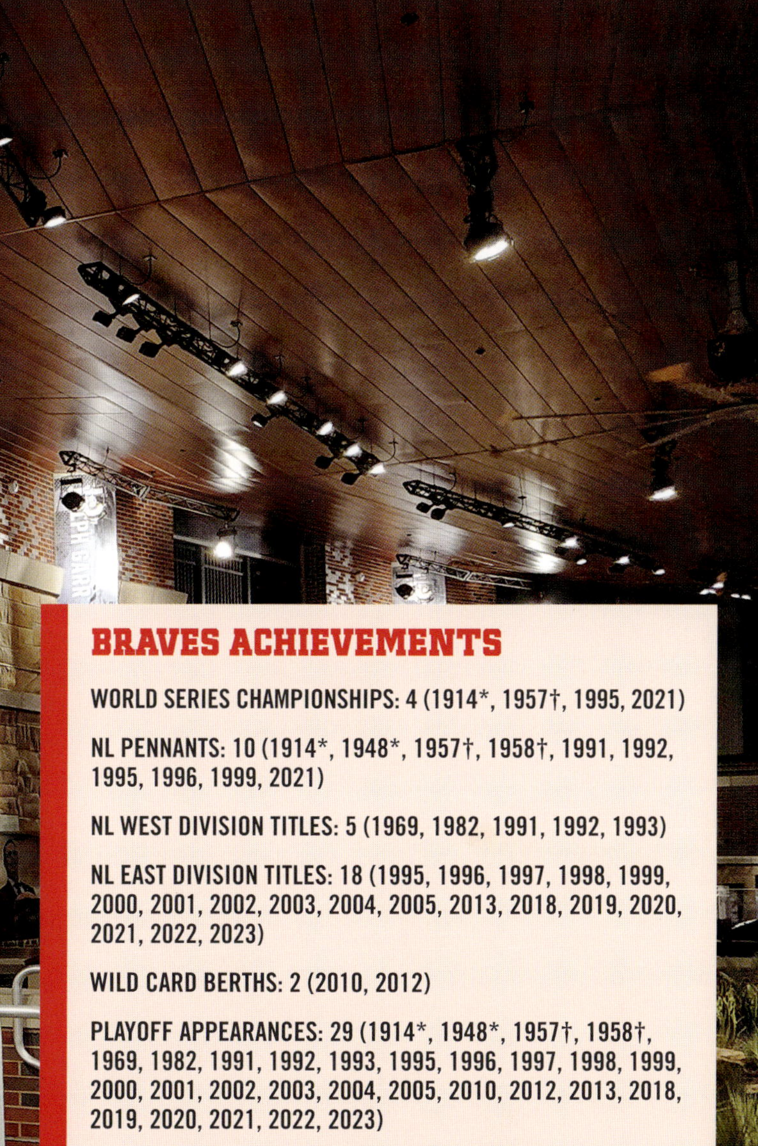

BRAVES ACHIEVEMENTS

WORLD SERIES CHAMPIONSHIPS: 4 (1914*, 1957†, 1995, 2021)

NL PENNANTS: 10 (1914*, 1948*, 1957†, 1958†, 1991, 1992, 1995, 1996, 1999, 2021)

NL WEST DIVISION TITLES: 5 (1969, 1982, 1991, 1992, 1993)

NL EAST DIVISION TITLES: 18 (1995, 1996, 1997, 1998, 1999, 2000, 2001, 2002, 2003, 2004, 2005, 2013, 2018, 2019, 2020, 2021, 2022, 2023)

WILD CARD BERTHS: 2 (2010, 2012)

PLAYOFF APPEARANCES: 29 (1914*, 1948*, 1957†, 1958†, 1969, 1982, 1991, 1992, 1993, 1995, 1996, 1997, 1998, 1999, 2000, 2001, 2002, 2003, 2004, 2005, 2010, 2012, 2013, 2018, 2019, 2020, 2021, 2022, 2023)

WORST SEASON RECORD: 1928*, 50–103 (.327)

BEST SEASON RECORD: 1998, 106–56 (.654)

* as Boston Braves † as Milwaukee Braves

Truist Park has won numerous awards, including a Best Projects Award–Sports/Entertainment from *Engineering News-Record* and the title of Ballpark of the Year from both Baseballparks.com and Ballparkdigest.com, all in 2017, and Ballpark of the Decade in 2019 from *Ballpark Digest*.

FEATURES AND AMENITIES

Truist Park was designed with the fans in mind, and that also goes for the concourses and eateries. And in terms of team history . . . as the *Atlanta Business Chronicle* reported in 2017, the stadium "won't have a museum, it will *be* a museum."

BRAVES HISTORY One of the park's main draws is the Monument Garden on the lower level behind home plate, which takes fans on a stroll down memory lane to learn about the club's history and relive its brightest moments. The spacious area includes Braves jerseys from different eras, the 1995 World Series trophy, artifacts from significant team events, a wall honoring individual award winners, and, naturally, a number of displays devoted to Hank Aaron. There are also 300 examples of Braves-themed art found throughout the grounds, including statues of several notable Braves—Warren Spahn, Phil Niekro, and manager Bobby Cox—that surround the perimeter of the stadium.

SEATS AND SUITES Seating options include the 4,000 premium seats found in the Truist Club, Delta Sky360 Club, and Terrace Club. The top deck is split, which allows fans to view the field while they are strolling the concourse. The 90-foot wide (27.4 m) canopy that stretches across the upper deck ensures protection from the hot summer sun. The largest such canopy in the pro leagues, it amplifies crowd cheers back down to the field, letting the players know they are appreciated. The park also provides air-conditioning on every level to ensure fans stay cool. Left-center field is home to one of the most distinctive features in any ballpark—the Home Depot Clubhouse, a premium suite that resembles a tree house. It features bleacher-style seating in the front with garage-style doors in the back.

FOOD AND DRINK The facility offers a number of dining options in addition to the concessions, including the three-level Chop House in right field. This area contains a restaurant, two party decks, and one group area directly on the field behind the outfield fence.

While playing in Boston, the team competed under a number of different names. Between 1885 and 1906 they were the Boston Beaneaters, then they changed to the Doves (1907), Rustlers (1911), Braves (1912), and Bees (1936). In 1941 they were back to the Braves, the name they still use. Shown above are the 1885 Beaneaters. Also of note is Charles "Old Hoss" Radbourn (standing, far left) giving the finger to the camera, the first-known photo of the gesture.

HOPE & WILL'S SANDLOT Behind the grandstand in left field is Hope & Will's Sandlot. This is a large kid-friendly area that has a zipline and numerous baseball-themed activities and games.

THE BATTERY ATLANTA Adjacent to the stadium lies The Battery Atlanta, which opened in 2017. This unique entertainment district, which includes a street lined with retail shops, restaurants, and bars, was designed by Wakefield Beasley & Associates, with HGOR overseeing the public areas of the 60-acre mixed-use project. By combining sports, music, dining, water features, and more, the Battery Atlanta provides an exciting, attractive entertainment hub that draws Braves fans, locals, and tourists. The complex, which also contains the Coca Cola Roxy Theatre, a luxury hotel, tower apartments, and corporate centers, was financed by the Braves organization and its development partners at a cost of $400 million. Referred to as "the South's preeminent lifestyle destination," the Battery Atlanta is open all year, not just on game days.

> **“The most exciting thing for me is seeing the number of fans here really early and enjoying the place for a full day.”**
>
> —ROB MANFRED, MAJOR LEAGUE BASEBALL COMMISSIONER

[ABOVE] The entrance to the Battery Atlanta shopping and entertainment district is an explosion of color that adds to this stadium’s theme-park ambiance.

[RIGHT] A statue commemorating Phil Niekro, who played for the Braves from 1964 to 1983 (and again in ’87), stands in front of the 3rd Base Gate. Nicknamed “Knucksie,” this Hall of Famer is generally acknowledged as the greatest knuckleball pitcher of all time.

[OPPOSITE PAGE] The stadium’s lights come up on a gorgeous spring evening with the Atlanta Braves playing the Los Angeles Dodgers.

[BELOW] Braves team members watch the play from the home team dugout.

OTHER HOMES OF THE BRAVES

ATLANTA–FULTON COUNTY STADIUM

1966–1996

This multipurpose stadium, which opened on April 9, 1965, as Atlanta Stadium—in 1966 became home to the MLB Atlanta Braves and the NFL Atlanta Falcons. It had been specifically constructed to attract a Major League ball club to Georgia and had a seating capacity of 52,000. Atlanta's ploy worked when the Milwaukee Braves decided to leave Wisconsin and head south.

The stadium was designed by Heery & Heery and FABRAP and was constructed on a site in a formerly wealthy neighborhood—Washington–Rawson—which a half-century before had been home to Georgia's governor, but it had fallen on hard times by the 1960s. The location was chosen in part due to its proximity to the state capital, major highways, and downtown businesses.

In February 1975, Atlanta Stadium officially became Atlanta–Fulton County Stadium, a change effected after the county threatened to withdraw its financial support from the franchise. Fans and sportswriters also referred to it as "the Launching Pad" and "the House that Aaron Built."

The Braves shared the field with the Falcons for 26 years, until 1992, when the football team moved to the new Georgia Dome. The Braves stayed at the stadium for five more years. During their tenure there, they would thrive: the NL West title in 1969, and an All-Star Game in 1974, with a nice bonus for hometown fans when Hank Aaron hit a home run. Two years later, Aaron would tally his record-breaking 715th career home run. In the 1980s, Dale Murphy emerged as a star, and in 1991 the Braves won the first of 14 consecutive division titles (six were played here). They made World Series appearances at the stadium in 1991, 1992, 1995, and 1996. It was here, too, that names like Greg Maddux, Tom Glavine, John Smoltz, Chipper Jones, and Fred McGriff became famous.

The stadium saw its final game on October 24, 1996, when the New York Yankees defeated the Braves 1–0 in the fifth game of the World Series. The site of the old stadium became a parking lot for Turner Field.

The Atlanta Fulton County Recreation Authority published this commemorative booklet about the rebuilding of the stadium in 1965 and reviewed the baseball Braves and football Falcons, who would share the facilities.

The stadium's design followed that era's trend for cookie-cutter venues that, from above, looked like donuts.

[above] A sign and part of the original wall of Atlanta–Fulton County Stadium marks the spot where home run king Hank Aaron broke the all-time home run record set by Babe Ruth. He went on to end his career in 1976 with an astounding total of 755 home runs. After his death on January 22, 2021, fans placed flowers, balloons, and other mementos to pay tribute to "Hammerin' Hank."

[left] Hank Aaron at bat, circa 1970s

TURNER FIELD
1997–2016

Fans begin to gather at Turner Field for a July 12, 2013, game. According to a poll in the *Atlanta Journal-Constitution,* Atlanta residents preferred “Hank Aaron Stadium” as the name for the new ballpark. It was instead named after team owner Ted Turner (nicknamed “the Ted” by fans). The city offered some consolation with its address, renaming the section of Capitol Avenue on which the stadium sits “Hank Aaron Drive” and giving it the street number “755” after Aaron’s home run total.

Turner Field was named for former Braves owner and media mogul Ted Turner. Originally known as Centennial Olympic Stadium, it was constructed by the Atlanta Committee for the Olympic Games (ACOG) to host the track-and-field events after the city of Atlanta was chosen to host the 1996 summer games. The original cost of the stadium was $207 million, which was financed by ACOG. The Braves organization, eager to abandon obsolete Atlanta–Fulton County Stadium, arranged with ACOG to become the tenants of the new stadium once the games were over. It was remodeled as a baseball park by architect George T. Heery in time for the 1997 MLB season. Nearly half the temporary bleachers were removed as the structure morphed into an open-air baseball park, similar in feeling to Baltimore’s retro Oriole Park at Camden Yards, which had become the sports’ *beau ideal* since its opening in 1992.

Attractions at Turner Field included Coca-Cola Sky Field; the Braves Fun Zone; the interactive Scouts Alley; Turner Beach; Monument Grove, which displayed the retired numbers of Braves players; the Ivan Allen Jr. Braves Museum and Hall of Fame, named for a former Atlanta mayor; Tooner Field; and the “My South Cooks” Suite. The venue also hosted many non-baseball events, including concerts, weddings, holiday parties, product launches, and student proms. The parking lot even hosted vehicle ride-and-drive events, road races, and a circus.

In 2015, after the Braves moved out of downtown Atlanta, a group of developers along with Georgia State University won a bid to turn the site into a southern expansion of Georgia State’s campus and a privately held commercial and residential hub. Turner Field was converted into a Georgia State football stadium in 2017 and renamed Center Parc Stadium in 2020.

[TOP] Fans turn out for a night game at Turner Field.

[MIDDLE TOP] Greg Maddux’s No. 31 was one of the retired number tributes along Monument Grove.

[MIDDLE BOTTOM] “Homer the Brave” before fans at Turner Field. Homer has been retired and a new mascot, Blooper, was introduced in 2018, at an Atlanta Braves fan fest. Blooper, a tall, fuzzy, beige creature with extendable ears, won over fans with his on-field antics and goodwill appearances.

[BOTTOM] After the final game, in front of a sold-out crowd, the video board displayed a thank-you message to Turner Field following the conclusion of the post-game ceremonies.

CLOSE-UP

EVOLUTION OF THE BALLPARK

"The field is now almost a perfect level, covering at least some six acres of ground, all of which is well drained, rolled, and in a few weeks will be in splendid condition . . ."

—THE *BROOKLYN EAGLE* ON UNION GROUNDS, 1862

[ABOVE] **Players at Brooklyn's Union Grounds. Union Grounds became the first enclosed ballpark in 1862 and included a permanent pagoda in short center field (*shown at right*), the central structure of the venue's winter ice rink.**

[TOP LEFT] **An 1866 Currier & Ives lithograph depicts "The American National Game of Base Ball" at Elysian Fields in Hoboken, New Jersey.**

Baseball lore insists the game was invented in Cooperstown, New York, in 1839. Whatever its source, this game quickly became a favorite recreational sport in New York City and the Northeast. Impromptu teams would co-opt any flat expanse of parkland or pasture and often found themselves cheered on by gatherings of friends, families, and passersby. Eventually, dedicated ballparks were constructed with stands to offer proper seating to the spectators. From those first makeshift fields where pickup teams played to the age of the ornate wooden "baseball palaces" to the soaring modern franchise parks with their multilevel concourses, historical displays, and family-friendly entertainment centers, the humble ballpark expanded to accommodate the needs of a game that grew more popular—and more commercial—with each new generation of fans.

THE FIRST FIELDS

Although baseball scholars argue about Abner Doubleday and the origins of the game, Cooperstown, New York, is still widely considered the "Birthplace of Baseball," where Doubleday purportedly oversaw the very first game. Cooperstown's Doubleday Field, a former cow pasture owned by Elihu Phinney, has been used for baseball since 1920, and it has remained hallowed ground for more than 10 decades.

Elysian Fields was the iconic Hoboken, New Jersey, ballfield where on June 19, 1846, the first officially recorded, organized baseball match was played under Alexander Joy Cartwright's rules. On that day the New York Base Ball Club defeated the Knickerbockers 23–1.

[RIGHT] ***The Sandlot Kid* stands outside the Doubleday Field in Cooperstown, New York.**

SIZE MATTERS

There was a lack of consistency when it came to field dimensions in early facilities, nothing like the modern-day average of 330-400-330 feet (100.6-122-100.6 m) for left, center, and right field. In some parks, center field ran 600 feet (183 m) deep and ended at a pond. Yet, down the foul lines, fences might be only 200 feet (61 m) away, leading to "cheap" home runs being declared doubles. When in 1884 the Chicago White Stockings (later the Cubs) voided this rule as applied to their 180-foot (54.8 m) left field wall, they improved their home run record from 13 the previous year to an astonishing 142.

Sheet music published in 1867 for the "Baseball Polka" gives a sense of the developing baseball diamond, but it would be a while before dedicated ballparks would standardize distances.

Hoboken is often lauded as the place "Where Baseball Was Born."

Located in London, Ontario, next to the Thames River, Labatt Memorial Park—formerly Tecumseh Park—is considered the world's oldest ballpark that is still in operation. The first game took place in 1877, and it is currently home to the London Majors of the Intercounty Baseball League. In 1994, the city of London named the 5,200-capacity stadium an Ontario Heritage Landmark Site.

In 1862, when William Cammeyer, the owner of an outdoor ice-skating rink in Brooklyn, wanted an off-season money stream, he converted the rink into a ball field, surrounded it with a fence, and added bleachers as an enticement to paying spectators. It became the first enclosed ballpark in the country. The players loved the setup at Union Grounds . . . and even managed to field grounders and flies around the skating rink's central pagoda, located in short center field.

As more teams began to coalesce, the need for ballparks increased. But the pickings were slim. Most venues were crude, with rough grandstands and field hazards like slopes, trees, swamps, and lakes.

Sited on the Thames River in London, Ontario, Labatt Park has seen dedicated use for baseball since at least 1877, making it the oldest continuously used baseball field in the world.

> "The new grounds are nearly complete in every respect of any of the kind in Canada, and but few American cities have such a convenient playing field."
>
> —THE *LONDON ADVERTISER*, ON THE OPENING OF TECUMSEH PARK, MAY 4, 1877

“The handsomest grounds in the country”

—*CINCINNATI ENQUIRER*, 1902, ON THE PALACE OF THE FANS

Demolition of Palace of the Fans. Although initially lauded for its elegance and beauty, Cincinnati’s neoclassical Palace of the Fans had a short life, with the Reds calling it home only between 1902 and 1911. Never a great venue for the team, it had quickly developed structural issues, and then a fire broke out on October 12, 1911, catastrophically damaging the 1901 grandstand. This day was the last time the Reds played there, a game coincidentally against the Cubs, whom they had played for the Palace’s first game. The charred remains were demolished the next month to make way for a new ballpark.

Main grandstand at Palace of the Fans, circa 1902–1911

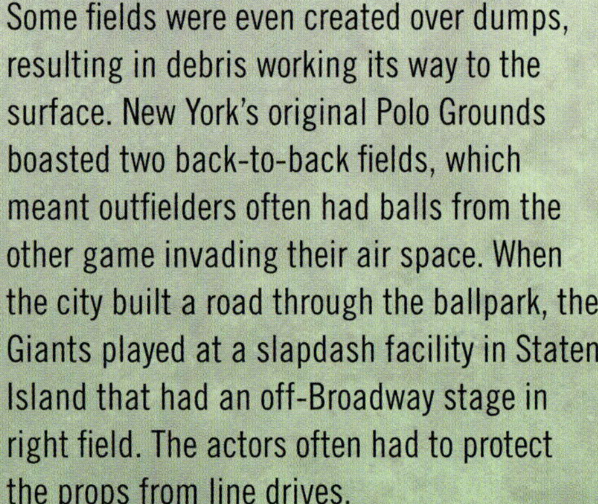

Some fields were even created over dumps, resulting in debris working its way to the surface. New York’s original Polo Grounds boasted two back-to-back fields, which meant outfielders often had balls from the other game invading their air space. When the city built a road through the ballpark, the Giants played at a slapdash facility in Staten Island that had an off-Broadway stage in right field. The actors often had to protect the props from line drives.

ARCHITECTURAL UPGRADES

Around the late 1800s, ballpark grandstands began to truly warrant the term “grand,” as ornate or historical details were added to the wooden structures. Whimsical touches like medieval spires and turrets competed with imposing palatial entryways, making some fans feel like they were entering Versailles. Finally, at the turn of the century, the neo-classical purity of Cincinnati’s celebrated Palace of the Fans replaced “castle-core” and set a trend for more restrained ballpark architecture that lasted the next 20 years.

In addition to architectural upgrades, special amenities were added to some parks to lure wealthier fans to the games—Chicago’s Lakefront Park had private boxes built atop the grandstand, early iterations of today’s luxury suites, and the Palace of the Fans offered ground-level boxes that accommodated buggies, or even automobiles. In 1882 the St. Louis Browns built the original Sportsman’s Park and transformed a house near right field into a beer garden with handball courts and lawn bowling. The 1891 version of the venue offered an amusement park, roller coaster bicycle track, and sideshow.

THE PERILS OF WOOD

Although ballparks grew grander and more aspirational, there remained one ever-present menace. Up until the late 1900s, these structures were made almost totally of wood. In a society where nearly half the male population smoked in public, it is not hard to imagine the danger to wooden grandstands, which were also vulnerable to overheated machinery and lightning strikes. Ballpark fires became a common occurrence and were especially dreaded during a game. In 1894 alone, fires burned four Major League parks, and at Chicago’s West Side Grounds, players had to rescue fans trapped within the flaming structure. Fortunately, most fires did not result in mass casualties. The worst accident took place in 1903 at Philadelphia’s brick-and-steel Baker Bowl, when hundreds of fans shifted away from the game to watch a street fight. The surge caused a wooden overhang behind third base to collapse, killing 12 and injuring more than 200.

The obvious need for safer ballparks was brought into focus by the creation of the American League in 1901—their rivalry with the National League produced a fresh wave of popularity for the game, plus the establishment of the “world series” in the autumn raised the stakes and boosted fan attendance throughout the season. Owners were forced to take note of potential ballpark hazards.

THE AGE OF CONCRETE AND STEEL

The year 1909 marked a seismic shift in the baseball community. Two new stadiums ushered in the concept of ballparks as beautiful, imposing monuments to the game. Philadelphia’s Shibe Park and Pittsburgh’s Forbes Field were constructed like skyscrapers of concrete and steel. With their impressive facades and ornate ironwork, they resembled art museums or opera houses . . . and signaled that America's pastime had achieved new respectability and even a level of gravitas.

The trend swept the country. No more ramshackle wooden grandstands with rickety seating; the old structures were either razed, burned down, or rebuilt with iron and concrete. Detroit's Bennett Park became Navin Field, later Tiger Stadium; Cincinnati's Palace of the Fans became Redland Field, later Crosley Field; and Washington's American League Park became Griffith Stadium. Steel-and-concrete makeovers served Cleveland's League Park as well as Sportsman's Park in St. Louis and the Polo Grounds in New York. Brand-new stadiums were also erected, including Boston's Fenway Park, Brooklyn's Ebbets Field, and Chicago's Comiskey Park. The ballpark would henceforth become a beacon of sports—on a par with the stadiums of ancient Greece and Rome. Likewise, the lowlifes and hooligans who once frequented ballparks were now ousted by solid citizens and their families.

The apex of this trend was surely the construction of Yankee Stadium in 1923, a fitting home for the team's stellar home-run king, Babe Ruth. The massive grandstand featured three decks, a roof, and an electronic scoreboard and could seat 58,000 fans.

[TOP] During the early years of the 20th century, newly built ballparks matched the current vogue for historical-revival styles in civic architecture. Elegant Ebbets Field in Brooklyn broke ground in 1912, and then held its first game on April 5, 1913, between the Dodgers and the Yankees.

[ABOVE AND LEFT] Pennsylvania rivals Philadelphia and Pittsburgh erected two of the first of the concrete-and-steel stadiums that were true monuments to the sport of baseball. The year 1909 saw both Philly's Shibe Park (*above*) and Pittsburgh's Forbes Field (*left*) host their first games.

But not everything was rosy in these new venues. Some of the stadiums were built in downtown neighborhoods—locations orchestrated by wealthy owners with political clout—and as a result the playing fields were often asymmetrical, while the distance to center field might be 400 feet (122 m) or even 500 feet (152.4 m). The days of the "cozy" outfield were surely lamented by some players. Fielders also ran the risk of injury after slamming into unforgiving concrete walls while chasing fly balls.

THE DEPRESSION YEARS

After its "golden age" at the turn of the century, the sport of baseball continued to flourish. Still, hard years were ahead, and the Great Depression of the 1930s and the subsequent world war in the 1940s did little to move the industry forward. Although the games provided a great distraction from woes on the home front and the world stage, with construction material so dear, most teams maintained the status quo as far as stadium improvements or innovations. Some franchises did enlarge their ballparks, and many added lighting to facilitate night games.

THE MULTIPURPOSE TREND

During the early 1960s to the mid-1970s, MLB created 10 new franchises and arranged five relocations. This was occasioned when the Dodgers and the Giants moved from their New York homes to California, as the fans now expected Major League play from coast to coast.

Due to the postwar prosperity in America, however, prices for everything were rising. Team owners now had to contend with escalating construction costs. The days of the $100,000 "bargain ballpark" were over. By the swinging '60s a baseball venue might cost tens of millions of dollars. There was also the question of location. Many cities had grown in size and also undergone suburban sprawl. Finding enough land for a baseball complex was increasingly difficult, even for owners who could threaten to move their teams if the cities didn't meet their demands for new venues. Public funding was one answer, but it came with a proviso—to save taxpayer money, the town fathers insisted on building multipurpose stadiums, ones that would cater to both baseball and to the increasingly popular sport of football.

This concept was initially daunting to architects, who would need to somehow blend the wedge-shaped baseball field with the rectangular gridiron. Many opted for enclosed, circular stadiums similar to Rome's Colosseum, where the lower decks would create the typical V shape for baseball, then swivel back for viewing football.

Another key change during this era was the introduction of artificial turf. In stadiums where the lower decks moved back and forth over the field, it made sense to use synthetic grass. Not to mention, the cost of upkeep for real grass was a constant financial drain. But nobody consulted the players, who suffered concussed knees from running on the hard surfaces and "rug burns" after making sliding catches. Artificial turf was also notoriously bouncy whenever fly balls hit the field.

The resulting dozen or so circular venues all appeared so similar they were dubbed "cookie cutter" stadiums or "concrete donuts." Players on the road swore they didn't know where they were half the time. The fields were symmetrical, with few distinguishing features. Personality had disappeared with the nickel hot dog. The last "cookie cutter" used was Oakland Coliseum, but the MLB Athletics are moving to Las Vegas, following the Raiders, who moved in 2020.

Four famous "cookie cutter" venues were Three Rivers Stadium in Pittsburgh (*top left*), Riverfront Stadium in Cincinnati (*top right*), Busch Stadium in St. Louis (*bottom left*), and Veterans Stadium in Philly (*bottom right*), whose bland exteriors belied the fans' loyalty and passion.

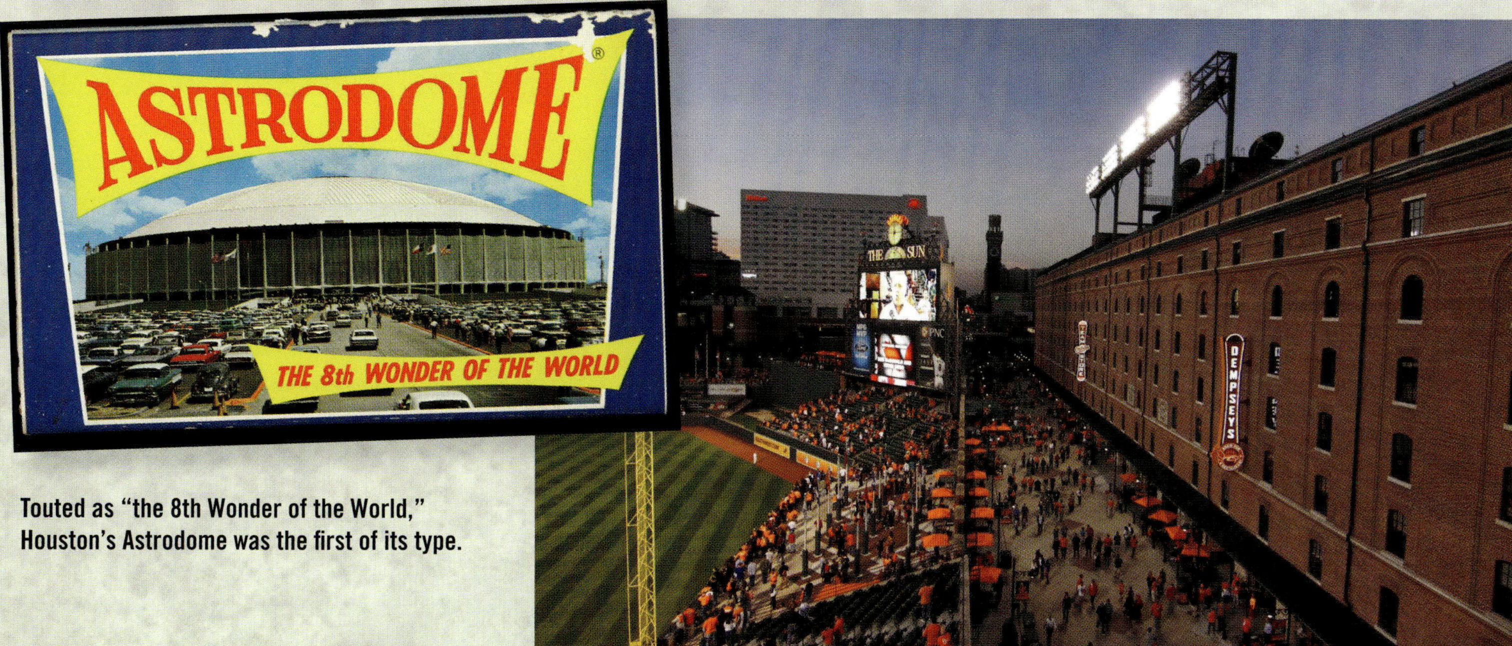

Touted as "the 8th Wonder of the World," Houston's Astrodome was the first of its type.

The B&O Warehouse looms behind the Orioles' outfield with Eutaw Street between, offering pedestrian strolling space and creating a neighborhood feel. Baltimore's Camden Yards won the hearts of the public and made HOK, later Populous, the go-to choice for creating retro-style ballparks.

UNDER THE DOME

During the 1960s and 1970s, some stadiums built in urban neighborhoods began to see a rise of crime outside their walls. The former exchange of culture between the stadium and its neighbors disappeared. Fans on the inside felt mostly safe, barricaded behind the concrete walls and separated from danger by the sprawling, fenced-in parking lots.

Another aspect of this era was the debut of the domed stadium. The first example, the Houston Astrodome, astonished fans and reviewers alike. Built to Texas scale and on an oil baron's budget, it was truly spectacular—with air-conditioning, padded seats, a huge electronic display, the first luxury boxes, a presidential suite, and even a bowling alley. Four more covered stadiums appeared in the next few decades, but none were without issues. In the Astrodome, the black-painted roof killed the grass; when made translucent, its glare obscured fly balls. In Seattle, ceiling tiles plummeted from the roof of the Kingdome, while a heavy snowfall ripped the Minneapolis Metrodome's fabric roof. The retractable roof of Toronto's Skydome often failed, while the roof at Olympic Stadium in Montreal never functioned.

THE RETRO MOVEMENT

During the political and economic turmoil of the 1980s, Americans had a yen to look backward, toward a time they imagined had been less fraught. Nostalgia swept the nation; ballparks that were once considered relics—Fenway Park and Wrigley Field, among others—were now looked upon as charming and comforting "jewel boxes." It's not surprising that architects took note of these sentiments. The first result, Camden Yards in Baltimore, the work of architects HOK, would soon become the beau ideal for subsequent builds. In spite of its modern amenities, the ballpark had a distinctly "old-timey" feel, especially with the vintage B&O warehouse looming massively beyond the outfield fences and adding instant character. (Conversely, in 1991 the White Sox chose to replace Comiskey Park with a modern-style structure with little charm and a steep upper deck fit only for mountain goats, labeled by columnist George Will "the last stupid ballpark.")

FUTURE TRENDS

The vogue is now for ballparks that offer a full package of entertainment and events. Franchises want families or groups of friends to spend an entire day at the stadium, enjoying historical displays, immersive activities, live entertainment, shopping, and a range of dining experiences along with the game. The addition of corporate and residential housing to these properties is not unusual, and concourses have been expanded into actual retail malls in some instances. Forecasters predict even more of this diversification of spaces—furnishing alternate sources of revenue—taking place in the future.

Unfortunately, with the advent of high-definition TV and multiple cable and streaming outlets allowing people to watch games at home, MLB attendance has dropped some 10 percent since its peak in 2007. Teams need to think about melding home theater technology with the live ballpark experience. Perhaps giant video screens could offer close-ups of action on the field and display the progress of other games between innings, or before the game. Multiple screens could even show other games in their entirety—say the fan's spouse or best friend supports another franchise—similar to the setup found in sports bars.

Seats could also offer outlets for mobile devices and tablets, so fans can listen to broadcast coverage of the game, check on their fantasy teams, get results of other games, and order food or drinks. Once seats allow for these updates, youthful fans are likely to feel a greater connection to the whole ballpark experience.

Fans crowd the stands for a June 22, 2017, match between the Yankees and Angels. The white frieze that wraps around the entire upper deck re-creates the look of the frieze that topped the original House That Ruth Built.

pitcher Mariano Rivera. The Yankees made the playoffs in 1995 and won four of the next five World Series—in 1996 and from 1998 to 2000, the last MLB team to accomplish such a feat.

STEINBRENNER'S CAMPAIGN

In spite of all the history and hoopla attached to the original Yankee Stadium, Steinbrenner began campaigning for a new venue in the early 1980s—just a few years after a remodeled Yankee Stadium reopened. Steinbrenner hinted he was considering a move to the Meadowlands Sports Complex in New Jersey, home of the NFL New York Giants and the NHL New Jersey Devils. Although Jersey Governor Thomas Kean authorized the use of land there for a baseball stadium in 1994, the state legislature refused to provide financing. Then, in 1987, New Jersey taxpayers rejected $185 million in public financing for a baseball stadium. Undeterred by the rejections, Steinbrenner maintained his threats to move as a means of negotiating with New York City.

YANKEES ACHIEVEMENTS

WORLD SERIES CHAMPIONSHIPS: 27 (1923,1927, 1928, 1932, 1936, 1937, 1938, 1939, 1941, 1943, 1947, 1949, 1950, 1951, 1952, 1953, 1956, 1958, 1961, 1962, 1977, 1978, 1996, 1998, 1999, 2000, 2009)

AL PENNANTS: 40 (1921,1922, 1923,1926, 1927, 1928, 1932, 1936, 1937, 1938, 1939, 1941, 1942, 1943, 1947, 1949, 1950, 1951, 1952, 1953, 1955, 1956, 1957, 1958, 1960, 1961, 1962, 1963, 1964, 1976, 1977, 1978, 1981, 1996, 1998, 1999, 2000, 2001, 2003, 2009)

AL EAST DIVISION TITLES: 20 (1976, 1977, 1978, 1980, 1981, 1996, 1998, 1999, 2000, 2001, 2002, 2003, 2004, 2005, 2006, 2009, 2011, 2012, 2019, 2022)

WILD CARD BERTHS: 9 (1995, 1997, 2007, 2010, 2015, 2017, 2018, 2020, 2021)

PLAYOFF APPEARANCES: 58 (1921,1922, 1923,1926, 1927, 1928, 1932, 1936, 1937, 1938, 1939, 1941, 1942, 1943, 1947, 1949, 1950, 1951, 1952, 1953, 1955, 1956, 1957, 1958, 1960, 1961, 1962, 1963, 1964, 1976, 1977, 1978, 1980, 1981, 1995, 1996, 1997, 1998, 1999, 2000, 2001, 2002, 2003, 2001, 2001, 2006, 2007, 2009, 2010, 2011, 2012, 2015, 2017, 2018, 2019, 2020, 2021, 2022)

WORST SEASON RECORD: 1908, 51–103 (.331)

BEST SEASON RECORD: 1998, 114–48 (.704)

One by one New York's mayors tried to address the problem—in 1988, Mayor Ed Koch agreed to have city taxpayers spend $90 million on a second renovation of Yankee Stadium. Steinbrenner, unsatisfied, backed out of the deal. In 1993, Mayor David Dinkins expanded on Koch's proposal, but no agreement was forthcoming.

> **“I kind of wish I would have been able to see the old Yankee Stadium after seeing the new one.”**
>
> —AARON JUDGE, YANKEE BATTING PHENOM

In 1993, Governor Mario Cuomo proposed using Manhattan's 30-acre (12 ha) West Side Yard, a former rail yard. But a few months later, Cuomo lost his re-election bid and was gone. By 1995, Steinbrenner had rejected 13 proposals to keep the Yankees in the Bronx or bring them to Manhattan.

In January 2002, outgoing Mayor Rudy Giuliani announced “tentative agreements” for both the Yankees and Mets to receive new stadiums at a cost of $2 billion, with city and state taxpayers contributing $1.2 billion. New mayor Michael Bloomberg called Giuliani's proposal “corporate welfare” and used an escape clause to back out of both deals. But Giuliani's contract contained a clause loosening the teams' leases, giving them the ability to leave New York if the city did not provide new venues. In 2004, a hamstrung Mayor Bloomberg released his blueprint for a new Yankee Stadium and the new Citi Field for the Mets, projects that would cost more than $3.1 billion, with taxpayer subsidies of $1.8 billion. The location of the new Bronx ballpark would be the 24-acre (9.7 ha) former site of Macombs Dam Park, one block north of the original stadium.

SEATING CHART

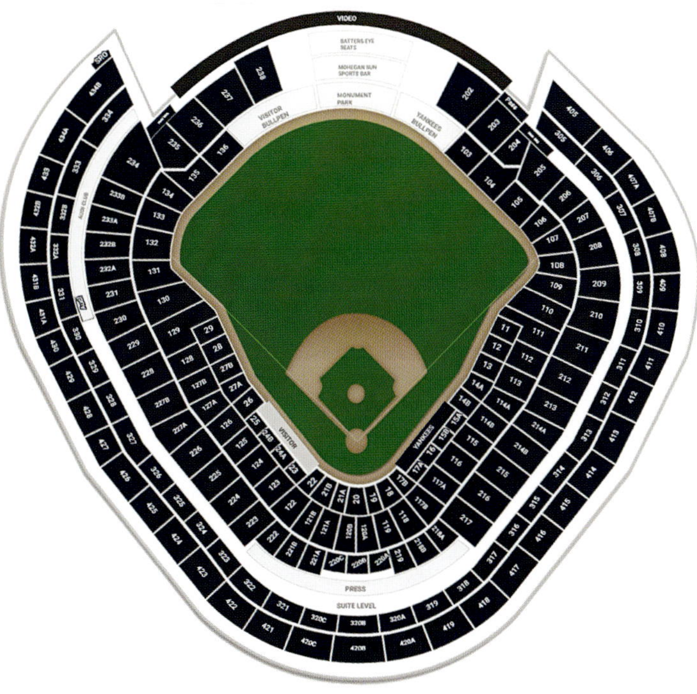

Gate 4 lit up in the evening. The Indiana limestone exterior at Gates 4 and 6 mirrors that used on the original Yankee Stadium in 1923.

DESIGN AND CONSTRUCTION

Designed by HOK Sport (Populous), the new Yankee Stadium replicated design elements from the first iteration, including both the original and the renovated versions. For instance, the new exterior reflects the original's classical style, and both facades utilized Indiana limestone for that distinguished and stately "civic monument" effect. The trademark frieze that lined the roof of the original Yankee Stadium from 1923 to 1973 is reproduced on the current stadium's roof. And just as it was at the former field, the wall beyond the bleacher seats is "cut out" to reveal the elevated subway trains as they pass by. Yet, the new build also managed to incorporate fan-friendly expanded spaces and desirable modern amenities.

Construction finally began in August 2006, but progress was slow. The builders and backers had to contend with many controversies, including the high cost to the taxpayers and the loss of public park land. The completed facility ended up costing $2.3 billion, including $1.2 billion in public subsidies, making it one of the most expensive stadiums ever built.

The new stadium had a capacity of approximately 52,000, with 52 luxury suites. Approximately two-thirds of the seating is found in the lower bowl, the inverse of the arrangement at the original Yankee Stadium. The new ballpark's seating is spaced outward in a bowl shape, unlike the "stacked tiers" design at the old stadium. Today there is seating for 46,537 fans—the sixth-largest capacity of the 30 MLB stadiums—with a standing room capacity of 52,325.

[ABOVE] The stadium is visible from the elevated platform of the NYC subway. The 161st Street stop takes fans directly to the ballpark.

[OPPOSITE PAGE] An aerial view of the stadium at night. In the shadow of the famous stadium lies Macombs Dam Park, with its three grass ballfields, built for softball, baseball, and Little League. The southern field at the park was laid in the footprint of the old stadium, giving amateur players the chance to step up to the plate in the same spot Babe Ruth, Joe DiMaggio, Yogi Berra, Mickey Mantle, Derek Jeter, and all the Yankee pros once batted.

Yankee Stadium opened for regular season play on April 16, 2009, with Yankee catcher—and arguably the most quotable ballplayer of all time—Yogi Berra throwing out the first pitch. At an earlier exhibition game on April 3, Reggie Jackson, "Mr. October" himself, did the honors.

In addition to serving the Bronx Bombers, since 2015 the stadium has been interim home to the Major League Soccer expansion club New York City FC. This franchise is owned by City Football Group and the Yankees and is awaiting a soccer-specific facility. Yankee Stadium also occasionally hosts college football games, including the annual Pinstripe Bowl, as well as concerts and other athletic, religious, and entertainment events. Although the original Yankee Stadium was often called "the House That Ruth built"—referring to the legendary Babe Ruth—the new incarnation has been nicknamed "the Stadium," "the House That Jeter Built," and "the House That George Built," the latter referencing the pugnacious Steinbrenner.

PUBLIC REACTION

Positive reviews for the new ballpark included accolades for its spacious, comfortable grandstand compared to the cramped, claustrophobic predecessor. The design references to the earlier park were not overlooked. Yet, the size prevented some of the intense, personal feeling fans got in the old stadium, the vibe and the energy. While the older version had one giant loudspeaker stack blaring out announcements, the new ballpark has loudspeakers over every section, making noise pollution a real issue. The franchise has also been widely criticized for high ticket prices—the average is more than $60, the highest price in baseball, and Legends Suite tickets—for seating behind home plate—run from $150 to $2,600 each. These suites are often seen to be empty during televised games. The "cheap seats," the bleachers, left fans disappointed because some sections were obstructed. These sections were replaced in 2017 with standing room areas featuring outdoor bars and several patios.

FEATURES AND AMENITIES

The stadium welcomes fans to browse their historical displays, take a tour of the facility, shop for mementos at the team stores, sample the variety of food at the concessions, and honor past Yankee associates with a visit to Monument Park.

YANKEE STADIUM FIRSTS

FIRST MLB GAME: 4/3/2009, Yankees over Chicago Cubs, 7–4 (exhibition)

FIRST HOME RUN: 4/3/2009, Robinson Cano (Chicago Cubs)

FIRST NO-HITTER: 6/25/2022, Cristian Javier (7 innings), Hector Neris (1 inning), Ryan Pressly (1 inning) (Houston Astros)

FIRST PLAYOFF GAME: 10/7/2009, Yankees over Minnesota Twins, 7-2

FIRST WORLD SERIES GAME: 10/28/2009, Philadelphia Phillies over Yankees, 6–1 in Game 1

The Great Hall at the stadium is a truly impressive space, with a sun-drenched promenade decorated with player banners.

GREAT HALL The Great Hall is situated along the southern front of the stadium and is festooned with large banners celebrating great Yankees. Vaulted arches overhead flood the space with natural light. It can accommodate 1,500 guests and is often used for cocktail receptions, corporate gatherings, dinners, and concerts.

MONUMENT PARK One of the most revered destinations at the stadium is Monument Park, an open-air museum beyond the center-field fence. Along a winding walkway are displayed the jersey numbers and biographical plaques of top players, as well as notable owners, managers, and coaches, and dignitaries like Nelson Mandela. Monuments on red granite blocks honor manager Miller Huggins, owner George Steinbrenner, and players Lou Gehrig, Babe Ruth, Mickey Mantle, and Joe DiMaggio. Much of the collection was transplanted from the old stadium.

NEW YORK YANKEE MUSEUM Fans delight in the New York Yankee Museum, which is found on the main level. Artifacts and artwork showcased here include Yankees captain Thurman Munson's locker; a display highlighting the career and awards of another Yankees captain, Derek Jeter; a statue of pitcher Don Larson that celebrates his perfect game; a display covering the

A plaque dedicated to long time public address announcer Bob Sheppard, "the Voice of Yankee Stadium," hangs on the wall of Monument Park. Much of the old memorabilia had been transplanted here from the old stadium, with displays such as the team's retired numbers exhibited in pinstriped balls.

team's "Home Run Heritage," including bats, jerseys, and signage going back to Babe Ruth; a collection of World Series trophies; and a scaled-down model of the stadium. There is a Ball Wall composed of autographed baseballs, and for true Yankee geeks there is even a showcase covering the history of team hats.

KID'S CLUBHOUSE Shaped like a minibaseball field, the Kid's Clubhouse is outfitted with Yankees-themed playground equipment—oversized baseballs, bases, and baseball cards. Here children are able to climb, slide, and play hide-and-seek among colorful fixtures that include a 6-foot (1.8 m) replica World Series trophy.

FOOD AND DRINK The food concessions offer a mix of baseball fare and specialty items. Fan favorites include Streetbird by Marcus Samuelsson, Bobby Flay's "Bobby's Burgers," Lobel's, Mighty Quinn's, Chickie's & Pete's, City Winery, The Halal Guys, Sumo Dog, Benihana, and Oatly and Wings of New York. The stadium's signature Pinstripe Shake is a thick vanilla milkshake topped with blue and white sprinkles. The Yankee's food court is at third base, next to Benihanas.

STADIUM MILESTONES

Many historic milestones and records have taken place or been set at Yankee Stadium. By any standards, the late 2000s was a high-water mark. In 2009, Derek Jeter got his 2,722nd hit and became the Yankees' all-time hits leader, surpassing Lou Gehrig's 72-year record. The following year, Alex "A-Rod" Rodriguez dinged his 600th home run at the stadium, the youngest player to accomplish this feat. Three milestones occurred at the ballpark In 2011—in July, Jeter became the first Yankee to join the 3,000-hit club, collecting all his career hits playing for that team; the next month the Yankees became the only team in MLB history to hit three grand slams during the same game. Finally, near the end of the season, superb relief pitcher Mariano Rivera earned his 602nd save, becoming the all-time leader in regular season saves.

"It gets late early out there."

—YOGI BERRA, REFERRING TO THE BAD SUN CONDITIONS IN LEFT FIELD AT THE STADIUM.

[ABOVE] Members of the Yankees 1950s team stand on the field while a picture of Yogi Berra, who could not attend, appears on the big screen at Old Timers' Day, July 17, 2010.

[LEFT] Derek Jeter salutes the crowd after becoming the all-time Yankees hits leader in 2009.

OTHER HOMES OF THE YANKEES

POLO GROUNDS

1913–1922

When the early Yankees were known as the Highlanders, they played at American League Field from 1903 to 1912. Located in Manhattan's Washington Heights neighborhood, the facility was called Hilltop Park for the ridge it sat atop. The Giants also played here for several months in 1911 while their home field, the Polo Grounds, was rebuilt after a fire. In 1913 the Yankees themselves moved to that fourth iteration of the Polo Grounds, subletting the field that lay in Coogan's Hollow beneath Coogan's Bluff. The team called Polo Grounds home until after the 1922 season, when they moved across the Harlem River to their new home at the original Yankee Stadium. (*See* Polo Grounds, New York Giants, pages 280–281.)

Babe Ruth taking batting practice at the Polo Grounds, circa 1920s. The Babe's enormous talent drew in large crowds—so large, in fact, that team owners saw that it was time for the Yankees to build a stadium of their own.

OLD YANKEE STADIUM

1923–2008

Even though the Yankees shared the Polo Grounds with the Giants, relations between the teams were not cordial. Yankee fans wondered when the team would see a permanent home of their own. After wildly popular long-ball hitter Babe Ruth started bringing droves of spectators to the Polo Grounds, Yankee owners Tillinghast L'Hommedieu Huston and Jacob Ruppert agreed it was time. The new stadium would fittingly be referred to as the "House That Ruth Built." The timing might have been iffy—the Black Sox scandal was slowing attendance at many clubs, but the two men followed their instincts and took the risk. The final cost of the structure would end up around $2.5 million.

After exploring several options, Huston and Ruppert settled on a 10-acre (4.0 ha) lumberyard in the Bronx within sight of Coogan's Bluff across the Harlem River. Huston and Ruppert purchased the property from tycoon William Waldorf Astor for $600,000—equal to $10.5 million today—and construction began May 5, 1922. Erected with almost lightning speed, the stadium debuted on April 18, 1923. It was the first three-tiered venue in MLB baseball and one of few ballparks given the illustrious title "stadium," derived from *stadia,* the sporting structures of the ancient Greeks. The facility seated an astounding 58,000 fans; it would later hold more than 70,000. On Opening Day, Babe Ruth stepped to the plate and hit a home run. The fans expected nothing less.

Designed by Osborn Engineering Corporation,

[ABOVE] Yankee Stadium in the 1920s, shortly after it was built. The original Yankee Stadium had many nicknames, among them "the House That Ruth Built," "the Cathedral of Baseball," and "the Bronx Zoo."

[BELOW] The stadium in 2006, as viewed from Macombs Dam Park. The park became the site of the new stadium.

the facility's exterior was constructed of pale, creamy Indiana limestone, with classical detailing in the roofline, entries, and arched windows. According to author Joseph Durso, the stadium's walls were built of "an extremely hard and durable concrete that was developed by Thomas Edison." Their new home seemed to galvanize the team—they won their first World Series that same year.

As the stadium aged, a number of renovations took place—during the 1926–1927 off season and from 1936 to 1938, when more extension changes were made. The stadium became home to the NFL Giants from 1956 to 1973, requiring more updates. After George Steinbrenner bought the Yankees from CBS in 1973, the stadium closed for two years to undergo a major facelift. Changes included the removal of 118 columns reinforcing each tier of the stadium's grandstand, replacing the roof with a new upper shell, adding new lights, lowering the field about 7 feet

JOE LOUIS AT THE STADIUM

On the night of June 22, 1938, the stadium played host to possibly the most ideological prize fight in American history when, during their rematch, Black boxer Joe Louis reclaimed his heavyweight title by knocking out champion Max Schmeling, who was a native of Germany and who embodied the Aryan "superman" so admired by Adolf Hitler and the Nazis. The two had fought previously on June 19, 1936. The "Brown Bomber" also appeared at Yankee Stadium in a 1937 fight against British Empire champion Tommy Farr, Billy Conn in 1946, Jersey Joe Walcott in 1948, and Ezzard Charles in 1950.

"To play 18 years in Yankee Stadium is the best thing that could ever happen to a ballplayer."

—LEGENDARY NO. 7, MICKEY MANTLE

[ABOVE LEFT] Monument Park at Old Yankee Stadium in the stadium's final season. Henry Louis "Lou" Gehrig, legendary manager Miller James Huggins, and George Herman "Babe" Ruth adorned the entrance to the area, which memorialized Yankee baseball player greats and other key figures.

[ABOVE RIGHT] A retired Joe DiMaggio stops by the old Yankee Stadium to chat with Mickey Mantle in 1956.

(2.1 m), and replacing the wood seats with larger molded plastic seats. A new concourse was situated above the old one, and a middle tier was built with a larger press box and luxury suites.

In spite of all the upgrades and renos over the years, the stadium did not offer the modern amenities and premium seating that many fans expected, and the decision to build a replacement was finally made. The Yankees played their last game there on September 21, 2008. During the closing ceremonies, home plate and the pitcher's mound plate were dug up and moved to the new stadium. Demolition of the beloved landmark was completed on May 13, 2010. A 10-acre (40,000 m^2) park complex called Heritage Field was constructed on the site.

[BELOW] Remains of old Yankee Stadium just as it was being torn down for the new stadium in 2010. Across the road is the new stadium.

[BOTTOM] The old Yankee Stadium, looking out to center field at the start of an Old-Timers' Day at the park. This is an MLB tradition, when the early afternoon preceding a weekend game is reserved to honor the team's retired players. The players compete in an exhibition game, usually lasting three innings. These days the Yankees are the only team to uphold this tradition. The names that appear here on the scoreboard reflect how they split up the players: The Clippers are named after the legendary Joe DiMaggio (the "Yankee Clipper"), and the Bombers are named after the Yankees nickname, the "Bronx Bombers."

American Family Field • Milwaukee Brewers

Busch Stadium • St. Louis Cardinals

Comerica Park • Detroit Tigers

Great American Ball Park • Cincinnati Reds

Guaranteed Rate Field • Chicago White Sox

Kauffman Stadium • Kansas City Royals

CENTRAL DIVISION

NATIONAL LEAGUE CENTRAL • Chicago Cubs • Cincinnati Reds • Milwaukee Brewers • Pittsburgh Pirates • St. Louis Cardinals

AMERICAN LEAGUE CENTRAL • Chicago White Sox • Cleveland Guardians • Detroit Tigers • Kansas City Royals • Minnesota Twins

This 10-team division was created in 1994 by moving franchises from the East and West Divisions.

THE AMERICAN LEAGUE CENTRAL Division was created by recruiting three teams from the AL West Division and two from the AL East. The AL Central was responsible for the all-time-winningest regular season team in the 2000s, when the Chicago White Sox finished higher in the standings than any team up to that time. The White Sox currently find competition from the Minnesota Twins and the Cleveland Guardians; all three franchises have gone into recent playoffs, and Cleveland has made it to multiple World Series.

THE NATIONAL LEAGUE CENTRAL Division was created by moving the Cincinnati Reds and Houston Astros from the NL West and the Chicago Cubs, Pittsburgh Pirates, and St. Louis Cardinals from the NL East. In 1998, the Milwaukee Brewers switched from the American League Central to this division. In 2013, the Astros moved to the NL West. This division has generated some of the most dramatic stories in baseball history. From the Chicago Cubs breaking their World Series title drought in 2016 to the St. Louis Cardinals' comeback over the Texas Rangers, this division has generated a great deal of postseason intensity—and the fans love it.

PNC Park • Pittsburgh Pirates

Progressive Field • Cleveland Guardians

Target Field • Minnesota Twins

Wrigley Field • Chicago Cubs

2001–PRESENT
AMERICAN FAMILY FIELD

HOME OF THE MILWAUKEE BREWERS

NATIONAL LEAGUE (1998–PRESENT)

HOME TO THE BREWERS SINCE 2001, *this unique ballpark blends elements of the past, including the nostalgic brick facade and grass field, with soaring modern architecture that incorporates massive exterior arches, industrial steel trusses, and a retractable roof, thus offering fans a satisfying game-day experience.*

The Brewers ball club was originally formed in 1969 as a Washington state expansion team named the Seattle Pilots. The club, which played at Sick's Stadium, was plagued nearly from the start by serious stadium and financial issues. They had only one season in the American League West Division before being acquired in bankruptcy court by Bud Selig, a local Milwaukee businessman and minority owner of the Milwaukee Braves. Selig and his investment group were eager to return Major League Baseball to their town after the Braves' departure for Atlanta in 1965, and they had unsuccessfully tried to purchase the Chicago White Sox in 1969. The following year they succeeded in acquiring the Pilots for $10.8 million, and the group relocated them to Milwaukee. This was during spring training in 1970, and there was no time to order new uniforms. So the team ripped the Pilots insignia off their existing uniforms, and the franchise ended up adopting the Pilots colors of blue, white, and yellow, instead of Selig's choice, the red and navy blue of the Milwaukee Braves.

Now named the Brewers in honor of the city's renown as a beer producer, the team first played in Milwaukee County Stadium. They remained there until the end of the 2000 season, when a brand-new field was built for them in a parking lot behind their current stadium. Ground was broken on November 9, 1996, initiating one of the largest construction projects ever seen in Wisconsin. The new stadium was to feature a retractable, fan-shaped roof, with panels that swept open and closed simultaneously from the first- and third-base sides toward center field. This complex and massive roof was a significant factor in the $392 million cost of the stadium. But it also created some serious problems for the organization.

For much of its history the stadium was known as Miller Park, as part of a naming rights deal with the Miller Brewing Company, which expired in 2020. Since the start of the 2021 season it has been called American Family Field after a 15-year deal was struck with Madison-based American Family Insurance.

BALLPARK STATS

ADDRESS
1 Brewers Way, Milwaukee, WI 53214

FORMER NAME
Miller Park (2001–2020)

OWNER/OPERATOR
Southeast Wisconsin Professional Baseball Park District

ARCHITECT
HKS, Inc.; NBBJ; Eppstein Uhen Architects

CAPACITY
41,900

RECORD BASEBALL ATTENDANCE
46,218 on 9/6/2003 (vs. Chicago Cubs)

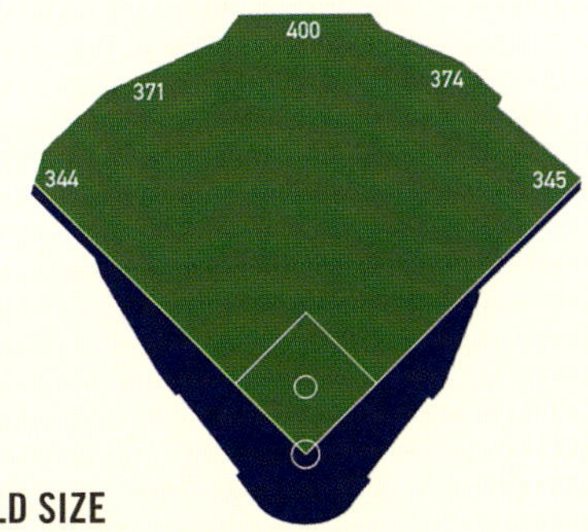

FIELD SIZE

Left field 342 feet (104 m)

Left-center 371 feet (113 m)

Center field 400 feet (122 m)

Right-center 374 feet (114 m)

Right field 337 feet (103 m)

Backstop 56 feet (17 m)

SURFACE
Kentucky bluegrass

TEAM MASCOT
Bernie Brewer

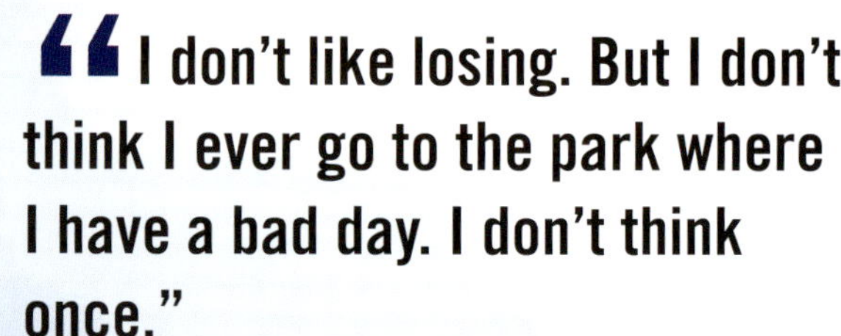

"I don't like losing. But I don't think I ever go to the park where I have a bad day. I don't think once."

—CATCHER / BREWER BROADCASTER BOB UECKER

Originally scheduled to open for the 2000 season, the ball field's construction was delayed when a huge Lampson Transi-Lift crane, nicknamed "Big Blue," collapsed on July 14, 1999, while lifting a 450-ton section of roof in high winds. Sadly, three ironworkers were killed. A safety inspector filming the progress of the new stadium actually captured the collapse on video. The necessary repair work, plus an investigation into the disaster, pushed the opening back another year. Today, a sculpture called *Teamwork* stands outside the ballpark's entrance and commemorates the men, William DeGrave, Jerome Starr, and Jeffrey Wischer, who died in the accident. Other problems that arose in the complicated fan-shaped roof required replacing elements of the pivot system behind home plate and the outfield roof track.

Initially called Miller Park, after a 15-year, $40 million naming rights deal with Miller Brewing Company—makers of the "beer that made Milwaukee famous"—the new field finally debuted on April 6, 2001. In 2019, American Family Insurance agreed to pay the Milwaukee Brewers approximately $4 million a year over 15 years for the naming rights of the ballpark. The original naming deal with Miller Brewing Company, which eventually became Miller Coors, had been for $2 million per year over 20 years.

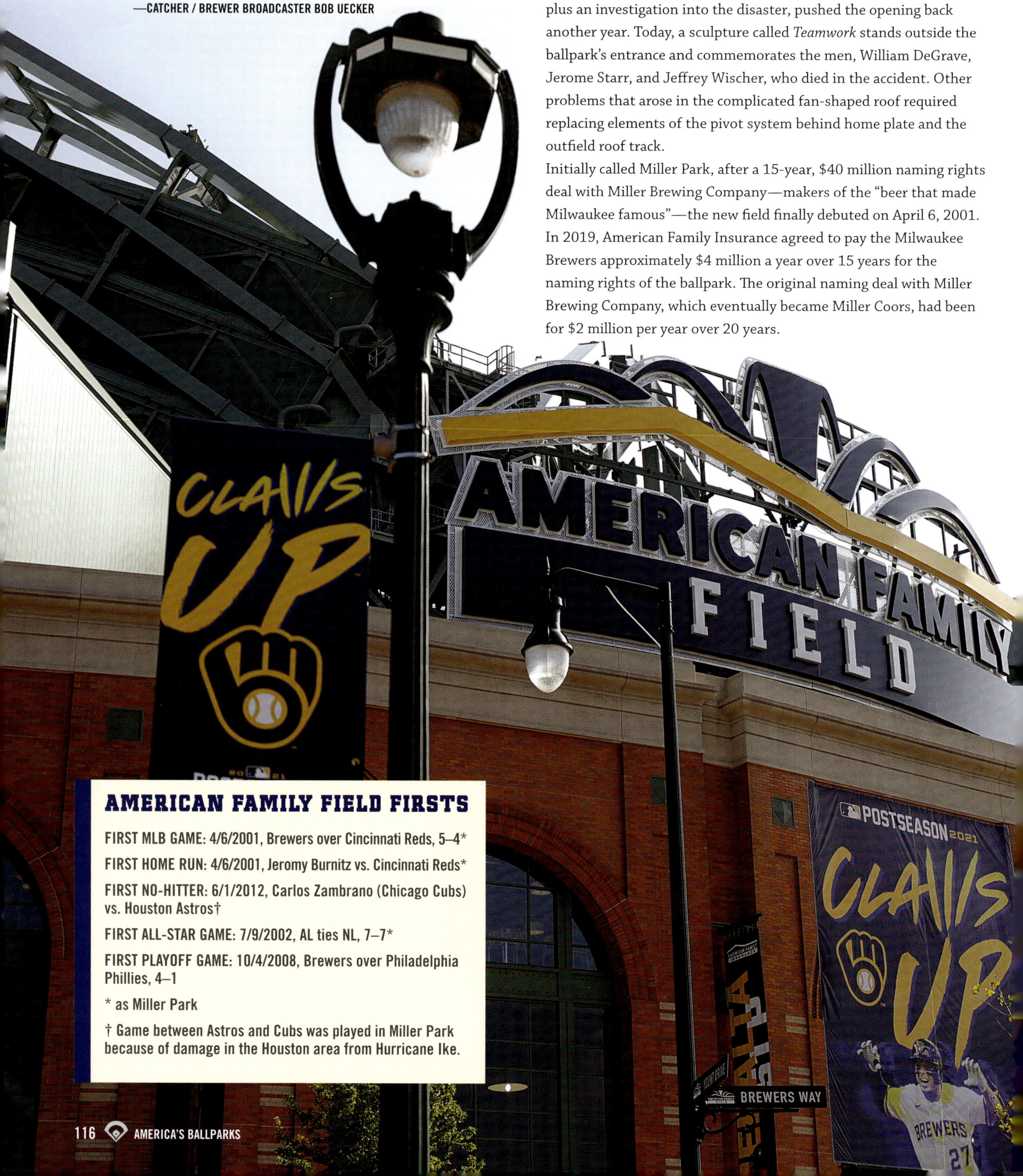

AMERICAN FAMILY FIELD FIRSTS

FIRST MLB GAME: 4/6/2001, Brewers over Cincinnati Reds, 5–4*

FIRST HOME RUN: 4/6/2001, Jeromy Burnitz vs. Cincinnati Reds*

FIRST NO-HITTER: 6/1/2012, Carlos Zambrano (Chicago Cubs) vs. Houston Astros†

FIRST ALL-STAR GAME: 7/9/2002, AL ties NL, 7–7*

FIRST PLAYOFF GAME: 10/4/2008, Brewers over Philadelphia Phillies, 4–1

* as Miller Park

† Game between Astros and Cubs was played in Miller Park because of damage in the Houston area from Hurricane Ike.

DESIGN AND CONSTRUCTION

In the mid-1990s, a competition was held to determine who would design the new stadium. The architectural plans were ultimately developed by Los Angeles-based NBBJ, sports and entertainment specialists. They in turn worked closely with LA-based Arup, a team of engineers responsible for every stage of the structural and building services stadium design, except for the mechanisms that controlled the roof. Originally these were designed by Mitsubishi Heavy Industries America, but they were replaced by new designs after their failure. Executive architect, HKS, Inc., of Dallas, was responsible for delivering the final stadium to the people of Milwaukee. Local firms that contributed to the project included Eppstein Uhen Architects.

Not surprisingly, the design of Miller Park was influenced by the retro trend begun by Oriole Park at Camden Yards, which wowed critics and fans when it opened in 1992. Miller Park's outfield grass was installed in March 2001, while the infield dirt and home plate were taken from County Stadium.

PUBLIC REACTION

Opinions were somewhat mixed when the ballpark finally opened, although the overall consensus was positive. Most remarked upon were the engineering marvels—the breathtaking steel arches and the retractable roof. On the other hand, the novel design is still considered the most controversial in MLB, with some critics remarking the steel arches stick out "like a sore thumb" or look like a "deformed tarantula." Advocates insist the sprawling spans are elegant and that the design team should be commended for attempting to give the roofline some aesthetic integrity . . . unlike other covered stadiums.

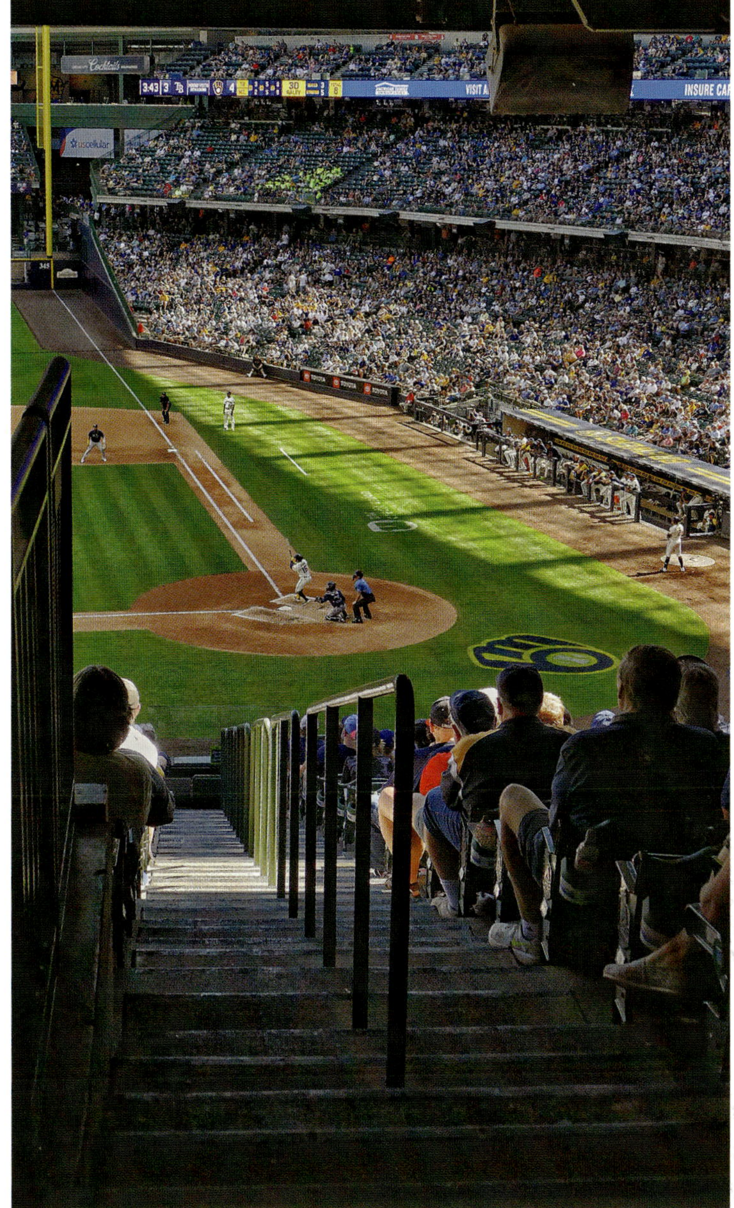

After climbing what seemed like forever, the photographer captured the distant image of home plate on August 10th, 2022, from what are called the "Uecker Seats" in the upper deck. This slang term for the cheap seats farthest from the field originated from a Miller Lite commercial featuring broadcaster Bob Uecker getting directed to his actual seat in the nosebleed section. There is now a statue of Uecker in the last row.

BREWERS ACHIEVEMENTS

WORLD SERIES CHAMPIONSHIPS: 0

AL PENNANTS: 1 (1982)

AL EAST DIVISION TITLES: 1 (1982)

NL CENTRAL DIVISION TITLES: 4 (2011, 2018, 2021, 2023)

WILD CARD BERTHS: 3 (2008, 2019, 2020)

PLAYOFF APPEARANCES: 9 (1981, 1982, 2008, 2011, 2018, 2019, 2020, 2021, 2023)

WORST SEASON RECORD: 2002, 56–106 (.346)

BEST SEASON RECORD: 2018, 96–67 (.589)

More kudos went to the tailgating experience in the parking areas ("Awesome!") and the concessions, which feature fantastic regional food along with popular restaurants and bars. In general the atmosphere at the ballpark was rated very highly. Location was also considered a plus. While not a downtown ballpark, this stadium is only 7 miles (11 km) from central Milwaukee and is easily accessible by car or metro transit.

Negative reviews pointed out the disregard for interior ambiance, lack of intimacy, the overwhelming scale of the structure in terms of the rather tame cityscape, an upper deck pushed too far back from the field, and a main concourse that is confusing and difficult to navigate, although rarely crowded. Also noted is the disconnect between the retro red-brick facade and the rest of Milwaukee—the "Cream City," known for its use of light-colored local clay brick.

In spite of the gripes and swipes, Brewers' fans love their ballpark and arguably have the strongest fan base for their home field outside Chicago or Boston. Fan polls consistently place this stadium near the top of the list.

The *Teamwork* sculpture is a poignant tribute to Miller Park workers Jeffrey A. Wischer, William R. DeGrave, and Jerome W. Starr, who died while building the park.

FEATURES AND AMENITIES

American Family Field, as its name suggests, prides itself on offering entertainment for fans of all ages, from kids to adult to seniors.

WALK OF FAME The Walk of Fame is located on the plaza outside the ballpark and near the statues of Hank Aaron, Robin Yount, Commissioner Emeritus Allan H. "Bud" Selig, and Bob Uecker. This site commemorates some of the greatest names in Milwaukee baseball history with a granite "home plate" set into the ground.

Reporters and fans came to American Family Field after baseball great Hank Aaron died in Atlanta. A statue of Aaron is in front of the stadium, and his plaque is shown upper left on the Brewers Wall of Honor outside the stadium.

WALL OF HONOR This is a permanent exhibit on an exterior wall adjacent to the entrance in left field. It commemorates Milwaukee Brewers and Braves players, coaches, and executives who were notable for their career accomplishments or their service to the organizations. Honorees receive a bronze plaque with their image and a brief synopsis of their career highlights. The initial 58 inductees were honored on June 13, 2014, with an unveiling ceremony and a program on the field.

WALKING TOUR The Brewers invite fans to take an exclusive Walking Tour of the stadium that features behind-the-scenes attractions that include the Selig Experience, playing field, visitors' clubhouse, visitors' dugout, the Brewers' bullpen, luxury suite level, press box, Bob Uecker's broadcast booth, and many other special, non-public locations.

THE SELIG EXPERIENCE This is a state-of-the-art attraction that honors former Brewers owner and Commissioner Emeritus Allan H. "Bud" Selig. The exhibit is located on American Family Field's Loge Level in the left-field corner. A highlight of the attraction is a multimedia show that relates the story of Selig's role in returning Major League Baseball to Milwaukee and his work to promote the game in his hometown. Fans can even share a 3-D encounter with Selig himself in a reproduction of his County Stadium office. The Selig Experience is available after the gates open and is included in certain ballpark tours.

SWITCHEROO!

In 1998, the AL Milwaukee Brewers joined the National League Central Division. They are the only franchise to play in four different MLB divisions since the 1969 advent of divisional play—AL West, AL East, AL Central, and NL Central. They are also one of only two current MLB franchises to switch leagues in the modern era, the other being the Houston Astros, who switched from the NL West to the NL Central and then to AL West in the 2013 realignment.

> “On June 27, 1993, as the Sausages approached Milwaukee County Stadium on the scoreboard video, the left field doors swung open—and much to the surprise of players and fans—out came larger-than-life mascots. Polish, Brat, and Hotdog were the new mascots the Milwaukee Brewers cooked up for a new marketing gimmick. Nearly 30 years later, the racing sausages are still a hit.”
>
> —EBAY LISTING FOR THE ORIGINAL SET OF COSTUMES

During each game in the middle of the sixth inning, fans are treated to the spectacle of the Sausage Race. The current “racing sausages” are the Italian, the Chorizo, the Hot Dog, the Bratwurst, and the Polish.

SEATING CHART

FAMILY AMUSEMENTS A ride down Bernie’s Slide Experience will add a thrill to a Brewers fan’s game day. X-Golf at American Family Field is located on the site of the previous Stadium Club on the Club Level. X-Golf is first-of-its-kind entertainment, offering the most innovative and accurate golf simulator in the world. It features seven state-of-the-art indoor golf simulator bays on two floors, with three of the bays providing expansive views of the field.

TEAM STORE The Brewers Team Store, located in Left Field Corner, is a fan-favored destination that offers a large selection of exclusive items—with the new Brewers branding—including jerseys, apparel, headgear, novelties, and much more.

HELFAER FIELD This is a beautiful, premier youth baseball and softball facility that lies in the shadow of American Family Field and on the site of the former County Stadium. Complete with a big-league scoreboard, sound system, and lighted field for night games, it creates a perfect setting for softball, youth baseball, kickball, employee outings, corporate events, birthday parties, and more. The field is named for Evan Helfaer, a part owner of the Brewers when they first arrived in Milwaukee.

SAUSAGE RACES In the middle of the sixth inning the Brewers stage Sausage Races, an amusing competition between oversized sausage mascots that entertains fans during home games. The tradition began in the early 1990s as a promotion for Klement’s Sausage Company of Milwaukee, whose products were served at the field. Featured were bratwurst, Polish sausage (kielbasa), and Italian sausage. Today Johnsonville sausages are served at the ballpark, and two newcomers, the hot dog and chorizo, have joined the group. The five racing sausages are known as “Brat,” “Polish,” “Italian,” “Hot Dog,” and “Chorizo.” From third base they hustle down the warning track and around home plate to first base. On Sundays, the oversized mascots relay to the human-size “Little Weenies,” who finish the race.

OTHER HOMES OF THE BREWERS

MILWAUKEE COUNTY STADIUM
1953–2000

After the Braves left for Atlanta, Bud Selig and other local businessmen who wanted to keep Major League Baseball alive in their city invited other teams to play at County Stadium. In 1967, an exhibition game was set up between the Chicago White Sox and the Minnesota Twins. It proved so successful that Selig contacted White Sox owner Arthur Allyn to arrange nine home games there in 1998. Fans flocked to these games, and so the following season, 11 more games were scheduled.

Finally in 1970 the Brewers moved into the stadium and again made it a proper Major League field. It saw a World Series win against the St. Louis Cardinals in 1982 and hosted Games 3, 4, and 5.

Baseball icon "Hammerin'" Hank Aaron, who debuted as a Milwaukee Brave in 1954,

[RIGHT] Fans watch a game in 1960.

[BELOW] Hank Aaron receives a standing ovation April 11, 1975, as he is introduced on Opening Day at County Stadium, his first game as a Brewer. He returned to Milwaukee, where his career had started, after playing with the Atlanta Braves following their move from Milwaukee in 1965.

spent his final two years as a ballplayer in Milwaukee, where the American League Brewers allowed the designated hitter position. This allowed the aging Aaron to extend his career. The powerhouse slugger hit his final home run at County Stadium on July 10, 1976, making a career total of 755. The stadium also hosted major rock concerts, including the Rolling Stones, Pink Floyd, and Paul McCartney, as well as ice skating exhibitions, religious services, and other special events.

By the 1990s, the stadium was judged to be outdated—it lacked revenue producing luxury boxes and other desirable amenities, and so in July 1992, Selig revealed plans to build a new ballpark adjacent to County. Because the funding for the new site ended up being quite controversial, ground was not broken until 1996, and the Brewers did not move in until the 2001 season. After a touching ceremony featuring Braves, Brewers, and Packers players who had called County Stadium home, the aging venue was officially closed. It was demolished between December 2000 and February 2001.

[TOP] The crowd celebrates as balloons rise over the stadium.

[ABOVE] Milwaukee County Stadium marquee sign, third-base grandstands, taken September 2000. Pictured are the logos of eight National League teams (including the Brewers) and the National League itself. The advertisement in the upper right was a "countdown clock" to the new stadium.

HOME OF THE ST. LOUIS CARDINALS

NATIONAL LEAGUE (1892–PRESENT)

THE SUCCESSFUL CARDINALS BALL CLUB *has always been affiliated with St. Louis, Missouri, another metropolitan center like Milwaukee that became famous for its beer breweries . . . and baseball. Even their stadium honors the Busch family, the name behind such popular adult beverage brands as Budweiser, Bud Light, Busch Beer, Michelob, Rolling Rock, and Shock Top.*

The official history of the St. Louis Cardinals began in 1881, when German American entrepreneur Chris von der Ahe bought a barnstorming baseball team called the Brown Stockings. An earlier iteration of the ball club started in 1875 as part of the National Association, then became charter members of the National League, until they were expelled after a game-fixing scandal, and the team went bankrupt. They then resorted to semipro barnstorming to eke out a living. Due to the confusion of this early period, the franchise's actual history is judged to begin in 1881.

Von der Ahe renamed the club the St. Louis Browns and made them charter members of the American Association league, where they remained from 1882 to 1891. After winning four league championships, they were eligible to play in the professional baseball championships, a precursor to the World Series. Twice they played the Chicago White Stockings, the future Chicago Cubs, which launched their historic rivalry with that team. During this era the franchise met with great success, winning four consecutive AA pennants from 1885 to 1888.

The team transferred to the National League in 1892, after the AA went bankrupt the previous year, and in 1899 they became the Perfectos. In 1900, owners Frank and Stanley Robison named them the Cardinals. This was after St. Louis Republic sportswriter Willie McHale reported a female fan's reaction to their uniforms: "What a lovely shade of cardinal." Fans quickly adopted the nickname. In 1902, the American League Milwaukee Brewers relocated to St. Louis and took the name the Browns. This sparked a 50-year rivalry with the Cardinals, themselves the former Browns.

The team's lackluster early years were poor indicators of their upcoming achievements, with a win-loss percentage of .406. But by the late 1920s, they'd hit their stride, winning the World Series in 1928, 1930, and 1931. Their streak continued, and in 1934, nicknamed "the Gas House Gang," they won 95 games, the NL pennant, and the World Series. This was under the leadership of that season's MVP, pitcher Dizzy Dean. Fans now spoke of "Cardinal Nation," as the team's popularity spread far beyond St. Louis. The Cards kept their momentum into the 1940s, making that decade one of the club's most prosperous. They even pulled off World Series wins in 1942, 1944, and 1946.

The year 1953 was a momentous one for the Cardinals. The Anheuser-Busch brewery bought the team, making August "Gussie" Busch the team's president. And the detested Browns left for Maryland to become the Baltimore Orioles, leaving the Cardinals to reign as the only MLB ball club in St. Louis. They went on to win five more World Series Championships in 1964, 1967, 1982, 2006, and 2011.

STADIUM SEARCH

The early Cardinals first competed at Sportsman's Park (Busch Stadium I), then played in two more ballparks named Busch Stadium. The current incarnation, also known as New Busch Stadium or Busch Stadium III, occupies a portion of the footprint of its predecessor, Busch Memorial Stadium. The adjacent Ballpark Village, a dining and entertainment district, occupies the rest of this footprint.

BALLPARK STATS

ADDRESS
700 Clark Avenue, St. Louis, MO 63102

OWNER/OPERATOR
St. Louis Cardinals

DESIGNER/CHIEF ARCHITECT
HOK Sport (now Populous); Kennedy Associates/Architects Inc.

CAPACITY
44,383

RECORD BASEBALL ATTENDANCE
48,581 on 8/6/2022 (vs. New York Yankees)

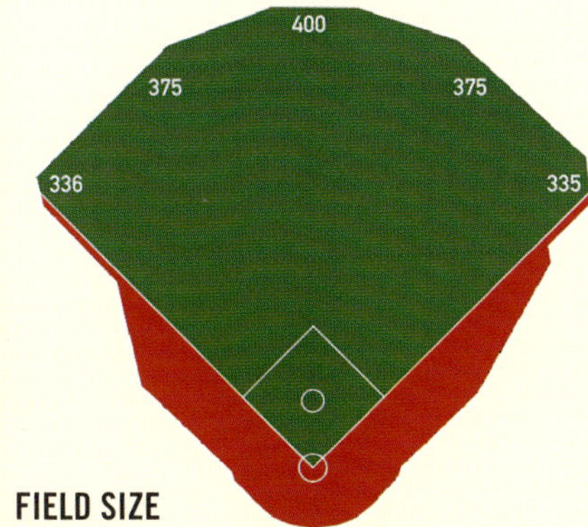

FIELD SIZE

- **Left field** 336 feet (102 m)
- **Left center field** 375 feet (114 m)
- **Center field** 400 feet (122 m)
- **Right center field** 375 feet (114 m)
- **Right field** 335 feet (102 m)

SURFACE
Bermuda grass

TEAM MASCOT
Fredbird

The need for replacing Busch Memorial was apparent by 1995, but the team struggled to acquire the funding until 2001, when the State of Missouri signed a contract proposing a downtown stadium for the Cardinals. But in 2002 the funding bill was struck down, leaving the team to consider a move to Gateway International Raceway near Madison, Illinois. Alarmed by this potential defection, the City of St. Louis responded by drafting a financing plan for the team that would allow them to construct a stadium in the downtown area. This project would be financed through private bonds, bank loans, a long-term loan from St. Louis County, and money from team owners. The total development, including the adjacent Ballpark Village, was projected to cost approximately $665 million, with the stadium itself costing $365 million.

Construction on the new ballpark began in December 2003. In August 2004, the Cardinals and Anheuser-Busch agreed on a 20-year naming rights contract in order to keep the Busch Stadium name alive. The team played their first official game there, quite fittingly, against the Milwaukee Brewers on April 10, 2006. By the end of the stadium's first season, every Cardinal game had been sold out, giving the venue a total attendance of 3,407,104, the second highest in team history. The Cardinals also ended their inaugural season on a high note—by winning the 2006 World Series, the first team to so christen their new home since the 1923 New York Yankees.

DESIGN AND CONSTRUCTION

The stadium's throwback design was by HOK Sport (Populous), the firm that set the standard for retro parks, and was in part created by Jim Chibnall, the sports architect who also worked on Progressive Field, Heinz Field, Globe Life Field, and Sydney Olympic Stadium, among others. The plans for the venue incorporated a facade of red brick with black steel arches over each entrance. The interior would feature three main seating decks, a main concourse, loge concourse, and terrace concourse. The bleachers, located in both left and right field, allowed fans two different views of the game. All concourses were open and provided views of the field. Beyond the outfield spread the breathtaking skyline of downtown St. Louis and the soaring curve of the Gateway Arch.

PUBLIC REACTION

Cardinal's fans loved the ballpark as a fitting place to stomp, cheer, and whistle for their favorite team—and clever gimmicks and fancy amenities be damned—but other members of the public were not so forgiving. A number of critics dismissed the new stadium as another retro ballpark based on the much-admired Camden Yards template, just one more brick-and-exposed-steel-girder assemblage meant to evoke the glorious days of yesteryear. The venue's rather bland appearance was faulted for lack of imagination when it came

to taking architectural chances. On the plus side, its location in the heart of the city—with stirring urban vistas in the near distance and a view of the Gateway Arch from home plate seating—and the pure enthusiasm of Cardinals fans did a lot to make up for the lack of innovative design or concourse extras.

The ruddy brick facade did a good job of conveying "Cardinal red" to the fans, while the exposed beams were black here, not the green seen in some other retro stadiums. The structure fit in well with the surrounding neighborhood, with the facade echoing the nearby Cupples Warehouse. A number of the architectural embellishments reflected St. Louis history. Ornamental terra-cotta panels on the main facade recalled the city's venerable Merchants Building, once considered the Wall Street of the Midwest.

FEATURES AND AMENITIES

It cannot be overstated that Busch Stadium caters to its highly passionate fans—who religiously flock to the stadium to the tune of three million attendees annually. The ballpark is brimming with historical references, and beyond its gates lies a lively entertainment and dining district.

HONORED PLAYERS The stadium offers a gallery of statues, showcasing team luminaries and furnishing prime spots for group selfies. Outside the Gate 3 entrance stands a bronze statue of

[ABOVE] Two bright-red cardinals flank the clock over the ballpark's scoreboard. Although the name "Budweiser Stadium" was nixed, signs throughout the stadium display the name of the "King of Beers," the flagship brand of brewing company Anheuser-Busch, the team's former owner.

[LEFT] The exterior of Busch Stadium, informally known as New Busch Stadium or Busch Stadium III. This retro-style park has been home to the St. Louis Cardinals since 2006.

> "I believe in the organization. I believe in the culture. I believe in the fans. I believe in the city. I believe in the traditions that have been created here."
>
> —SONNY GRAY, CARDINALS PITCHER

Cardinals legend Stan "the Man" Musial. The Cardinals statues that previously surrounded Busch Memorial Stadium are now displayed at the corner of Clark and 8th Streets, outside the Cardinals' team store. These statues represent former Cardinal players and Hall of Fame inductees Enos Slaughter, Dizzy Dean, Rogers Hornsby, Red Schoendienst, Lou Brock, Bob Gibson, Ozzie Smith, and Ted Simmons; former St. Louis Browns player George Sisler; former Negro League Stars player and Hall of Fame inductee Cool Papa Bell; and Cardinals radio broadcaster and Hall of Fame honoree Jack Buck.

BALLPARK VILLAGE The newest addition at Busch Stadium was completed in 2014. Beyond center field, on the site of the old Busch Stadium, lies the Ballpark Village. Phase I of the village opened in 2014 and included a three-story, 30,000-square-foot building containing the St. Louis Cardinals Hall of Fame and Museum and Cardinal Nation Restaurant. The museum is open year-round and covers the team's evolution during its occupancies of Busch Stadiums I, II, and III. There are 300 seats located atop the structure, allowing fans to watch the Cardinals in action from 500 feet (152 m) away. Also included in Phase I is the Budweiser Brew House, showcasing Anheuser-Busch's connection to the franchise, featuring a beer garden and 100 different beers. In addition, Live! at Ballpark Village and PBR St. Louis are a part of the Ballpark Village. In 2018 the Budweiser Terrace was added in the upper right field section of the stadium. This multilevel area includes two bars, lounge seating, and standing areas for fans. Approximately 1,000 seats were removed to make room for this space.

SEATING CHART

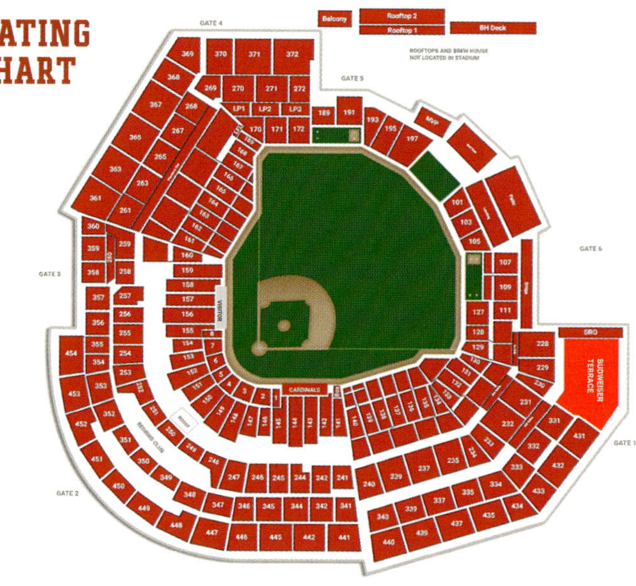

BUSCH STADIUM FIRSTS

FIRST MLB GAME: 4/10/2006, Cardinals over Milwaukee Brewers, 6–4

FIRST HOME RUN: 4/10/2006, Bill Hall, vs. Milwaukee Brewers

FIRST ALL-STAR GAME: 7/14/2009, AL defeats NL, 4–3

FIRST PLAYOFF GAME: 10/7/2006, San Diego Padres over Cardinals, 3–1

FIRST WORLD SERIES GAME: 10/24/2006, Cardinals over Detroit Tigers, 5–0 in Game 3

Located on 10 acres (4 ha) just north of Busch Stadium, Ballpark Village occupies a portion of the old Busch Memorial Stadium's former footprint. One of the top restaurant and entertainment districts in the region, Ballpark Village is the first master-planned development designed around a new Major League Baseball ballpark.

[ABOVE] Mascot Fredbird, a cardinal wearing a team jersey, was introduced in 1979 as a way to entertain younger fans. One of the best-known MLB mascots, he makes hundreds of goodwill appearances all over the St. Louis area.

FAMILY- AND KID-FRIENDLY OPTIONS Along with the popular Coca Cola Rooftop Deck and the Backstop Bar, there are also many gathering spots and party areas at the venue where fans will find interactive games and activities. For parents with kids in tow, the ballpark offers fun distractions like sharing photo ops with the giant player bobbleheads, visiting Fredbird at Ford Plaza during the third inning, and trying out the sensory room, which provides a safe, relaxing environment for people to chill out. There is also Kid's Club, which, for a fee, offers two game tickets, a Kid's Club T-shirt, a squishy Fredbird, a bucket hat, a Cardinals poster, and TOPPS baseball cards. The Hall of Fame is also extremely kid-friendly.

CARDINALS ACHIEVEMENTS

WORLD SERIES CHAMPIONSHIPS: 11 (1885*, 1886*, 1926, 1931, 1934, 1942, 1944, 1946, 1964, 1967, 1982, 2006, 2011)

AA PENNANTS 4 (1885*, 1886*, 1887*, 1888*)

AL PENNANTS: 19 (1926, 1928, 1930, 1931, 1934, 1942, 1943, 1944, 1946, 1964, 1967, 1968, 1982, 1985, 1987, 2004, 2006, 2011, 2013)

NL East Division Titles 3 (1982, 1985, 1987)

NL CENTRAL DIVISION TITLES: 15 (1996, 2000, 2002, 2004, 2005, 2006, 2009, 2013, 2014, 2015, 2019, 2022)

WILD CARD BERTHS: 3 (2012, 2021, 2022)

PLAYOFF APPEARANCES: 132 (1926, 1928, 1930, 1931, 1934, 1942, 1943, 1944, 1946, 1964, 1967, 1968, 1982, 1985, 1987, 1996, 2000, 2001, 2002, 2004, 2005, 2006, 2009, 2011, 2012, 2013, 2014, 2015, 2019, 2020, 2021, 2022)

WORST SEASON RECORD: 1908, 49–105 (.318)

BEST SEASON RECORD: 1885, 79–33 (.705)*

* as St. Louis Browns

[ABOVE] Outside Busch Stadium stands a statue of "Stan the Man" Musial. Hall of Famer No. 6 played 22 seasons with the Cardinals. Over the years, team nicknames have included "the Cards," "the Birds," and the "Redbirds."

[BELOW] Fans can relax before a game at outdoor picnic tables with the landmark Gateway Arch as a backdrop.

OTHER HOMES OF THE CARDINALS

SPORTSMAN'S PARK
1902–1966

The first Sportsman's Park was originally called the Grand Avenue Ball Grounds or Grand Avenue Park. The first grandstand was built in 1881. In the mid-1880s, the park was leased by the St. Louis Brown Stockings, or "Browns," an up-and-coming ball club. Soon they went looking for a new ballpark, finding a site a few blocks northwest of the old field and calling it New Sportsman's Park, which was later renamed Robison Field. They also changed their team colors from brown to cardinal red—and created a new identity.

When the AL Milwaukee Brewers moved to St. Louis in 1902 and took the Browns name, they built another version of Sportsman's Park, with a steel-and-concrete grandstand, the third such stadium in the Majors, and the second in the American League, after Shibe Park. The Cardinals began to play there in the mid-1920s, as tenants of the Browns, after abandoning the outdated, wooden Robison Field. Thus, the ballpark witnessed the 1926 World Series, with the Cardinals—not the resident Browns—upsetting the Yankees in a memorable seventh game.

[LEFT] Team photo of the 1885 St. Louis Browns, who later morphed into the Cardinals, set against a backdrop of the first Sportsman's Park.

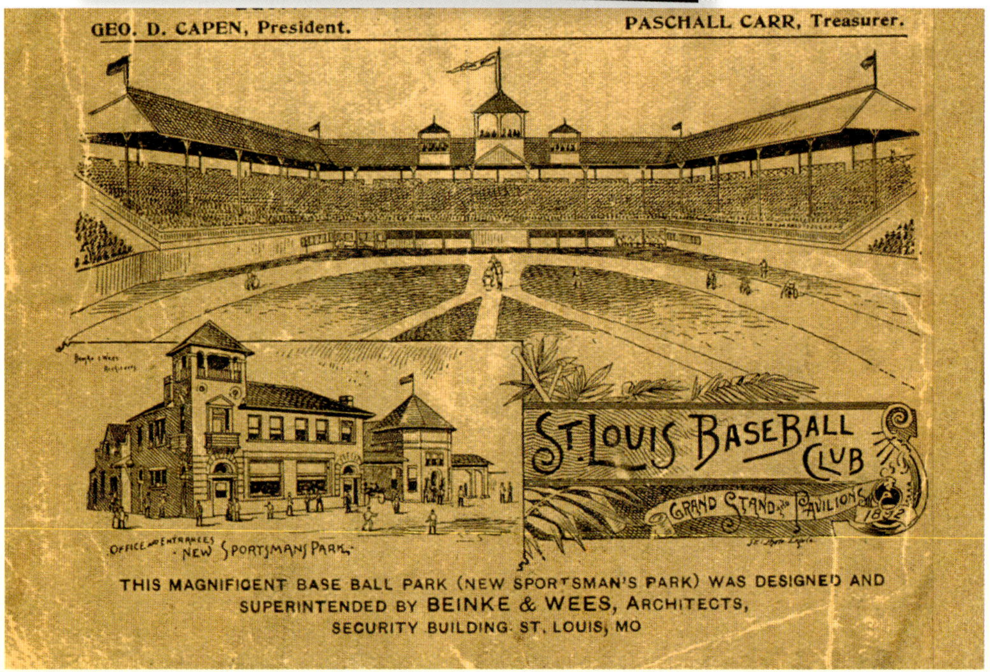

[BELOW] Cover illustration for the official score book used for a game against Washington at Sportsman's Park in 1893 shows both a field and a street view of the ballpark.

Sportsman's Park was renamed Busch Stadium in 1953 to honor the Cardinals' new owner, the city's brewing giant, Anheuser-Busch. This came about after plans to name it Budweiser Stadium were scotched by league rules that prohibited naming ballparks after alcoholic drinks. It was also home to pro football—in 1923, it hosted St. Louis's first NFL team, the All-Stars, and later the NFL St. Louis Cardinals. The Cardinals' last game there was May 8, 1966. Sportsman's Park/Busch Stadium was demolished not long after.

[ABOVE] A view of the concrete-and-steel version of Sportsman's Park in 1926, where the Cardinals lost the fourth game of the World Series to the NY Yankees. Babe Ruth had three home runs in the game.

[LEFT] The site of Sportsman's Park is currently the site of the Herbert Hoover Boys' Club, which includes an athletic field in the same spot as the original playing field. A sign marks the stadium's former location, listing some of the park's baseball highlights.

BUSCH MEMORIAL STADIUM
1966–2005

Busch Memorial Stadium, a.k.a. Busch Stadium II, was a multipurpose sports facility in St. Louis that operated from 1966 to 2005. Built during the era of the "cookie cutter" arenas, Busch was enclosed on all sides, similar in style to Riverfront, Veterans, Three Rivers, and Atlanta–Fulton County Stadiums.

The new venue was designed by Sverdrup & Parcel and built by Grün & Bilfinger. Edward Durell Stone designed the roof, with its 96-arch "Crown of Arches," paid tribute to the St. Louis Gateway Arch. Just weeks after opening, the new stadium hosted the All-Star Game, followed by a performance by the Beatles.

Like all good multipurpose stadiums, Busch II served as home to the MLB St. Louis Cardinals baseball team for its entire operating existence, while also serving as home to the football St. Louis Cardinals for 22 seasons, from 1966 to 1987, and the NFL St. Louis Rams during part of the 1995 season. After serving the baseball Cardinals for 40 seasons, the stadium was demolished by wrecking ball in late 2005, and part of its former footprint was occupied by its replacement—the new Busch Stadium. As a testimonial to its design and durability, Busch II was one of the last venues built in the 1960s to be torn down.

[TOP] An aerial shot of the park shows the Gateway Arch rising behind the stadium. From above, the "Crown of Arches," a design element that was inspired by the shape of this St. Louis icon, is clearly visible.

[MIDDLE] Cardinals fans gather at Busch Memorial Stadium to watch a game in 2001.

[BOTTOM] After nearly 40 years of hosting multiple sports teams of the city of St. Louis, Busch Memorial Stadium was demolished in late 2005.

CLOSE-UP

MAINTAINING THE BALLPARK

The Chicago White Sox groundskeeping crew puts the finishing touches on the infield and home plate before a game.

It's not surprising that to many sports fans, ballparks seem like cathedrals or other sites of veneration. They possess beauty, character, spaciousness, and an almost palpable atmosphere. And, like other venues frequented by the public, ballparks and stadiums require a great deal of after-hours upkeep. This is when busy workers clean and disinfect surfaces, as well as inspect the structure and the field for problems—all out of the sight of the fans. Yet, the efforts of these crews contribute greatly to the levels of comfort and enjoyment experienced by visitors.

In a ballpark there are two distinct areas that require maintenance—the seating areas and facilities that are part of the stadium, and the ballfield itself. The average annual maintenance cost for a sports facility is around $200,000 to $300,000 per year, but costs can vary significantly depending on facility age, materials used, quality of construction, and frequency of use.

On average, a well-maintained modern stadium might have a lifespan of 30 to 50 years or even more. In order to ensure such a long life, many stadiums undergo periodic renovations and upgrades that accommodate changing industry standards, enhance spectator experience, introduce new technologies, and comply with safety regulations.

KEEP IT CLEAN

For those who might be wondering how many people it takes to clean a stadium, a well-attended game could require up to 150 workers picking up trash. A smaller crowd might need something like 80 cleaners. Roughly 50 to 75 people then spray down the seats and concourses with pressure washers and use a special vacuum to suck up the water on the seats and surrounding areas, leaving everything clean and dry. To sanitize the seats, they are sprayed with industrial-strength disinfectant. The cleaning crews also attend to the premium suites and food service areas.

STADIUM-CLEANING CHECKLIST

- Establish and follow regular cleaning schedules and checklists.
- Thoroughly clean high-traffic areas, such as restrooms and concessions.
- Use disinfectants to prevent the spread of germs and viruses.
- Train and certify stadium cleaning staff to ensure quality results.

GREEN FIELDS

As fans stream out of the dim entrance tunnels and into the sun-filled ballpark, few sights can compare to the expanse of verdant green playing field bisected by crisp brown paths that lies before them. First-time visitors, especially younger fans, often have their breath taken away at the view.

But that sea of grass requires constant upkeep by a crew of groundskeepers who are responsible for field preparation and in-game maintenance. Their duties might include watering, repairing bases, and maintaining pitching mounds, batter's boxes, infield playing surfaces, and warning tracks.

To keep the grass healthy, the grounds crew needs to avoid standing water, clean or aerate the field properly, mow and edge natural turf regularly, manage disease control, and implement natural turf fertilization. They must also be ready to draw a large tarp over the field to keep it dry if it begins to rain during a game. This is because playing on fields that are too wet is the number one cause of damage to the grass and also the top reason for player injury. Once the rain stops, the tarp is removed. Some clubs tarp their fields to ensure they are ready for games and to keep the clay in the pitcher's mound and batter's and catcher's boxes from drying out.

FIELD MAINTENANCE CHECKLIST

- Make sure that at least 75 percent of field is covered with turf grass.
- Check that there are no bare spots, leaving hard soil exposed.
- Strive for turf grass that has a uniform color, density, and height.
- Remove burrs, thistles, or thorns from surface.

Dancing on the field: The grounds crew at some stadiums put on a show for the fans—the Yankee crew famously performs to "YMCA" (shown above) and the Mariners' crew dances between the innings—not to mention the players there lock arms and dance the hora after a win!

CARING FOR ARTIFICIAL TURF

Some stadiums with synthetic turf use a Clean Sweep Turf Maintenance Machine, which lifts and loosens the infill to soften the surface. This also helps the grass fibers spring back to their original position. The machine then goes across the top layer of turf, sweeping up loose infill and any debris. The infill is replaced on the surface, and the debris is discarded. Soiled turf can also be spot cleaned with Simple Green All-Purpose Cleaner, which removes both mess and odor, or with a sprayed-on mixture of white vinegar and water followed by a water rinse.

Even an artificial turf field requires occasional watering. Obviously, this is not to help maintain live grass; rather, it serves to regulate field temperature. During hot summer weather, the surface of the turf may actually become warm to the touch. A nice hose-down is a quick and easy way to cool things off.

Because the backing on artificial turf is extremely porous, it allows more water to reach the underlying soil than actual grass does. High-quality turf will drain at a rate of 1,200 inches (3,048 cm) per hour, which is more than enough to prevent any rain from pooling on the field.

A water hose is being used to spray down Canvas Alley, the open alley behind the first-base line at Fenway Park, where the grounds crew sits.

The Atlanta Braves groundskeeping crew perform various duties to make sure the playing field is in perfect shape before the start of a game.

The grounds crew at Yankee Stadium sweep and smooth the infield dirt area during the brief intermission between innings of the game.

San Francisco Giants grounds crew uses a tarp to cover the infield to save it from rain after a Giants win at AT&T Park, now known as Oracle Park.

HOME OF THE DETROIT TIGERS

AMERICAN LEAGUE (1901–PRESENT)

THE DETROIT TIGERS *are one of the American League's eight charter franchises and date back to their founding in 1894 in the minor league Western League. They are the only members of the Western League still found in their home city, and the oldest "one-name, one-franchise" team playing in the American League.*

The Detroit Tigers are an historic team that has completed 123 seasons as a professional franchise. Since their entry into the Major League, they have won four World Series, 11 American League pennants, three East Division titles, and four Central Division championships. Through their many years of play, the Tigers have recorded 71 seasons at .500 or better, 69 of which have been winning campaigns.

The earliest Detroit Tigers franchise was founded as a member of the reorganized Western League in 1894. They originally played at Boulevard Park, sometimes called League Park. Their first game at the new Bennett Park was on April 28, 1896. It was located at the corner of Michigan Avenue and Trumbull Avenue, west of downtown Detroit, a humble site that would go on to become the team's base of operations for more than 100 additional seasons.

In 1900, the Western League renamed itself the American League, but it was still considered a minor league according to the National Agreement, a pact that governed relations between rival major leagues, allowing them to respect one another's player contracts. The upstart American League broke from the confines of the National Agreement the next year, declaring itself a major league, and began to compete with the National League for players and fans.

The Tigers became charter members of the American League in 1901, playing their first Major League game against the Milwaukee Brewers on April 25 in a close match, which they won 14–13. The Tigers ultimately finished third in the eight-team league. That initial season, the Tigers were the first Major League team to have a mascot on their ball cap—a red tiger on a dark background. In 1903, it was replaced by the letter "D," and the iconic Old English letterform appeared the following year.

In the first decade of the 20th century, team executive and eventual owner Frank Navin helped the Tigers acquire a number of talented players that would put the team on the map. In 1905, the Tigers acquired future Hall of Famer Ty Cobb to join a team that had already contracted powerful assets like Sam Crawford, Hughie Jennings, and Bill Donovan. Cobb remained with the team for 21 years and would help them reach the World Series three times.

The Tigers played and made history in the same ballpark since 1912—and at the same location since 1895—but by the early 1990s, the beloved venue was past its prime. Originally known as Navin Field, then Tiger Stadium, the structure was deteriorating badly. Club owner Mike Ilitch—an entrepreneur and founder of the Little Caesar's Pizza franchise—expressed his desire to build a luxurious new ballpark for his team. He eventually played a key role in designing the post-modern facility and was able to bring his years of family entertainment experience to the process. Groundbreaking for the $300 million project took place on October 29, 1997, in downtown Detroit, on the former site of the Detroit College of Law. More than 60 percent of the cost was privately financed, and the balance was contributed by public sources. The ballpark design would combine classic seating areas with unique amusement and entertainment areas.

The final game at Tiger Stadium was played on September 27, 1999, and the club moved to its new ballpark at the end of that season. That venue had been christened Comerica Park after a December 1998 agreement with Comerica Bank, which agreed to pay $66 million over 30 years for the naming rights. In 2018, Comerica extended its agreement with the Tigers through 2034.

DESIGN AND CONSTRUCTION

The ballpark, which opened on April 11, 2000, was designed by HOK Sport (Populous); SHG, Inc.; and Rockwell Group, along with team owner Mike Ilitch. The brick-clad, concrete-and-steel structure featured soaring light towers and tiger-themed embellishments and, in some ways, resembled a massively overgrown version of a traditional ballpark.

The stadium's structure conforms to the configuration of the playing field, with all seating designed to prioritize fan sight lines.

BALLPARK STATS

ADDRESS
2100 Woodward Avenue, Detroit, MI 48201

OWNER
Detroit/Wayne County Stadium Authority

OPERATOR
313 Presents

ARCHITECT
HOK Sport (then Populous); SHG, Inc.; Rockwell Group

CAPACITY
41,083

RECORD BASEBALL ATTENDANCE
45,280 on 7/26/2008 (vs. Chicago White Sox)

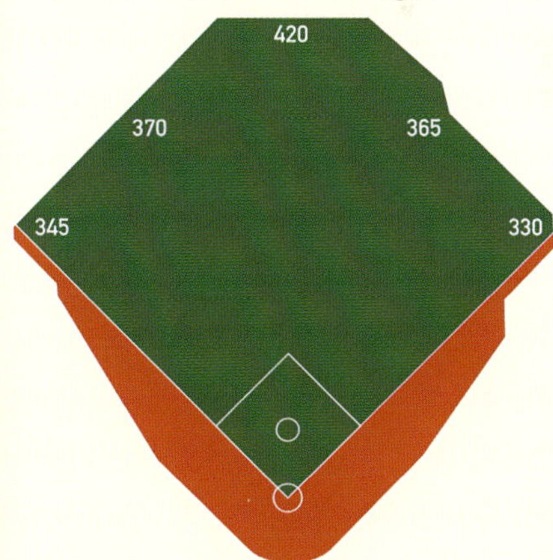

FIELD SIZE

- **Left field** 342 feet (104 m)
- **Left center** 370 feet (110 m)
- **Center field** 412 feet (126 m)
- **Right center** 365 feet (111 m)
- **Right field** 330 feet (100 m)

SURFACE
Kentucky bluegrass

TEAM MASCOT
Paws

> **“If the fans feel the pride that this is their park, and a pride of ownership, then we’ve accomplished what we set out to do.”**
>
> —MIKE ILITCH, TIGERS OWNER

COMERICA PARK FIRSTS

FIRST MLB GAME: 4/11/2000, Tigers over Seattle Mariners, 5–2

FIRST HOME RUN: 4/14/200 Juan Gonzalez vs. Devil Rays

FIRST NO-HITTER: 6/12/2007, Justin Verlander vs. Milwaukee Brewers

FIRST ALL-STAR GAME: 7/12/2005, Al over NL, 7–5

FIRST PLAYOFF GAME: 10/3/2011, Tigers over NY Yankees, 5–4

FIRST WORLD SERIES GAME: 110/21/2006, St. Louis Cardinals over Tigers, 7–2 in Game 1

[ABOVE] An overhead shot shows the lines of the stadium following the contours of the diamond-shaped playing field.

[BELOW] The exterior is clad in brick, giving it the look of a classic ballpark.

The park’s main entrance on Witherell Street is located across from the Fox Theater and two iconic churches, St. John’s Episcopal Church, and Central United Methodist Church. Outside this entrance, a roaring tiger statue stands an imposing 15 feet (4.6 m) high and offers fans a prime spot for taking selfies or capturing the expanse of the stadium in the background. The main gate also features two immense 80-foot-high (24.4 m) baseball bats, while parts of the exterior displays classic Detroit Pewabic tile accents. The three other main entrances are the Rocket Mortgage Entry on Adams and Witherell, the Gallagher Entry at the corner of Brush and Adams Streets, and Gate D on Montcalm Street.

The field itself, which is sown with Kentucky bluegrass, has undergone a number of alterations since its creation, including a decrease in the dimensions of the outfield. On the basis of its spacious initial layout, Comerica was clearly a pitcher’s paradise. Tigers’ outfielder Bobby Higginson once sarcastically referred to the venue as “Comerica National Park.” After the walls and fences were drawn in closer to home plate, however, the ballpark became the third-most batter-friendly stadium in MLB. The field also features a distinctive dirt strip running between home plate and the pitcher’s mound, sometimes known as the “keyhole.” This was a common feature in early ballparks, but today it is rarely seen, and Comerica Park is the only MLB stadium to feature one. Another anomaly—the home plate area is not a standard circle, but instead follows the shape of the plate itself.

Comerica Park offers stadium-goers a range of premium seating areas: In descending order of price, they include Home Plate Suites,

Diamond Suites, Legends Suites, Party Suites, Championship Club, On-Deck Circle, Tiger Den/Tiger Club, and Right Field Balcony and Tables. The Tiger Den area was the first of its kind in baseball—resembling the fashionable boxes with movable chairs found at old-time sporting stadiums.

PUBLIC REACTIONS

Fans of Comerica consider it a combination of ballpark, entertainment venue, and museum. Lovers of the old Tigers Stadium even admit that they enjoy making "new memories" at their team's updated home.

Visitors often comment that the field appears to lie at the center of an urban village, one that includes shops, restaurants, offices, and other attractions. A number of the buildings that make up this village house the service facilities surrounding the park, but the layout also includes 70,000 square feet (6,503 m^2) of retail space and another 36,000 square feet (3,345 m^2) dedicated to Tigers' offices. And because there are no upper deck outfield seats, few venues offer a better vista of the downtown skyline.

One of the statues at the park captures pitcher Hal Newhouser mid-throw. The Hall of Famers whose names adorn the wall at Comerica Park are Ty Cobb, Sam Crawford, Mickey Cochrane, Harry Heilmann, and Hughie Jennings, although they do not have retired numbers.

FEATURES AND AMENITIES

The generous proportions of the concourses include a 40-foot (12 m) main concourse that expands in certain areas. Tiger Stadium's lower concourses ranged from only 17 to 27 feet (5–8.2 m). The current upper concourse measures roughly 34 feet (10.3) in width, compared to 11 feet (3.35 m) at the former ballpark.

CARNIVAL RIDES AND KIDS FUN The Hi-Chew Carousel, located near Comerica Bank Big Cat Court at Section 119, adds to the carnival atmosphere the park fosters. Here, patrons young and old ride atop prowling tigers instead of the usual prancing horses. And behind the Brushfire Grill at Section 131 stands the 50-foot (15.24 m) Fly Ball Ferris Wheel with its baseball-shaped cars. For children 4 through 14, Kids Run the Bases gives them the opportunity to run the bases after all Sunday home games throughout the season.

BASEBALL HISTORY Historical enticements include a walking tour of baseball and lifestyle history that is divided into different eras of the 20th century. "Decade monuments," towering displays celebrating two decades each, are spaced throughout the concourse and feature photos and artifacts from their eras.

HONORED PLAYERS On the left field wall are six action-based statues of esteemed Tigers' players Al Kaline, Hal Newhouser, Charlie Gehringer, Hank Greenberg, Ty Cobb, and Willie Horton. These Detroit legends stand from 11 to 13 feet (3.35–4 m) tall, including their granite bases. This is a favorite spot for fans to stand along the fence and watch the Tigers from the outfield.

CHEVROLET FOUNTAIN The center-field wall Chevrolet Fountain produces a stunning "liquid fireworks" display with flashing lights that are synchronized to music. It is used to celebrate home runs and other special moments.

FOOD AND DRINK When it comes to food concessions, most ballparks have a point-of-sale register for every 200 fans, while Comerica Park speeds the wait time with one register for every 125

TIGERS ACHIEVEMENTS

WORLD SERIES CHAMPIONSHIPS: 4 (1935, 1945, 1968, 1984)

AL PENNANTS: 11 (1907, 1908, 1909, 1934, 1935, 1940, 1945, 1968, 1984, 2006, 2012)

AL EAST DIVISION TITLES: 3 (1972, 1984, 1987)

AL CENTRAL DIVISION TITLES: 4 (2011, 2012, 2013, 2014)

WILD CARD BERTHS: 0

PLAYOFF APPEARANCES: 10 (1969, 1973, 1986, 1988, 1999, 2000, 2006, 2015, 2016, 2022)

WORST SEASON RECORD: 1934, 43–119 (.265)

BEST SEASON RECORD: 1984, 104–58 (.656)

fans. Popular dining spots include the Brushfire Grill barbecue area behind third base and the Big Cat Court behind first base, which offer a range of range of snacks, sandwiches, frozen treats, and other munchies. In 2023, the Tigers began partnering with several small local businesses—Bert's Marketplace, Breadless, Green Dot Stables, Taqueria El Rey, the Lobster Food Truck, and Yum Village—which will all have a presence at Comerica Park.

SEATING CHART

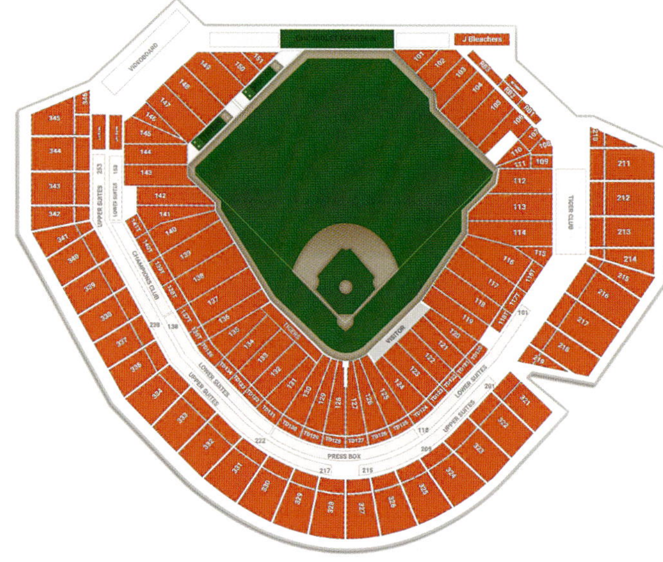

THE TIGERS OF COMERICA PARK

Befitting the team name and identity as "Tiger Town," a tiger theme pervades the park. Along with the roaring tiger that greets stadium-goers at the main entrance, eight other oversize tiger statues adorn the park, including two at the Gate B entrance (*below*) and two on the scoreboard in left field. Whenever a Tiger player hits a home run or the home team wins, their eyes light up while tiger growls are played through the sound system. Outside the park, the brick walls display 33 tiger heads with lit baseballs in their mouths (*right*). Other embellishments include the Pewabic Tile baseballs, tigers, and Old English "D" logos in the team's colors that decorate the exterior walls (*above*), the tiger-themed carousel, and—of course—Paws, the team mascot.

[ABOVE] Park goers use the growling tiger statue as a readily recognizable meet-up spot.

[LEFT] Families take a ride on the park's Hi-Chew Carousel.

[ABOVE] Paws, an anthropomorphic Bengal tiger dressed in a Tigers jersey and cap, made his debut as the official team mascot on May 5, 1995. He began entertaining fans at Tiger Stadium and made the move to Comerica Park along with the team.

[LEFT] Menacing rooftop tigers loom over the grounds.

third base, increasing capacity to 30,000, and a press box was added on the roof.

After Walter O. Briggs became the Tigers' sole owner in 1935, he expanded and renovated the stadium, including a double-decker grandstand. It was then renamed Briggs Stadium. The revamped stadium, which now had the look it would retain for many decades, could seat 36,000 fans. After an additional expansion the following year, Briggs Stadium, which was now enclosed, had a seating capacity of 54,500, making it one of baseball's largest stadiums.

The team began night games on June 15, 1948, and that same year, the press box was extended around the third deck. It was rechristened Tiger Stadium in 1961, when John Fetzer bought the team. In 1972, Fetzer outraged fans by announcing plans to build a new multipurpose stadium, but city voters united to reject the bonds to construct the complex along the Detroit River. And so Tiger Stadium remained the team's home until 1999. Certainly one of the most popular stadiums in baseball history, under its various names this venue housed the Detroit Tigers for nearly a century and became a mecca for generations of Tiger fans.

After the construction and opening of Comerica Park in 2000, Tiger Stadium sat empty for nearly a decade. Several preservation groups tried to save and renovate some portion of the venue. But the City of Detroit had no interest in saving the ballpark and scheduled it for demolition. In October 2007, seats and other items were removed, and in September 2008, partial demolition was completed. Still, advocates pushed to salvage the remainder, but the last sections were razed in September 2009. For nearly another decade the site sat empty. All that remained of the Tigers' former home was the playing field and the center-field flagpole. Finally, in 2016 the Detroit Police Athletic League bought the property and built a youth complex, the Corner Ballpark, on the site. It included an 8,500-square-foot (790 m2) building, a baseball field on the footprint of Tiger Stadium's field, and the original flagpole from the ballpark.

[LEFT] The typography of the signage of Detroit Stadium shows the influence of the 1930s renovations.

[ABOVE] Demolition of the stadium began in 2007 and continued into 2009.

[LEFT] Detroit Stadium, circa 1980s. Although the team had vacated the premises before the 2000 season, the building would stand empty for another seven years.

“. . . Tiger Stadium has been home to this great game of baseball. But more than anything, it has been a cherished home to our memories. . . . Tonight we say goodbye. But we will not forget. Open your eyes, look around, and take a mental picture. Moments like this shall live on forever. It’s been 88 moving years at Michigan and Trumbull. The tradition built here shall endure along with the permanence of the Olde English D. But tonight we must say goodbye. Farewell, old friend Tiger Stadium. We will remember.”

—HALL OF FAME BROADCASTER ERNIE HARWELL, FAREWELL SPEECH, FINAL GAME AT TIGER STADIUM, SEPTEMBER 27,1999

2003–PRESENT

GREAT AMERICAN BALL PARK

HOME OF THE CINCINNATI REDS

NATIONAL LEAGUE (1890–PRESENT)

GREAT AMERICAN BALL PARK *is a soaring, 21st-century-style stadium situated along the winding banks of the Ohio River in Cincinnati's central business district. It is the home of the Reds baseball franchise, the fifth oldest continually operating MLB team and the one with the oldest origin.*

The foundational Reds club had an interesting start with the national pastime. The Cincinnati Base Ball Club, called the Red Stockings, was founded in 1866 and the following year joined the National Association of Base Ball Players (NABBP). They played at the Union Cricket Club Grounds, which was headed by George Ellard, a founding member of the ball club. A certain Harry Wright was a club professional in cricket, and so, primarily due to the efforts of Ellard and Wright, cricket players were recruited to play baseball. Local athletes also developed their skills, and so Cincinnati did well during its first year in the NABBP, losing only once in 17 matches.

[RIGHT] Next to the Hall of Fame and Museum is a commemorative gazebo erected as part of the team's 150th anniversary celebration. Cincinnati sculptor Tom Tsuchiya created relief figures of the members of the 1869 Red Stockings, the team that would later be known as the Reds.

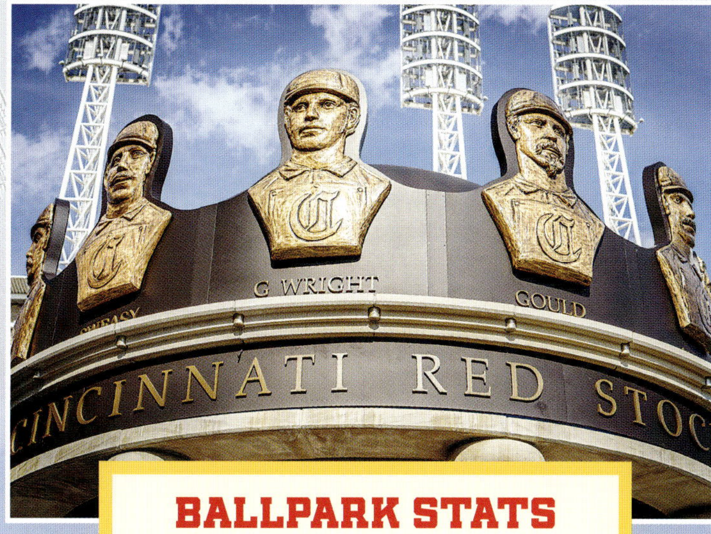

They became baseball's first professional team in 1869, but with only amateur teams as competition, they remained undefeated in their first 81 games. The pros team won their first match up by walloping Great Western of Cincinnati by a score of 45–9.

Throughout their early history, the Reds played in a number of smaller ball fields before settling into larger venues like the Palace of the Fans and Crosley Field by the middle of the 20th century. Since 1970, the Reds had been playing at Cinergy Field, formerly Riverfront Stadium, a "cookie cutter" arena they shared with the NFL Cincinnati Bengals. But by the mid-1990s, both tenants were complaining that the multipurpose field lacked the attractive amenities necessary for small-market professional sports teams to thrive, and they lobbied for their own stadiums. This was a common grievance in the 1990s, when nearly every professional baseball and football franchise desired a single-use stadium, one that featured seating closer to the field, additional luxury suites, and other features that drew fans.

BALLPARK STATS

ADDRESS
100 Joe Nuxhall Way, Cincinnati, OH 45202

OWNER
Hamilton County

OPERATOR
Cincinnati Reds

DESIGNER/CHIEF ARCHITECT
HOK Sport (Populous); GBBN Architects

CAPACITY
43,500

RECORD BASEBALL ATTENDANCE
44,599 on 10/10/2010 (NLDS, Game 3)

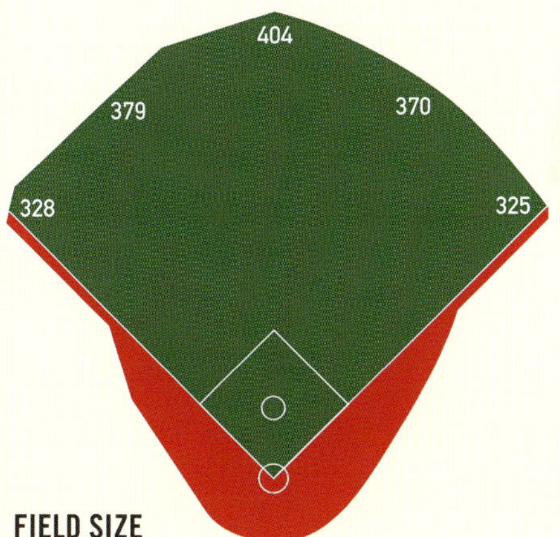

FIELD SIZE

Left field 328 feet (100 m)
Left-center 379 feet (116 m)
Center field 404 feet (123 m)
Right-center 370 feet (110 m)
Right field 325 feet (99 m)
Backstop 55 feet (17 m)

SURFACE
Kentucky bluegrass

TEAM MASCOTS
Mr. Red, Rosie Red, Mr. Redlegs, and Gapper

GREAT AMERICAN BALL PARK FIRSTS

FIRST MLB GAME: 3/31/2003, Pittsburgh Pirates over Reds, 10–1

FIRST HOME RUN: 3/31/2003, Reggie Sanders (Pittsburgh Pirates)

FIRST NO-HITTER: 7/2/2013, Homer Bailey vs. SF Giants

FIRST ALL-STAR GAME: 7/14/2015, AL over NL, 6–3

FIRST PLAYOFF GAME: 10/10/2010, Philadelphia Phillies over Reds, 2–0

FIRST WORLD SERIES GAME: 10/30/2015, NY defeats Kansas City, 9–3 in Game 3

[ABOVE] The main entrance to the Great American Ball Park features a plaza honoring the Reds' heroes of the Crosley Field era of 1912 to 1970. To the right are sculptor Tom Tsuchiya's statues of three legendary Reds: pitcher Joe Nuxhall, catcher Ernie Lombardi, and slugging outfielder Frank Robinson. To the left is first baseman Ted Kluszewski, who played from 1947 to 1957. An imposing physical specimen, "Big Klu" was a power hitter with bulging biceps that became the inspiration for Cincinnati's sleeveless uniforms.

[OPPOSITE PAGE] Fans begin to take their seats before a game on a rather gloomy day. The ballpark is sited alongside the Ohio River.

In 1996, voters in Hamilton County passed a 0.5 percent sales tax increase to fund the construction of new venues for both the Reds and the Bengals. The Bengals new home, Paul Brown Stadium—later known as Paycor Stadium—broke ground first, in 1998, and was opened for play on August 19, 2000. Two locations for a new Reds ballpark were proposed—Broadway Commons and an area between Riverfront Stadium and US Bank Arena known as the "Wedge." Reds officials were concerned about the cost of land at Broadway Commons, whereas the riverside land was already owned by Hamilton County.

To make room for the new stadium, part of Cinergy Field had to be demolished—almost 14,000 seats were removed from the outfield. Meanwhile, for two years the Reds continued playing baseball at their partially razed stadium while their new home was being constructed in view of fans at the old ballpark. The stadium was named for the Great American Insurance Company, which had purchased 30-year naming rights for $75 million. Cinergy Field was finally imploded in December 2002.

The stadium debuted on March 31, 2003. President George H. W. Bush threw out the first ceremonial pitch. Hall of Fame power hitter Ken Griffey Jr., a Reds outfielder, got the first hit in the new ballpark, a double.

DESIGN AND CONSTRUCTION

Designed in the popular "retro-modern" style by HOK Sport and GBBN Architects, the stadium cost a total of $290 million to complete. The facade presents a three-story exterior of brick and cast limestone, and atop it runs the phrase "Rounding third and heading for home," the signature sign-off of former broadcaster Joe Nuxhall. Banners representing great moments in Reds history line this area. The home plate entrance, where most fans access the stadium, is at the intersection of Second and Main Streets and opens to Crosley Terrace. Roughly an acre of concrete, the Terrace is paved with bricks purchased by fans and inscribed with personal messages. It is landscaped with grass and trees and features statues of Crosley Field–era players Joe Nuxhall, Ernie Lombardi, Ted Kluszewski, Joe Morgan, Johnny Bench, and Frank Robinson, as well as a 60-foot (18.3 m) stone sculpture, all meant to depict the romance of the game. The ballpark's interior space, with its signature scarlet-red seats and bright-green grass, may have been aiming for panoramic, but the colors clash when the stadium is empty. Ultimately, the new facility helped to revitalize the riverfront area, while at the same time becoming a showpiece in the center of downtown Cincinnati.

PUBLIC REACTION

The new venue received mixed reviews. The exterior was faulted for lacking a cohesive design—"trying to please too many at once"—and an interior that did not showcase the city or the river. One critic from Ballpark Ratings online wrote: "GABP has my least favorite interior aesthetics for a ballpark without a roof. How do you have the riverfront and the skyline, yet have good views of neither? The underlying design is disjointed and fragmented. In the outfield, riverfront views are blocked by oversized seating, clumsy signage, a new superfluous videoboard, the tackiest gimmicks in baseball, and an ugly black batter's eye." The aforementioned gimmicks included a fake riverboat and ornate "riverboat-style" smokestacks. The stadium was also criticized as quite complicated from a functional point of view; for instance, "Exploring the concourses here is like walking the Mall of America, with a twist and turn at every corner." The number of horizontal and vertical discontinuities were also noted.

Fan experience, on the other hand, was given much-higher marks. The main concourse was praised for being mostly wide and open to the field, and in spite of the high upper deck, the seating geometry there was considered superb. Also, the ballpark's downtown setting and local scene has gotten better and better every year, with numerous lively bars and restaurants now adjacent to the venue.

SEATING CHART

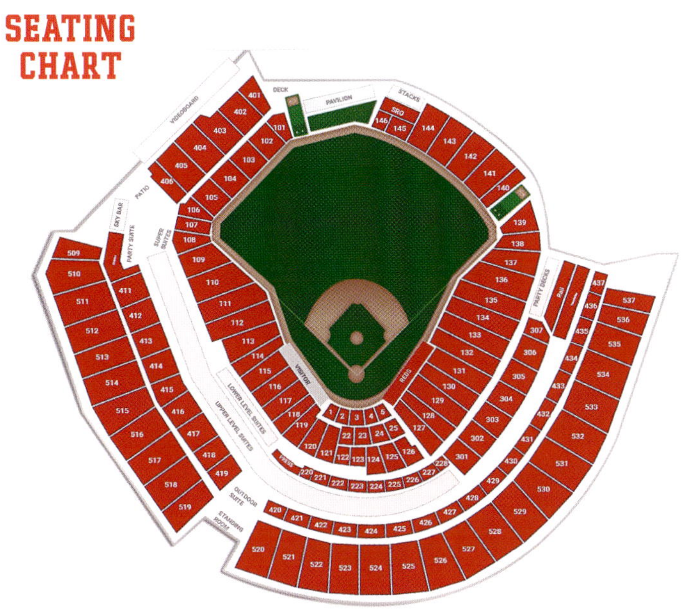

REDS ACHIEVEMENTS

WORLD SERIES CHAMPIONSHIPS: 5 (1919, 1940, 1975, 1976, 1990)

AA TITLES: 1 (1882)

NL PENNANTS: 9 (1919, 1939, 1940, 1961, 1970, 1972, 1975, 1976, 1990)

NL WEST DIVISION TITLES: 7 (1970, 1972, 1973, 1975, 1976, 1979, 1990)

NL CENTRAL DIVISION TITLES: 3 (1995, 2010, 2012)

WILD CARD BERTHS: 2 (2013, 2020)

PLAYOFF APPEARANCES: 16 (1919, 1939, 1940, 1961, 1970, 1972, 1973, 1975, 1976, 1979, 1990, 1995, 2010, 2012, 2013, 2020)

WORST SEASON RECORD: 1934, 52–99 (.344)

BEST SEASON RECORD: 1975, 108–54 (.667)

“In Cincinnati, baseball has always been less a sport than a kind of psychosis.”

—*THE NEW YORKER*

In 21013, Cincinnati Reds baseball fans camped out in front of Great American Ball Park on a Saturday morning a little after midnight for a chance to buy some of the 1,500 Opening Day tickets that would go on sale at 9:00 am.

Most recently, the ballpark has received much more positive updates. In 2009, the reviewer for *Stadium Journey* considered it “a wonderful place to watch a baseball game.” Online fans applauded the “great atmosphere,” “friendly, helpful staff,” “numerous amenities,” and “range of food choices,” and many reported that there was not “a bad seat in the house.” The convenient downtown location was also praised.

FEATURES AND AMENITIES

Along the stadium’s main concourse the aisles are spacious, and most stands have at least one television so fans don’t miss any of the action. Throughout the stadium there are also a number of event spaces available for special occasions, as well as tours of the park that provide a behind-the-scenes view of the private suites.

FIRST STAR FAN ZONE This area offers entertainment, such as live music, games, and activities. There are photo walls, giant baseball cards, a home run challenge video game, and even a kid-size playing field.

TRIHEALTH FAMILY ZONE This area, featuring activities for kids—including a playground and batting cages, and a lounge area with spectacular river views—is a must for families visiting Great American Ball Park. One of the two nursing suites designed exclusively as a place for mothers to feed and care for their babies—a first in MLB—are part of this addition on the former site of Redlegs Landing.

The Reds boast four mascots who roam the field during games and connect with fans before and after play. Above is Mr. Redlegs, a mustachioed “old-time” player with a baseball head; Rosie Red, a female humanoid in a Reds uniform with a baseball head; and Gapper, a furry red pet, sidekick to Mr. Red. Mr. Red, a humanoid figure in a Reds uniform with a baseball head, is the fourth.

FOOD AND DRINK Dining amenities include examples of local food, an impressive craft beer selection that places the park in the Top 10 by beer enthusiasts, and the Kroger Fan Zone, a favorite ballpark hangout. Fans recommend the Montgomery Inn for pulled pork or chicken; the three Skyline Chili locations for Cincinnati’s own Skyline Cheese Coney; LaRosa’s Pizza, found at three locations throughout the park; and the Machine Room Grille, with video games, a pool table, and indoor and outdoor seating.

MAIN STREET Adjacent to the stadium on Main Street are the Team Store and the Reds Hall of Fame and Museum, where fans can experience Cincinnati baseball year-round with changing exhibits, player appearances, interactive exhibits, and much more. Memorabilia includes team jerseys and World Series rings, as well as the enormous, bejeweled dog collar of Schottzie, former team owner Marge Schott’s St. Bernard.

EVOLVING NAMES

In 1869, Harry Wright formed the Cincinnati Red Stockings pro ball club, which played its home games at Union Grounds, just west of downtown. The name was based on the high red socks or stockings the team wore with its knee-length trousers. The name was first shortened to the Reds during the 1890 season. In 1954 the team became known as the Redlegs, as the term "reds" evoked Communist Russia and the "Red Scare" brought on by the McCarthy hearings on un-American activities. The team went back to calling themselves the Reds in 1959.

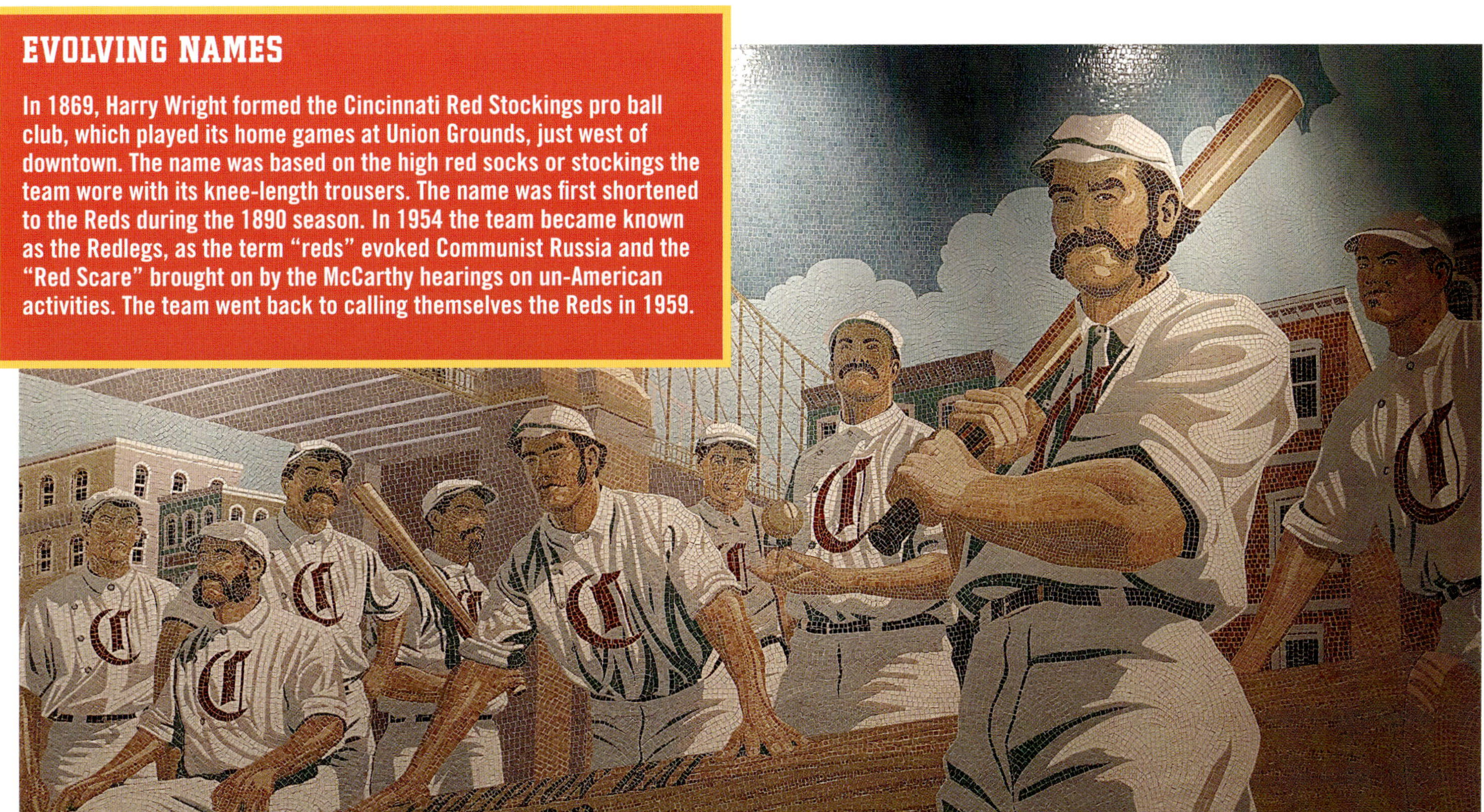

[ABOVE] *The First Nine* by Mark Riedy is one of two 16-by-10-feet (4.9 x 3.0 m) mosaic panels just inside the main gates off Crosley Terrace. It depicts the 1869 Red Stockings—the first professional baseball team in history with a record of 57–0 in their first season.

[BELOW] Standing out in right center field are two smokestacks that recall the steamboats that were common on the Ohio River in the 19th and early 20th centuries. During games the stacks flash lights, belch flames, and launch fireworks in response to the Reds' on-field efforts.

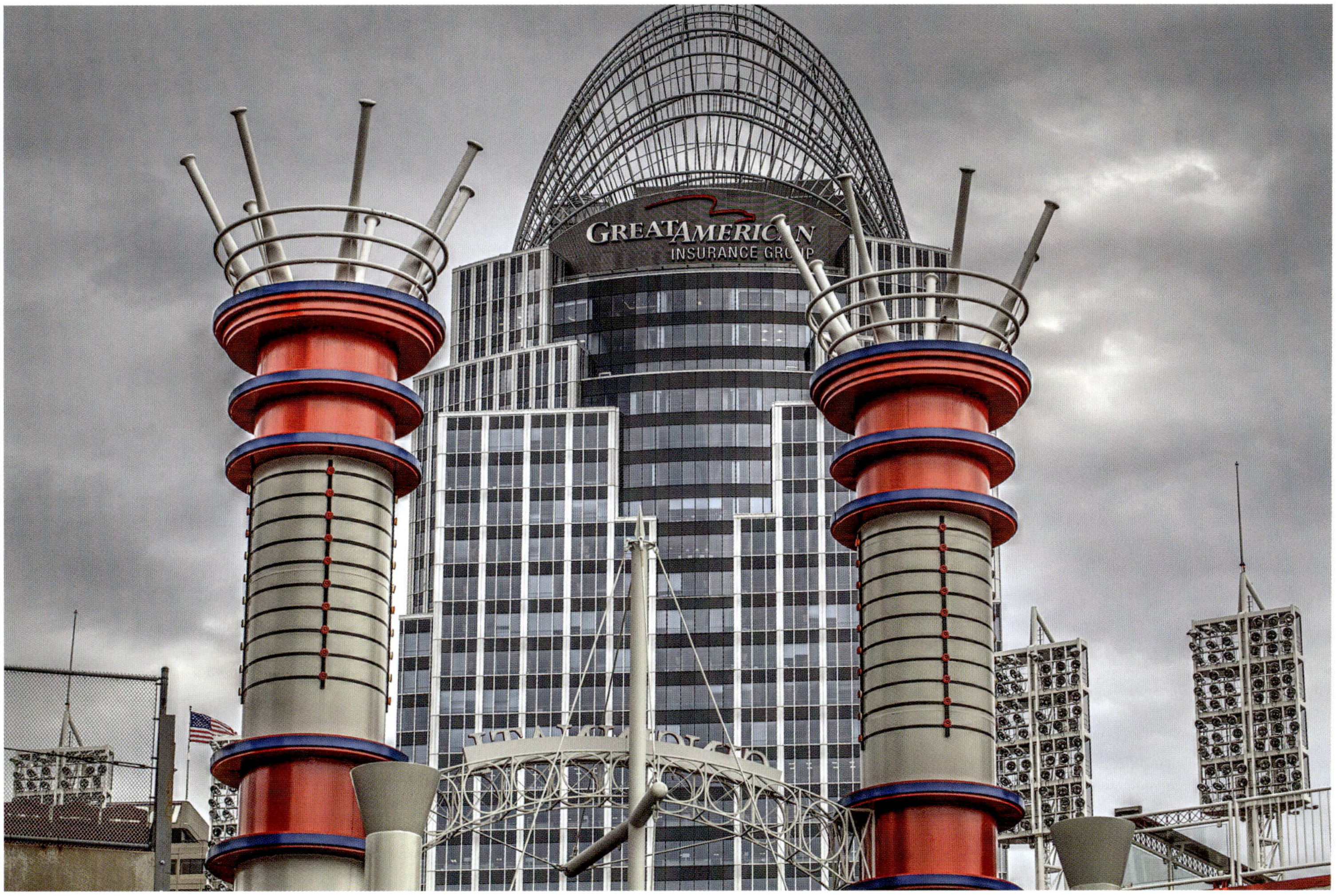

OTHER HOMES OF THE REDS

EARLY BALLPARKS
1869–1911

League Park was home to the Reds from 1884 to 1901.

This team has quite a collection of former homes to look back upon. They began playing at Union Grounds (1869–1870), followed by Avenue Grounds (1876–1879), Bank Street Grounds (1880–1883), then moved to League Park (1884–1901), and then the Palace of the Fans (1902–1911). Union Grounds, which saw the fledgling Red Stockings' first games, was also known as Lincoln Park Grounds, Union Cricket Club Grounds, and Lincoln Park. The park featured an ornate cupola-capped grandstand called "the Grand Duchess." The team's horse-drawn transport took the field through a double-gated entrance. To honor the uniform's red stockings, fans were often decked out in red from their hats to their parasols.

Bank Street Grounds was home to three major league baseball teams—the National League Cincinnati Stars in 1880, the Cincinnati Red Stockings from 1882 to 1883, and the Cincinnati Outlaw Reds of the Union Association in 1884. The Stars were a new NL entry, but their trajectory was brief. They were expelled from the league for selling beer and playing on Sundays, thus violating the league's "blue laws." In 1882, the Red Stockings franchise was formed as an American Association club. Because the American Association had no rules against Sunday play or beer sales, it was known informally to fans as "the beer-and-whiskey league."

When the Reds lost their lease to Bank Street in 1883, they moved to League Park, less than a mile from their former home in Cincinnati's West End. In 1894, Reds owner, John Brush, built a new grandstand and added an amphitheater. He also shifted the diamond from the southeast to the southwest corner, a change that left some people calling the venue League Park II. The center-field fence was painted black in 1895 to form a "batter's eye" screen. Some sports scholars maintain this was the first such screen in baseball.

After Brush's grandstand burned down in 1900 it was replaced by the neoclassical grandstand called Palace of the Fans, a name soon being applied to the ballpark itself. The concrete structure featured an ornate facade, Corinthian columns, and luxury "fashion" boxes, including ground-level enclosures where wealthy patrons watched the games from their carriages. At field level was rowdy "Rooter's Row," where 640 spectators could intrude on field conversations. This unique grandstand suffered fire damage in 1911 and was demolished to build Redland Field, which would later bear the name Crosley Field.

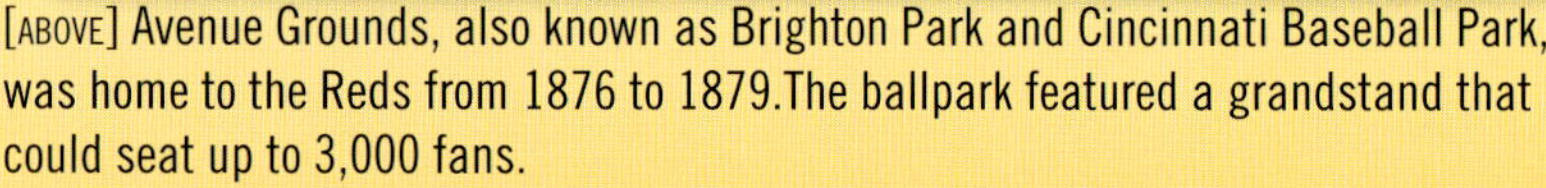
[ABOVE] Avenue Grounds, also known as Brighton Park and Cincinnati Baseball Park, was home to the Reds from 1876 to 1879.The ballpark featured a grandstand that could seat up to 3,000 fans.

The Reds called the stately Palace of the Fans home from 1902 to 1911.

CROSLEY FIELD
1912–1970

In the footprint of the Palace of the Fans, the National League's third steel-and-concrete stadium was constructed. It offered a double-decker grandstand and single-deck covered pavilions, with bleachers in right field. The configuration of the covered areas created a V shape, leading to the park's nickname the "Old Boomerang." It was also one of the smallest venues in baseball, seating 30,000 fans at most. The Reds struggled for success in their new home, and attendance waned. When local inventor and entrepreneur Powel Crosley Jr. bought the team in 1934, team president Larry MacPhail insisted the stadium be named for their would-be savior.

By the late 1930s, some good fortune had returned, in part due to Major League owners allowing the Reds to hold the first-ever night games. On Friday, May 24, 1935, President Franklin D. Roosevelt hit a ceremonial switch in the White House that "lit up" Crosley Field, where the Reds would defeat the Phillies 2–1. During the 1950s the "Ragamuffin Reds" returned to mediocrity, and even after making it to the World Series in 1961, they were dispatched by the potent Yankee duo of Mickey Mantle and Roger Maris.

In the 1970s, when baseball was again dominated by the "Big Red Machine," the team left Crosley Field for Riverfront Stadium, which they would share with the city's new NFL franchise, the Bengals. On April 19, 1972, Crosley Field fell to the wrecking ball.

[ABOVE] Players assemble for the *Star-Spangled Banner* at Crosley Field, circa 1960s.

[BOTTOM] Reds players observe the field action from the team's dugout, 1959.

RIVERFRONT STADIUM
1970–2002

The team's new venue was one of many multipurpose, circular, cookie-cutter arenas built in the 1970s that allowed communities to save money by housing two professional sports teams in one space. Similar structures included Three Rivers Stadium in Pittsburgh, Shea Stadium in New York, and Veterans Stadium in Philadelphia. As was often the case, these venues were not a perfect fit for either sport. But the Reds prospered here, becoming one of the best teams in baseball history—making the World Series after their first season and winning the Series back to back in 1975 and 1976.

In 2000 the Bengals departed, but the Reds continued playing in Riverfront, now called Cinergy Field, as they awaited their new stadium, which would open in 2003. Cinergy Field was demolished by implosion on December 29, 2002. In part of its footprint lies Great American Ball Park, along with the National Underground Railroad Freedom Center.

[ABOVE] A panorama of the Cincinnati riverfront. The aptly named Riverfront Stadium once stood at the end of the Roebling Suspension Bridge over the Ohio River.

[BELOW] Riverfront Stadium, by then known as Cinergy Field, was imploded on December 29, 2002.

[ABOVE] Johnny Bench and Pete Rose of the Reds flank President Gerald Ford and Atlanta Brave Hank Aaron for a photo op before the start of the Riverfront Stadium season opener on April 4, 1974. Aaron hit his historic 714th home run later in the game, tying Babe Ruth's record.

[OPPOSITE PAGE] A game at Cinergy Field (a.k.a. Riverfront Stadium) between the Reds and the New York Mets on April 27, 2001. To make room for the Great American Ball Park, seating sections of the outfield had been removed, offering great views of the construction. Riverfront Stadium was built on a site that had included a 2nd Street tenement, the birthplace of Roy Rogers. The cowboy actor and singing star often joked that he was born "somewhere between second base and center field."

HOME OF THE CHICAGO WHITE SOX

AMERICAN LEAGUE (1901–PRESENT)

RATE FIELD *on Chicago's South Side is the current home of the White Sox. Completed at a cost of $137 million, the park opened on April 18, 1991, as the second iteration of Comiskey Park, taking its name from the former ballpark where the Chi Sox played since 1910.*

One of the American League's eight charter franchises, the White Sox got their start in 1900 as the Chicago White Stockings, shortened to White Sox in 1904. The team originated as the minor league Sioux City Cornhuskers of the Western League, and when owner Charles Comiskey moved them to St. Paul, Minnesota, they played as the St. Paul Saints. Comiskey then relocated them to his hometown Chicago neighborhood of Armour Square. Here they became the White Stockings, which was the former name of the city's National League team, the Orphans (now the Cubs).

In 1901 the Western League changed its name to the American League, declaring itself a "major league," and that same year the

Sox finished as league champions. By 1906 they were World Series Champions after besting their rivals, the Chicago Cubs. They repeated this feat in 1917, this time against the New York Giants. Initially the team played at Southside Park, but in 1910 they moved into their new stadium, soon dubbed Comiskey Park after their owner.

In 1991, after eight decades playing in Comiskey Park, the White Sox found themselves anticipating life in a modern stadium. Alas, age had caught up with their venerable former home, and it fell to the wrecking ball in several stages over summer 1991. In its honor, the new venue was also christened Comiskey Park. Completed at a cost of $137 million, it was built across the street from the site of the original ballfield, which would now be used as a parking lot. The location of the former home plate is represented by a marble plaque embedded in the sidewalk of the new stadium, while painted versions of the earlier foul lines run across the parking lot. The spectator ramp is even angled to resemble the contours of Old Comiskey's first-base grandstand.

In 2003 the stadium was renamed U.S. Cellular Field when the Chicago-based telecom company purchased naming rights for $68 million over 20 years. Their contract ended early, and in 2016 local mortgage company Guaranteed Rate purchased naming rights for 13 years at a cost of $20.4 million.

"If there is any justice in this world, to be a White Sox fan frees a man from any other form of penance."

—BILL VEECK, *VEECK AS IN WRECK*

BALLPARK STATS

ADDRESS
333 West 35th Street, Chicago, IL 60616

FORMER NAMES
Comiskey Park (II) (1991–2003)
U.S. Cellular Field (2003–2016)

OWNER/OPERATOR
Illinois Sports Facilities Authority

ARCHITECT
HOK Sport (now Populous); Devrouax & Purnell Architects - Planners

CAPACITY
40,615

RECORD BASEBALL ATTENDANCE
46,246 on 10/5/1993 (ALCS Game 1)

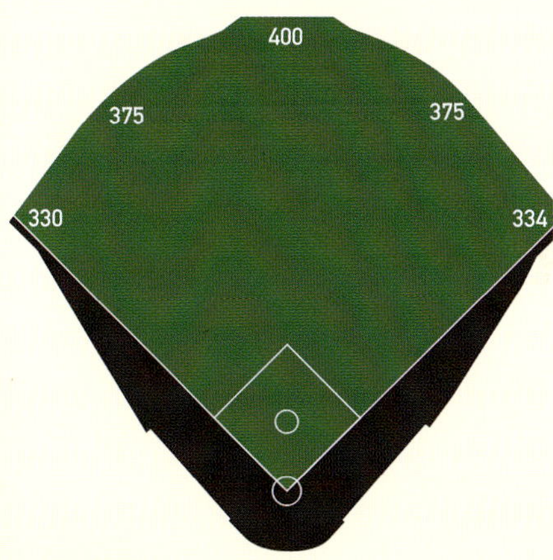

FIELD SIZE

- **Left field** 330 feet (100 m)
- **Left-center** 375 feet (114 m) (not posted)
- **Center field** 400 feet (120 m)
- **Right-center** 375 feet (114 m) (not posted)
- **Right field** 335 feet (102 m)
- **Backstop** 60 feet (18 m)
- **Outfield wall height** 8 feet (2.4 m)

SURFACE
Kentucky bluegrass blend

TEAM MASCOT
Southpaw

> "Charm, intimacy, and the idea of weaving the stadium into the fabric of its surroundings—all the things that retro parks have come to represent—were not high on the agenda of the White Sox or the agency that built Comiskey, the Illinois Sports Facility Authority."
>
> —BLAIR KAMIN, "10 YEARS LATER, COMISKEY STILL HAS A BAD REPUTATION," *CHICAGO TRIBUNE*, JULY 22, 2011

The Chicago skyline is off in the distance in an aerial shot of the ballpark. It has faced much criticism over the years. Blair Kamin of the *Chicago Tribune* described it as "a soulless, modern object stuck in the middle of a parking lot."

GUARANTEED RATE FIELD FIRSTS

FIRST MLB GAME: 4/18/1991, Detroit Tigers over White Sox, 16–0*

FIRST HOME RUN: 4/22/1991, Frank Thomas vs. Orioles*

FIRST NO-HITTER: 4/18/2007, Mark Buehrle vs. Texas Rangers†

FIRST ALL-STAR GAME: 7/15/2003, AL over NL, 7–6†

FIRST PLAYOFF GAME: 10/5/1993, Toronto Blue Jays over Chicago White Sox, 7–3*

FIRST WORLD SERIES GAME: 10/22/2005, White Sox over Houston Astros 5–3, in Game 1†

* as Comiskey Park (II)

† as U.S. Cellular Field

DESIGN AND CONSTRUCTION

This postmodern stadium was the first major sports facility built in the city since Chicago Stadium in 1929. It was also the last ballpark built before the wave of "retro-classic" styles swept baseball in the 1990s and 2000s. Several design features from the old Comiskey Park were retained—the front facade of the exterior features similar arched windows, and the "exploding scoreboard" pays tribute to the original, installed by owner Bill Veeck at the old park in 1960.

When it first opened, the new stadium was criticized over the height of the upper deck. Because the original architects, HOK Sport, wanted to eliminate the overhang problems found in many venues built since the 1970s, they set the upper deck back over the lower deck, with the stands rising gradually. This did allow the upper level unobstructed views of the field, but the new upper deck was now one of the highest in the Major Leagues. In fact, the *lowest* seats in the current upper deck were as high as the *highest* upper deck seats in the former stadium. This was partially remedied in 2004, when 6,600 "nosebleed" seats at the apex of the upper deck were removed.

A number of alterations were made to the field and the stands each season from 1996 to the present during various building phases, updating some existing elements or adding new ones, many of them intended to make the park more fan-friendly. Among the most novel was a "rain room" in right field that allowed fans to cool off during hot summer games. Blue seats in the upper and lower decks were changed to green in 2004, replicating the seating from the earlier stadium. On April 8, 2008, the stadium unveiled the first environmentally friendly parking lot with permeable paving to be installed by a Major League facility. The special absorbent surface saves taxpayer money by reducing runoff into Chicago's stormwater system.

PUBLIC REACTIONS

The stadium opened to lukewarm reviews, and initially it often appeared near the bottom of ballpark rankings. The construction had come in under budget—and it showed. The resulting venue was judged as lacking both character and pleasing aesthetics, especially the ad-plastered outfield. “No visual sense of place,” one reviewer reported. Yet others approved the simplicity of the space and the lack of busy gimmicks found in the new “retro” parks.

After decades of periodic renovations, most critics concede that the ballpark has definitely gotten better. There is still that steep upper deck and cumbersome ramps for vertical circulation, and exploring the park can be a chore. Ticket holders for the upper deck are not allowed access to the main concourse, which has always been problematic. But there is a lot more to please the fans now, including “a great selection of delicious food and a wide selection of beers,” according to one online review. There are multiple lounges and bars on the main concourse, historical sites and statues to explore, and a kid’s section offering baseball-related activities.

SEATING CHART

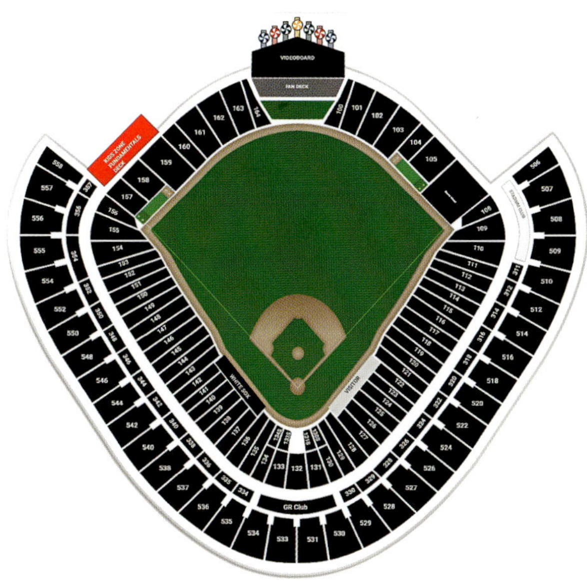

FEATURES AND AMENITIES

This stadium offers a number of special features both on and off the field, including flickering LED lights that signal when the White Sox first take the field, hit a home run, or win a game. Other stadium amenities include speed pitch machines, the “rain rooms,” the Scout Seats behind home plate, the Xfinity Zone, Chicago Sports Depot, the Scoreboard Shop, the Home Plate Shop, and the New Era Cap Corner.

PREMIUM SEATING The stadium’s premium seating offers 103 luxury seats on two levels and 1,822 “club seats” between the lower and upper decks. These sections provide wait staff and feature multiple TV viewing areas and bar-style concessions. (A lack of revenue-generating premium seating was one reason Old Comiskey was torn down.) The 12 escalators and 15 elevators ensure rapid movement of crowds.

SPECIAL SEATING AND DINING The two-tiered Fan Deck accommodates up to 150 people and offers a panoramic view of the field from the top of the center-field concessions. It provides catered food and beverages, including chicken sandwiches, hot dogs, hamburgers, potato chips, popcorn, beer, soda, and water. Miller Lite Landing offers a section of 326 seats in right field. There is running water on all four sides, comfortable seating, spaces for parties,

Rate’s distinctive center-field scoreboard is a replica of the old Comiskey Park’s “Exploding Scoreboard” designed by Bill Veeck. When the White Sox hit a homer, the pinwheels light up and spin, and then fireworks explode from the tops.

and a standing room area near the outfield concourse. The Patio is located at fence level behind the right center field fence. It is ideal for group outings and can accommodate from 50 to 100 guests. Home Plate Club is located behind home plate and features a restaurant buffet, open bar, outdoor seating in padded seats, private restrooms, numerous flat-screen TVs, a private elevator, and early admittance to the park for certain games to watch batting practice. The stadium also offers #SoxSocial Tap Room, the Pizza Pub, and ChiSox Bar and Grill.

TWO BLUE SEATS These have been placed amid the green seating to indicate where Paul Konerko hit his grand slam and Scott Podsednik landed his game-winning home run in Game 2 of the 2005 World Series. Both are the original seats from that game.

HONORED PLAYERS Historical features to look for include dramatic statues of White Sox players Minnie Miñoso, Carlton Fisk, Luis Aparicio, Nellie Fox, Billy Pierce, Harold Baines, Frank Thomas, Paul Konerko, and owner Charles Comiskey.

WHITE SOX CHAMPIONS PLAZA Located at the main entrance, this area is dedicated to the 2005 World Champion team and their fans. Legacy bricks inscribed with personalized messages are part of the baseball diamond-shaped space. The Plaza also features a life-size white bronze sculpture weighing more than 25 tons that celebrates the historic win.

KID'S ZONE Located in left field, this 15,000-square-foot (1,394 m^2) feature is geared to young White Sox fans. It provides a hands-on learning experience about the fundamentals of baseball and offers a whiffle ball diamond for coaching clinics, batting "swing" boxes, and areas for skills instruction.

WHITE SOX ACHIEVEMENTS

WORLD SERIES CHAMPIONSHIPS: 3 (1906, 1917, 2005)

WL PENNANTS: 1 (1894)

AL PENNANTS: 7 (1900, 1901, 1906, 1917, 1919, 1959, 2005)

AL WEST DIVISION TITLES: 2 (1983, 1993)

AL CENTRAL DIVISION TITLES: 6 (1969, 1973, 1986, 1988, 2006, 2015)

WILD CARD BERTHS: 1 (2020)

PLAYOFF APPEARANCES: 11 (1906, 1917, 1919, 1959, 1983, 1993, 2000, 2005, 2008, 2020, 2021)

WORST SEASON RECORD: 1932, 49–102 (.325)

BEST SEASON RECORD: 1917, 100–54 (.649)

[ABOVE] Rate Field is this ballpark's fourth name. When it opened it was called Comiskey Park, after its predecessor, and then in 2003 U.S. Cellular bought the naming rights. It was called U.S. Cellular Field until 2016, when Guaranteed Rate purchased naming rights. The team also has a few nicknames, including the Sox, the Chi Sox, the South Siders, the Pale Hose, and the Black Sox (from the 1919 betting scandal).

[OPPOSITE PAGE] Champions Plaza makes an imposing display in the open space in front of the Gate 4 entrance to the park. Below the Championship Moments monument, the plaza is paved with hundreds of inscribed bricks.

[ABOVE] Southpaw, the furry green mascot of the White Sox, was introduced to the fans in 2004. He wears a black cap, a Sox uniform with pinwheel buttons, and black shoes with pinwheel decorations.

[LEFT] Early-arriving fans begin to fill the seats above and below the ballpark's press box.

OTHER HOMES OF THE WHITE SOX

SOUTH SIDE PARK III
1900–1910

The early White Sox teams originally played at South Side Park, on the north side of 39th Street. This was the best-known and longest-lived of three fields that bore this same name. Also known as the 39th Street Grounds, during the 1893 World's Fair, South Side Park I served as the playing field of the Chicago Wanderers cricket team.

After Charles Comiskey erected a wooden grandstand there in 1900 it became home to his Chicago White Stockings, a minor league team that in 1901 graduated to the Majors as members of the newly minted American League. The team remained there until the middle of the 1910 season, when Comiskey debuted the concrete-and-steel ballpark that would eventually bear his name that was located only three blocks from the team's former field. In 1911 South Side Park III became the home of the newly formed Negro League baseball club, the Chicago American Giants.

The White Sox take on their crosstown rivals, the Chicago Cubs, in the City Championship Series on October 9, 1909, at Southside Park III.

COMISKEY PARK
1910–1990

To say that at its peak Comiskey Park was popular is a massive understatement. On good days the stadium was virtually overflowing with fans, with 55,000 people or more lining the aisles and even standing up for a full nine innings. The enclosed stands had the ability to capture the crowd noise and reverberate loudly.

In 1909, team owner Comiskey purchased the building site for his new stadium, a former city dump in the Armour Square neighborhood on the southwest side of the city. Originally called White Sox Park when it opened in 1910, within three years it was renamed for Comiskey himself. The original name was restored in 1962, then changed back to Comiskey Park in 1976.

Designed by Zachary Taylor Davis, the venue was considered quite modern—it was only the third concrete-and-steel stadium in the Majors to be built after 1909. It originally seated nearly 32,000 fans, which was an MLB record during that era. With its gleaming white facade—echoing the pristine "White City" created for Chicago's popular 1893 World Columbian Exposition—Comiskey Park matched many fans' idea of a proper ball field. It was even nicknamed "the Palace of Baseball" for a time.

The well-loved Comiskey Park, also called White Sox Park, in 1972. The stadium took its cues from the White City of the 1893 Columbian Exposition with its brilliant white exterior cladding that befits the team name.

From the start the venue was known for its pitcher-friendly proportions, to the point that no player ever hit 100 home runs there; White Sox catcher Carlton Fisk got the closest with 94. It was also the site of four World Series, three featuring the White Sox and one, in 1918, when the Cubs borrowed the ballpark with its larger capacity to face—and lose to—the Red Sox. The park hosted three All-Star Games and, from 1933 to 1960, was also the most frequent home to the Negro League's East-West All-Star Game. Perhaps most impressive of all, more than 6,000 Major League games took place there.

The field also entered the history books as the site of one of the century's most famous boxing matches, the 1937 title fight between "Brown Bomber" Joe Louis and champion James J. Braddock. Louis ended up defeating Braddock in eight rounds and so began his astonishing 11-year run as heavyweight champion.

Bill Veeck, the White Sox owner from 1959 to 1961, was responsible for a number of the park's features, including the "exploding" scoreboard, with its flashing lights and spinning pinwheels, and a screened picnic area in left field where picnic tables were set up. He and an ownership group repurchased the team in 1975—preventing owner John Allyn from moving the Sox to Seattle, Washington—and among other "stunts" Veeck installed showers near the center field bleachers for fans to use on hot summer days.

THE LAST GAME . . .

By the late 1980s, Comiskey Park was the oldest stadium in baseball and clearly in need of replacement, yet, in its final eight years it had still managed to attract more than two million fans three times. Then owner Jerry Reinsdorf threatened to move his team away from the aging venue—and Chicago—if no new stadium were in the offing. At the time he was being courted by St. Petersburg, Florida, a town in search of a franchise, which was promising him a stadium. In 1988 Reinsdorf got his wish, receiving $200 million in public financing from the City of Chicago.

The White Sox played their last game at Comiskey Park on September 30, 1990, with 42,849 loyal fans watching them best the Seattle Mariners 2–1. At the game, Mayor Richard M. Daley threw out the first pitch and ballpark organist Nancy Faust played crowd favorites. At the end, the fans joined Faust in singing a final chorus of their traditional victory song, "Na Na Hey Hey (Kiss Him Goodbye)."

> **"Wrigley Field *yayed* and Comiskey Park *roared*."**
>
> —CHICAGO SPORTSWRITER ALAN SOLOMON IN A CHILDHOOD RECOLLECTION

Fans take in a White Sox game at old Comiskey Park, circa 1910

BLACK SOX SCANDAL

In 1920, the White Sox were accused of fixing the outcome of the 1919 World Series. After an investigation of the huge bets placed on their opponents—the Cincinnati Reds—eight White Sox players were believed to have thrown the series in exchange for payment from a gambling syndicate. As a result of the "Black Sox Scandal," the eight suspected players were acquitted in court but were banned from baseball by the judge. Recovery from this low-water mark was slow; it took the team 40 years to win another pennant.

VISIT THE REAL FIELD OF DREAMS

Even those people who never saw the cherished baseball film *Field of Dreams* will recognize the line, "If you build it, they will come." In this iconic film the protagonist sees a vision of "Shoeless" Joe Jackson (*above right*)—one of the players embroiled in the infamous Black Sox Scandal—and a baseball diamond in his cornfield. For lovers of the movie, or baseball fans in general, the actual field can be seen in the small town of Dyersville, in northern Iowa.

CLOSE-UP

NEGRO LEAGUE BALLPARKS

Due to the strict segregation practiced by the Major Leagues, players of color were banned from ball clubs until 1947. Not to be cowed, Black and Latino players formed their own teams and leagues and even played in their own ballparks. Everyone was welcome at these venues, while many parks in the Majors were segregated, with grandstands off limits to Black fans. From 1920 to 1951, a number of these Black teams traveled around the country "barnstorming," playing wherever there was a ball field—be it urban sandlot or country pasture. These leagues proved to be a great success and a source of pride for many Black Americans. They also generated iconic players like Josh Gibson, Satchel Paige, Buck Leonard, Cool Papa Bell, Oscar Charleston, and Martín Dihigo, who drew Black and white fans alike.

The color line that kept Black players from the Majors was perpetuated by powerful baseball commissioner and federal judge Kenesaw Landis, a staunch advocate of segregation. After his death in 1944, Branch Rickey, owner/manager of the Brooklyn Dodgers, decided to challenge the color barrier. He chose Jackie Robinson, a former army captain and talented fielder from the Kansas City Monarchs, to help open the door to other athletes of color. As a Dodger, Robinson put up with plenty of offensive, racist comments but always handled himself with dignity and poise. His behavior on and off the field helped convince other team owners that the days of segregation were over.

A mural on the Paseo YMCA building in Kansas City, Missouri, depicts the Kansas City Monarchs, the longest-running franchise in the history of the Negro Leagues. The Monarchs also produced more Major League players than any other Negro League team.

NEGRO LEAGUE STADIUMS

Negro League venues were often less glossy than the parks built for white fans, but the spirit and gamesmanship found inside them was no less genuine. The teams also occasionally played in MLB fields like Fenway Park and Comiskey Park while the home teams were away.

PASEO YMCA Established in 1914 in Kansas, City, Missouri, the Paseo YMCA was the birthplace of the Negro National League (NNL). There, several African American baseball club owners, led by Rube Foster, a former baseball player and founder of the Chicago American Giants, met in 1920 and decided to create their own league. The first all-Black league to survive more than a single season, the NNL included franchises such as the Birmingham Black Barons, Cuban Stars, Dayton Marcos, Detroit Stars, Indianapolis ABCs, Louisville White Sox, Memphis Red Sox, Milwaukee Bears, and Nashville Elite Giants. Eventually pressures from the Great Depression saw its demise in 1931.

RICKWOOD FIELD One of a few surviving Negro League stadiums, this field in Birmingham, Alabama, was built in 1910, making it older than Fenway Park and Wrigley Field. Home to the Birmingham Black Barons of the Negro Southern League, it also served minor league baseball and the powerful industrial leagues that flourished in the '20s, '30s, and '40s. In 1987, when the local AA-team Barons moved on, the crumbling stadium seemed destined for demolition. But the citizens of Birmingham had the stadium declared a historic landmark, and Rickwood was restored. In 1996 the Barons agreed to play one game each year in their old field—the Rickwood Classic—an official game, not an exhibition.

LEAGUE PARK Built in Cleveland, Ohio, in 1910, this field served the National League Spiders, the future Cleveland Indians, before their move to Municipal Stadium. The Negro League Cleveland Buckeyes used the park from 1943 to 1948, then again in 1950.

J. P. SMALL PARK This park was built in 1912 in Jacksonville, Florida. At the home-side entrance, a statue of Black ballplayer Buck O'Neil was dedicated in 2006 in recognition of the historical significance of this park to Negro League baseball. O'Neil lived in Jacksonville with relatives throughout high school when, in 1934, he left to play barnstorming baseball. The Jacksonville Red Caps of the Negro American League were long-time residents of the ballpark. Formed by a group of local train porters, the team at one time wore their red porter's caps as part of their baseball uniform.

MUZZY FIELD Located in Bristol, Connecticut, this grand old park with its brick-faced grandstand has been in use since 1912. Muzzy Field hosted many professional ball clubs as far back as the 1940s, including the Bristol Owls (1949–1950), Bristol Red Sox (1972–1982), and Nighthawks (1994–1995). During the 1940s and '50s the New York Black Yankees played here.

League Park was home field to the Cleveland Buckeyes of the Negro American League. Although the Buckeyes had some great successes, such as sweeping the powerhouse Homestead Grays in a best-of-seven series to earn the title of Negro American League World Series champions in 1945, in the history of Cleveland baseball their legacy was overshadowed by the integration of baseball by 1947.

BOSSE FIELD Built in 1915 and beautifully maintained, Bosse Field in Evansville, Indiana, has a classic, red-brick, roofed grandstand that curves in a huge semicircle around the field. It hosted Black players for the first time on June 21, 1917, then again 33 years later for a Negro American League game. It was also a location used in the film *A League of Their Own.*

Once home to the Birmingham Black Barons, Rickwood Field is one of the few Negro League ballparks still standing and is now listed on the National Register of Historic Places.

Ruppert Stadium, home to first the Newark Stars and then the Newark Eagles, once stood in what is now the Ironbound area of the city.

> **"The Eagles were to (black) Newark what the Dodgers were to Brooklyn."**
>
> —EAGLES STAR MAX MANNING

MCCORMICK FIELD Built in 1924 in Ashville, North Carolina, this picturesque field provided baseball to the nearby mountain communities, hosting the Asheville Tourists for almost 100 years. The Negro Southern League's Asheville Blues played here during the 1940s.

DURHAM ATHLETIC PARK This field, constructed in Durham, North Carolina, in 1926, was home to minor league and Negro League baseball from 1926 through 1994. Scenes from the classic baseball film *Bull Durham* were shot in and around the park.

LAGRAVE FIELD Built in 1926, this Texas ballpark served the Fort Worth Cats of the Central League and the Negro League Black Cats in the 1930s and the Black Panthers in the 1940s. The Fort Worth Cats once played an exhibition game here against their parent team, the Dodgers, and Black fans could finally cheer for heroes Jackie Robinson and Roy Campanella. After 2014 the field was abandoned.

POINT STADIUM Set among the hills of Johnstown, Pennsylvania, this atmospheric stadium was built in 1926. In June 1945, eight future Hall of Famers were on view to the crowd as the KC Monarchs faced the Homestead Grays . . . and Jackie Robinson ripped a double.

RUPPERT STADIUM Located in Newark, New Jersey, Ruppert Stadium was built in 1926. It was home to the Negro League Newark Stars in 1926 and the Newark Eagles from 1936 to 1948. Among its notable alumni was Don "Newk" Newcombe, who was an Eagle in 1944 and 1945 before being signed to the Brooklyn Dodgers.

WORLD WAR MEMORIAL STADIUM Greensboro, South Carolina, is home to this art deco stadium from 1926. Although constructed with football and track and field in mind, the facility was also home to the Carolina League's Greensboro Red Wings in the 1940s, who played other African American teams in North Carolina and Virginia.

HAMTRAMCK STADIUM The field debuted in 1930 as the new home of the Detroit Stars of the Negro National League. After that league folded, other Negro League teams played there, including the Detroit

World War Memorial Stadium was built in a classical modern style with a three-arch entrance. It still stands today near the campus of North Carolina A&T University.

Although Hamtramck Stadium (also known as Roesink Stadium) was listed on the National Register of Historic Places in 2012, a photograph from 2013 shows its grandstand falling apart. Dating to 1930, it was originally built as a home to the Detroit Stars, and it is one the few major Negro Leagues home ballparks left in the United States. In 2022 the historic grandstand reopened after a $3 million rehabilitation.

Wolves (1932), Detroit Stars (1933), and Detroit Stars again (1937).

MUNICIPAL STADIUM Built in 1930, in Hagerstown, Maryland, as a minor league venue, this field is currently home to the single-A Southern League Suns. Sadly, little has been done to preserve the park. During the 1940s and 1950s, three Negro League teams—the Homestead Grays, the Indianapolis Clowns, and the Pittsburgh Crawfords—all played here.

HALL OF FAMERS

The National Baseball Hall of Fame in Cooperstown, New York, includes 37 members who were inducted mainly or entirely based on the basis of their achievements in the Negro Leagues. Other inductees started in these leagues but made their mark in the integrated Major Leagues. Examples of the latter include Hank Aaron, Ernie Banks, Roy Campanella, Larry Doby, Elston Howard, Sam Jones, Willie Mays, Minnie Miñoso, Don Newcombe, and Jackie Robinson.

JOHN O'DONNELL STADIUM Built in 1931 in Davenport, Iowa, and now called Modern Woodmen Park, this once-impressive brick-and-steel field was home to the Quad City River Bandits of the Midwest League. In 1936, it hosted an exhibition game between MLB stars and the Negro League All-Stars. Players included Satchel Paige, Cool Papa Bell, Johnny Mize, and Rogers Hornsby.

RAY WINDER FIELD This 1932 field was the longtime home of the Arkansas Travelers of the Texas League. It boasted large wooden seats and metal bleachers. The section down the right field line was once reserved for African Americans, but for games with large crowds the bleachers were integrated. In 1945 the field was used by the Little Rock Black Travelers, and the venue also hosted a number of barnstorming Negro League teams.

[ABOVE] Legendary player Buck Leonard spent his entire 17-year career with the Washington Homestead Grays. He was elected to the National Baseball Hall of Fame in 1972.

[BELOW] Eastern Colored League champion Hilldale Athletic Club and the Negro National League champion Kansas City Monarchs line up at Muehlebach Field for an Opening Day photo before Game 6 of the 1924 Colored World Series, a best-of-nine match-up. Kansas City's Muehlebach Park had several name changes over the years; the last was Municipal Stadium in 1954. The ballpark was demolished in 1976.

GREENLEE FIELD Home to The Pittsburgh Crawfords, Greenlee was located in the 2500 block of Bedford Avenue. It officially opened on April 29, 1932, when the Crawfords lost a

tough game to the New York Black Yankees, 1–0. It had a modest interior, with spartan amenities, but stood out for the brick facade and three arched entryways. Most notably, it was designed by a Black architect, Louis Arnett Stuart Bellinger, and was one of the few ballparks designed and constructed by African Americans for a Negro league team.

BOVERINI STADIUM This Passaic, New Jersey, stadium from 1934 played host to the New York Black Yankees of the Negro Leagues. The team included double-threat Clarence "Fats" Jenkins, a daunting lead-off hitter in baseball and a Hall of Fame point guard in professional basketball.

PHIL WELCH STADIUM Built in 1939 in St. Joseph, Missouri, this WPA stadium was a minor league field and barnstorming stop for the Negro League Kansas City Monarchs. It has hosted the likes of players such as Mickey Mantle, Yogi Berra, Dizzy Dean, and Stan Musial, as well as Black icons Satchel Paige and Buck O'Neil.

VICTORY FIELD in Indiana, originally called Perry Stadium, was home to the Indianapolis Clowns from 1944 to 1948. Some of the greatest names in Negro Leagues baseball played here, including Hank Aaron.

MAJOR LEAGUE FIELDS
A number of Major League ballparks were also utilized by the Negro Leagues. Fenway Park (1912) hosted the Boston Royal Giants of the Boston Park League. The dominant Chicago American Giants played in Comiskey Park (1910) from 1910 to 1956. Wrigley Field (1914) hosted Sunday double-headers for the Chicago American Giants and other Negro League teams. Cleveland Stadium served the Cleveland Giants and the Cleveland Buckeyes. On July 5, 1930, Yankee Stadium (1923) witnessed a double-header between the NY Lincoln Giants and the Baltimore Black Sox. Tiger Stadium (1912) served the Detroit Stars, Chicago American Giants, and Indianapolis ABCs. Memorial Stadium (1950) hosted the Baltimore Elite Giants, the former team of Dodger Roy Campanella.

[ABOVE] **The 1935 Pittsburgh Crawfords team photo shows the exterior of Greenlee Field, with three arched entries cut into the brick facade. The Crawfords produced some well-known players, including Cool Papa Bell (*seventh from right*), Josh Gibson (*fourth from right*), and Satchel Paige (*second from right*).**

[RIGHT] **A poster advertises an exhibition game held at Victory Field featuring baseball great Satchel Paige, then playing as a KC Monarch, and Reece "Goose" Tatum, playing as a Harlem Star. Tatum, a.k.a. "the Clown Prince of Baseball," is best remembered as a member of the Harlem Globetrotters, an exhibition basketball team.**

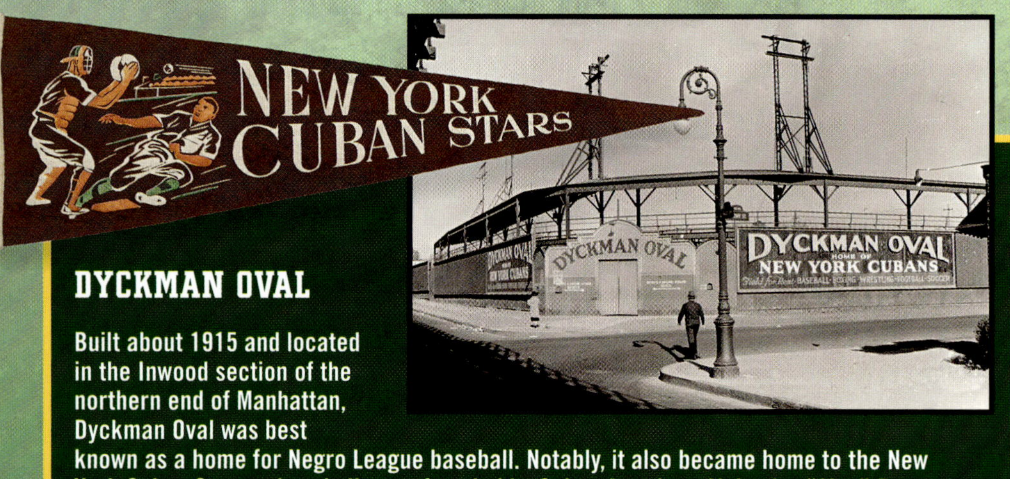

DYCKMAN OVAL

Built about 1915 and located in the Inwood section of the northern end of Manhattan, Dyckman Oval was best known as a home for Negro League baseball. Notably, it also became home to the New York Cuban Stars, a baseball team founded by Cuban American Alejandro "Alex" Pompez in 1916, which, until 1935, employed only Caribbean and Latin American players. The team was also generally known as the Cuban Stars (East) because they shared a named with a contemporaneous Cuban baseball team that primarily played in the Midwest, which became known as the Cuban Stars (West).

HINCHLIFFE STADIUM RECLAIMED

Another surviving Negro League ballpark is Hinchliffe Stadium in Paterson, New Jersey, which was built in 1932. A product of the 1920s "stadium movement," it was built as an elegant, classical-inspired amphitheater. Paterson, the "Silk City," had struggled as the Great Depression hit the industrial Northeast, but under a New Deal financed program, many laid-off workers were employed to provide enhancements to the stadium. Over the years the New York Black Yankees, the Newark Eagles, and the New York Cubans considered the stadium their home base.

Abandoned in 1997, the structure had become overgrown and crumbling and was facing the wrecking ball. In a comeback worthy of Hollywood, in 2014 the stadium was recognized as a National Historic Landmark and in 2019 the City of Paterson approved a deal for Hinchliffe to be redeveloped. After a $100 million renovation the reborn Hinchliffe was rededicated on May 19, 2023, in a ceremony attended by city officials, former baseball players Omar Minaya and Harold Reynolds, Whoopi Goldberg, Senator Cory Booker, Congressman Bill Pascrell, and plenty of fans. It is now the home field of the New Jersey Jackals of the Frontier League. The Charles J. Muth Museum of Hinchliffe Stadium will showcase the stadium's rich history, with a special focus on the proud but troubled history of the Negro Leagues.

[TOP] Jackie Robinson (*left*) and Larry Doby (*right*). Robinson is remembered for breaking the MLB color barrier in 1957 with the National League Dodgers, but Paterson native Doby, a standout student at Eastside High School, became the American League's first Black player after being scouted by Cleveland. Doby was discovered by the Negro League's Newark Eagles at a Hinchliffe Stadium tryout.

[ABOVE] Art deco elements, such as decorative tiles of stylized Olympic athletes and bronze relief plaques set around the outside walls, lent this stadium a beauty that was rarely found in Negro League stadiums.

[LEFT] Fans filled the stands in the early years of the stadium's history.

[BELOW] Hinchliffe Stadium in 2020, before the restoration was complete. Perched above the majestic Great Falls of the Passaic River, it has been revitalized and is now part of the Paterson Great Falls National Historical Park.

"With its white-washed concrete walls, red terracotta roof tiles and five gabled towers, Hinchliffe Stadium made for an elegant horseshoe of dreams."

—*SPORTS ILLUSTRATED*, ON THE BUILDING OF HINCHLIFFE STADIUM

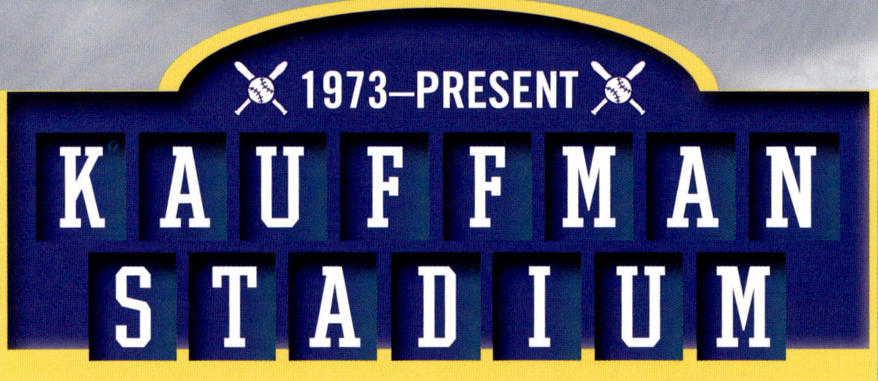

HOME OF THE KANSAS CITY ROYALS

AMERICAN LEAGUE (1969–PRESENT)

IN 2023, THE KANSAS CITY ROYALS—*an early expansion team that became known for their grit and "come-from-behind attitude" during a roller-coaster history—celebrated their 51st season at Kauffman Stadium. A venue of great beauty, "The K" has always been one of the crown jewels of Major League Baseball. Even as the Royals franchise considers replacing it, its memory will remain in the hearts of players and fans.*

Kansas in the mid-1960s was home to both the MLB Athletics and the NFL Chiefs, who shared multipurpose Municipal Stadium. Conditions were deteriorating at the aging venue, however, and it was clearly time to relocate the two teams. In 1967, Jackson County voters approved bonds to construct the Truman Sports Complex, which would feature a ballpark for the Athletics and a stadium for the NFL Chiefs. At that time this was an unusual move—multiuse venues had become the standard, because supporting separate stadiums was not considered financially feasible for owners. The plan seemed like a go, but in 1968, Athletics owner Charles O. Finley, who had recently signed a lease to remain in Kansas City, abruptly moved his ball club to Oakland, California, and into a brand-new multipurpose stadium.

Kansas City was now without Major League Baseball or, for the first time since 1883, any professional baseball at all. Missouri senator Stuart Symington was outraged by the move and threatened to press for revocation of baseball's cherished anti-trust exemption

[RIGHT] Built in the early 1970s, Kauffman Stadium is reminiscent of Googie architecture, a style especially popular in the 1950s and '60s, which favored a futurist look influenced by car culture, jets, the atomic age, and the space age.

if MLB did not find a new team for Kansas City. The league quickly granted expansion franchises to four cities, including one for a KC team owned by pharmaceutical magnate Ewing Kauffman. Meanwhile, the county carried on with its plans for the new ballpark. Royals Stadium opened on April 10, 1973, with 39, 464 fans in attendance to watch their team nail down a 12–1 win over the Texas Rangers. Twenty years later the venue would be renamed in honor of Kauffman. It is currently the only stadium still named after an individual and not a company, and it is one of only nine stadiums that has not sold naming rights.

While waiting for their new stadium to be finished, the Royals played in Municipal Stadium, former home of the KC Athletics, from 1969 to 1972. The expansion team was graciously welcomed by Kansas City, and nearly a million fans flocked to watch them during their first season. (*See* Oakland Athletics, Municipal Stadium, page 273.)

DESIGN AND CONSTRUCTION

Designed by architects Kivett and Myers, along with Populous, and built by three construction firms, Sharp, Kidde, and Webb, Royals Stadium cost $70 million to build. From 1996 to 1991, it was the lone baseball-only park built in the Majors, one of the few constructed during the era of the cookie-cutter multipurpose stadiums. It is one

BALLPARK STATS

ADDRESS
1 Royal Way, Kansas City, MO 64129

FORMER NAME
Royals Stadium (1973–1993)

OWNER/OPERATOR
Jackson County Sports Complex Authority

ARCHITECT
Kivett and Myers; Populous

CAPACITY
37,903

RECORD BASEBALL ATTENDANCE
42,633 om 10/9,/1980 (ALCS Game 2)

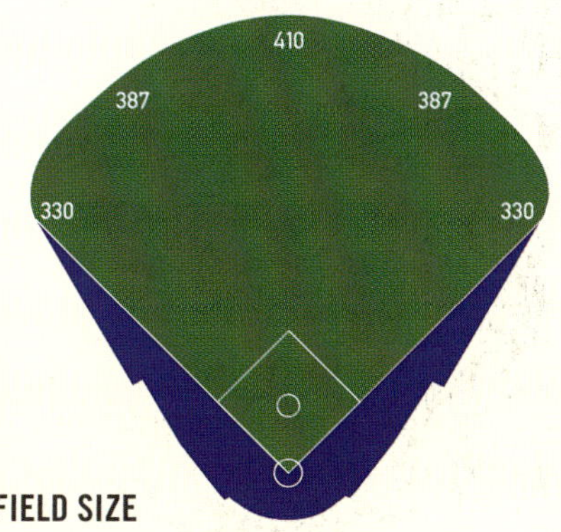

FIELD SIZE

- **Left field** 330 feet
- **Left-center** 387 feet
- **Center field** 410 feet
- **Right-center** 387 feet
- **Right field** 330 feet
- **Height of fence** 8 feet

SURFACE
Kentucky bluegrass/perennial ryegrass

TEAM MASCOT
Sluggerrr

On August 1, 2020, when the COVID-19 pandemic forced MLB teams to play to empty stadiums, organizers placed cardboard cutouts of fans to take the place of the unfilled seats before the Kansas City Royals took on the Chicago White Sox on Opening Day in Kauffman Stadium.

ROYALS ACHIEVEMENTS

WORLD SERIES CHAMPIONSHIPS: 2 (1985, 2015)

NL PENNANTS: 4 (1980, 1985, 2014, 2015)

NL WEST DIVISION TITLES: 6 (1976, 1977, 1978, 1980, 1984, 1985)

NL CENTRAL DIVISION TITLES: 1 (2015)

WILD CARD BERTHS: 1 (2014)

PLAYOFF APPEARANCES: 9 (1976, 1977, 1978, 1980, 1981, 1984, 1985, 2014, 2015)

WORST SEASON RECORD: 2005/2023, 56–106 (.346)

BEST SEASON RECORD: 1977, 102–60 (.630)

of two dedicated parks, along with Dodger Stadium, that are still active and were never converted for multiple use.

Still, the designers did borrow several stylistic features from multipurpose venues, as well as from the space age "Googie" style that was so popular in the 1950s. The stadium's sleek facade is mainly smooth, uncovered concrete. Inside the park, the stands wrap around the infield, ending at the foul poles, where smaller bleachers are located. The stadium's seating bowls and sight lines still serve as industry models today. Writers have described Kauffman as "one-third of a cookie-cutter stadium," containing only the seats necessary to provide the best views of baseball. The upper deck is quite steep, though not so high as some other stands of that time. Its influence can be seen in Guaranteed Rate Field in Chicago, as well as in many minor league ballparks. The field also has the second most playable square footage in MLB, after Colorado's Coors Field.

Perhaps the best-known feature of Kauffman Stadium is the waterfall and fountain display called the Water Spectacular, located behind the right field fence. The largest privately funded fountain in the world, it is 322 feet (98 m) wide. The waterfall flows continuously, but the fountains are active only before and after games and between innings.

MAJOR UPGRADES

In 2006, voters approved funds for the renovation of the entire Truman Sports Complex. This included a $250 million renovation of the stadium. Expectations were high that the updated venue would offer visitors unsurpassed amenities and state-of-the-art technology. On Opening Day in 2009, fans were greeted by a host of improvements and alterations, including four new entry ticket gates and wider concourses. Two vomitorium portals in the upper deck and two on field level were also widened. Seating capacity was reduced to 37,903, but there was now enhanced vertical circulation to all seating levels, and new and upgraded concessions and toilet amenities were added on all concourses. Other improvements and additions included new press facilities; new HD scoreboard, dubbed "Crown Vision," and control room; 360-degree outfield concourse; fountain-view terraces; an outfield kids' area; a right-field sports bar-themed restaurant; and a left-field Hall of Fame and conference center.

FEATURES AND AMENITIES

Upon entering, visitors can explore the stadium via a 360-degree expanded concourse while still in sight of the action on the field. And with access to 74 concession stands and 67 restroom facilities, fans need to spend the minimum time away from their seats.

THE OUTFIELD EXPERIENCE This feature is geared for kids and consists of the Price Chopper Little K, Sluggerrr's Mini Golf at the K, Pitching Mound, Batting Challenge, Base Run, and the Carousel. It is also the location of the Rivals Sports Bar, Blue Moon Tap Room, New Era Cap Store, the Royals Boutique and Fountain Team Store, Belfonte Ice Cream, the Miller Lite Fountain Bar, Sweet Baby Ray's BBQ Pit, Sonic Slam Section, Pepsi Party Porch, Boulevard Concession, Price Chopper Patio, and the Bally Sports Kansas City Broadcast booth.

ROYALS HALL OF FAME Presented by Commerce Bank, the Royals Hall of Fame is located inside Gate A. Established in 1986, it celebrates individuals who have made exceptional contributions to Kansas City Royals baseball, both on and off the field. On view are the Royals' 1985 and 2015 World Series Championship trophies; the 1980, 1985, 2014, and 2015 American League Championship trophies; artifacts from Cy Young Awards; and Rawlings Gold Gloves.

SEATING CHART

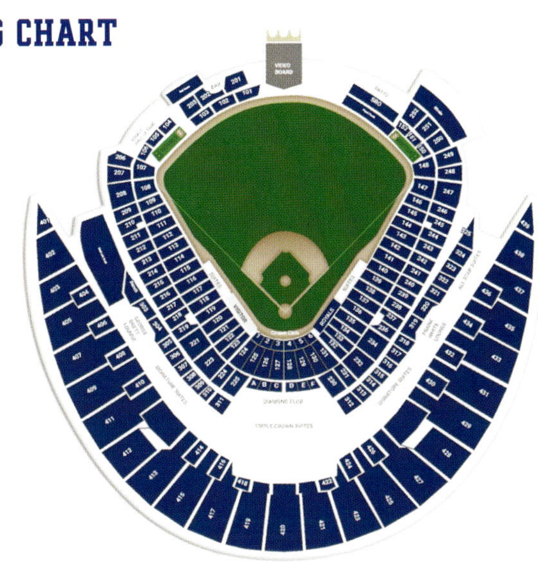

[BELOW] The one-of-a-kind Kauffman "Water Spectacular" sits above the Pepsi Party Porch. The fountain wall follows the natural curve of the outfield wall and is composed of wings on each side of the scoreboard.

THE TEAM NAME

The name "Royals" is a nod to the American Royal, a livestock show, horse show, rodeo, and championship barbecue competition that has been held annually in Kansas City since 1899. Sanford Porte from Overland Park, Kansas, submitted the name as a tie-in with Missouri's billion-dollar livestock industry. Royals was also the name of two former Negro League baseball teams that played in the first half of the 20th century.

HONORED PLAYERS Four statues stand behind the fountains in the outfield concourse—players George Brett, Dick Howser, and Frank White are in right field, while the fourth, former owner Ewing Kauffman and his wife, Muriel, is in left field.

THE BUCK O'NEIL LEGACY SEAT This was established during the 2007 season. The Royals had a red seat placed behind home plate among the blue seats to honor Buck O'Neil, who played in the Negro Leagues for the Kansas City Monarchs from 1937 to 1955 and later became a beloved fixture in the city. At each game a person who embodies his spirit is selected to sit in that seat, which was once occupied by O'Neil as both a scout and as an ambassador of baseball.

PREMIUM SEATING This includes the UMB Dugout Suites, which offer a unique vantage point to the game. Located next to the Royals and visiting team dugouts, these suites—which can host from 25 to 35 guests—make a memorable setting for any event.

KAUFFMAN STADIUM FIRSTS

FIRST MLB GAME: 4/10/1973, Royals over Texas Rangers, 12–1*

FIRST HOME RUN: 4/10/1973, John Mayberry vs. Texas Rangers*

FIRST NO-HITTER: 5/15/1973, Nolan Ryan (California Angels)*

FIRST ALL-STAR GAME: 7/24/1973, NL over AL, 7–1*

FIRST PLAYOFF GAME: 10/9/1976, NY Yankees over Royals, 13–7*

FIRST WORLD SERIES GAME: 10/19/1985, St. Louis Cardinals over Royals, 3–1 in Game 1*

* as Royals Stadium

SENSORY ROOMS PRESENTED BY JE DUNN These rooms are located inside each dugout concourse along the first- and third-base sides closest to the elevator. Each Royals-themed room is enclosed, furnished, and features several sensory-friendly features like puzzles, fidget items, bean bags, textured walls, activity panels, and wall art.

ROYALS SHOPPING The Team Store, located at Gate C, sells Royals merchandise and souvenirs. Upper level locations include the Loge Level Store on the Third Base Side and the View Level Store behind Home Plate. In the Outfield you will find Throwbacks near the Royals Hall of Fame and the Fountain Team Store and the New Era Store. The Show, featuring official on-field merchandise, is in left center field. A New Era Kiosk is also located on the Plaza Level near First Base. The Royals Team Store features exclusive products from Nike, New Era, 47 Brand, Homage, and much more. The Royals Authentics Store, located on the third-base side of the Plaza/Field Level near section 225, offers guests exclusive one-of-a-kind memorabilia—Major League Baseball authenticated items, including game-used bats, baseballs, bases, jerseys, caps and more . . . as well as collectibles autographed by current and past Royals players. A portion of all proceeds benefit Royals Charities.

FUTURE PLANS . . .

In 2021, the Royals announced plans to leave aging Kauffman Stadium, which has been suffering structural and mechanical problems. Their intention is to create both a ballpark and an entertainment district, which they claim would be an economic boon for the region, creating a potential 20,000 jobs.

In August 2023, plans were revealed for two widely different locations, each rated equal in appeal. The first location, in East Village, would include a downtown ballpark anchoring a 27-acre (11 ha) development. It would be only blocks away from the thriving Power and Light District, home to T-Mobile Center. The other option is a 90-acre (36.4 ha) parcel in Clay County, across the Missouri River, which would give the team more ability to develop commercial and residential properties. The KC franchise estimates the overall development—a ballpark and surrounding entertainment district—would cost more than $2 billion at either site. "The K has been the home to the Royals for 50-plus years—been a great home—but it's time for a new one," said Brooks Sherman, the Royals' president of business operations. "It's actually incredible that we have these two locations to even consider as a future home and sustain ourselves as a Major League city."

Both plans were produced by Populous, the Kansas City-based sports architecture giant responsible for more than 20 MLB stadiums. Their proposed design tentatively features swooping roof lines reminiscent of Kauffman Stadium. There is even an homage to the fountains for which the current park is famous. But the path toward a solution has been a winding one, given the multitude of factors involved in the ambitious proposal. As of today the goal is still to have a new stadium.

> "Nosotros Creamos!"
>
> —MANAGER TONY PENA, 2003 RALLYING CRY, "BELIEVE!"

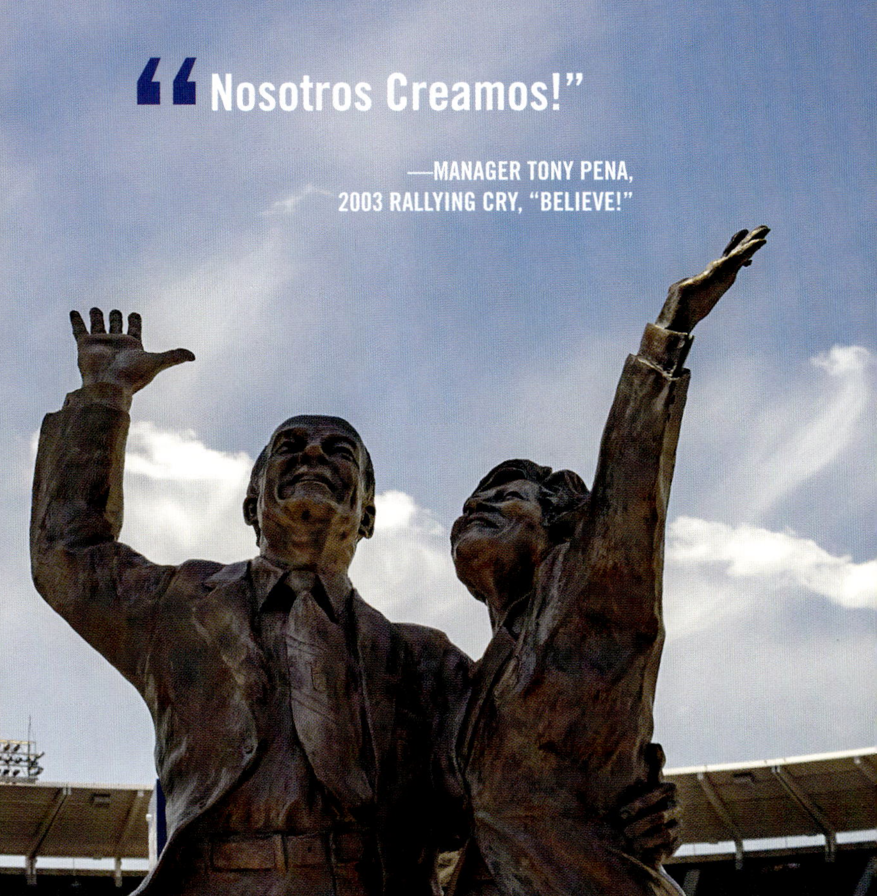

[ABOVE] Unveiled in 2009 on the left-center field concourse stands the larger-than-life-sized bronze sculpture commemorating former Royals owner, Ewing Kauffman, and his wife, Muriel. World-renowned artist Harry Weber depicted the smiling couple dressed in their Sunday best and waving to Royals fans.

[ABOVE] The Outfield Experience features kid-and-family-friendly activities like Slugerrr's Mini Golf.

[OPPOSITE PAGE] The stadium's lighting and scoreboard illuminate the deep-blue sky as fans take in a night game at Kauffman Stadium.

[RIGHT] Sluggerrr with his version of mini-me before a game against the Minnesota Twins on July 2, 2017. In 1996, the lovable lion made his MLB debut at Kauffman Stadium as the official mascot of the Royals. He now entertains millions of baseball fans both at the stadium and during Royals road trips across the country and is one of the highest-paid mascots in the Majors.

HOME OF THE PITTSBURGH PIRATES

NATIONAL LEAGUE (1887–PRESENT)

PITTSBURGH HAS A LONG HISTORY *with the MLB Pirates—who are now housed in their fifth ballpark. The city also has a strong association with Black teams—two of the premier teams in the Negro Leagues, the Pittsburgh Crawfords and the Homestead Grays, played there. How fitting then that the Pirates were the first Major League team to field an all-Black lineup on September 1, 1971.*

The Pirates baseball team was founded in 1881 as the Pittsburgh Alleghenys of the American Association, who then joined the National League in 1887. The team later became part of the NL East Division from 1969 to 1993, then were moved to the Central Division, where they remain.

At the start of the 20th century, the Pirates were one of the best teams in pro ball, making it to the very first World Series in 1903, and winning the series against the Detroit Tigers behind their star shortstop Honus Wagner in 1909. But after some legendary mid-century games—like the Bill Mazeroski walk-off home run to end the 1960 World Series, and another championship win in 1971 with Latino batting ace Roberto Clemente—the team endured an epic slump. There were 20 years of losing seasons, 1993 to 2012, the longest streak in American professional sports, and they have made it to the post season only three times since 1992. Regardless of this record, Pirates fans remain loyal and express their support at games, even when their team is having an off season—or decade.

Over their long history the Pirates have played in five different venues—Exposition Park I and II, Recreation Park, Exposition Park III, Forbes Field, Three Rivers Stadium, and PNC Park. Since 2001 they have called PNC Park home, and though it has not exactly proved to be a potent charm for the team, it has plenty of amenities to keep fans and visitors happy. Located on the scenic banks of the Allegheny River, the park is often lauded as one of the best in the Major League, in terms of location, ambience, and design.

During their shared tenure with the Steelers in Three Rivers Stadium, the ball club realized the venue was far better suited to football. Making matters worse, their once-devoted fans stopped coming to the park, and attendance numbers began to flag. By the 1990s the team threatened to leave the city unless the city built a dedicated baseball stadium. After the passage of a 1997 referendum, dedicated stadiums were approved for both the Pirates and the Steelers. The Pirates played their final game at Three Rivers on October 1, 2000, and moved to their new downtown ballpark, PNC Park, on March 31, 2001. The facility is named for the PNC Financial Services Group, Inc., an American bank holding company and financial services corporation based in Pittsburgh. Their original 20-year naming rights deal, reportedly worth $30 million, was set to expire ahead of the 2021 season, but it has now been extended to 2031.

> **"We said when construction began that we would build the best ballpark in baseball, and we believe we've done that."**
>
> — STEVE GREENBERG, PIRATES' VICE PRESIDENT

BALLPARK STATS

ADDRESS
115 Federal Street, Pittsburgh, PA 15212

OWNER
Sports & Exhibition Authority of Pittsburgh and Allegheny County

OPERATOR
Pittsburgh Pirates

DESIGNER/CHIEF ARCHITECT
HOK Sport (now Populous); L.D. Astorino & Associates

CAPACITY
38,747

RECORD BASEBALL ATTENDANCE
40,889 on 10/7/2015 (vs. Chicago Cubs)

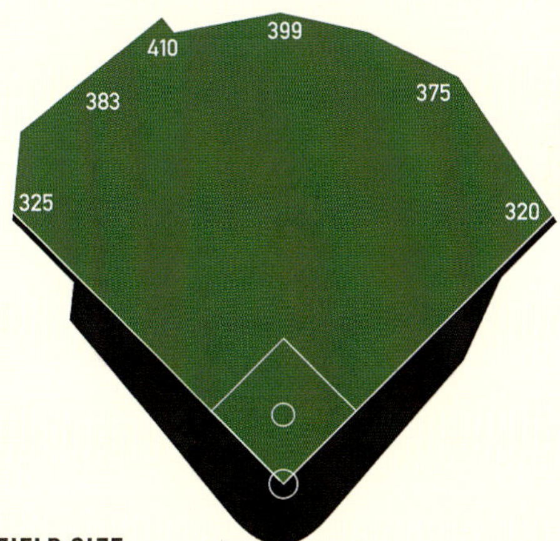

FIELD SIZE

- **Left field** 325 feet (99 m)
- **Left-center** 383 feet (117 m)
- **Deep left-center field** 410 feet (125 m)
- **Center field** 399 feet (122 m)
- **Right-center** 375 feet (114 m)
- **Right field** 320 feet (98 m)
- **Backstop** 51 feet (16 m)

SURFACE
Kentucky bluegrass

TEAM MASCOT
The Pirate Parrot

DESIGN AND CONSTRUCTION

The stadium was designed by architects HOK Sport (now Populous) and L. D. Astorino & Associates and constructed at a cost of $216 million. The Pirates decided they wanted a classic "jewel box" stadium, a park that was actually intimate—not one made just to look that way through sunken exterior landscaping. Owner Kevin McClatchy desired an authentically low-scale "35,000-to-37,000-seat park with natural grass and no roof, bells, or whistles." So the architects kept things simple. As a result, the two-deck stadium became known for its sense of intimacy—fans in the upper deck are closer to the plays than in most stadiums, while those in the lower deck are also closer to the field, and the batter is closer to the seats behind home plate than to the pitcher. Meanwhile, a large, four-level steel rotunda provides plenty of standing room down the left field line.

Often called "the most beautiful park in baseball," the completed PNC Park had a comforting vintage feel that jibed nicely with its state-of-the-art technologies. While the Kasota limestone and American-made raw-steel facade reflect the aesthetic of the "Steel City," the outfield offers spectators a commanding view of the city's actual skyline. The visual mix of bridges, skyscrapers, winding river, and North Shore neighborhood creates a powerful sense of place.

PUBLIC REACTION

The new stadium certainly acquired plenty of admirers in its first few decades. In 2010, an unranked list of "America's 7 Best Ballparks" from ABC News reported that PNC Park "combines the best features of yesterday's ballparks—rhythmic archways, steel trusswork, and a natural grass playing field—with the latest in fan and player amenities and comfort." In 2017, a group of *Washington Post* sports writers named PNC Park the second-best stadium in MLB, and a 2018 article in *Parade* dubbed it, "The Jewel of the Allegheny." And speaking of the river, there is even a ferryboat that brings fans right to the park.

UPDATES AND ALTERATIONS

Even a highly regarded ballpark needs occasional refurbishing, and PNC Park is no exception. Improvements made for the 2015 season included a left-field terrace with two levels of standing room—with 250 feet (76 m) of drink rails—that is open to any fan with a ticket. A patio dubbed the "The Porch" was added next to the terraces; it overlooks center field, has bar tables and outdoor sofa-style seating, and accommodates up to 25 people. Other additions included The Corner, a sports bar at the base of the left-field rotunda; the

PNC PARK FIRSTS

FIRST MLB GAME: 4/9/2001, Cincinnati Reds over Pirates, 8–2

FIRST HOME RUN: 4/9/2001, Sean Casey (Cincinnati Reds)

FIRST NO-HITTER: 9/28/2012, Homer Bailey (Cincinnati Reds)

FIRST ALL-STAR GAME: 7/11/2006, AL defeats NL, 3–2

FIRST PLAYOFF GAME: 10/1/2013, Pirates beat Cincinnati Reds, 1–0

The bright lights of the ballpark add to the glowing Pittsburgh skyline and reflect into the river during a night game.

NICKNAMES AND SLOGANS

The Pirates are often referred to as the "Bucs" or the "Buccos" (taken from "buccaneer," a synonym for pirate), and as "the Lumber Company." Emmy-winning sportscaster Greg Brown, known for his love of the ball club, has made the phrase "Raise the Jolly Roger!" the cry for a Pirates' victory and "Clear the deck; cannonball coming!" his signature home run call.

Terrace Bar in the upper concourse; and Pirates Outfitters, a merchandise shop beside the home-plate entrance.

Prior to the 2017 season, the manual out-of-town scoreboard on the right-field wall was replaced by an LED screen. The 2022 season saw several rows of seats in center field, and the security booth next to the batter's eye replaced by two open-air bars. Ahead of the 2023 season the Pirates replaced and expanded the main scoreboard.

FEATURES AND AMENITIES

If fans' reactions online are anything to go on, this stadium offers a superlative game-day experience. Between the competition on the field, the sense of history, the artwork, the team merchandise, and a host of snack stops, restaurants, patios, and bars, PNC Park has something for almost everyone.

HONORED PLAYERS The team's legacy is never far from the minds of the fans. Statues commemorating Hall of Famers Roberto Clemente, Willie Stargell, Bill Mazeroski, and Honus Wagner are positioned at different locations outside the stadium, making great backdrops for selfies. Near the center-field entrance the Pirates now have a display commemorating the team's retired numbers, while large baseballs spaced along the Allegheny River bear the names of Pittsburgh-based members of the Baseball Hall of Fame, including players from the local Negro League franchises, the Homestead Grays and Pittsburgh Crawfords.

HALL OF FAME In September 2022 the Pirates unveiled their own Hall of Fame, located in the Legacy Square area near the left field rotunda. The inaugural class featured 15 members.

[ABOVE] A deep-toned statue of Johannes Peter "Honus" Wagner stands out against the pale limestone walls of the exterior of the ballpark. Shortstop Wagner, also nicknamed the "Flying Dutchman," played 21 seasons in Major League Baseball, from 1897 to 1917, almost entirely for his hometown Pirates.

SEATING CHART

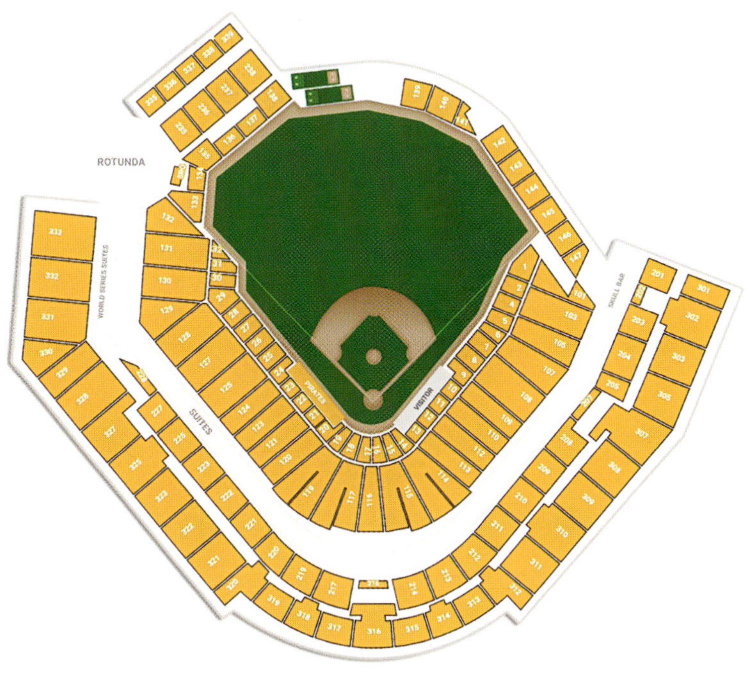

KIDS' PLAYGROUND A pirate-ship-themed playground for kids is located behind center field, along with signs and plaques detailing the club's history and its five championships.

FOOD AND DRINK Choices include a variety of specialty burgers and hot dogs, Nashville Hot Chicken sandwiches, BBQ bacon waffles, pizza, cheese curds, pierogies, fried pickle curds, and nachos. The stadium prides itself on its wide selection of artisanal beers from local breweries. The popular Bullpen Tap serves Fat Heads beer, Cinderlands, and Threadbare Cider.

PREMIER SEATING These include the Luxury Suites on the wrap-around Suite Level; World Series Suites that are perfect for entertaining clients, colleagues, and friends; and the Real Azul VIP Lounge, which offers indoor and outdoor seating and serves food and nonalcoholic drinks. The Home Plate Club seats fans in the first 12 rows behind the plate and includes a buffet. The Pittsburgh Baseball Club level features three clubs, Gunner's, Keystone Corner, and Club 3000.

PIRATES ACHIEVEMENTS

WORLD SERIES CHAMPIONSHIPS: 5 (1909, 1925, 1960, 1971, 1979)

NL PENNANTS: 9 (1901, 1902, 1903, 1909, 1925, 1927, 1960, 1971, 1979)

NL CENTRAL DIVISION TITLES: 9 (1970, 1971, 1972, 1974, 1975, 1979, 1990, 1991, 1992)

WILD CARD BERTHS: 3 (2013, 2014, 2015)

PLAYOFF APPEARANCES: 17 (1903, 1909, 1925, 1927, 1960, 1970, 1971, 1972, 1974, 1975, 1979, 1990, 1991, 1992, 2013, 2014, 2015)

WORST SEASON RECORD: 1890, 23–113 (.169)

BEST SEASON RECORD: 1909, 110–42 (.724)

[ABOVE] Pittsburgh Pirates mascot, the Parrot, prior to a 2009 game between the Reds and the Pirates. The costumed Pirates Parrot was introduced in 1979 in response to the popularity of the Phillie Phanatic, which had debuted one year earlier. This was but one example of the fierce intrastate rivalry between the two Pennsylvania ball clubs.

[RIGHT] Fans watch the Pirates take on the Milwaukee Brewers on a summer night as a Gateway Clipper paddle boat cruises on the Allegheny River.

A CONTROVERSIAL DECISION

In 2006, the pirates honored Pittsburgh's historic Negro League teams in an exhibit called Highmark Legacy Square. It featured statues of seven players from the city's Homestead Grays and Pittsburgh Crawfords, including Josh Gibson, Satchel Paige, and James "Cool Papa" Bell. The 25-seat Legacy Theatre featured a film about Pittsburgh's history with the Negro Leagues. Then in 2015, in the face of much controversy, the Pirates closed Legacy Square and donated the statues to the Josh Gibson Foundation. Yet, in the fall of 1988, Pirates management were the first franchise to celebrate the Negro Leagues at the 40th anniversary of the Homestead Grays winning the Negro League Championship. The Pirates brought the former players back to Three Rivers Stadium, and owner Carl Barger apologized for MLB preventing Black ball players from joining the Major Leagues. Legacy Square at PNC Park is now a rather empty space, with just banners depicting both Negro League and present-day Pittsburgh ballplayers.

[ABOVE] A statue of Josh Gibson, catcher and power hitter who played for both the Homestead Grays and Pittsburgh Crawfords, was one of the tributes to the Negro Leagues that once graced Legacy Square.

[BELOW] Fans gather before a game to peruse the wares available from vendors set up on the bridge leading to the ballpark. The Roberto Clemente Bridge (also known as the Sixth Street Bridge) becomes a pedestrian thoroughfare during Pirates' home games, leading people straight to PNC Park.

EARLY BALLPARKS
1876–1909

Professional baseball came to the Pittsburgh region on April 15, 1876, when the independent Allegheny Base Ball Club was organized in Allegheny City (later North Side, Pittsburgh) and played their first game at Union Park. After they disbanded, a new Allegheny Base Ball Club of Pittsburgh was chartered in 1881 and began play in 1882 as a founding member of the American Association. They played at Exposition Park, which was a few blocks west of the current PNC Park, and also at Recreation Park, a sporting field and stadium in Allegheny City. The latter park was also home to the Western University of Pennsylvania's football team, and one of its claims to fame is that in November 1892, it hosted the first known American football game that included a professional player. In 1891 the Alleghenys officially became the Pirates, named for their habit of "plundering" players from other teams. That same year they made Exposition Park their permanent home, a venue that would enter sports history in 1903 as the site of the first World Series game. By 1909 the facility had become too small for the Pirates' increasing fanbase, so in mid-season they moved to Forbes Field. And although Exposition Park is now a parking lot and site of several restaurants, there is a historical marker to indicate its location.

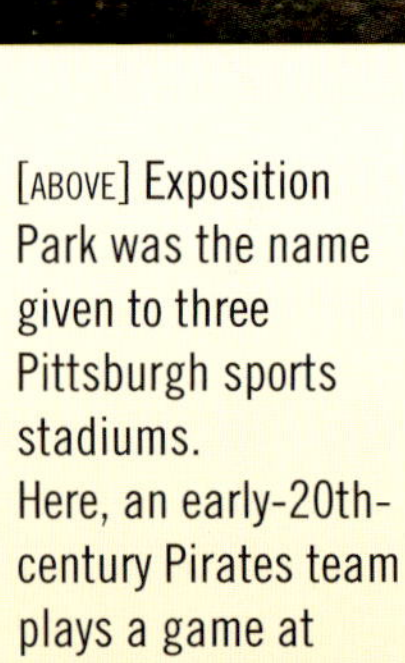

[ABOVE] Exposition Park was the name given to three Pittsburgh sports stadiums. Here, an early-20th-century Pirates team plays a game at Exposition Park III.

[RIGHT] Due to its location along the Allegheny River, the stadium was flooded numerous times during ts history, and, consequently, the roof was torn off twice. In this photo, Exposition Park is inundated with water from the Great Flood of 1913.

FORBES FIELD
1909–1970

Forbes Field earned the nickname "the House of Thrills" as home to the Pirates for 61 years. Other fond appellations included "the Old Lady of Schenley Park" and "the Oakland Orchard." The venue was named for a British general, John Forbes, who fought in the French and Indian Wars. It was Forbes who named the city Pittsburgh in 1758, in honor of British statesman William Pitt. The stadium was the first example of America's three-tiered steel-and-concrete stadiums, specifically built for longevity. Located on 7 acres (2.8 ha) of low-cost land near the Carnegie Library, it cost $1 million to build and boasted a capacity of 23,000 seats. Team owner Barney Dreyfuss signed a contract agreeing to "make the ballpark . . . of a design that would harmonize with the other structures in the Schenley Park district." Dreyfuss hated "cheap" home runs, so he insisted on a large playing field. Yet, in spite of that impediment, Forbes was known for several significant home runs, including Babe Ruth's final three homers on May 25, 1935.

After 1933 this venue was also home to the NFL Pittsburgh Steelers, which were known as the Pirates until 1940. Unfortunately, their three decades spent at Forbes were often fraught with struggle and disappointment. In 1963 they moved to the larger Pitt Stadium, home of the University of Pittsburgh's football Panthers.

Among the innovations introduced at Forbes were ramps and elevations to ease movement through the park, an umpire's room, and a clubhouse for the visiting team similar to the Pirates' own. The exterior of the ballpark used buff terra-cotta to spell out "PAC," which stood for Pittsburgh Athletic Company. The light-green steelwork nicely set off the red slate roof. After Dreyfuss died, a monument honoring him was placed in center field.

[BELOW] Forbes Field, circa 1963, before a game. Designer Charles Wellford Leavitt Jr. was contracted to design the grandstand at Forbes Field. Trained as a civil engineer, Leavitt gained experience in steel-and-concrete constructs while designing the Belmont and Saratoga Racetracks and their grandstands. Forbes Field was the only ballpark he developed. By the time of its closing, it was one of the oldest baseball fields in MLB, second only to Philadelphia's Shibe Park.

“The ceremonies were witnessed by the largest throng that ever attended an event of this kind in this or any other city in the country. . . . Forbes Field is so immense—so far beyond anything else in America in the way of a baseball park—that old experts, accustomed to judging crowds at a glance, were at a loss for reasonable figures.”

—*PITTSBURGH PRESS*, ON FORBES FIELD OPENING DAY, JUNE 30, 1909

[ABOVE] Spectators crowd into the Forbes Field grandstands, 1910.

[TOP] The exterior of Forbes Field, circa 1910–1920

THREE RIVERS STADIUM
1970–2000

In 1970, the Pirates ball club moved into the new Three Rivers Stadium, which they would again share with the football Steelers. Three Rivers was the first of the bland, circular, multipurpose stadiums constructed during that era, and the first in both the NFL or MLB to feature 3M's Tartan Turf, a competitor of popular Astro Turf. Like other "cookie cutter" stadiums, Three Rivers offered extensive box seats and moveable seating sections to accommodate both football and baseball. It was also the site of several "super group" concerts—the Rolling Stones, Pink Floyd, the Who, Led Zeppelin, and Alice Cooper. In 2001 the Steelers, who had been lobbying for their own stadium, moved to Heinz Field, later Acrisure Stadium. Meanwhile the Pirates relocated to PNC Park in time for the 2001 season. Three Rivers was razed in February 2001, and the site is now home to the entertainment complex known as Stage AE, as well as several parking lots.

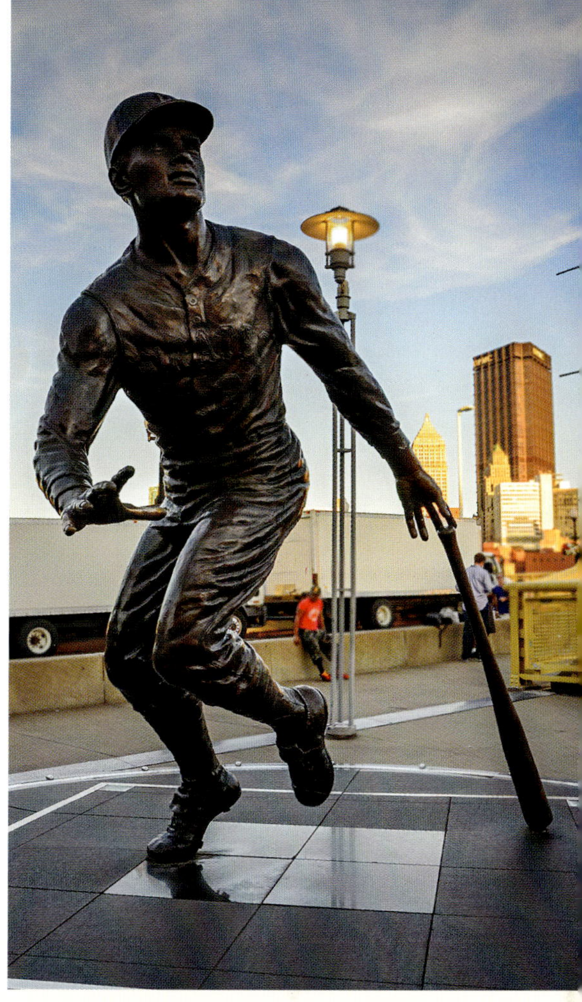

[RIGHT] On September 30, 1972, in his final regular season at-bat, right fielder Roberto Clemente achieved his long-awaited 3,000th hit. The Pirates—the defending World Champions—were taking on Yogi Berra's Mets at Three Rivers Stadium. A statue paying tribute to this Hall of Famer first stood outside Gate B at Three Rivers. When PNC Park became home to the Pirates, the statue was reinstalled just beyond center field.

[BELOW] Three Rivers got its name from its location at the confluence of the Allegheny River and Monongahela River, which forms the Ohio River.

"He could field the ball in New York and throw out a guy in Pennsylvania."

– SPORTSCASTER VIN SCULLY, ON PIRATE ROBERTO CLEMENTE

HOME OF THE CLEVELAND GUARDIANS

AMERICAN LEAGUE (1901–PRESENT)

LOCATED IN DOWNTOWN CLEVELAND, *Progressive Field is the third home field of the Guardians, the team formerly known as the Indians. The franchise goes all out to entertain their fans—the game-day experience might include live music and great concessions—and visitors swear there is not a bad seat in the park.*

This historic franchise originated in 1894 as the Grand Rapids Rippers, a minor league team based in Michigan that played in the Western League. After relocating to Cleveland in 1900, they were renamed the Lake Shores. The team became a Major League franchise in 1901 and played as the Cleveland Bluebirds/Blues (1901–1902), Cleveland Broncos (1902), Cleveland Napoleons/Naps (1903–1914), and Cleveland Indians (1915–2021) before their current stint as the Guardians. The Ohio teams first played in League Park and then Cleveland Stadium on the shores of Lake Erie, which they shared with the NFL Cleveland Browns. A new downtown stadium, Jacobs Field, opened in 1994 as a replacement for the latter venue and was located in the Gateway Sports and Entertainment Complex. Named for then owners Richard and David Jacobs, the ballpark quickly became known as "The Jake." In 2008 it was renamed for Progressive Corporation, a major insurance company based in the Cleveland suburb of Mayfield, which gained the naming rights for $58 million over 16 years.

The new ballpark was constructed with a combination of public and private funding, including a 15-year Cuyahoga County "sin tax" on tobacco and alcohol from 1990, tax-exempt Gateway Bonds, and prepaid leasing on the luxury boxes. The tax on cigarettes and alcohol expired in 2005, only to start up again the next day. That is because, in 1995, Cuyahoga County voters authorized a 10-year extension of the tax to help fund a new stadium for the Cleveland Browns football team.

Fans are able to access the ballpark from a number of gates, but many enter through the Gate C entrance in center field. The area was revamped after the 2014 season, and it now connects the ballpark with downtown Cleveland.

DESIGN AND CONSTRUCTION

Progressive Field is an urban ballpark with a sophisticated style, traditional appeal, and modern amenities. Designed by architects HOK Sport (Populous), Whitley & Whitley Architects, and Triad Design, it cost $175 million to build. The base of the exterior facade consists of Atlantic green granite, while the remainder is a mix of Kasota stone, limestone, and buff-colored brick. It is also known as a fan-friendly facility that offers an intimate environment. The stadium occupies 12 acres (4.9 ha) of the 28-acre (11.3 ha) Gateway Sports & Entertainment Complex, a $362 million project that was intended to revitalize downtown Cleveland. The complex also includes the multipurpose Rocket Mortgage FieldHouse, home to the NBA Cleveland Cavaliers and the AHL Cleveland Monsters, as well as a transitional space known as Gateway Plaza and the Gateway East parking garage.

With the architect firm of Populous on board, it's not surprising Progressive Field is similar in look and feel to their Baltimore triumph, Camden

BALLPARK STATS

ADDRESS
2401 Ontario Street, Cleveland, OH 44115

FORMER NAME
Jacobs Field (1994–2007)

OWNER
Cuyahoga County

OPERATOR
Gateway Economic Development Corporation

ARCHITECT
HOK Sport (now Populous); Devrouax & Purnell Architects - Planners

CAPACITY
34,830

RECORD BASEBALL ATTENDANCE
45,274 on 10/4/1997 (ALDS Game 5 vs. NY Yankees)

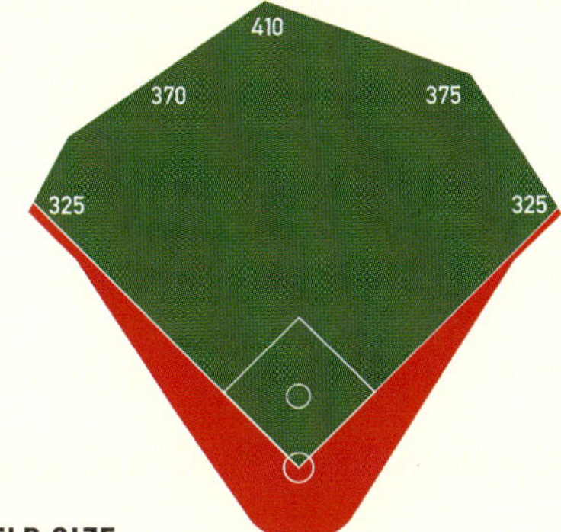

FIELD SIZE

Left field 325 feet (99 m)
Left-center 370 feet (113 m)
Center field 400 feet (122 m)
Deep center field 410 feet (125 m)
Right-center 375 feet (114 m)
Right field 325 feet (99 m)
Backstop 60 feet (18 m)
Fence height
Left field 19 feet (6 m)
Center and right fields 9 feet (3 m)

SURFACE
Kentucky bluegrass

TEAM MASCOT
Slider

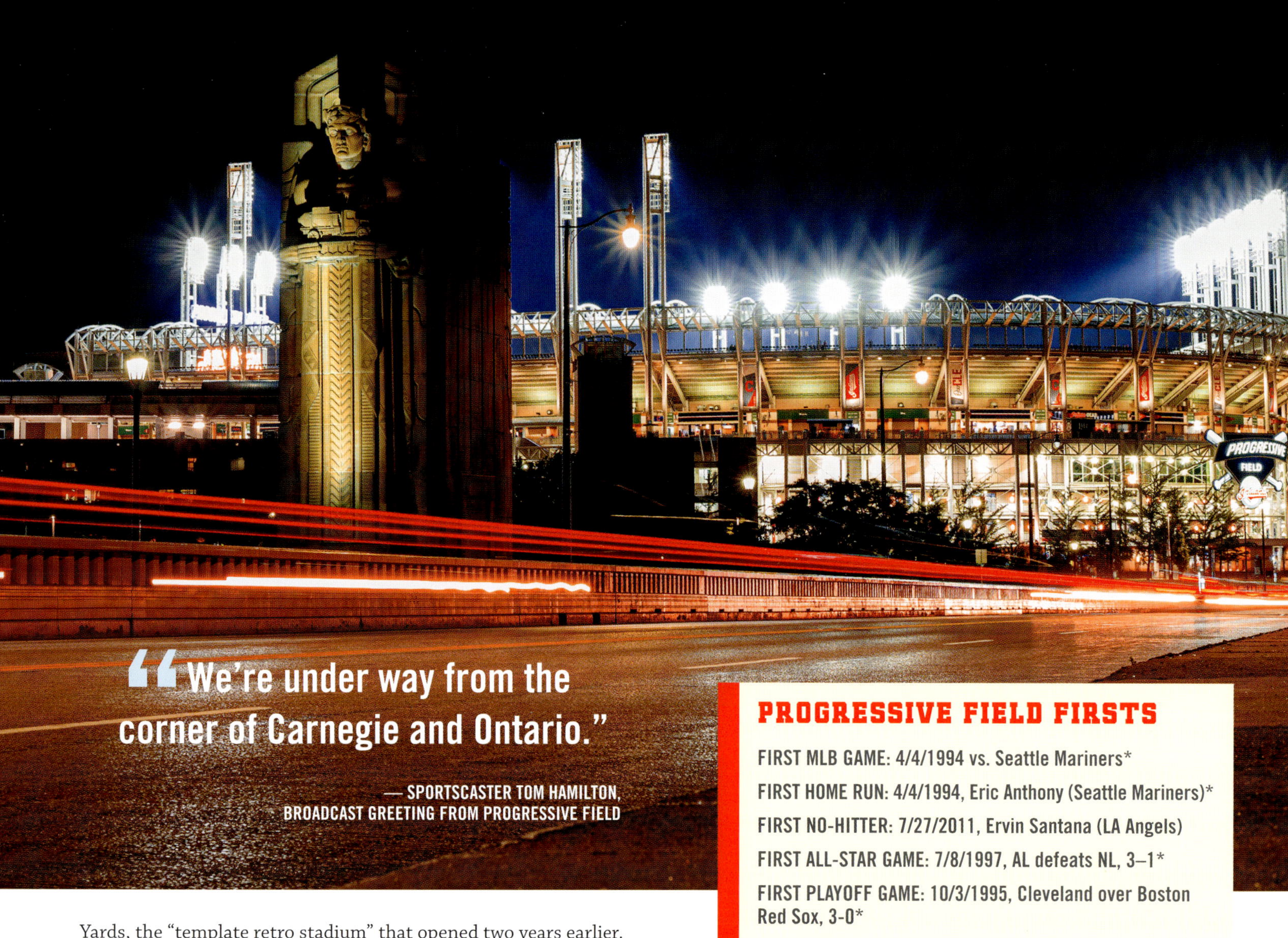

> “We're under way from the corner of Carnegie and Ontario.”
>
> — SPORTSCASTER TOM HAMILTON, BROADCAST GREETING FROM PROGRESSIVE FIELD

PROGRESSIVE FIELD FIRSTS

FIRST MLB GAME: 4/4/1994 vs. Seattle Mariners*

FIRST HOME RUN: 4/4/1994, Eric Anthony (Seattle Mariners)*

FIRST NO-HITTER: 7/27/2011, Ervin Santana (LA Angels)

FIRST ALL-STAR GAME: 7/8/1997, AL defeats NL, 3–1*

FIRST PLAYOFF GAME: 10/3/1995, Cleveland over Boston Red Sox, 3-0*

FIRST WORLD SERIES GAME: 10/30/2015, Cleveland over Atlanta Braves, 7–6 in Game 3

* as Jacobs Field

Yards, the “template retro stadium” that opened two years earlier. The Cleveland site provides some features of classic ballparks—the field is asymmetrical, and the bleachers perch atop a 19-foot (5.8 m) left-field wall, and because the park isn't completely enclosed, fans can view the skyline of downtown Cleveland. But the Indians made some alterations in their ballpark that the Orioles didn't. The seats down both lines are angled toward home plate, meaning fans don't need to crane their necks to view the batter's box. An area behind first base is designated Kidsland, with special concessions and features, and the bullpens feature three mounds. As in Baltimore, they are raised above the field so that fans can watch pitchers warming up. And like Baltimore, a picnic area is located behind the outfield fence. The site also boasts a 42-panel, 8.4-kWh Solar Pavilion in section 541, which produces enough electricity per year to power an average home.

PUBLIC REACTIONS

When Progressive Field first opened, the ballpark was greeted with praise from critics and the public. The fans certainly approved—for 455 straight games, from 1995 to 2001, the Indians sold out every game at Jacobs Field. In 2008, Progressive Field was voted MLB's best ballpark in a *Sports Illustrated* fan opinion poll. The venue continues to earn high marks today for its food and drink options, the number of standing room spaces, the friendly and helpful staff, and the venue's general atmosphere. “It's a ballpark, not a mallpark,” as one online reviewer noted.

FEATURES AND AMENITIES

Progressive Field is considered one of the better ballparks in terms of recognizing past players. There are historical markers and monuments throughout the stadium, while the Memorial area is beautifully landscaped, with lots of trees and plants providing shade and a welcome touch of nature. Many of the public gathering spots are gathered into districts, making them easier to locate on the stadium map.

THE LEFT FIELD DISTRICT This area includes a variety of game viewing options, including public drink rails and bleacher seating. It is also the site of the very popular Home Run Porch.

THE RIGHT FIELD DISTRICT This area connects the ballpark with the city of Cleveland, offering stunning views of the skyline. The concourse features food and beverage from favorite local restaurants. The Stacked Bullpens in the Right Field District are one of the most distinctive layouts in Major League Baseball, providing up-close views of player warmups and thrilling access to the players.

BLOCK PARTIES These are held in right field on most Fridays and Saturdays during the season. They feature live pregame entertainment, from DJs to live bands to performers, making them the perfect way for groups to get geared up for the game.

HERITAGE PARK This two-tiered park, located in the center field area near Gate C, displays monuments that honor the greatest names in club history and celebrates the Guardians' memorable moments; features include the Guardians Hall of Fame and statues of Cleveland greats Bob Feller and Jim Thome. Also showcased is the "Top 100 Guardians" roster, selected during the team's 100th Anniversary Celebration in 2001. It's open to fans before, during, and after games and is available for special events.

SMUCKER'S KIDS CLUBHOUSE This is located near the Family Deck and features two stories of child-oriented activities. A Sensory Room for those who become overstimulated at the game opened in 2019 and is located on the first floor of the Kids Clubhouse. The wall art is uneven to the touch and has a calming effect, while the bubble wall morphs into soothing colors.

TEAM STORES The latest Cleveland Guardians apparel and souvenirs are carried at the Official Team Store and at souvenir and concession stands. Locations include the Main Team Store; Ballpark Novelty stands; Main Concourse; Mezzanine, Kids Store; Club Lounge; Upper Deck; New Era Hat Stand; and Game-Used/ Memorabilia stand. For kids there is even a Make Your Own Mascot store. The Guardian's mascot, Slider, is one of only three MLB mascots inducted into the Mascot Hall of Fame.

SEATING CHART

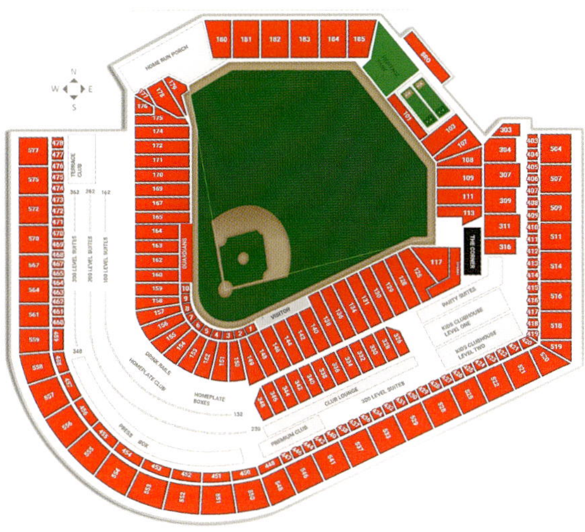

[RIGHT] Plaques honoring Satchel Paige and Bob Feller. Heritage Park, located in the center-field area, hosts the Guardians Hall of Fame, which pays tribute to the greatest players in franchise history. It has served as the Cleveland team's museum, celebrating its rich 100+ years of history.

[BELOW] Progressive Field now displays the new team name.

[ABOVE] The Guardians' team mascot, Slider, has bright fuchsia-colored fur, with a large yellow nose and shaggy yellow eyebrows. Created in 1990, his look was inspired by the Phillie Phanatic.

[RIGHT] One of the faces of the Guardians of Traffic. These towering pylons were installed on the Lorain-Carnegie Bridge in 1932. Each of the four pylons has images front and back, for a total of eight representations. The bridge was later renamed the Hope Memorial, and these art deco landmarks supplied the inspiration for the new team name of the former Indians.

FOOD AND DRINK The ball park is known for its range of tasty choices when it comes to food, drink, and snacks. The Corner, a new two-story bar, is the perfect place for fans to gather. The Terrace Club, as of the 2022 season, offers buffet-style-only service. The Infield District features a dozen local eateries for fans, including Happy Dog, Ohio City Burrito, Butcher + Brewer, Momocho, Dante's Inferno, Fat Head Brewery, and the Brew Kettle. It is also home to the Great Lakes Beer Garden and the Home Plate Club. The ballpark's new concession area represents popular neighborhoods that exemplify Cleveland's exciting food and beverage scene. Ohio City is home to Great Lakes Brewing Company and their award-winning lagers and ales. Tremont is where to find Barrio, with its inventive, fresh, and flavorful tacos. Dynomite Burgers in University Circle fires up premium patties topped with bacon, barbecue mayo, or caramelized onions. In Cleveland Heights, grilled cheese goodness is found at Melt Bar and Grilled. Gordon Square's Sweet Moses offers old-fashioned sundaes and other yummy ice cream concoctions. Many fans also appreciate that they can take in the nearby Rock & Roll Hall of Fame after visiting the ballpark.

A NEW IDENTITY

In 1915, sportswriters were asked to come up with a name for the Cleveland club. They chose Indians, referring back to the nickname "Indians" applied to the Cleveland Spiders when Native American Louis Sockalexis played for them. Naming sports teams after America's Native peoples was already a trend—Chiefs, Braves, Indians, and Redskins were all popular. Yet, for decades American Indians were treated poorly, and having their names associated with sports franchises was hardly a boon. Plus the team mascots or logos often reflected Hollywood or cultural stereotypes. The Cleveland Indians faced controversy over their logo image of Chief Wahoo, a cartoonish ethnic stereotype. He was retired in 2018, but the team name remained problematic . . . and fans continued to wear war paint and feathered headresses to games. On July 23, 2021, the team announced their new name—the Cleveland Guardians. This fresh identity arose from the stately art deco *Guardians of Traffic* statues on the Hope Memorial Bridge next to their home field. Each guardian holds a different vehicle: a hay wagon, a covered wagon, a stagecoach, and a 1930s automobile, plus four construction trucks.

GUARDIANS ACHIEVEMENTS

WORLD SERIES CHAMPIONSHIPS: 2 (1920, 1948)

AL PENNANTS: 6 (1920, 1948, 1954, 1995, 1997, 2016)

AL CENTRAL DIVISION TITLES: 11 (1995, 1996, 1997, 1998, 1999, 2001, 2007, 20016, 2017, 2018, 2022*)

WILD CARD BERTHS: 3 (2013, 2020, 2022*)

PLAYOFF APPEARANCES: 16 (1920, 1948, 1954, 1995, 1996, 1997, 1998, 1999, 2001, 2007, 2013, 2016, 2017, 2018, 2020, 2022*)

WORST SEASON RECORD: 1991, 57–105 (.352)

BEST SEASON RECORD: 1954, 111–43 (.721)

* as Guardians (all others as Indians)

[ABOVE] "Minnie" and "Paul" shake hands across the Mississippi River whenever the Twins hit a home run.

[RIGHT] Located in the historic warehouse district of downtown Minneapolis, Target Field has the smallest footprint in Major League Baseball, at only 8.5 acres (3.4 ha). The designers chose a hearty, weather-resistant—but lovely—native Minnesotan limestone to cover most of the ballpark's facade.

lines from Twins broadcasts are etched in wood planks outside the press box. The celebration sign in center field features the original Twins logo from 1961—two players in old-time uniforms, one from Minneapolis, one from St. Paul. Whenever a Twins player gets a homer, the sign lights up, making it look like "Minnie" and "Paul" are shaking hands across the Mississippi River.

The architects also made their design for Target Field environmentally friendly, incorporating conservation, sustainability, and energy efficiency. And since it opened, the ballpark has earned kudos for its sustainability and urban design. Its positive effect on the area can be seen in the increased demand for construction permits, while condo sales and hotel occupancy are up. It could be said that Target Field "hit the bull's-eye," helping the Twins become one of baseball's most successful operations.

Changes for 2023 include a great deal of updated technology and a new baseball medallion with the "TC" logo positioned at the top of the Twins Tower in right field.

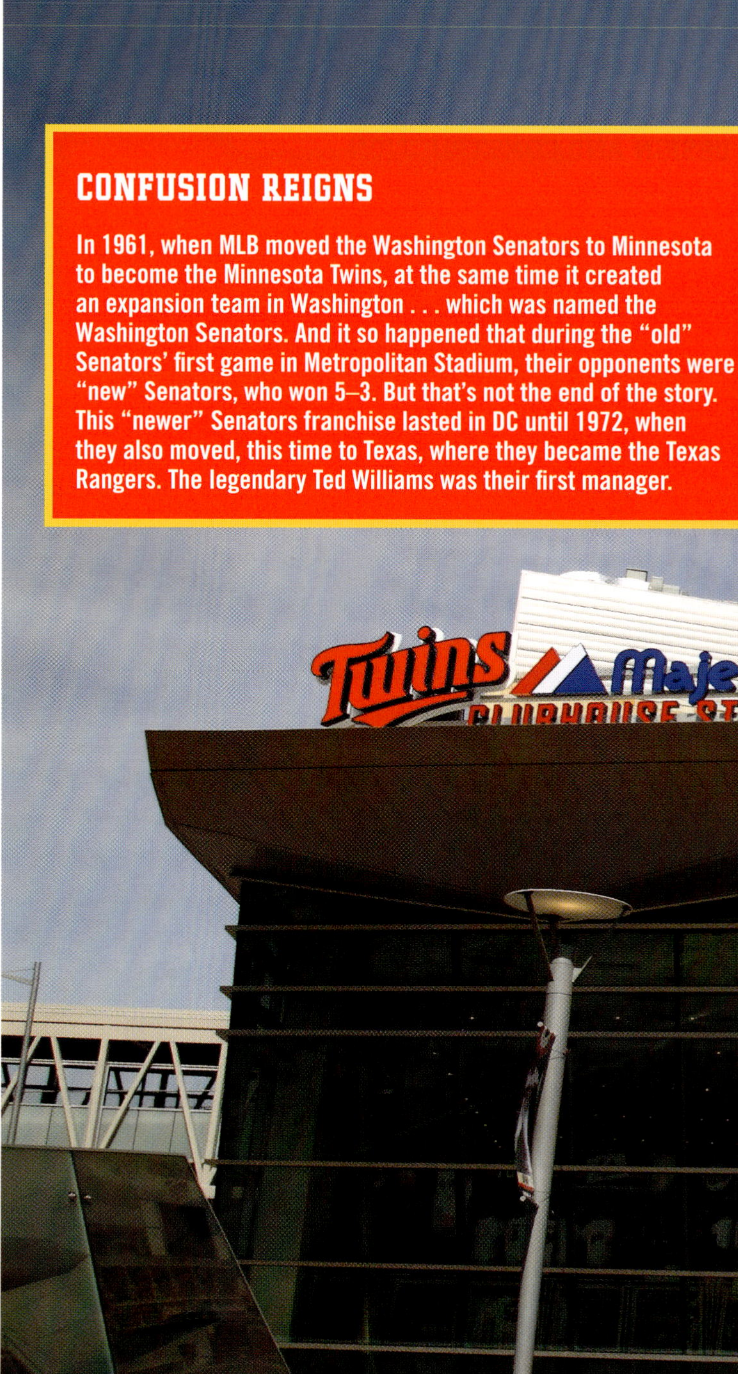

CONFUSION REIGNS

In 1961, when MLB moved the Washington Senators to Minnesota to become the Minnesota Twins, at the same time it created an expansion team in Washington . . . which was named the Washington Senators. And it so happened that during the "old" Senators' first game in Metropolitan Stadium, their opponents were "new" Senators, who won 5–3. But that's not the end of the story. This "newer" Senators franchise lasted in DC until 1972, when they also moved, this time to Texas, where they became the Texas Rangers. The legendary Ted Williams was their first manager.

TARGET FIELD FIRSTS

FIRST MLB GAME: 4/12/2010, Twins over Boston Red Sox, 5–2

FIRST HOME RUN: 4/12/2010, Jason Kubel vs. Boston Red Sox

FIRST ALL-STAR GAME: 7/15/2014, AL over NL, 5–3

First playoff game: 10/6/2010, NY Yankees over Twins, 6–4

FEATURES AND AMENITIES

The ballpark has a number of fan-pleasing attractions and concessions.

HONORED PLAYERS Outside the stadium, fans enjoy viewing the bronze statues of Hall of Famers Harmon Killebrew, Rod Carew, Kirby Puckett, and Tony Oliva. The Twins own Hall of Fame membership is permanently displayed in the Hall of Fame Gallery on the United Healthcare Suite Level.

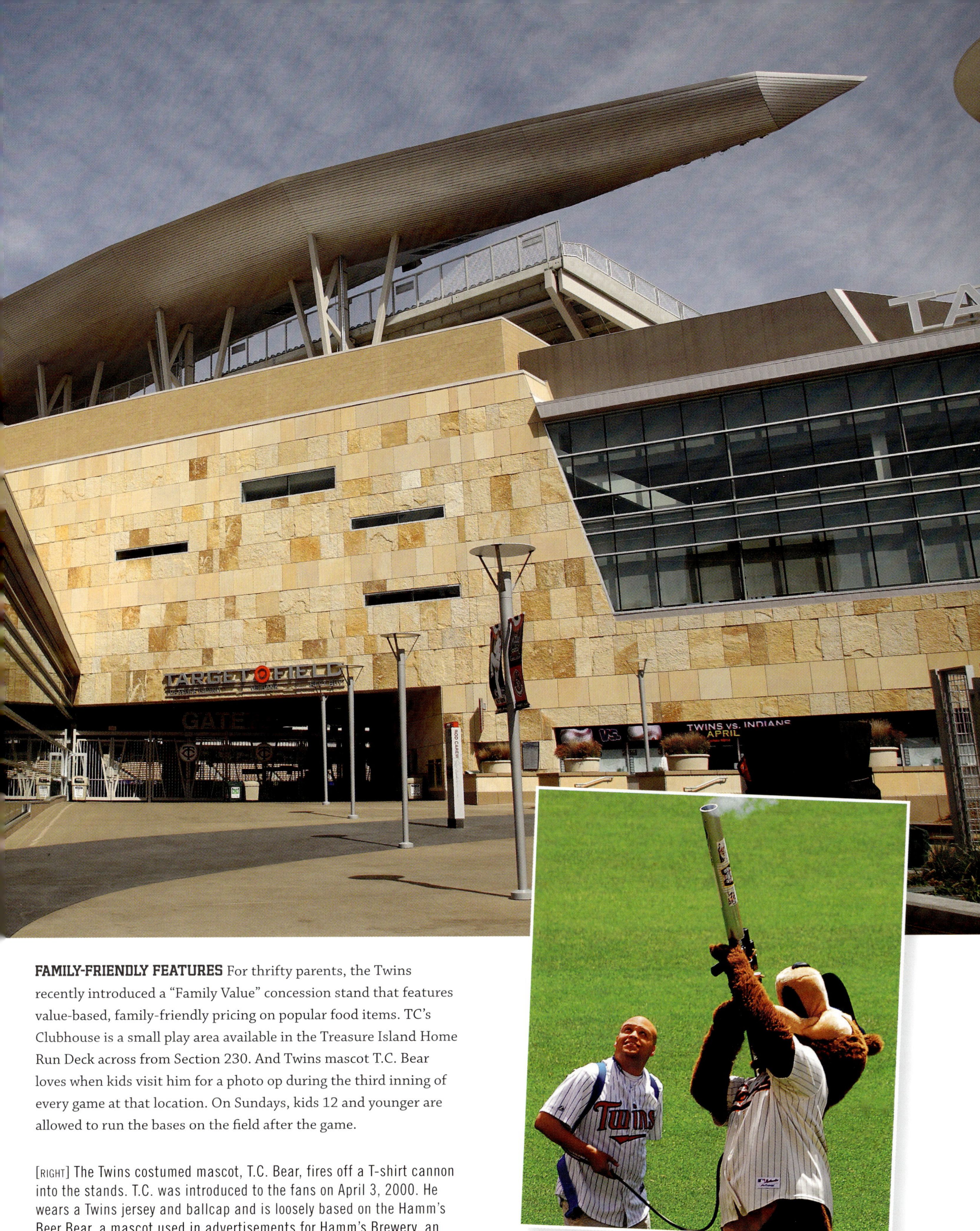

FAMILY-FRIENDLY FEATURES For thrifty parents, the Twins recently introduced a "Family Value" concession stand that features value-based, family-friendly pricing on popular food items. TC's Clubhouse is a small play area available in the Treasure Island Home Run Deck across from Section 230. And Twins mascot T.C. Bear loves when kids visit him for a photo op during the third inning of every game at that location. On Sundays, kids 12 and younger are allowed to run the bases on the field after the game.

[RIGHT] The Twins costumed mascot, T.C. Bear, fires off a T-shirt cannon into the stands. T.C. was introduced to the fans on April 3, 2000. He wears a Twins jersey and ballcap and is loosely based on the Hamm's Beer Bear, a mascot used in advertisements for Hamm's Brewery, an early Twins sponsor. A previous Twins mascot, a loon named Twinkie, lasted only from 1980 to 1981.

[ABOVE] The popular left-field Budweiser roof deck features mostly standing room. Hanging below are the player jersey numbers that have been retired, including Twins Harmon Killebrew (No. 3), Rod Carew (No. 29), Tony Oliva (No. 6), Kent Hrbek (No. 14), Kirby Pucket (No. 34), Bert Blyleven (No. 28), and Tom Kelly (No. 10). Since this image was shot, Joe Mauer (No. 7) and Jim Kaat (No. 36) have been added. On April 15, 1997, while the Twins still played at the Metrodome, Jackie Robinson's No. 42 was retired throughout MLB.

[LEFT] Charlie Brown dons a Twins uniform outside Target Field. His creator, Charles Schulz, was a Minnesota native.

CREATOR'S CORNER In 2023, the Twins and U.S. Bank introduced Creator's Corner, a unique retail space inside Gate 34. It will host three different businesses each year, showcasing entrepreneurs from underserved communities in Twins Territory. The inaugural trio that launched the project were Must Be Ruff from Brooklyn Park, Native Roots Trading Post from St. Paul, and SJC Body Love from St. Paul.

FOOD AND DRINK With more than 40 spots to eat or drink, including sites with specialty menus like Italian, Mexican, Cajun, Indian, Hmong, and vegetarian, Target Field is a diner's delight. Truly On Deck, located on the Club Level in Right Field, is the perfect place to meet for a meal or a drink before, after, or during a game. It offers both indoor and outdoor seating. The popular Budweiser Roof Deck, found in left field, features mainly standing room and boasts the only bonfire in the Major Leagues. Townball Tavern is a burger and sandwich restaurant known for serving cocktails engineered for baseball fans. Keeper's Heart Double Play, anyone?

“You gotta have heart, all you really need is heart . . .”

—INSPIRATIONAL PLAYERS' ANTHEM FROM BROADWAY'S *DAMN YANKEES*

[ABOVE] A statue of Kent Hrbek celebrating the Twins 1987 World Series victory stands outside Target Field's Gate 14 entrance.

[LEFT] On the plaza level, there is the giant “Gold Glove,” a nod to former Twins players to receive this award. The Gold Glove is given annually to the MLB players judged to have exhibited superior individual fielding performances at each fielding position in both the NL and AL.

SEATING CHART

TWINS ACHIEVEMENTS

WORLD SERIES CHAMPIONSHIPS: 2 (1991, 1987)

AL PENNANTS: 6 (1924*, 1925*, 1933*, 1965, 1987, 1991)

AL WEST DIVISION TITLES: 4 (1969, 1970, 1987, 1991)

AL CENTRAL DIVISION TITLES: 9 (2002, 2003, 2004, 2006, 2009, 2010, 2019, 2020, 2023)

WILD CARD BERTHS: 3 (2017, 2020, 2023)

PLAYOFF APPEARANCES: 18 (1924*, 1925*, 1933*, 1965, 1969, 1970, 1987, 1991, 2002, 2003, 2004, 2006, 2009, 2010, 2017, 2019, 2020, 2023)

WORST SEASON RECORD: 1904, 38–113 (.252)*

BEST SEASON RECORD: 1965, 102–60 (.630)

* as Senators

OTHER HOMES OF THE TWINS

METROPOLITAN STADIUM

1961–1981

[ABOVE] Metropolitan Stadium was located where the sprawling Mall of America is today. The Home Plate plaque is placed there in the exact spot where the real thing had sat at the stadium.

[LEFT] Metropolitan Stadium was referred to as the “Met,” “Met Stadium,” or the “Old Met” to distinguish it from the Metrodome.

[BELOW LEFT] Uniformed spectators watch a spring 1972 game during Armed Forces Day at Metropolitan Stadium.

This sprawling venue, located just outside downtown Minneapolis, was the home of the Minnesota Twins for 20 years. During the 1950s, hoping to attract a MLB club, city officials began scouting for a likely site, and in 1955 they acquired a 160-acre (64.7 ha) parcel in Bloomington, Minnesota, at a cost of $458,000. After its completion in 1956, Metropolitan Stadium first housed the minor league Minneapolis Millers, a sports staple of the city for more than seven decades.

The new stadium featured 18,200 seats and a three-tier grandstand, with a press box on the upper deck, which also displayed a row of light towers. The following year, additional seating brought capacity to 21,000, increasing the venue’s appeal to an MLB franchise. Over the next few years a number of MLB games were played there—Calvin Griffith brought his Washington Senators to the stadium and called it “one of the finest in baseball.” This alerted the city to the notion that Griffith might be amenable to a move, and so they courted him over the next two years. Things were not rosy in Washington—attendance was flagging and Griffith Stadium was showing its age. Finally, Griffith was allowed to relocate his team after the 1960 season. The newly christened Twins played their first game at Metropolitan on April 21, 1961, ironically against the new Washington Senators, one of the recent expansion franchises. That same year the stadium welcomed the NFL expansion Minnesota Vikings.

In 1962 and 1965, more construction took place to enlarge the stadium, including a double-decked grandstand in left field that increased seating capacity to just under 48,000. There were also bleachers in right field where the scoreboard was located, and a large section of bleachers ran from third base to the left field foul pole. Still, the Vikings felt constrained by the size of Metropolitan and began looking for an alternative. By the 1970s it was falling into disrepair, and the city realized it needed to act fast to keep its two pro teams in Minneapolis. Another factor was the upcoming merger of the AFL and NFL, which mandated that all pro stadiums have a capacity of 50,000. In light of this, the Minnesota state legislature passed a bill in 1977 that authorized construction of a multipurpose domed stadium. The resulting Hubert H. Humphrey Metrodome, a downtown venue set on 25 acres (10.1 ha), opened April 3, 1982 . . . with a capacity of 55,000 seats.

As a memorial to the fondly remembered Metropolitan Stadium, its original flagpole was installed on Target Plaza.

HUBERT H. HUMPHREY METRODOME
1982–2009

The H.H.H. Metrodome, named after Minnesotan Vice President Hubert H. Humphrey, was only the third domed stadium to open. The 16-story dome consisted of an air-supported, Teflon-coated fiberglass fabric roof that had a 340-ton cover that was stabilized by air-pressure-generated fans as well as steel cables. There were even snow-melting ducts to prevent the structure from collapsing, although it collapsed five times due to snow.

In addition to the 48,678 blue seats that circled the stadium for baseball, the right field wall of the venue was made up of 7,600 retractable seats that allowed the conversion to football. A massive scoreboard/video display sat above the left field upper deck. In 1996 a gathering spot for fans to meet, eat, and drink was added along Kirby Puckett Place.

Starting in the mid-1990s, the Twins began pushing for their own ballpark. Like a number of other ball clubs before them, they felt the multipurpose stadiums favored football, while giving short shrift to baseball. Finally in May 2006, the state okayed financing for a dedicated ballpark. Target Field opened in April 2010 . . . and the Twins at last had their own home.

Meanwhile, on December 12, 2010, a particularly heavy fall of snow tore a hole in the roof of the Metrodome, signaling the eventual—and inevitable—demise of the Vikings' home field. The team played there until the end of the 2013 NFL season, and the stadium was then demolished in the winter of 2014 to free up the site for the Vikings' new venue, U.S. Bank Stadium.

[ABOVE] The Metrodome had several nicknames, including "the Dome," "the Thunderdome," "the Homer Dome," and "the Technodome."

[BELOW] A photo by Bobak Ha'Eri captures the Metrodome after its air-supported roof, made of Teflon-coated fiberglass fabric, tore in two spots and deflated in December 2010 due to a heavy snow burden from the Twin Cities' worst snow storm in over a decade.

HOME OF THE CHICAGO CUBS

NATIONAL LEAGUE (1876–PRESENT)

IT'S NOT SURPRISING *that the second-oldest ballpark in America has taken on legendary status. Home to one of the most beloved—and beleaguered—teams in the Majors, Wrigley Field has nonetheless bolstered the Chicago Cubs, buoying them up during lean times . . . and offering them a celebratory venue when victories came their way.*

The Cubs predecessors, originally known as the White Stockings, began playing in 1870. By 1871 they were located at West Side Grounds, but the team lost its stadium and equipment when the Great Chicago Fire swept through the city. The team finished out their season on the road, but then dropped out of the league while the city attempted to recover. The team eventually began playing at 23rd Street Park, followed by a jockeying back and forth between parks in Chicago's South Side and West Side. The team joined the brand-new National League in 1876, and during the league's first 11 years they finished first six times. Due to the proliferation of young players, the club was frequently referred to by the press as the Colts, Orphans, Infants, and Remnants. When the *Chicago Daily News* began referring to them as the "Cubs," this nickname really caught on among the fans, and it became the official team name in 1907.

In 1906, despite losing the World Series in six games, the Cubs set a Major League record with 116 wins. That is still the best winning percentage in baseball history at 76 percent. They won 107 games in 1907 and went on to win their first World Series. The following year they earned their second Series title. But then the team began to falter. Even their move to Wrigley Field in 1916 didn't give them much of a boost.

Things got really bad after Billy Sianis, the owner of the Billy Goat Tavern, was asked to leave Game 4 of the 1945 World Series with his smelly goat. On the way out, he predicted that the Cubs would never win . . . and thus was born the "Curse of the Billy Goat." During the next two decades the Cubs never finished higher than fifth in the National League. Even winning seasons from 1967 seasons from 1967 to 1969 did not result in a championship. (A black cat appearing on the field of Shea Stadium in 1969 on a day the Mets beat the Cubs started the "black cat curse.") The Curse of the Billy Goat finally ended in 2016, when the Cubs gained a World Series victory over Cleveland.

DESIGN AND CONSTRUCTION

Originally named Weeghman Park (1914–1920) and Cubs Park (1920–1926), Wrigley Field was built on Chicago's North Side community of Lakeview, on the site of a former theological seminary (this may account for why so many people consider it holy ground). Baseball executive and restaurant entrepreneur Charles Weeghman hired his own architect, Zachary Taylor Davis, to design the park. It opened in 1914 as home to Weeghman's Chicago Whales of the Federal League, which unfortunately folded after the 1915 season. Weegham then formed a syndicate, including chewing gum tycoon William Wrigley Jr., to buy the Cubs from owner Charles P. Taft. The Cubs then left the dilapidated West Side Grounds for Wrigley Field.

In 1921, Wrigley himself purchased controlling interest in the team, and in 1927 the venue then called Cubs Park was renamed Wrigley Field. On a related note, the gum magnate owned another Wrigley Field, a Los Angeles ballpark that opened in 1925. Also designed by Zachary Taylor Davis, it was home to Weeghman's farm team, the Los Angeles Angels, and in 1961 it hosted the first season of a Major League expansion team, also called the Los Angeles Angels.

Chicago's Wrigley Field was constructed on an irregular block, with Clark and Addison Streets to the west and south, and Waveland and Sheffield Avenues to the north and east. An upper deck was added in 1927. In 1937, Bill Veeck Jr., son of the club president,

> **"Wrigley, beyond its status as a baseball icon, has an undeniable positive energy all its own, which penetrates all who enter its gates."**
>
> —GABE KAPLER, MLB OUTFIELDER/MANAGER

BALLPARK STATS

ADDRESS
1060 West Addison Street, Chicago, IL 60613

OWNER
Thomas S. Ricketts

OPERATOR
Chicago Cubs

ARCHITECT
Zachary Taylor Davis and Charles G. Davis

CAPACITY
41,649

RECORD BASEBALL ATTENDANCE
47,171 on 8/31/1948 (vs. Brooklyn Dodgers)

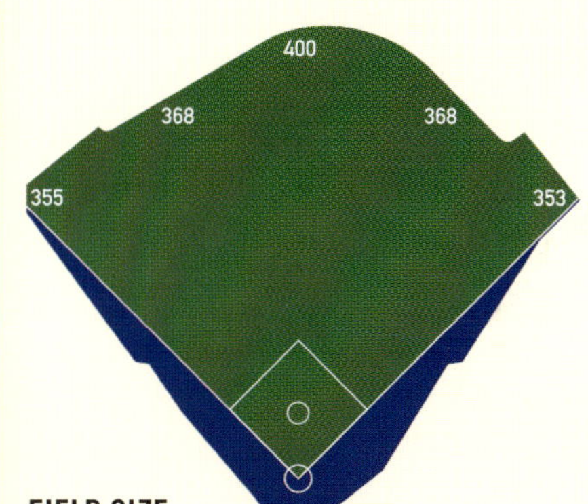

FIELD SIZE

- **Left field** 355 feet (108.2 m)
- **Left-center** 368 feet (112.2 m)
- **Center field** 400 feet (121.9 m)
- **Right-center** 368 feet (112.2 m)
- **Right field** 353 feet (107.6 m)
- **Backstop** 55 feet (16.8 m)
- **Outfield wall height:**
- **Bleachers** 11 feet 6 in (3.5 m)
- **Corners** 15 feet (4.6 m)

SURFACE
Merion bluegrass

TEAM MASCOT
Clark the Cub

[ABOVE AND RIGHT] "Mr. Cub," Hall of Famer Ernie Banks. Also called "Mr. Sunshine," Banks starred as a shortstop and first baseman for the Chicago Cubs between 1953 and 1971.

[BOTTOM RIGHT] A statue of "Sweet Swinging" Billy Williams outside the southeast entrance of the ballpark portrays him finishing his trademark left-handed swing. Lined up near Gallagher Way is Statue Row, which features Williams, along with other Cubs legends Ernie Banks, Ron Santo, Ferguson Jenkins, and Harry Caray. The Cubs plan to honor Hall of Famer Ryne Sandberg in 2024.

In 2016, the stadium's drab exterior of concrete panels was updated to appear the way it did in the 1930s. There would now be terra-cotta roofing on the street-level facade, and ornamental steel grill work topped with sunburst patterns. The green-and-white stadium would again be as attractive on the outside as it had always been from the seats.

Today the ballpark is noted for its ivy-clad brick outfield wall, the hand-turned scoreboard, and the red marquee over the main entrance. And after a Cubs victory, the white "W" flag is still hoisted aloft atop the scoreboard. (Another "feature" that fans have been dealing with since the early days of the stadium is the distinctive

The Wrigley Field home team locker room is ready for the players' arrival.

CUBS ACHIEVEMENTS

WORLD SERIES CHAMPIONSHIPS: 3 (1907, 1908, 2016)

NL PENNANTS: 11 (1906, 1907, 1908, 1910, 1918, 1929, 1932, 1935, 1968, 1945, 2016)

NL EAST DIVISION TITLES: 2 (1984, 1989)

NL CENTRAL DIVISION TITLES: 6 (2003, 2007, 2008, 2016, 2017, 2020)

WILD CARD BERTHS: 3 (1998, 2015, 2018)

PLAYOFF APPEARANCES: 21 (1906, 1907, 1908, 1910, 1918, 1929, 1932, 1935, 1938, 1945, 1984, 1989, 1998, 2003, 2007, 2008, 2015, 2016, 2017, 2018, 2020)

WORST SEASON RECORD: 1962; 1966, 59–103 (.364)

BEST SEASON RECORD: 1906, 116–36 (.763)

wind patterns off Lake Michigan.) These traditional elements continue to add retro character to Wrigley Field, the oldest standing National League field and the only remaining Federal League park. In recognition of its iconic status in the Windy City, the ballpark was designated a National Historic Landmark in 2020.

FEATURES AND AMENITIES

Not surprisingly, this ballpark's features include several exhibits that look back over its long history.

HALL OF FAME The Cubs established their Hall of Fame in 1982, which honored 41 members over the next four years. Nine more members were inducted six years later to the Cubs Walk of Fame. It was paused in 1998, but revived in August 2021, now with a total of 56 commemorative plaques. Induction is open to players, managers, owners, executives, and broadcasters and requires a minimum of five years as a Cub and significant contributions to the franchise. The current exhibit is in the Left Field Budweiser Bleacher concourse.

SEATING CHART

Crowds gather in the stadium's bleachers and on the rooftops surrounding Wrigley Field.

THE C.D. PEACOCK TROPHY ROOM This space houses the 2016 World Series Championship trophy. Open to fans on game days, it is located inside the Marquee Gate entrance.

HONORED PLAYERS Statues that honor outstanding players and announcers are found around the stadium. These include legendary Cubs broadcaster Harry Caray; "Mr. Cub" Ernie Banks, who played shortstop and first base from 1953 to 1971; Billy Williams, the Hall of Famer who played outfield and first base from 1959 to 1974; Ron Santo, the Hall of Famer who played third base from 1960 to 1973 and was a Cubs broadcaster for 21 seasons; and Fergie Jenkins, the Hall of Fame pitcher who played from 1966 to 1973 and 1982 to 1983. The next statue to be installed will be in honor of player, coach, and manager Ryne Sandberg.

WRIGLEYVILLE This former working-class neighborhood on Chicago's North Side surrounds the stadium. These days it is a hub of activity that offers fans a bounty of cool eateries and fine dining, upbeat sports bars and cozy pubs, and plenty of baseball-themed gift shops. The intimate Metro is a concert space for indie or alternative music that has played host to bands like Nirvana and R.E.M.

WRIGLEY ROOFTOPS This name refers to the 16 rooftops of residential buildings that dot the neighborhood of Wrigleyville. These have views looking out over the playing field and have bleachers or seating on them to watch games. Roofs on Waveland Avenue overlook left field, while those along Sheffield Avenue have a view over right field. Fans have watched games from these perches since 1914, but not in significant numbers until the team's popularity surged in the 1980s. Cubs managment wasn't too thrilled when building owners began charging for the seats, but since the early 2000s, rooftop owners and the Cubs have hammered out revenue-sharing agreements.

GALLAGHER WAY Adjacent to Wrigley Field lies Gallagher Way, an open-air space located on Clark Street. This is a destination where family, friends, and neighbors can join together as part of the Wrigleyville experience.

FOOD AND SNACKS When it comes to food and snacks, the ballpark and its surroundings offer a selection of menus and price ranges. Houndstooth Saloon is a massive space for gatherings that is known for its bargain drinks. El Jardin is the place to stop for tacos and margaritas, while Cheba Hut prepares towering sandwiches. A block from the field, Graystone Tavern's enclosed patio is popular for gatherings; it offers drink specials and a Baseball Stadium menu with nachos, popcorn, and pretzels. Almost Home Tavern is a new Wrigleyville eatery that fans need to check out. On Clark Street, try Deuce's Major League Bar for fishbowl cocktails and casual dining, Country Club for their pre-game burger and beer combo, or Yak-Zies Bar & Grill for zesty wings, pizza, cheese curds, and chili.

TEAM STORES The Cubs Team Store is located behind home plate on the main concourse on the first-base side of the Marquee Gate. Cubs Gear stores and kiosks are located at Section 107–108, at Section 133–138, and in the lower level of the Budweiser Bleachers. New Era Team stores and kiosks are found in Section 104 and the upper level of the Budweiser Bleachers.

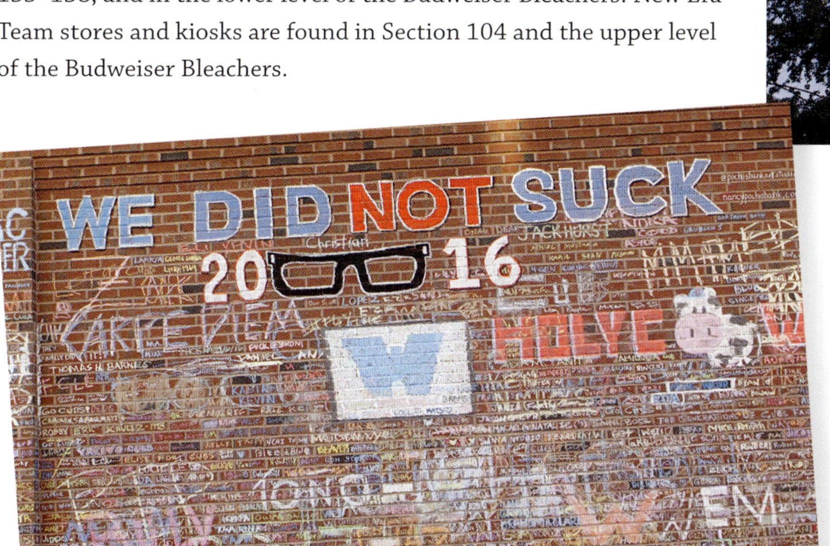

[ABOVE] NIke captured the mood of Chicago after the Cubs' 2016 World Series victory broke the 108-year drought with the simple "Good Bye Someday" TV spots, other ads, and billboards all over town. These were bidding farewell to the "Someday" mantra that had long consoled fans, along with the dreaded Curse of the Billy Goat.

[LEFT] Fans covered Wrigley Field's exterior outfield brick walls with chalk artwork and messages as postseason memorials after the World Series win. The organization thanked its loyal fans, saying, "You have developed what we hope will become a Wrigley Field postseason tradition. . . . We also are very appreciative of the use of chalk, which produces a creative and colorful display that does not damage our historic brick walls, which include bricks dating back to the 1920s."

EARLY CHICAGO FIELDS

During the formative years of the Cubs and their predecessors, the Chicago White Stockings, they played in a number of different parks, some with the same name. When the White Stockings were founded in 1870, their fields included Ogden Park (on Ontario Street near Lake Michigan on the city's North Side) and Dexter Park (next to the Union Stock Yards on the South Side). Neither site was very satisfactory: Ogden Park had no benches or seats, and Dexter Park was actually a horse racing track, with a baseball diamond located outside the track oval. It was also too far from the city for easy travel.

In 1871, the City of Chicago leased part of Lake Park to the ball club for a new field. White Stocking Grounds, also known as Union Base-Ball Grounds or Lakefront Park, saw only a few months of use before it was consumed by the Great Chicago Fire in October, which also destroyed the homes of most of the players. In 1872, the newly formed Chicago Base Ball Association staged games on their new field, 23rd Street Grounds, also called State Street Grounds. In 1874, the White Stockings finally reformed and began to play there.

In 1878, the team was offered a ballpark at the same location they had played on before the fire. Called Lake Front Park, Lake Shore Park, or Lake Park—and dubbed Grant Park in 1901—the field was home to the team until Al Spalding of the Chicago Ball Club relocated them to the new West Side Park. This could have been a permanent venue for the former White Stockings, now called the Colts, but in 1882, their management moved them to South Side Park, where attendance would be higher. In 1893, millions of visitors flocked to Chicago's World's Columbian Exhibition, also located in the South Side, and the team hoped many of them would flock to the ballpark as well. The first West Side Park was sold to finance a new version of West Side Park, or West Side Grounds, which opened in May 1893. It became the Colt's new home that same year, and they remained there until their move to Weeghman Park—later Wrigley Field—in 2016. West Side Park II (*above*) saw some incredible action from the team—from 1906 through 1910, the newly christened Cubs won four National League pennants and two World Series championships. The next time they won a World Series, it would be 108 years later.

Angel Stadium • Los Angeles Angels

Chase Field • Arizona Diamondbacks

Coors Field • Colorado Rockies

Dodger Stadium • Los Angeles Dodgers

Globe Life Field • Texas Rangers

Minute Maid Park • Houston Astros

WEST DIVISION

NATIONAL LEAGUE WEST • Arizona Diamondbacks • Colorado Rockies • Los Angeles Dodgers • San Diego Padres • San Francisco Giants

AMERICAN LEAGUE WEST • Houston Astros • Los Angeles Angels • Oakland Athletics • Seattle Mariners • Texas Rangers

These new divisions were created after MLB expanded in 1969 and split the National and American Leagues into two divisions each.

THE AMERICAN LEAGUE WEST had only four teams from 1994 to 2012, as opposed to other divisions that had five or six teams. But in 2013 the Houston Astros joined this division, resulting in six divisions of five teams each. The AL West standings are often unpredictable, with no clear star, but rather a variety of teams rising to top of the division in recent years. The Los Angeles Angels, Astros, Texas Rangers, Seattle Mariners, and Oakland Athletics have all experienced sustained, successful runs.

THE NATIONAL LEAGUE WEST was created in 1969, when the National League expanded to 12 teams by adding the San Diego Padres and Montreal Expos to their roster. The league ended up putting half the teams in the East Division and half in the new West Division. The NL West is one of the more predictable divisions in the baseball standings, with the Los Angeles Dodgers as the division powerhouse. Their competition includes the San Diego Padres, the Colorado Rockies, the Arizona Diamondbacks, and the San Francisco Giants.

Oakland–Alameda County Coliseum • (former) Oakland Athletics

Oracle Park • San Francisco Giants

Petco Park • San Diego Padres

T-Mobile Park • Seattle Mariners

HOME OF THE LOS ANGELES ANGELS

AMERICAN LEAGUE (1961–PRESENT)

BUILT IN ANAHEIM, CALIFORNIA, *in 1966, Angel Stadium is the fourth-oldest active ballpark to host MLB games after Fenway Park (1912), Wrigley Stadium (1914), and Dodger Stadium (1962). Its affectionate nickname, "the Big A," which was originally coined when the venue was called Anaheim Stadium, currently applies to the shape of the scoreboard.*

The Major League Los Angeles Angels were founded in 1960 by popular singing cowboy Gene Autry, who had become wealthy through his movies and many record-breaking hit songs, including the first ever Gold Record. Autry was a minority owner in the Pacific Coast League Hollywood Stars and was interested in branching out into the Majors. The Angels were one of two early expansion teams and the first originating in California—the other was the second incarnation of the Washington Senators. The team's name was derived from another ball club in the Pacific Coast League, the Los Angeles Angels, who were at that time the top farm team of the Chicago Cubs. They played in a field named after their owner, chewing gum magnate William Wrigley Jr., who also owned the Cubs. Autry's Angels actually spent their first season in the LA version of Wrigley Field. Then, from 1962 to 1965, they shared the new Dodger Stadium in Chavez Ravine with their crosstown rivals.

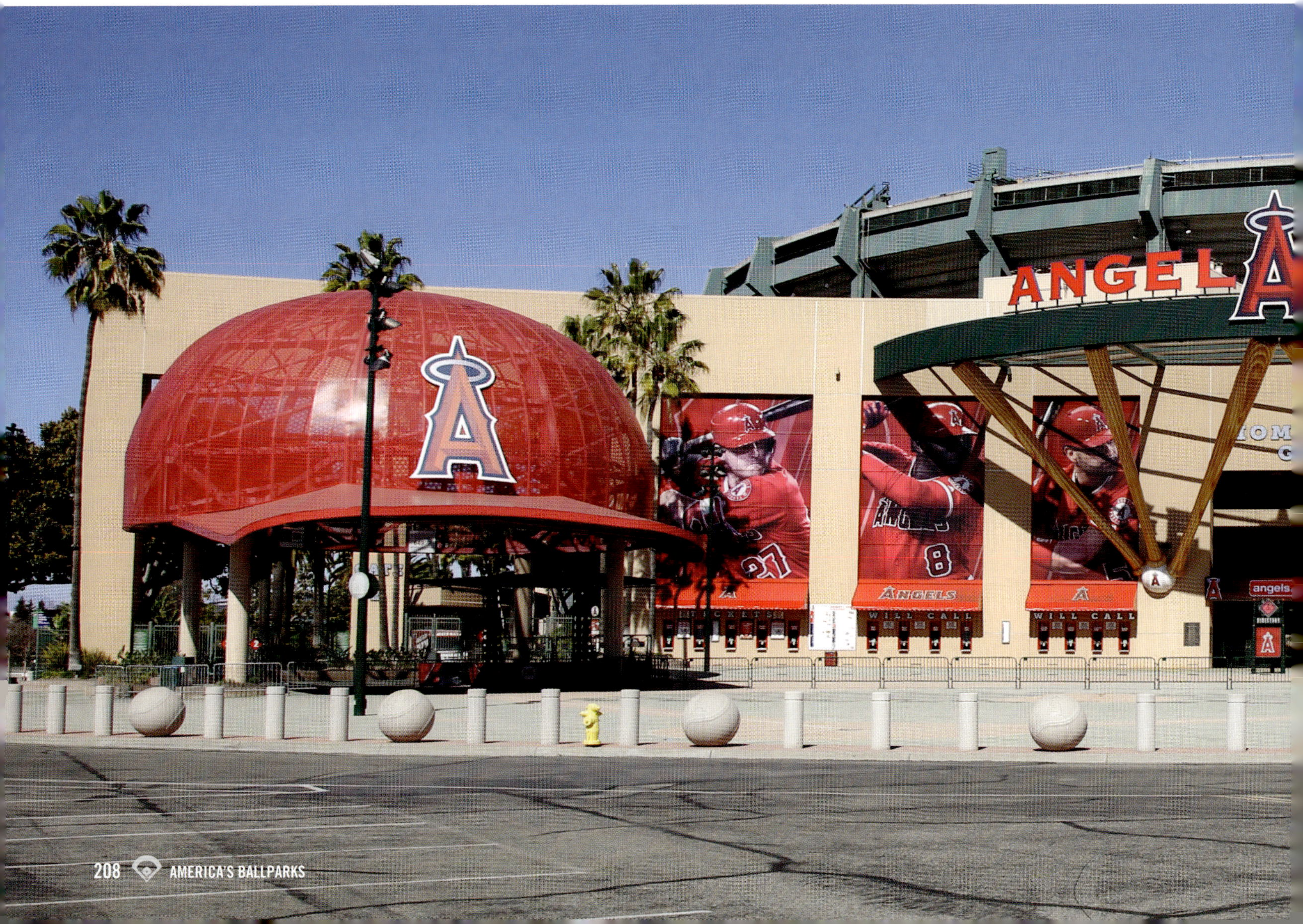

Singing cowboy and film star Gene Autry was the founding owner of the Major League Baseball club, then called the California Angels.

Several fantastic seasons at their temporary quarters highlighted their need for a ballpark of their own. Finally, in 1966, the team got their wish and moved to the new Anaheim Stadium. It had a seating capacity of 43,204, which was later modified to 43,250. The first ball game held there was an exhibition match between the Angels and the San Francisco Giants on April 9, 1966. Their first American League game was April 19, 1966, against the Chicago White Sox, whom they beat.

BALLPARK STATS

ADDRESS
2000 East Gene Autry Way, Anaheim, CA 92806

FORMER NAMES
Anaheim Stadium (1966–1997)
Edison International Field of Anaheim (1998–2003)

OWNER
City of Anaheim

OPERATOR
Angels Baseball LP

ARCHITECT
Noble W. Herzberg and Associates (1966); HOK Sport; Robert A. M. Stern

CAPACITY
45,517

RECORD BASEBALL ATTENDANCE
64,406 on 10/5/1982 (ALCS Game 1 vs. Brewers)

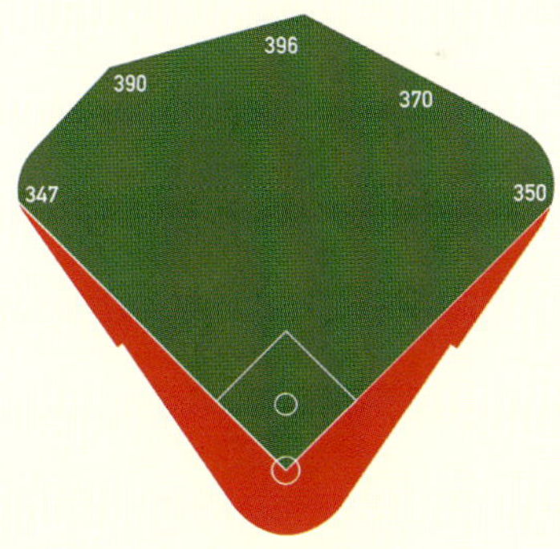

FIELD SIZE
- **Left field** 347 feet (105.8 m)
- **Left-center** 390 feet (118.9 m)
- **Center field** 396 feet (120.7 m)
- **Right-center** 370 feet (112.8 m)
- **Right-center** (shallow) 365 feet (111.3 m)
- **Right field** 350 feet (106.7 m)
- **Backstop** 60.5 feet (18.4 m)

SURFACE
Tifway 419 Bermuda grass

TEAM MASCOT
The Rally Monkey

HOME OF THE CALIFORNIA ANGELS

A 1967 postcard shows the brand-new ballpark, then called Anaheim Stadium.

ANGEL STADIUM FIRSTS

FIRST MLB GAME: 4/19/1966, Chicago White Sox over Angels, 3–1*

FIRST HOME RUN: 4/19/1966, Rick Reichardt vs. Chicago White Sox*

FIRST NO-HITTER: 7/3/1970, Clyde Wright vs. Oakland Athletics*

FIRST ALL-STAR GAME: 7/11/1967, NL over AL, 2–1*

FIRST PLAYOFF GAME: 10/5/1979, Angels over Baltimore Orioles, 4–3*

FIRST WORLD SERIES GAME: 10/20/2002, Angels over San Francisco Giants, 11–10 in Game 2†

* as Anaheim Stadium † as Edison International Field of Anaheim

In the mid-1970s, the NFL Los Angeles Rams began looking for a new venue. After playing at the Los Angeles Coliseum for more than 30 years, the Rams were upset that their home stadium would not add luxury suites. They finally announced that they would be moving to Anaheim. To accommodate the arrival of the Rams, the stadium underwent construction, including being enclosed, in 1979 and 1980. Upon completion of the project in 1981, the stadium seating had expanded to 65,158, later 64,593.

DESIGN AND CONSTRUCTION

The ballpark was built at a cost of $24 million and was located in a suburban neighborhood between Katella Avenue to the north and the Orange Freeway to the east. There was not much around the facility except highways, office buildings, and parking lots.

When approaching the home plate entrance to the ballpark, fans walk between two oversized helmets. Within this space are bricks outlining a regulation-size infield, with a pitcher's mound exactly 60 feet, 6 inches (18.44 m) from home plate. This is a favorite spot for fan photos.

The walls inside Angel Stadium display images of various Angels players, both present and past. Team merchandise shops are located throughout the various sections of the stadium, and the main concourse wraps around the outfield, offering fans a great view of the action on the field.

UPDATES AND RENOVATIONS

On October 1, 1996, after the Rams departed for St. Louis, Missouri, work began at Anaheim Stadium to return the 30-year-old structure to a baseball-only facility. A number of companies were enlisted in the project: Walt Disney Imagineering—a division of the Walt Disney Company that owned the Angels at that time—served as the manager of the design and construction; HOK Sports Facilities Group (now Populous) and Robert A. M. Stern Architects oversaw the architectural planning, design, and renovation; and Turner Construction directed and provided construction services.

During this phase the exterior of the stadium was also refreshed. The concrete structure and ramps were painted a combination of deep green and sandstone, while much of the facade was torn down to provide a more open aspect for visitors. Perhaps the most memorable part of this renovation was the water feature in center field, a rock fountain where geysers erupt and a stream cascades down a mountainside adorned with real trees. This waterfall, which reflects California's pride in its wild spaces, flows over a rugged rock formation in the shape of an "A." It also features pyrotechnics that go off during player introductions and after Angel home runs and wins.

[ABOVE] The Rally Monkey rallies Angels fans.

[RIGHT] Rally Monkey plushies, which fans wear to games. The Angels' mascot, introduced to fans in 2000, was based on a clip from the 1994 movie *Ace Ventura: Pet Detective*. The ball club even hired a similar white-haired capuchin monkey named Katie to star in the entertaining Jumbotron videos.

[BELOW] A reminder of the stadium's Disney days, a colorful statue of Mickey Mouse dressed in an Angels' baseball uniform greets visitors at the entrance of to the stadium.

On September 15, 1997, the franchise announced that the renovated stadium would be called Edison International Field of Anaheim. This reflected a 20-year, $50 million naming rights deal with the utility company. The total cost for the renovation was roughly $100 million, and the project was completed in time for the Angels' Opening Day, April 1, 1998. After the 2003 season, Edison International exercised its option to exit the sponsorship deal, so on December 29, 2003, the Angels announced that the stadium would henceforth be known as Angel Stadium, or more properly, Angel Stadium of Anaheim. The Walt Disney Company sold their interest in the Angels around this time as well.

[RIGHT] Angels manager Bill Rigney is flanked by Disney characters Goofy and Mickey Mouse at the groundbreaking ceremonies for Anaheim Stadium.

In addition to baseball and pro football, the stadium has hosted high school and college football, soccer matches, the short-lived World Football League, two crusades by evangelist Billy Graham, 20 consecutive annual crusades by evangelist Greg Laurie, Eid el Fitr celebrations, concerts, Monster Jams, and two to three AMA Supercross Championship races a year. The stadium also houses the studios and offices of the Angels' flagship radio station, KLAA (830 AM).

As for the ballpark's future, the Angels' lease on the stadium will expire in 2029. It is likely the team will remain in Anaheim, but whether or not the franchise will end up in a new stadium has not been determined.

FEATURES AND AMENITIES

Angel Stadium is said to be home to some of the most welcoming fans in the Majors. And while it might be lacking modern touches found in other ballparks of the post Camden Yards era, the stadium's size ensures that visitors are never too far from the action. Plus the stadium's interior offers a number of historical exhibits.

ANGELS MEMORABILIA The team's 2002 World Series Trophy and other Angels memorabilia are on display inside the entrance to the team store beyond the main gate. There are also other exhibits that highlight player and team accomplishments that can be viewed in the field and terrace level concourse.

FAN MESSAGES Angel Bricks, inscribed with messages from fans or memorials for loved ones, are a permanent fixture in the entry diamond of Angel Stadium.

[ABOVE] Cement baseballs inscribed with the Angels insignia line the front entrance of the stadium, while giant baseball caps provide shade.

[OPPOSITE PAGE] The Angels are nicknamed "the Halos." A halo is featured on the towering "A" outside the stadium, and it is part of the team logo.

[BELOW] Twilight softens the skies over a 2019 game.

ANGELS ACHIEVEMENTS

WORLD SERIES CHAMPIONSHIPS: 1 (2002)

AL PENNANTS: 1 (2002)

AL WEST DIVISION TITLES: 9 (1979, 1982, 1986, 2004, 2005, 2007, 2008, 2009, 2014)

WILD CARD BERTHS: 1 (2002)

PLAYOFF APPEARANCES: 10 (1979*, 1982*, 1986*, 2002, 2004, 2005, 2007, 2008, 2009, 20014)

WORST SEASON RECORD: 1980, 65–95 (.406)

BEST SEASON RECORD: 2008, 100–62 (.617)

* as California Angels

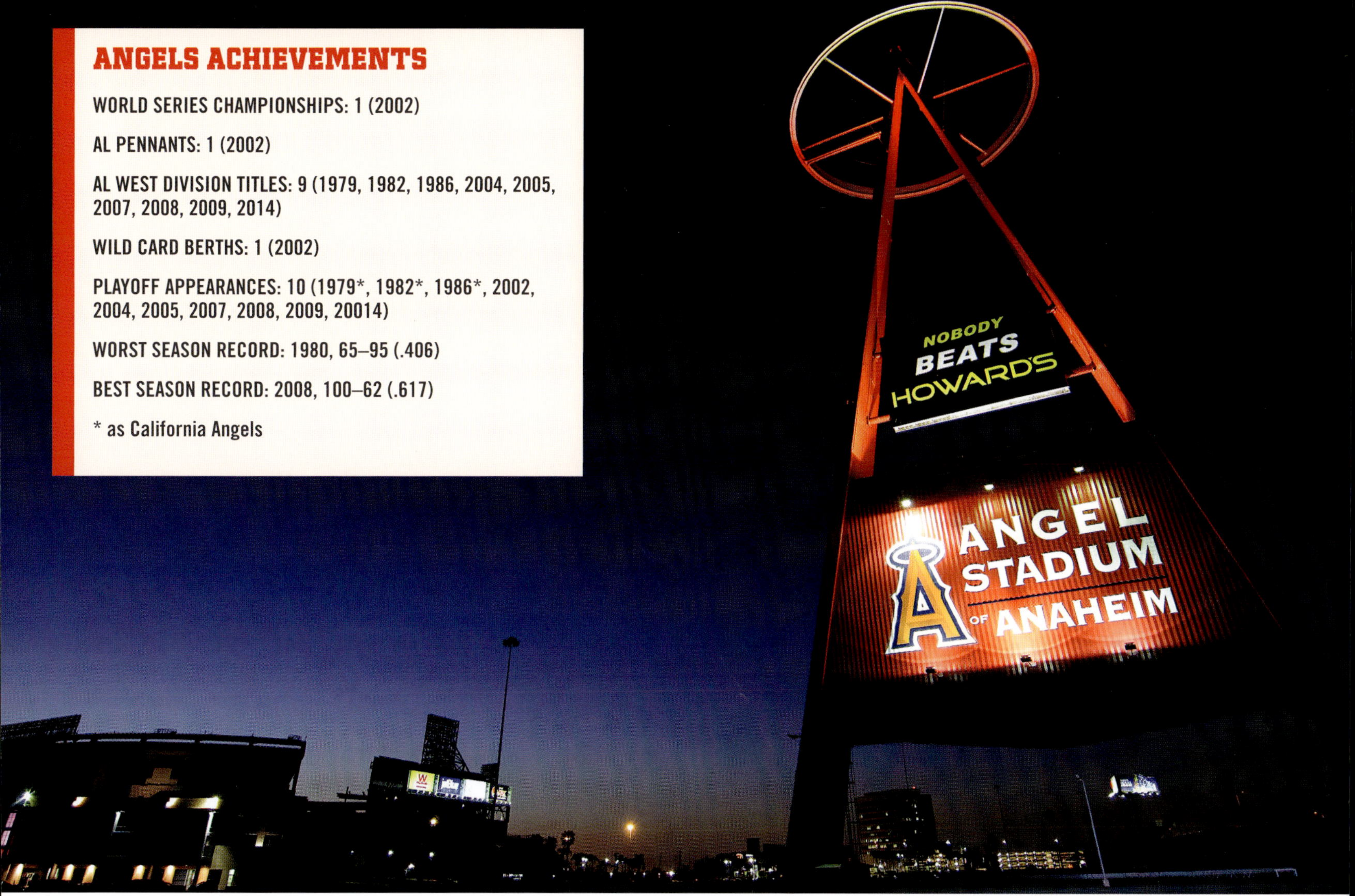

> **"Disneyland and Disneyworld, that was their world. The quirky part of Angel Stadium is the outfield. We set that aside for them, and they came up with the look and feel."**
>
> —EARL SANTEE, POPULOUS ARCHITECT, ON THE CREATION OF THE ROCKPILE

[ABOVE] The center-field Rock Pile gives the ballpark a Disneyland-style quirk, which seems fitting given its proximity to the "happiest place on Earth."

[OPPOSITE PAGE] Six gigantic baseball bats balance on baseballs to hold up the marquee at the stadium's home plate entrance.

ROCK PILE A truly notable feature of this ballpark is the Rock Pile, also known as the California Spectacular. This Disney-imagined sculpture was installed behind the left-center field fence during renovations. The rock formation is adorned with fake boulders, real trees, dancing fountains, and a geyser that spouts water.

STADIUM TOURS Tours of Angel Stadium take place at 10:30 a.m., 12:30 p.m., and 2:30 p.m. on select days while the Angels are on the road. Highlights of the 75-minute tour may include a trip down to the field, a visit into the Angels dugout, a walk through the visitors' clubhouse, access to the Clubhouse Press Conference Room, and an exclusive look at the Gene Autry Suite, broadcast booth, and a Dugout Suite. Pregame tours allow fans to experience an exclusive introduction to Angel Stadium before the start of the game. This tour runs for approximately 60 minutes and may include visits to the Courtyard statues, World Series and MVP trophy cases, a photo op behind the center field rocks, and early entry into the stadium to watch the Angels at batting practice or warm-up exercises.

DOWNTOWN DISNEY This area offers a variety of dining destinations and shopping opportunities and is only a short drive from the stadium. While visiting Downtown Disney guests are able to view the nightly fireworks display that takes place inside Disneyland during the summer.

DINING OPTIONS For hungry fans, dining options include sit-down restaurants like Brewery X and La Rotisserie, as well as a food court and plenty of snack concessions. Stadium-goers can nosh on tacos, nachos, chicken tenders, vegan dishes, hot dogs, burgers, sausages and brats, pizza, loaded potatoes, and hot and cold sandwiches.

SEATING CHART

CONFLICTING NAMES

The team's name has seen a number of variations over the years—in 1965 the Los Angeles Angels were renamed the California Angels. When the Walt Disney Company took control of the team in 1997, it renovated Anaheim Stadium, which was then called Edison International Field of Anaheim. The City of Anaheim contributed $30 million to the $118 million renovation, with the understanding that the names of both the stadium and team contain the word "Anaheim." The team became the Anaheim Angels and the ballpark was dubbed Anaheim Stadium. In 2005, new owner Arturo Moreno added Los Angeles to the name, and the team was officially called the Los Angeles Angels of Anaheim. A lawsuit brought by fans and both cities objecting to the clunky name was eventually dropped. The team typically refers to itself as the Angels or Angels Baseball in the media, and the words "Los Angeles" never appear in the stadium or on team merchandise. Furthermore, the uniforms traditionally say just "Angels," with no mention of a city or state. Since 2016 the team has been commonly referred to as the Los Angeles Angels.

HOME OF THE ARIZONA DIAMONDBACKS

NATIONAL LEAGUE (1998–PRESENT)

THE ARIZONA DIAMONDBACKS, *one of the National League West's expansion teams, play at Chase Field in Phoenix. Debuting in 1999, they entered the new millennium as their division champs. In spite of an up-and-down record, the team keeps fans coming back to Chase for more of that "snake juice."*

The Arizona Diamondbacks ball club was established on March 9, 1995, when the city of Phoenix was awarded an expansion franchise that would begin play in 1998. After a fee of $130 million was paid to MLB, the team was voted into the National League on January 16, 1997. The name Diamondbacks, inspired by the indigenous western diamondback rattlesnake, was chosen from among thousands of name contest entries. The team's first Major League game was played against the Colorado Rockies on March 31, 1998, at Bank One Ballpark, later Chase Field.

The "D-backs" are one of the newest baseball teams along with the Tampa Bay Rays. And although they may have been a recent addition to the Majors, they left the starting gate at a run—racking up one Wild Card series, five NL West Division titles, two NL pennants, and the 2001 World Series by defeating the Yankees in Game 7, thus becoming the youngest team in MLB history to clinch the title. In 2023 they again made it to the Series, falling to the Texas Rangers 4 games to 1, with their final game played at home.

The Diamondbacks' stadium, Bank One Ballpark, opened in 1998, just in time to welcome its new tenants. The naming rights had been purchased by Bank One of Chicago, Illinois, for $100 million over 30 years., but when Bank One merged with New York's JPMorgan Chase and Co. in 2005, the stadium became Chase Field. It could be said that the Diamondbacks love their stadium, and in some seasons it's to the point where their hitting record at home is notably higher than while they are on the road.

The stadium has been the site of pop music concerts, including acts like Elton John, Black Sabbath, Billy Joel, Kenny Chesney, NSYNC, Pink, and Bad Bunny. It has also been the site of international soccer games. To accommodate both football and soccer, the field is configured so that the end lines are perpendicular to the third-base line, and temporary bleacher seating is set up on the east side of the field.

Chase Field has also hosted first-round games in the 2006 and 2013 World Baseball Classic tournaments and hosted first-round games in the 2023 tournament, which had been postponed from 2021 due to the COVID-19 lockdown. Starting in 2000, the organizers of the Insight.com Bowl moved the game from Tucson's Arizona Stadium to Phoenix beginning in 2000, and Chase Field became the game's venue. Chase Field has staged nine women's college basketball games and hosted an annual "Challenge at Chase," a college baseball game series between Arizona State and the University of Arizona that lasted two years. The Arizona Wildcats were the victors in both contests. Other events held at Chase include Professional Bull Riders competitions, Supercross Monster Jams, and a WWE Royal Rumble.

BALLPARK STATS

ADDRESS
401 East Jefferson Street, Phoenix, AZ 85004

FORMER NAME
Bank One Ballpark (1998–2005)

OWNER
Maricopa County Stadium District

OPERATOR
SMG

ARCHITECT
Ellerbe Becket; Wyatt/Rhodes; Castillo Company; Cox James

CAPACITY
48,405

RECORD BASEBALL ATTENDANCE
50,180 on 8/31/2019 (vs. LA Dodgers)

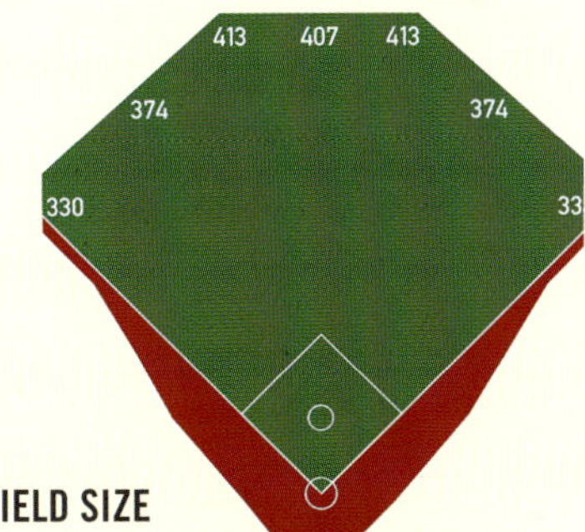

FIELD SIZE

- **Left field** 330 feet (101 m)
- **Left-center** 374 feet (114 m)
- **Left-center** (deep) 413 feet (126 m)
- **Center field** 407 feet (124 m)
- **Right-center** (deep) 413 ft (126 m)
- **Right-center** 374 feet (114 m)
- **Right field** 334 feet (102 m)

SURFACE
Shaw Sports B1K

TEAM MASCOT
D. Baxter the Bobcat

CLOSE-UP

THE AGE OF CORPORATE BRANDING

The concept of a business, company, or corporation paying a sports team or athlete to promote their interests is not new. This method of generating revenue goes back to the 1870s, when famous athletes were employed to tout various products. For instance, baseball players endorsed cigarettes or other tobacco products on trading cards, which are still collected today.

By the dawn of the 20th century, many businesses understood the wisdom of having professional teams and popular athletes connected to their brand, with Coca Cola paving the way by advertising at the 1928 Olympic Games. For their 1932 Summer Olympics sponsorship, the soda company distributed three million miniature cutouts of Olympic athletes, with a history of Olympic records on the back. A larger cut-out was displayed in store windows across the host city of Los Angeles.

Ballparks and their sponsors also generated income by prominently displaying advertising signs on the fences of the ball field. Early sponsors included tobacco companies, breweries, distilleries, insurance companies, candy-makers, restaurant chains, watchmakers, men's shaving products, tire companies, and gas stations. Today, not only are ads in Major League stadiums posted in the outfield, they are flashed on giant screens or scrolled across LED signs. While tens of thousands of spectators in the stands view them, so do millions of people watching on network television, cable, or streaming channels.

Other ways that ballparks allow sponsors to benefit include giveaways, logos placed on food and drinks, and replays and plays sponsored by specific companies.

THE RISE OF MEDIA MARKETING

With the growing popularity of radio shows in America and the subsequent rise of television, sports marketing took a huge leap forward. Radio's first sports broadcast was a 1921 boxing match between Johnny Ray and Dundee, while the first sporting event to be televised was a 1939 college baseball game between Ivy Leaguers Princeton and Columbia. The surge of

[TOP] Early example of a cigarette card showing Capt. Jack Glasscock, who played shortstop in Major League Baseball for several teams from 1879 to 1895.

[LEFT] In 1933 the Goudey Gum Company began to issue baseball cards with each stick of gum.

[BELOW] A 1955 Topps baseball card depicting Hall of Fame player Ted Williams with the Boston Red Sox. In 1952, Topps had introduced its first baseball cards, which included a player's name, photo, facsimile autograph, team name, and logo on the front, and the player's height, weight, bats, throws, birthplace, birthday, and stats, and a short bio on the back. They took off with the baseball fan base and the cards became highly collectible. The basic design is still in use today.

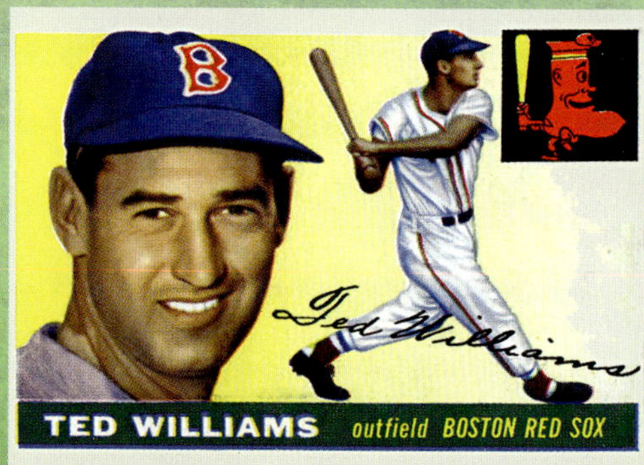

interest in these media debuts was not lost on corporate heads, and as broadcast technology improved, sports coverage created more openings for advertising and product placement. The sports marketing industry subsequently grew more sophisticated and increasingly more profitable.

It might be said that professional athletes were some of the earliest "influencers"—swaying the purchasing decisions of their many fans. Certain brands of cigarettes were praised by the likes of baseball legends Babe Ruth, Joe DiMaggio, and Ted Williams. DiMaggio also famously plugged for Mr. Coffee brewing machines. Athletes also became a familiar sight on boxes of the General Mills breakfast cereal Wheaties, especially baseball and football players.

The late 20th century saw the emergence of the sports superstar as corporate spokesperson. Entire media campaigns were formulated around these icons. Some of the more entertaining ads are still fondly recalled today, like Nike's tongue-in-cheek "Bo Knows" campaign featuring baseball and football Hall of Famer Bo Jackson.

[RIGHT] A 1938 Wheaties box front shows "Lefty' Grove of the Boston Red Sox. With its memorable "The Breakfast of Champions" slogan, General Mills Wheaties cereal is known for its images of sports stars on the front of a bright orange box. Wheaties' first association with sports came in 1927 with the typical outdoor ads at minor league baseball's Nicollet Park in Minneapolis. In 1934, baseball's Lou Gehrig became the first athlete depicted on a Wheaties box.

[BELOW] Advertising signs surround the grandstands during a 1920s World Series game at New York's Polo Grounds. Since baseball's earliest days, local businesses have used this space to sell their wares.

SWAYING THE FANS

If a ballpark advertisement is done properly, it will get the fans to think about the product past the time it takes them to read it. But ad placement is critical—the most effective advertisements are the ones that both stadium spectators and the home viewers can see. The most coveted ad spot is behind home plate, but the cost can be high; for instance, $750,000 at Camden Yards.

[ABOVE] Busch Stadium was a compromise name when the then baseball commissioner rejected the name "Budweiser Stadium."

[TOP RIGHT] An example of a long-term naming rights deal is Colorado's Coors Field. Coors Brewing purchased naming rights to the stadium as part of their $30 million investment in the Rockies in 1991 that will last through 2047.

[BOTTOM RIGHT] One of the problems of naming rights is that deals have expiration dates. The Milwaukee Brewers called their home Miller Park until 2020, before a new deal was struck with American Family Insurance. Although these deals are lucrative for the ballparks, fans often object to changes to their beloved stadiums.

THE DAWN OF NAMING RIGHTS

While product promotion enriched specific players or athletes, the idea of companies "branding" sports stadiums with their names would eventually offer a windfall to many franchises. This practice possibly started in 1912, with the naming of the new home of the Boston Red Sox, Fenway Park. The stadium's owner, John I. Taylor, also owned a realty company called Fenway Realty—named for a stretch of local parkland—and the stadium's name certainly helped promote this other business. Perhaps a more typical case of corporate branding—using the names of owners or founders—occurred in 1926, when William Wrigley Jr., chewing gum tycoon and owner of the Chicago Cubs, lent his name to his team's stadium, Wrigley Field. Similarly, in 1953, August Busch Jr., head of Anheuser-Busch Brewing and owner of the St. Louis Cardinals, first proposed changing Sportsman's Park to Budweiser Stadium. When baseball commissioner Ford C. Frick rejected the idea, the name Busch Stadium was submitted . . . and accepted. Then came Coors Field in Denver and Miller Park in Milwaukee, both named for companies that were investors in or sponsors of those franchises. An early example of a team selling naming rights to an outside corporation was the NFL New England Patriot's Foxboro Stadium, which was called Schaefer Stadium from its opening up to 1983.

These naming rights deals became increasingly common in the United States, but branded stadiums can also be found in Australia, Japan, China, Finland, Canada, Israel, and Germany. Even the tradition-loving United Kingdom has witnessed this trend—Arsenal Football Club's Arsenal Stadium became Emirates Stadium, and the Surrey County Cricket Club's famous Oval has had a series of corporate sponsors. It is currently known as the Kia Oval.

Fan reactions to corporate naming is understandably mixed. Branding seems to work best with new stadiums, where the fan base has never known the venue by another name. But with established fields, like San Francisco's Candlestick Park, the change to 3Com Park was never accepted by the public, who continued to use the former name. Another problem is that when one naming rights contract runs out, a new sponsor may appear, adding a level of confusion to the "identity" of the venue. Candlestick Park went from 3Com Park to Monster Park after cable company Monster Inc. bought the rights. In 2004, city voters passed an initiative that the name revert to Candlestick once that contract ran out, but, sadly, the ballpark was closed and demolished in 2014, still bearing the name Monster Park.

As of 2023, nine ballparks do not have corporate naming rights deals: Angel Stadium, Dodger Stadium, Boston's Fenway Park, Kansas City's Kauffman Stadium, Nationals Park, the Athletics' former Oakland-Alameda County Coliseum, Oriole Park at Camden Yards, the Chicago Cub's Wrigley Field, and Yankee Stadium.

BAD ASSOCIATIONS

Most often, naming rights offer a boon to a sports franchise. But sometimes the sponsors' brand or name loses its luster. This was the case with the Houston Astros in 1999, when they sold naming rights to their beautiful new stadium to a Houston energy company in a 30-year, $100 million deal. The company's CEO and chairman, Ken Lay, even threw out the ballpark's ceremonial first pitch. The energy giant was called Enron, and in 2001 it famously went bust due to massive corporate fraud. The Astros eventually bought the naming rights back from Enron for $2.1 million and sold them to Minute Maid for an estimated $100 million plus over 28 years.

HOW MANY AND HOW MUCH?

Roughly 95 percent of all American sports facilities constructed since 1990 have a naming rights deal. The fees run from $4 million to over $200 million, with the length of the agreements ranging from 5 to 31 years. In Major League Baseball there are currently 21 teams with corporate naming rights. One earlier venue, Wrigley Field, does not offer rights, but does bear its original "corporate" family name. Pundits point out that naming rights for Wrigley Field would hold little "brand association" value, since Chicago Cubs fans would never call the beloved venue by any other name.

"Step up to the plate. Out of left field. Come off the bench . . . Playing hardball. Are we talking baseball or business? Or both?"

—AMERICANMARKETING.COM

1995–PRESENT

COORS FIELD

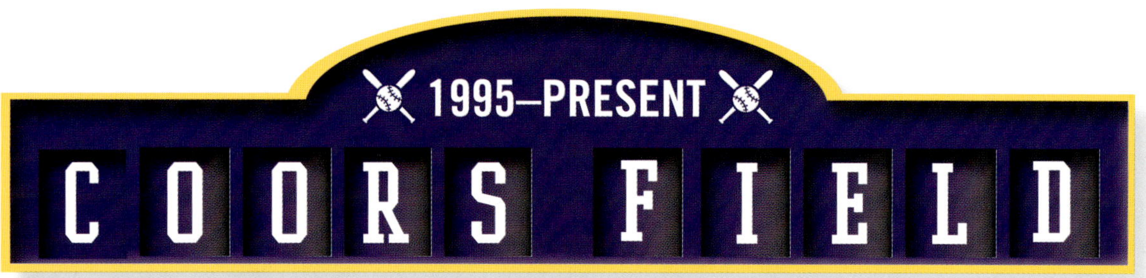

HOME OF THE COLORADO ROCKIES

NATIONAL LEAGUE (1993–PRESENT)

THE COLORADO ROCKIES, *members of the National League West, are a scrappy, underdog expansion team that plays baseball in Coors Field, a stately "throwback" stadium that reflects the rich heritage of the team's hometown of Denver. There is even a row of purple seats in the stadium that serve as a "mile-high" marker in honor of the city.*

Denver's long history with minor league baseball goes back 130 years—starting with the Denver Bears of the Western League in the late 1800s. Six decades later, in 1955, that team was replaced by a AAA ball club with the same name. It wasn't long before the city fathers and citizens were seeking a Major League franchise.

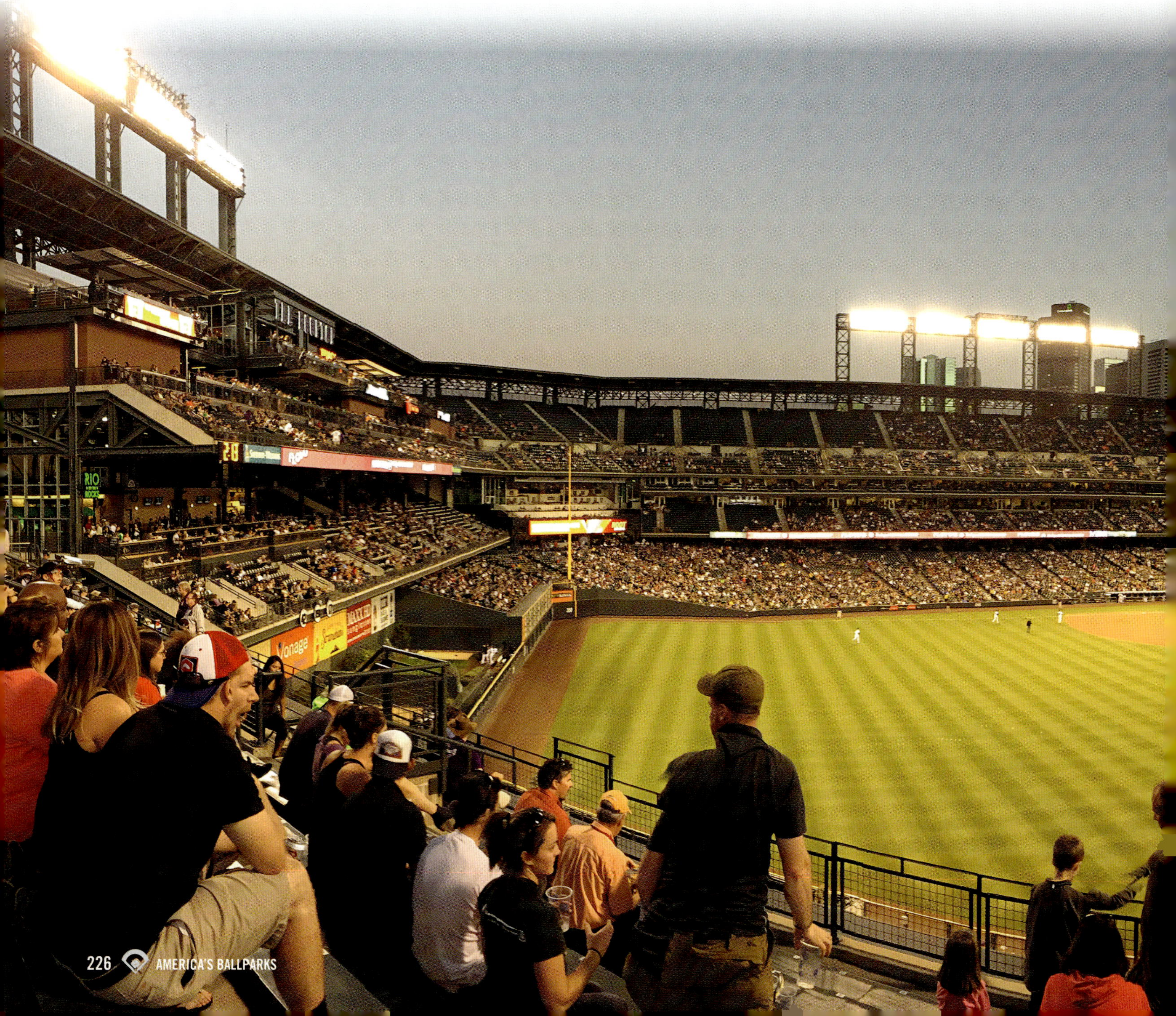

Although the city's Mile High Stadium was built as a minor league venue for the Bears, it could certainly be upgraded to Major League requirements. Things seemed hopeful when the new Continental League was formed in 1960, especially because it included a Denver team, but the organization vanished without playing a single game. This disappearing act occurred because the National League agreed to place expansion teams in New York and Houston. Denver, meanwhile, tried to purchase the Pittsburgh Pirates, but failed. Finally, in 1991, MLB approved another expansion; the result was the Florida Marlins and a Denver franchise called the Rockies, so named for the city's proximity to the Rocky Mountains. The same name had earlier been used by Denver's first National Hockey League team—which headed east and became the New Jersey Devils.

The Rockies first hit the field in 1993, spending their first two years in Mile High Stadium, since 1960 home to the revered Denver Broncos. That same year, they entered the National League West Division and went on to set the all-time Major League record for

BALLPARK STATS

ADDRESS
2001 Blake Street, Denver, CO 80205

OWNER
Denver Metropolitan Major League Baseball Stadium District

OPERATOR
Colorado Rockies

ARCHITECT
HOK Sport (now Populous)

CAPACITY
46,897 (50,144 with standing room)

RECORD BASEBALL ATTENDANCE
51,267 on 7/7/1998 (All-Star Game)

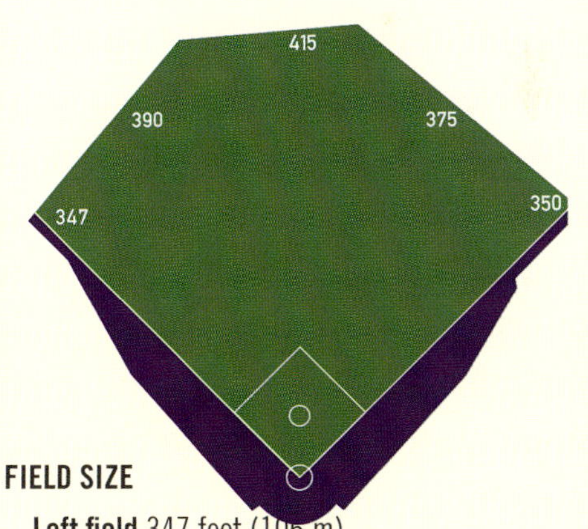

FIELD SIZE

Left field 347 feet (106 m)
Left-center 390 feet (119 m)
Center field 415 feet (126 m)
Right-center 375 feet (114 m)
Right field 350 feet (107 m)
Backstop 56 feet (17 m)

SURFACE
Kentucky bluegrass/perennial ryegrass

TEAM MASCOT
Dinger

annual attendance, attracting an incredible 4,483,350 fans to Mile High. It is a record that still stands. In the meantime, their new stadium build was underway, a project that would cost around $300 million and would include 63 luxury suites and 4,526 club seats. It would be the first baseball-only stadium built in the National League since Dodger Stadium was erected in 1962. In 1995, the new stadium was completed at a cost of roughly $300 million, and the team played their first game there on April 26.

DESIGN AND CONSTRUCTION

Coors Field is located on 20th and Blake Streets in Denver's Lower Downtown neighborhood, or LoDo. It was designed by the ubiquitous Populous firm of architects in the postmodern style. Yet, the rising brick facade conveys a strong sense of yesteryear . . . of 19th-century neighborhoods and doughty civic buildings that hark back to Denver's storied past and its role as the gateway to the West.

The stadium was originally supposed to be smaller, with seating for only 43,800 fans. But then the Rockies set attendance records at Mile High Stadium and the plans were changed, with new seats added to the right-field upper deck. Coors Field quickly gained a reputation as a hitter's park, mainly because the city's "mile-high" elevation—5,200 feet (1,580 m) above sea level—and its dry climate made hit balls really travel . . . 9 percent farther at 5,280 feet (1,609 m) than at sea level. The architects expected this phenomenon, so they placed the outfield fences an unusually long distance from home plate and, as a result, created the largest outfield in Major League Baseball.

MILE HIGH STADIUM

Mile High Stadium was originally built as a minor league venue for the Denver Bears ball club in 1948. But the stadium was later expanded to accommodate a professional football team, the Denver Broncos, as well as to attract a Major League Baseball franchise. Meanwhile, after changing their name to the Zephyrs in 1985, the former Bears continued to play in the stadium until 1992, when the franchise was moved to New Orleans. Denver finally got its Major League wish in 1991, when the new Rockies ball club arrived. The team quickly made itself at home at Mile High, where its two-year stay brought the fans out in staggering numbers.

By the turn of the 20th century, the aging stadium's fate was in flux. Broncos management finally decided that a new $2 billion state-of-the-art stadium with a retractable roof would substantially increase revenue by attracting the Super Bowl and other major events to Denver. The demolition of Mile High, which began in January 2002 and was completed in April, was covered by Denver newspapers and even broadcast live on television. The former site is now a parking lot for Empower Field, but there is a miniature of Mile High on display there, and the position of home plate is identified with a marker.

[LEFT] An overhead view of the ballpark shows how it sits within Denver's LoDo neighborhood, with the city's taller buildings framing it.

[RIGHT] A young man sells beer at Coors Field during a Colorado Rockies baseball game.

[BELOW] With its elegant brick exterior facing the street, Coors Field is a prime example of the "throwback" stadiums built by the Populous firm of architects.

COORS FIELD FIRSTS

FIRST MLB GAME: 4/26/1995, Rockies over New York Mets,11–9

FIRST HOME RUN: 4/26/1995, Rico Brogna (New York Mets)

FIRST NO-HITTER: 4/17/2010, Ubaldo Jimenez vs. Atlanta Braves

FIRST ALL-STAR GAME: 7/7/1998, AL over NL, 13–8

FIRST PLAYOFF GAME: 10/3/1995, Atlanta Braves over Rockies, 5–4

As with many urban venues, Coors Field was constructed for maximum accessibility. It is located near Interstate 25, with direct access to the 20th Street and Park Avenue exits. Nearby Union Station also offers light rail and commuter rail access. Inside the ballpark, the batter's eye is a large green, ivy-covered wall located in straight-away center field. The center-field bleacher section is named "The Rockpile." In 1993 and 1994, when the team was at Mile High, the Rockpile was located next to the south stands, in center field and a long way from home plate, so the same bleacher design was incorporated into Coors Field.

DIGGING UP THE BONES

During construction of Coors Field, workers unearthed a number of dinosaur fossils throughout the grounds. Rumors quickly spread that one of the finds was a 7-foot-long (2.1 m) 1,000-pound (450 kg) triceratops skull! But the fossil fragments were actually quite small, and they are now housed at the Museum of Science and Nature. But because of these discoveries, one of the first names considered for the new stadium was "Jurassic Park." The fossil finds did later lead to the selection of a triceratops as the Rockies' mascot, Dinger.

In 1991, Coors Brewing, a corporation synonymous with Colorado, purchased naming rights to the stadium as part of their $30 million investment in the Rockies. The Rockies club ownership signed a 2017 lease agreement with the stadium district to ensure that the Coors name would remain at least through 2047.

[ABOVE] *The Player* statue by George Lundeen stands at the Home Plate entrance to Coors Field. The Rotary Club of Denver donated the statue in honor of baseball pioneer Branch Rickey.

[RIGHT] Visitors strolling around Coors Field may find themselves up close and personal with a large purple dinosaur, specifically a triceratops. That would be Dinger, who has been the team's official mascot since he hatched from an egg at Mile High Stadium on April 16, 1994. He also is a reminder to fans of the many dinosaur bones unearthed during the excavation for the new ballpark.

[ABOVE] The Rock Pile section of Coors Field is famous for offering the cheapest seats in the house for a Rockies game.

[LEFT] For more than 25 years, *The Evolution of the Ball* by local artist Lonnie Hanzon welcomed Rockies fans. This imposing archway adorned the Wynkoop Street entrance to Coors Field. It was relocated during the development of McGregor Square, which takes up the entire square block just south of the ballpark.

ROCKIES ACHIEVEMENTS

WORLD SERIES CHAMPIONSHIPS: 0

NL PENNANTS: 1 (2007)

NL EAST DIVISION TITLES: 1 (2007)

WILD CARD BERTHS: 4 (1995, 2009, 2017, 2018)

PLAYOFF APPEARANCES: 5 (1995, 2007, 2009, 2017, 2018)

WORST SEASON RECORD: 2023, 59–103 (.364)

BEST SEASON RECORD: 2009, 92–70 (.568)

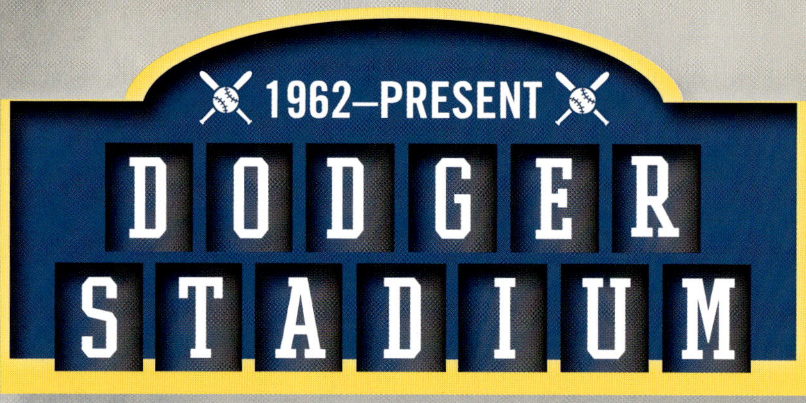

HOME OF THE LOS ANGELES DODGERS

NATIONAL LEAGUE (1890–PRESENT)

DODGER STADIUM HAS EARNED ITS LEGENDARY STATUS. *The oldest Major League ballpark west of the Mississippi, it is the third oldest overall following Boston's Fenway Park (1912) and Chicago's Wrigley Field (1914). As home to the Dodgers ball club, it more than lives up to that team's stellar history and charismatic appeal.*

Few teams have had as storied a run as the seven-time world champion Dodgers . . . who created one of the first baseball dynasties, were beloved by their Brooklyn supporters as "dem bums," and then abandoned New York for California, to the shock and dismay of the perplexed fans they left behind.

Founded in 1883 as the minor league Brooklyn Grays, the team then joined the American Association league in 1884 as the Brooklyn Atlantics, taking the name of a defunct Brooklyn team. Six years later they won the AA championship before joining the National League in 1890. Brooklyn was still an independent city at this time, not yet annexed as a borough of New York City. In the 1940s, a fierce rivalry with the Bronx-based Yankees sprang up. This was also the period when the Dodgers broke the color barrier by contracting Jackie Robinson in 1947, the first African American to play in the Majors since 1884. In 1956, Dodger Don Newcombe became the first player to win the Cy Young Award and the National League MVP during the same season.

The team's departure from New York at the end of the 1957 season was the result of team president Walter O'Malley's search to find a replacement for their aging ballpark. This was only one in a series of stadium shifts. During their first 15 years, the early Dodgers played in four different fields. Yet, after their 1913 move to Ebbets Field, the stadium with which they are most associated, they stayed put for 44 years.

Now O'Malley was hoping to build a domed stadium in Brooklyn, but was unable to reach an agreement with city officials regarding land acquisition. The city of Los Angeles promised him a new venue (and California sunshine), and so the Dodgers were off to the West Coast. While awaiting completion of their stadium, the team played at Los Angeles Memorial Coliseum, which had a staggering capacity of 90,000.

The Dodgers' new home would be located in a section of L.A.'s Elysian Fields known as Chavez Ravine. Earlier, in a controversial move that would later haunt them, the city had seized Chavez

Ravine from local homeowners through voluntary purchases or eminent domain, using funds from the Federal Housing Act of 1949. Many mostly Hispanic residents of the communities of Palo Verde, La Loma, and Bishop were forcibly removed from their homes. This land was originally earmarked for public housing, with plans calling for 24 apartment buildings and 160 townhouses, along with playgrounds, schools, and a college. But a conservative shift in the political climate occurred in 1953. Public housing projects were labeled "socialist," and many lost funding. The city repurchased the property from the Federal Housing Authority at a bargain price, agreeing that the land would still serve a public purpose. In 1958, after voters approved a "Yes on Baseball" referendum, the Dodgers were finally able to purchase 352 acres (142 ha) of Chavez Ravine.

This new stadium would be the first in MLB since the construction of the original Yankee Stadium to be built using only private funding, and the last of such until San Francisco's Oracle Park opened in 2000. Groundbreaking took place on September 17, 1959. Afterward, the landscape underwent some serious reconfiguring—tops of ridges were removed, with the soil then used to level Sulfur and Cemetery Ravines. Palo Verde Elementary School was not demolished; it was simply buried under a parking lot. Roughly 8 million cubic yards of earth (6,100,000 m^3) were moved to complete the build. Massive precast concrete units, some weighing 32 tons, were made on-site and lowered into place by crane to form the structural framework of the facility.

Dodger Stadium was completed in less than three years at a cost of $23 million. The stadium overlooked downtown Los Angeles and offered city views to the south, the green hills of Elysian Fields to the north and east, and the rounded contours of the San Gabriel Mountains beyond the outfield.

DESIGN AND CONSTRUCTION

When Dodger Stadium opened in 1962, it was clear that architect Emil Praeger had truly achieved Walter O'Malley's dream of a field with nearly perfect sight lines. By creating a cantilevered grandstand with no visible supporting structures to obstruct the action, Praeger had set a new standard for ballpark design. As

BALLPARK STATS

ADDRESS
1000 Vin Scully Avenue, Los Angeles, CA 90012

OWNER
Guggenheim Baseball Management

OPERATOR
Los Angeles Dodgers

ARCHITECT
Praeger-Kavanagh-Waterbury

CAPACITY
56,000

RECORD BASEBALL ATTENDANCE
57,099 on 4/13/2009 (Home Opener vs. SF Giants)

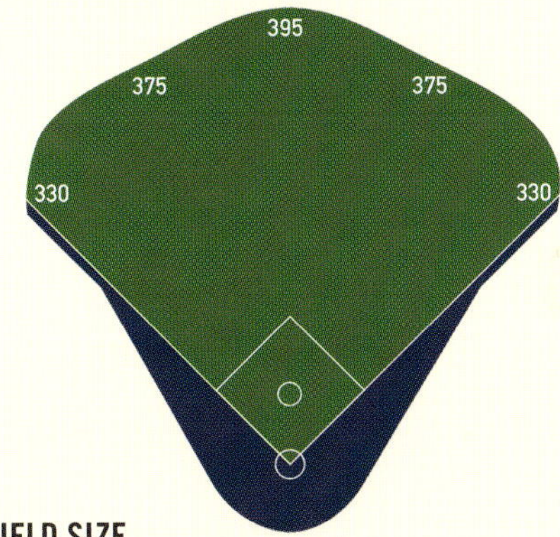

FIELD SIZE

- **Left field** 330 feet (101 m)
- **Medium left-center** 360 feet (110 m)
- **True left-center** 375 feet (114 m)
- **Center field** 395 feet (120 m)
- **True center field** 400 feet (122 m)
- **True right-center** 375 feet (114 m)
- **Medium right-center** 360 feet (110 m)
- **Right field 330 feet** (101 m)
- **Backstop** 55 feet (17 m)

SURFACE
Santa Ana Bermuda grass

TEAM MASCOT
None

A bifurcated staircase leads to the stadium's main entrance. Gorgeous So-Cal-style landscaping now surrounds the perimeter of the park. Dodger Stadium is sometimes referred to as "Blue Heaven on Earth," a nickname coined by Dodgers manager Tommy Lasorda. Some fans call it Chavez Ravine after the geographic site where it was built. This was how the L.A. Angels referred to the ballpark when they played there from 1962 to 1965, mainly to avoid speaking the name of their competition.

the largest baseball stadium in the world, on the basis of seating capacity, it was soon labeled a "pitcher's park." To take advantage of this defensive edge, the team assembled a cutthroat roster of pitchers. Since it opened, Dodger Stadium has witnessed 13 no-hitters, two of them perfect games.

PUBLIC REACTION

When it debuted, Dodger Stadium impressed fans and students of ballpark construction. Its understated simplicity had an elegance rarely seen in sports venues. Plus its "modernist" style held up well over the passing decades, while places like Kauffman Stadium and Angel Stadium succumbed to the lure of renovations that undermined their aesthetics for the sake of extra amenities and kitschy design. More recently, Ballparkratings.com proclaimed, "Architecturally and aesthetically, Dodger Stadium is a place that really exceeded my expectations, as I would put it shoulder-to-shoulder with the best of the retro parks and the best of the classic ones . . . emphasizing enduring structural assets over attention-grabbing gimmicks or contrived quirks, Dodger Stadium is the ideal combination of light and heavy."

Although Dodger Stadium has received multiple upgrades in recent years, the designers have been careful not to disrupt its timeless appeal. This decision apparently worked well—the venue has been declared the most popular MLB stadium by social media.

In contrast, the stadium's setting generally got lower marks. In spite of its admirable views of green hills, palm trees, and the San Gabriel Mountains, the park is separated from the city center and has little neighborhood ambiance. There are no bars, restaurants, shops, and the like in the vicinity. The complex system of entrances and exits at the stadium itself as well as traffic issues can still be a deterrent to visitors after one or two frustrating experiences. Another complaint was that the stadium lacked ramps for easy movement, forcing the crowd into multiple levels of stairwells. And for fans hitting the concessions during the game, the interiors lacked openings for viewing the field, compared to newer stadiums like Oracle Park or Petco Park.

There are also people in LA—and elsewhere—with a long memory, who still resent the presence of the stadium, who have not forgiven the city—and to some extent the club owners—for tearing the residents of Chavez Ravine away from their neighborhoods. A demand for proper restitution is currently being addressed in the courts.

UPDATES AND RENOVATIONS

Dodger Stadium has undergone a number of major renovations. A highly visible change took place during the 2005 off-season, when most of the seats were replaced. Dating to 1975, their palette of bright yellow, orange, blue, and red had helped give the venue its "space age" ambiance. The new seats, with more-toned-down versions of the colors, hark back to the original pastel color theme so in keeping with mid-1950s sensibilities.

During this same period, the baseline seating sections were converted into retro-style "boxes," adding leg room and a table, repairs were made to the concrete structure of the stadium, and the scoreboards were upgraded with LED video displays. In 2008, a $412 million project added Dodger Way, a tree-lined entrance leading to

SEATING CHART

[ABOVE] Post-2005 renovations included replacing the stadium's seats. The bright seats from 1975 were replaced with new ones in the original 1962 color scheme of yellow, light orange, sky blue, and turquoise. Fans were offered 2,000 of the old seats at a cost of $250 each, with the proceeds going to charity.

[BELOW] With the demolition of Shea Stadium in 2009, Dodger Stadium became the only ballpark with symmetrical outfield dimensions in the National League and only one of three in the MLB. The other two are Kansas City's Kauffman Stadium and Toronto's Rogers Centre, both in the American League. The stadium is also so large that there have only been five home runs hit out of the park in its 57-year history, and by only four players. Willie Stargell hit two of them, in 1969 and 1973; the others were Mike Piazza in 1997, Mark McGwire in 1999, and Giancarlo Stanton in 2015.

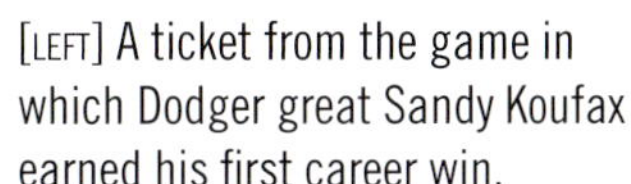

[LEFT] A ticket from the game in which Dodger great Sandy Koufax earned his first career win.

DODGER STADIUM FIRSTS

FIRST MLB GAME: 4/10/1962, Cincinnati Reds over Dodgers, 6–3

FIRST HOME RUN: 4/10/1962, Wally Post (Cincinnati Reds)

FIRST NO-HITTER: 5/5/1962, Bo Belinksy (LA Angels)

FIRST ALL-STAR GAME: 7/8/1980, NL defeats AL, 4–2

FIRST PLAYOFF GAME: 10/2/1962, Dodgers over SF Giants, 8–7

FIRST WORLD SERIES GAME: 10/5/1963, Dodgers over NY Yankees, 1–0 in Game 3

[ABOVE] Jumbo versions of player bobbleheads scattered through the grounds add a retro feel to the ballpark in keeping with its mid-century origins.

[BELOW] Fireworks light up the sky during a night game at the ballpark. In 2008, the Los Angeles City Council voted unanimously to give the Dodger Stadium area its own zip code, 90090, and to bestow upon it the name Dodgertown.

a landscaped grand plaza that connects to a promenade featuring restaurants, shops, and the interactive Dodger Experience Museum; Green Necklace, a beautiful, landscaped perimeter that allows fans to walk around the park, yet remain inside the stadium gates; and Top of the Park, a large-scale outdoor plaza featuring 360-degree views encompassing the downtown skyline and Santa Monica Bay, the Santa Monica and San Gabriel Mountains, and the Dodger Stadium diamond.

In 2012, as the stadium turned 50, the team hired architect, urban planner, and stadium specialist Janet Marie Smith to oversee renovations. Both video boards were replaced with high-definition screens, and new clubhouses and weight rooms were installed. The restrooms, concession stands, sound system, and batting cages were also upgraded. Other improvements included a new sound system, wider concourses, and more standing-room viewing areas.

Between the 2013 and 2014 seasons, renovations included wider concourses in the pavilions, new restaurants, dedicated team store buildings, and bullpen overlooks with overlook bars. In 2019 a $100 million renovation created a center field plaza with a children's playground that included the relocation of the Jackie Robinson

DODGERS ACHIEVEMENTS

WORLD SERIES CHAMPIONSHIPS: 8 (1955*, 1959, 1963, 1965, 1981, 1988, 2020, 2024)

NL PENNANTS: 19 (1941*, 1947*, 1949*, 1952*, 1953*, 1955*, 1956*, 1959, 1963, 1965, 1966, 1974, 1977, 1978, 1981, 1988, 2017, 2018, 2020)

NL WEST DIVISION TITLES: 21 (1974, 1977, 1978, 1981, 1983, 1985, 1988, 1995, 2004, 2008, 2009, 2013, 2014, 2015, 2016, 2017, 2018, 2019, 2020, 2022, 2023)

WILD CARD BERTHS: 3 (1996, 2006, 2021)

PLAYOFF APPEARANCES: 35 (1941*, 1947*, 1949*, 1952*, 1953*, 1955*, 1956*, 1959, 1963, 1965, 1966, 1974, 1977, 1978, 1981, 1983, 1985, 1988, 1995, 1996, 2004, 2006, 2008, 2009, 2013, 2014, 2015, 2016, 2017, 2018, 2019, 2020, 2021, 2022, 2023)

WORST SEASON RECORD: 1992, 63–99 (.389)

BEST SEASON RECORD: 2022, 111–51 (.685)

* as Brooklyn Dodgers

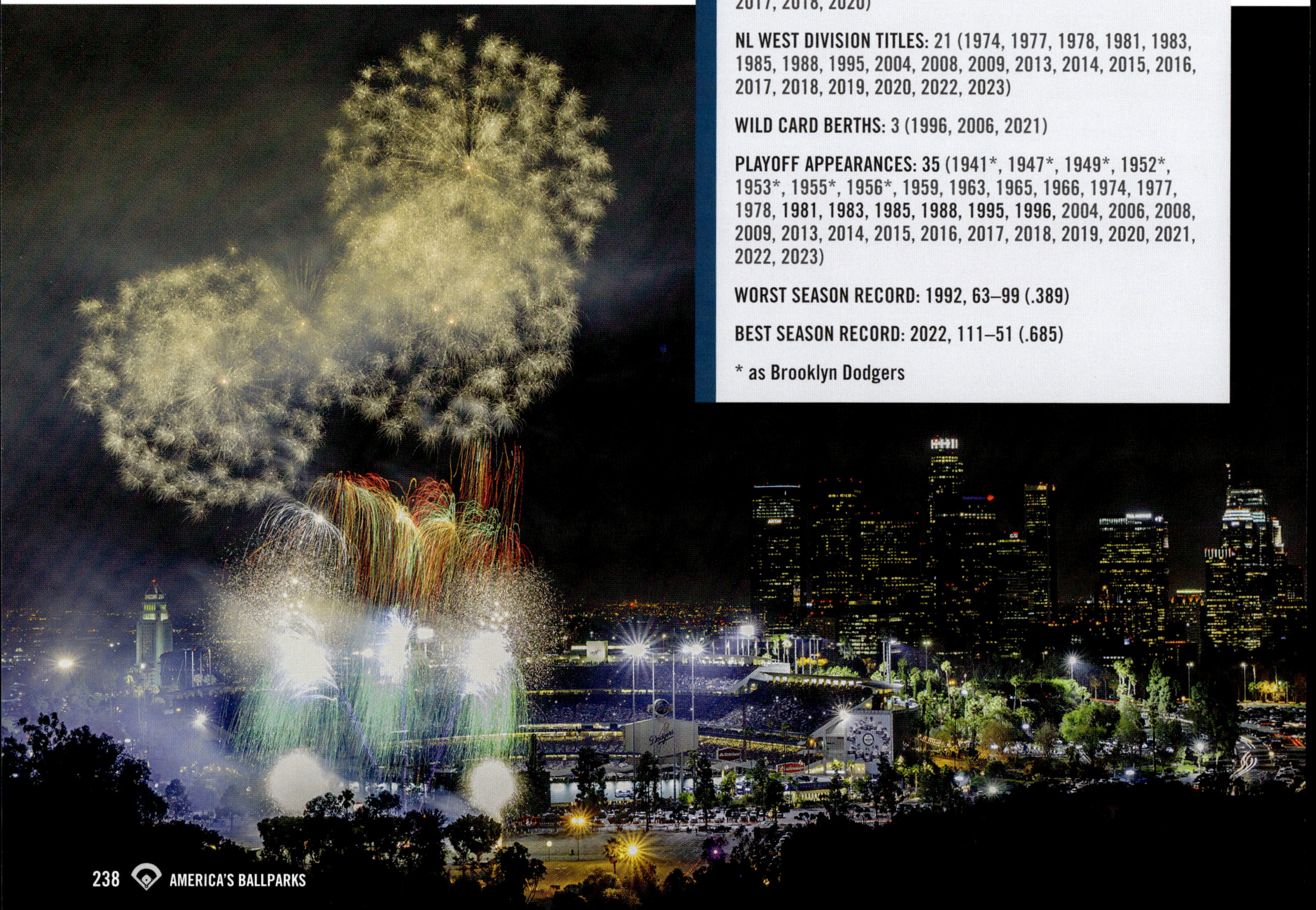

"I have never seen anything like this. Now you'll see baseball that is real baseball. You rip one out of the park here and you've really earned it. This is what I call a ball park."

—LEO DUROCHER, DODGER COACH

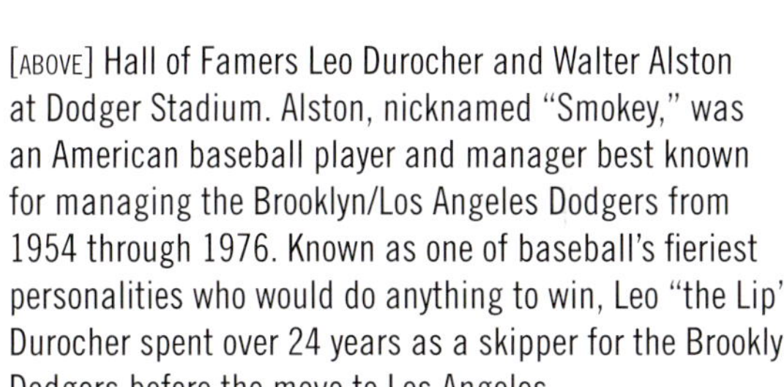

[ABOVE] Hall of Famers Leo Durocher and Walter Alston at Dodger Stadium. Alston, nicknamed "Smokey," was an American baseball player and manager best known for managing the Brooklyn/Los Angeles Dodgers from 1954 through 1976. Known as one of baseball's fieriest personalities who would do anything to win, Leo "the Lip" Durocher spent over 24 years as a skipper for the Brooklyn Dodgers before the move to Los Angeles.

[LEFT] The Dodgers Welcome Board posts messages to fans.

[BELOW] Designed to evoke the look of the world-famous Hollywood sign, the "Think Blue" sign was originally sited on the small hill just beyond the (then) center-field overflow parking lot. Put up by then owner Peter O'Malley as a promotion for Think Blue Week sometime around the 1997 season, the sign was taken down after the week-long promotion. It was later put back up—and stayed up—for a very long time, becoming a local landmark. "Think Blue" also became the team's identity, logo, and trademark. In December 2011, during one of SoCal's notorious Santa Ana windstorms, portions of the sign blew down—it then read "Ink Blje." It then disappeared for good.

[LEFT] The iconic sign for Dodger Dogs. It is believed that Dodger Dogs were first called that name in 1958, when the Dodgers first came to Los Angeles from Brooklyn.

[BELOW] A cotton candy vendor works his way through the crowd.

statue and a display honoring the Legends of Dodger Baseball, along with a sports bar and beer garden. New elevators and escalators connected the outfield bleachers with the field, loge, and reserve levels, and a new main entrance. This renovation was completed while the 2020 regular season was delayed due to COVID.

FEATURES AND AMENITIES

With each fresh renovation, Dodger Stadium has gained additional amenities and activities to enhance fan experience. In addition to concessions, shops, playgrounds, and historical displays, there are also special events held throughout the season.

BALLPARK TOURs A ballpark tour with a knowledgeable guide allows fans to go behind the scenes—and on to the field—and learn about the team's history. Options include a pre-game tour, clubhouse tour, a tour + photo op, a hands-on experience tour, a shortstop tour, a Jackie Robinson tour, a tour of the on-site botanic gardens, and private tours.

KID-FRIENDLY FEATURES Outfield Plaza provides plenty of space for lively kids to move around; plus it offers some great dining options. Kids who are between ages 5 and 14 can run the bases on the field after most Sunday home games. For new moms who attend the games with their babies, and who desire privacy, the stadium even has a nursing lounge located in center field under the Left Pavilion.

SPECIAL EVENTS Each season Dodger Stadium honors the diverse populations of Los Angeles and also offers fun themed celebrations. These special events even have their own themed "swag," and include fan favorites like USC Night, UCLA Night, Military Appreciation Night, Mexican Heritage Night, Yoga Day, Hello Kitty Night, Game of Thrones Night, Girl Scouts Day, Star Wars Night, Jewish Community Day, Japan Night, Korea Night, and Dog Lovers Night, among many others. The stadium has showcased a number of other sports, including boxing, basketball, soccer, hockey, and cricket. It also hosted the semifinals and finals of the 2009 and 2017 World Baseball Classics and exhibition baseball during the 1984 Summer Olympics. The venue, along with Angel Stadium, is currently scheduled to host softball and baseball for the 2028 Olympics. Pope John Paul II celebrated Mass there on September 16, 1987, while Greg Laurie held his Harvest Crusades at the stadium in 2011 and 2012. Tyler, the Creator's Camp Flog Gnaw festival has been regularly held outside Dodger Stadium since 2018.

FOOD AND DRINK In terms of eateries, the stadium has plenty of food concessions, stands, and food trucks; the Mediterranean-inspired LA Grille and LA Cheesesteak are two 2023 additions to the roster. Along with the usual burgers, hot dogs, nachos, and pizza, the stadium also offers many new food items each year. Some recent hits include deep-fried cheesecake and the Flamin' Hot Cheetos corn dog, both walk-away treats that are served on a stick.

STARRING DODGER STADIUM . . .

Considering its proximity to Hollywood, it is not surprising that the stadium has appeared in a number of films and TV productions, sometimes playing a key role in the action, as it did as the crash-landing site for Autobot Jazz in 2007's *Transformers*. Other productions featuring the stadium include *Naked Gun*, *The Fast and the Furious*, *Superman Returns*, *The Core*, *Rock of Ages*, and *Creed III*. TV shows that were shot at the stadium include *The Amazing Race* season 4, *Curb Your Enthusiasm*, *MasterChef*, and even the classic 1960s comedy *Mr. Ed*, when Mr. Ed gave batting tips to Dodgers coach Leo Durocher.

Additionally, many of the world's top rock, pop, and electronic music acts have performed at Dodger Stadium, including the Cure, KISS, the Rolling Stones, the Beatles, Simon and Garfunkel, David Bowie, Weezer, Madonna, Beyoncé, the Bee Gees, Genesis, Eric Clapton, U2, Bruce Springsteen, Elton John, Guns N' Roses, Michael Jackson, Blackpink, and Lady Gaga. The popular music video for Fleetwood Mac's song "Tusk" was recorded and filmed at the empty stadium in 1979.

“I am very proud to announce . . . the unveiling of the Sandy Koufax statue. . . . The statue will be located at our main entrance in the Centerfield Plaza, right next to Jackie Robinson’s statue, and fans entering those gates will be ‘greeted’ by Jackie and Sandy. Not only are both of these Hall of Famers part of our rich Dodger history, they are also continuously inspiring sports fans everywhere.”

— DODGER PRESIDENT AND CEO, STAN KASTEN

[ABOVE] Jackie Robinson broke the baseball color line when he started at first base for the Brooklyn Dodgers in 1947. The Los Angeles Dodgers count Robinson as one their own, although Robinson never actually played in LA. Shown here in its original position on the Reserve Level along the left-field line, the statue of Robinson has since been moved to the renovated Centerfield Plaza, which also offers three kids’ play areas, batting and pitching cages, and a virtual photo booth that lets fans take pictures with players.

[BELOW] Souvenir print from the 1963 World Series showing Dodger Stadium and star players like Sandy Koufax, Don Drysdale, and Maury Wills, who defeated the New York Yankees in four games to become World Champions.

[ABOVE] The Sandy Koufax Statue designed by Branly Cadet was unveiled June 18, 2022, at an dedication ceremony with the man himself in the Centerfield Plaza.

EARLY BALLPARKS
1884–1912

The early ball club that would become the Dodgers joined the Majors in 1884. At that time, they were playing in the first version of Washington Park, one of two fields of that name located in the Park Slope region of Brooklyn. The property contained an historic building called the Gowanus House. Known today in its restored state as the Old Stone House, it was once used as headquarters by George Washington. In 1894, the team moved to Ridgewood Park in Queens. Then 1898 saw them back in Brooklyn, in Eastern Park in the Brownsville neighborhood. This ballpark was considered too far away from the city center, and it eventually failed. Charles Ebbets, who'd bought the team in 1897, moved them to the other Washington Park, which was closer to downtown and cost less to rent. There they stayed until 1912.

For the record, Brooklyn featured the first two enclosed baseball parks—Union Grounds and the Capitoline Grounds. These fenced-in, dedicated ballparks helped to speed up baseball's evolution from a popular amateur game to a professional sport.

[ABOVE LEFT] The 1889 Brooklyn Bridegrooms take a team photo.

[ABOVE RIGHT] A program from the 1890 season shows that this iteration of the team played at the first Washington Park.

[LEFT] Pedestrians wait for a trolley to pass before crossing the road outside Ebbets Field.

[ABOVE LEFT] Even after "Trolley" was no longer part of the official name, the team still used images of them in promotional pieces.

[ABOVE RIGHT] Ross "Tex" Erwin at Ebbets Field, 1913. Erwin played in Brooklyn from 1909 to 1914. In his short stint there, his jersey sported a variety of team names: Superbas, Trolley Dodgers, Dodgers, and Robins.

MANY NAMES, MANY HOMES

Over the years the team has played under at least 12 different names. Their eventual moniker started as a nickname for the fans. Due to the electric trolley tracks in front of Eastern Park, game-goers often had to scramble to avoid trolley cars while heading for the stadium. In the early 1900s, sportswriter Charles Dryden began calling the team after those "trolley dodgers." In 1932, the team invited the Brooklyn baseball writers to select a permanent name, and on January 22 they chose Dodgers. Later in the 20th century they would be affectionately dubbed "The Boys of Summer" by sports author and Brooklyn native Roger Kahn.

- Brooklyn Grays (1883)
- Brooklyn Atlantics (1884)
- Brooklyn Grays (1885–1887)
- Brooklyn Bridegrooms (1888–1890)
- Brooklyn Grooms (1891–1895)
- Brooklyn Bridegrooms (1896–1898)
- Brooklyn Superbas (1899–1910)
- Brooklyn Trolley Dodgers (1911–1912)
- Brooklyn Dodgers (1913)
- Brooklyn Robins (1914–1931)
- Brooklyn Dodgers (1932–1957)
- Los Angeles Dodgers (1958–present)

It's no surprise that a team with roots stretching back to the 19th century has called so many ballparks "home."

- Washington Park I (1884–1890)
- Ridgewood Park (1886–1889)
- Eastern Park (1891–1897)
- Washington Park II (1898–1912)
- Ebbets Field (1913–1957)
- Roosevelt Stadium (1956–1957)
- Los Angeles Memorial Coliseum (1958–1961)
- Dodger Stadium (1962–present)

OTHER HOMES OF THE DODGERS

EBBETS FIELD
1913–1957

Its facade rising up from the streets of Brooklyn's Flatbush neighborhood like a distinguished Edwardian exhibition hall, Ebbets Field was home to one ball club . . . and possessed the hearts and minds of several generations of baseball fans. When Dodgers owner Charles Ebbets viewed the prospective stadium site on Bedford Street, he knew it was the ideal spot to build a steel-and-concrete replacement for the wooden grandstand of Washington Park. In 1908 he began buying up lots, including a garbage dump that was named Pigtown due to the stench. The site also contained derelict houses, shanties, and a herd of goats, and two of the bordering streets were not yet paved. Construction began on March 4, 1912, and a Connecticut granite cornerstone holding newspapers, photos of ballplayers, telegrams, and almanacs was laid on July 6. Reporters covering the opening in 1913 called the new park "A Monument to the National Game" and predicted it could "last 200 years."

Now named Ebbets Field in honor of the team's owner, the ballpark's distinctive exterior was made up of red brickwork and tall, arched, multi-paned windows picked out in white. The hallmark of the interior was the Rotunda at the home plate entrance. This 80-foot (24 m) circle,

> "The park as it stands today is the best tribute to Mr. Van Buskirk's tireless endeavor. He stuck on the job as if he were building the place for his very own . . ."
>
> —*BROOKLYN EAGLE*, ON ARCHITECT CLARENCE VAN BUSKIRK'S COMMITMENT TO BUILDING EBBETS FIELD

LATE

DAILY NEWS

NEW YORK'S PICTURE NEWSPAPER

4¢

THIS IS NEXT YEAR!

FOR MORE SERIES FOTOS PLEASE TURN TO CENTERFOLD AND BACK PAGE

[RIGHT] The *Daily News* announces the Dodgers' 1955 World Series win with Don Hoak and Johnny Podres going in for a hug with catcher Roy Campanella. Six future Hall of Famers—along with manager Walter Alston—played for Brooklyn that season: Campanella, Sandy Koufax, Tommy Lasorda, Pee Wee Reese, Jackie Robinson, and Duke Snider.

Ebbet's Field, Brooklyn, N. Y.

[LEFT] Ebbets Field in the 1950s

[BELOW] Jackie Robinson signs autographs for adoring young Brooklyn fans.

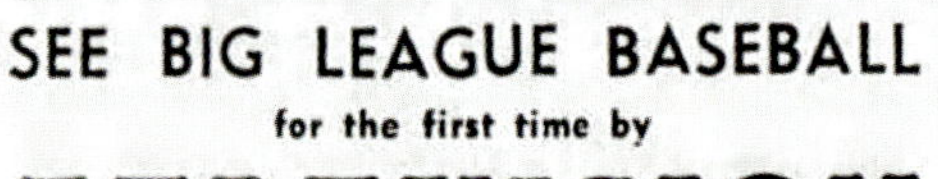

SEE BIG LEAGUE BASEBALL
for the first time by
TELEVISION
at any RCA Victor Television Dealer's Store
CINCINNATI REDS
vs.
BROOKLYN DODGERS
Saturday, August 26th
Both games will be televised by NBC direct from Ebbets Field, starting at 1:30 P.M. Daylight Time

A Service of the Radio Corporation of America

[LEFT] On August 26, 1939, the first televised MLB game took place at Ebbets Field between the Dodgers and the Cincinnati Reds. The first-ever broadcast had taken place earlier that year, when Princeton edged Columbia, 2-1, at Baker Field. It wouldn't be until the 1950s, when increasing numbers of Americans owned TV sets, that televised sports really took off.

enclosed in Italian marble, had a floor tiled to represent the stitches of a baseball, and a chandelier with 12 baseball bats holding 12 baseball-shaped globes. There were 12 turnstiles and 12 gilded ticket windows.

The stadium's capacity when it opened was 13,000; by its final years it had increased to 31,902. Still, as the team grew more popular—a strong start in the 1900s and 1920s was followed by some fallow years, but the team came roaring back in the 1940s with pennant wins in 1941, 1947, 1949, 1952, 1953, 1955, and 1956—the limitations of their ballpark became evident. Hemmed in by the surrounding neighborhood, Ebbets Field had no room to expand. There was only limited parking for automobiles in an era when people were increasingly moving to the suburbs and relying on cars for travel.

In the early 1950s, new team owner Walter O'Malley announced plans for a domed stadium at Atlantic Yards, where a large market was being demolished. Robert Moses, the New York City building commissioner, urged the club to move to the city-owned Flushing Stadium in Queens. This did not fly with O'Malley, who pronounced his team was "the Brooklyn Dodgers, not the Queens Dodgers." He began talks with the City of Los Angeles, primed for Major League Baseball and ready to build him a new stadium. When no Brooklyn venue was forthcoming, O'Malley accepted the West Coast offer and moved his team after the 1957 season.

Adding insult to injury, O'Malley tried to convince Horace Stoneham, owner of the Dodgers' crosstown rivals, the Giants, to head to California as well. Stoneham, who was suffering stadium and financial headaches of his own, took the advice and relocated his ball club to San Francisco that same year. New York baseball fans were stunned by the double desertion.

In its prime, Ebbets Field was also home to five professional football teams, including three NFL teams (1921–1948). After the Dodgers departed, the stadium occasionally hosted soccer matches, and high school, college, and Negro League ball games. The iconic ballpark was demolished in 1960 and replaced by the Ebbets Field Apartments. Before the structure was razed, an auction of the stadium's contents was conducted on April 20, 1960. Saul Leisner, a longtime Dodgers fan, was contracted to handle the sale. More than 500 people gathered in the marble rotunda to bid on locker room stools, benches, team banners, seats, bricks, bats, caps, team photos, balls, and a cornerstone of the stadium. Leisner later stated that it was the saddest day of his life.

In 1956, Brooklyn Dodgers owner Walter O'Malley sold Ebbets Field to real estate developer Marvin Kratter. Although the sale to Kratter included a lease that would mean the "Bums" had a potential home in the borough until 1961, O'Malley was already hammering out a deal with the City of Los Angeles. Eventually the ballpark was demolished in 1961, to be replaced by apartment housing.

LOS ANGELES MEMORIAL COLISEUM
1958–1961

When the Dodgers reached Los Angeles, their new stadium was still under construction. They found a temporary home from 1958 to 1961 at the multipurpose Coliseum in the Exposition Park neighborhood. Referred to as the "Greatest Stadium in the World," the Coliseum had been commissioned in 1921 to commemorate the city's World War I veterans, and upon its completion in 1923, Los Angeles viewed it as a beacon of civic pride. In 1932 the Coliseum hosted the Summer Olympics, and then again in 1984. As the scheduled host in 2028, it will then become the only venue to host the summer games three times.

Architects John and Donald Parkinson designed the exterior in the art moderne style, while the bowl-like structure of the field was likely inspired by the Yale Bowl, which dated from 1914. The original construction costs approached a million dollars, but the result was the largest sports venue in LA. Initial capacity was 74,144, but in 1930 the upcoming Olympics necessitated more seating. Capacity was expanded to 101,574 by extending the seats upward.

From the start, the Dodgers drew crowds to the Coliseum. They were, after all, the first Major League team to settle in California. And on April 15, 1958, the first Major League game ever played on the West Coast featured the Dodgers against the similarly uprooted Giants, who hosted the matchup.

The Coliseum was also home to professional and college football, including the Los Angeles Rams (1946–1979 and 2016–2019), the 1960 NFL Chargers, the NFL Raiders (1982–1994), and UCLA Bruins football. It also hosted a number of notable events, including the first AFL–NFL World Championship Game—later called Super Bowl I—as well as Super Bowl VII. Today the Coliseum serves the USC Trojans football team, which usually attracts a capacity crowd to home games.

"The Greatest Stadium in the World"

—COMMON ACCOLADE FOR THE LOS ANGELES MEMORIAL COLISEUM

[ABOVE] The facade of the coliseum shows elements of Egyptian, Spanish, and Mediterranean revival styles that architects John and Donald Parkinson incorporated into their monumental moderne structure. Still a source of civic pride for locals, it is one of only a handful of National Historic Landmarks in the entire city of Los Angeles.

[RIGHT] An aerial view of the coliseum

[BELOW] The Dodgers faced the Chicago White Sox at Los Angeles Memorial Coliseum for the 1959 World Series.

CLOSE-UP

JAPANESE BALLPARKS

Professional baseball is played in more than 100 countries. In addition to the United States and Canada, the game is especially popular in the Netherlands, China, the Dominican Republic, Cuba, and Italy. Yet, there is one country where baseball fever caught the imagination of the people more than a century ago—the island nation of Japan.

The Japanese baseball tradition goes back to the schoolyards of the late 19th century, when the game was first introduced to students at Kaisei Academy in 1872 by American professional Horace Wilson. The Shimbashi Athletic Club, the country's first organized team, was founded in 1888 by American-trained engineer Hiroshi Hiraoka. Early fans found heroes in "Ichiko," a team from the First Higher School of Tokyo that defeated a Yokohama-based team of American adults. The Yankees' Babe Ruth helped to inspire more interest in the game in 1934,

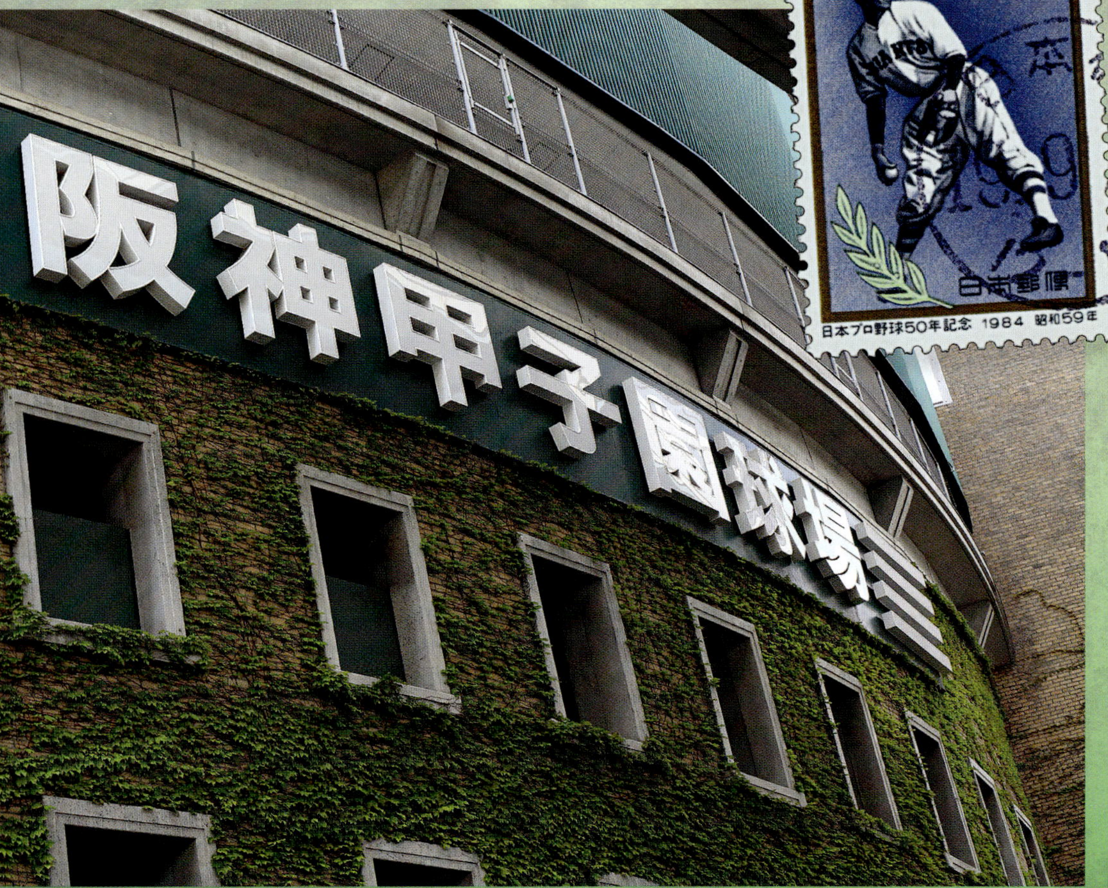

[ABOVE] Babe Ruth at bat during the 1934 Japan Tour. The sport of baseball got a boost from this 12-city barnstorming tour headlined by such stars as Ruth, Earl Averill, Lou Gehrig, Charlie Gehringer, Lefty Gomez, Connie Mack, Jimmie Foxx, and Moe Berg. Game venues included Meiji-Jingu Stadium in Tokyo, Koshien Stadium in Kobe, and Yagiyama Baseball Field in Sendai.

[ABOVE LEFT] Stamp shows Eiji Sawamura, the high school pitcher who struck out nine US batters, including Babe Ruth, during the 1934 tour.

[LEFT] When it was built in 1924, Hanshin Koshien Stadium was the largest stadium in Asia. Its design was modeled after New York's Polo Grounds. The Great Hanshin earthquake of 1995 affected Koshien, so it was remodeled, although it kept the distinctive ivy-covered walls inspired by Chicago's Wrigley Field.

One of the few stadiums left in the world where Babe Ruth played (the others are Wrigley Field, Fenway Park, and Koshien Stadium), Meiji Jingu is an old-school ballpark. Unfortunately, highly controversial plans to redevelop the area have called for this venerable stadium to be demolished.

ON-FIELD ENTERTAINMENT

Some American teams provide singing and dancing grounds crews, but Japanese stadiums also offer various entertainments. Besides the raucous bands, most of the teams have dancing cheerleaders who may be joined on the field by the team mascot. The Yakult Swallows' mascot, Tsubakuro, is a big black-and-white bird who excites the fans by throwing gifts and dancing.

when he led an all-star group of MLB players on a tour of Japan. The Americans played a Japanese team of professionals organized by Matsuko Shoriki, president of the *Yomiuri Shimbun* newspaper. The tour proved so successful that Shoriki kept the All-Nippon team together, naming them the Great Tokyo Baseball Club. They, in turn, became the Yomiuri Giants, who founded the first pro league in Japan in 1936. It was reorganized in 1950 as Nippon Professional Baseball. Today two leagues, the Central League and the Pacific League, field six teams each that play a 144-game schedule from March to October. The Western League and the Eastern League represent the NPB's affiliated minor league teams.

THE STADIUMS

There are differences between modern Japanese ballparks and US fields, but it is safe to say the level of fan loyalty and esteem for older stadiums is almost identical. The Nippon league uses a smaller strike zone and playing field. In fact, the dimensions of five Nippon League fields would violate American Official Baseball Rules. American food vendors specialize in salty, fried, high-calorie items. In Japanese parks there are hot dogs and popcorn, but there are also bento boxes, stir-fried vegetables, and rice balls. American crowds tend to be relatively quiet while watching baseball, savoring the tension. Meanwhile, crowds in Japan grow frenzied during games—clapping, flashing novelty symbols of their teams, and eagerly singing along to field bands with thundering drums and blaring trumpets.

HANSHIN KOSHIEN STADIUM The oldest ballpark in Japan, dating to 1924, Hanshin Koshien Stadium boasts a unique, all-dirt infield. Although it is home to the Hanshin Tigers, it is best known for hosting a legendary high school baseball tournament every spring and summer. Many of these talented athletes later become professional baseball stars.

MEIJI JINGU Built in 1926, Meiji Jingu is home to the Tokyo Yakult Swallows, but it is also famous for the Roku Daigaku tournaments for six Tokyo-based universities. Many Roku Daigaku players who moved on to professional baseball have become legends.

KUSANAGI STADIUM This has been around since 1930. It is also known as the Sawamura/Babe Ruth Memorial Stadium. In 1934, before professional baseball officially began in Japan, Eiji Sawamura, a 17-year-old Japanese pitcher, went up against Ruth's exhibition team of all-stars and struck out Ruth, Charlie Gehringer, Lou Gehrig, and Jimmie Fox. For fans of Japanese baseball, this ballpark means something special.

RAKUTEN MOBILE PARK MIYAGI This is another older stadium. Built in 1950, it serves the Tohuku Rakuten Golden Eagles. An amusement park with a Ferris wheel, Smile Glico Park, is integrated into the stadium's left-field seating.

YOKOHAMA STADIUM Also called Hama Suta, this ballpark is home to the powerful Yokohama DeNA BayStars. The stadium,

Primarily used as the home field of the Yokohama DeNA BayStars, Yokohama Stadium is a rare multipurpose stadium that also hosts American football games and live events.

[ABOVE] The illuminated roller coaster and Ferris wheel light the sky behind the Tokyo Dome. Its roof is an air-supported structure with a flexible membrane.

[BELOW] Fukuoka SoftBank HAWKS supporters enter Fukuoka PayPay Dome to watch a game. This stadium can boast of one of the largest domes in the world.

which opened in 1978 with a capacity of 34,046, hosted the baseball and softball games at the 2020 Summer Olympics.

BELLUNA DOME Since 1979 this has been home to the Saitama Seibu Lions. Although it is a covered stadium, it lacks a wall behind the stands, allowing fresh air on to the field.

KOBE SPORTS PARK This ballpark opened in 1988 as one of two homes to the Orix Buffaloes. The Hanshin Tigers also play there when Koshien Stadium is hosting high school baseball tournaments. It is one of three ballparks in Japan with an American-style field—an all-grass outfield and infield with dirt base paths.

TOKYO DOME Opened in 1988, this is the home of the Tokyo Yomiuri Giants. The Giants and Tigers are the oldest teams in Japan, and the original ballpark used to be called Korakuen Stadium. The original amusement park is still located at Korakuen, situated next to the Dome.

ZOZO MARINE STADIUM Built in 1990 on the Chiba City waterfront, ZOZO Marine Stadium serves the Chiba Lotte Marines. The

Fans watch the Hiroshima Toyo Carp vs. the Yokohama BayStars, member teams of Nippon Professional Baseball, at Mazda Zoom-Zoom Stadium in Hiroshima.

stands in this circular stadium can often be chilly—recalling San Francisco's Candlestick Park—but fans jump around for nine innings to keep warm.

FUKUOKA PAYPAY DOME This ballpark hosts the illustrious Fukuoka SoftBank Hawks, winners of five of the past six Japan Series. Built in 1993, it was the first stadium in Japan to feature a retractable roof. Near the park is the Sadaharu Oh museum, where the all-time home-run king's fans can view his living room and the samurai sword with which he practiced his mighty swing.

KYOCERA DOME OSAKA Built in 1997, Kyocera Dome Osaka is the second of two homes to the Orix Buffaloes. The stadium has also hosted mixed martial arts fights.

VANTELIN DOME NAGOYA The Vantelin Dome Nagoya was built in 1997 with a geodesic dome for a roof. It serves as headquarters for the Chunichi Dragons.

MAZDA ZOOM-ZOOM STADIUM This is home to the Hiroshima Toyo Carp. Opened in 2009, the stadium was originally a public arena before Mazda bought it and renovated it. It is now considered one of the best baseball venues in Japan.

ES CON FIELD HOKKAIDO The home of the Nippon Ham Fighters, this ballpark got a lot of buzz before it opened in 2023. It's eco-friendly and has many interesting features, such as the "sauna seats" that overlook the field and special sections where fans can bring their dogs.

The kids' diamond at Es Con Field. Japan's newest ballpark was designed by HKS, the same architectural firm that designed the newest US ballpark, Globe Life Field in Texas.

SINGING IN THE STANDS

Japanese fans sing *a lot*. For example, the Hanshin Tigers fans have an original song for each player, and they sing it every time that individual is up at bat. The lyrics are posted on the fan site so that the crowd can sing together. The Chiba Lotte Marines fans are also unique—they bob up and down when their players are at bat. Yakult Swallow fans hold tiny umbrellas and move them up and down as they sing "Tokyo Ondo"—a famous old festival song. The tradition possibly started in 1978 to keep fans from leaving before the game ended.

Yokohama Marinos fans sing during a game in the stands of the Yokohama Stadium.

2020–PRESENT

GLOBE LIFE FIELD

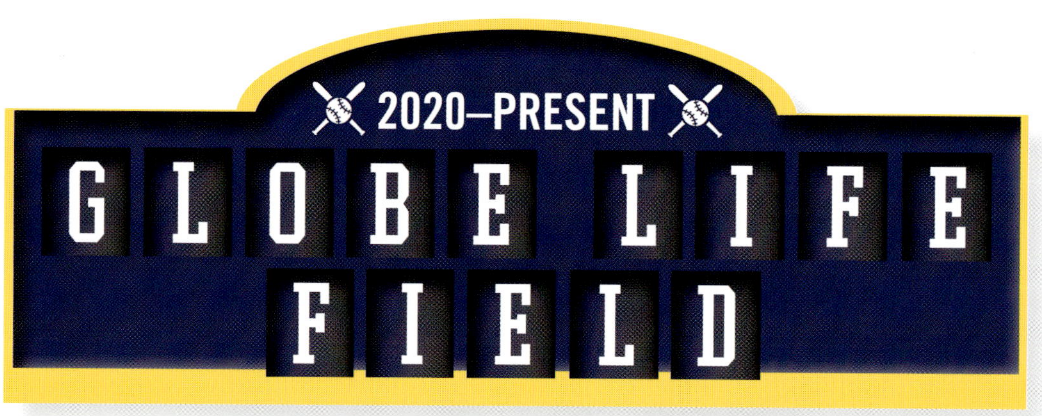

HOME OF THE TEXAS RANGERS

AMERICAN LEAGUE (1961–PRESENT)

THE TEXAS RANGERS' NEW COVERED STADIUM *is located in Arlington, not far from where they formerly played at Globe Life Park. Beside the stadium lies Texas Live!—an upbeat complex that offers a gathering place for fans and visitors along with eateries, bars, and entertainment venues.*

The Texas Rangers expansion ball club certainly "got around." They started life as the second iteration of the Major League Senators, in the nation's capital, where they called two stadiums home. They then moved to Arlington, a suburb of Dallas-Fort Worth, became the Texas Rangers, and played in three stadiums . . . so far. Their new name was based on the historic Texas law enforcement agency

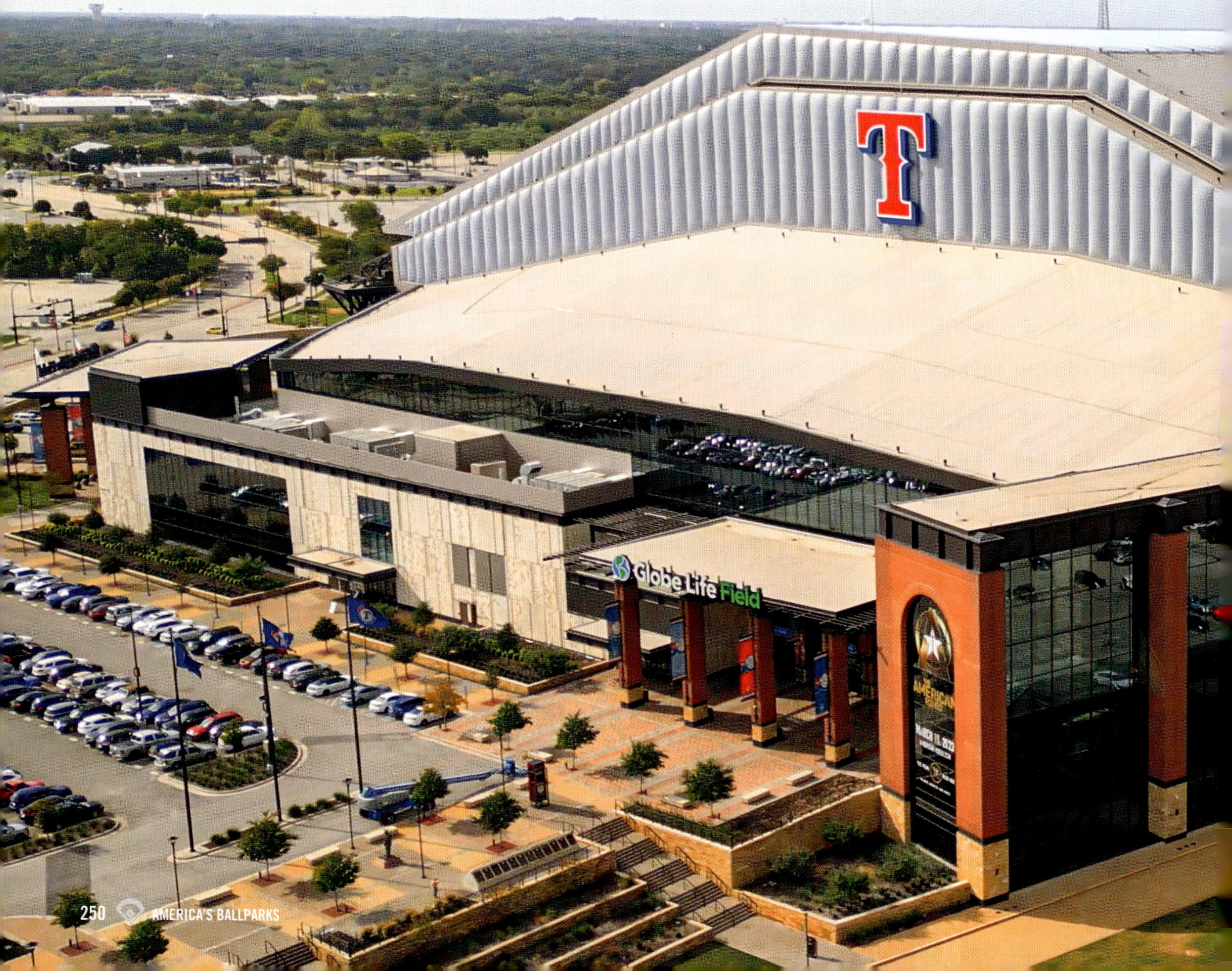

founded in 1823 by "Father of Texas" Stephen Austin. After claiming seven division titles and three American League pennants, and winning the 2023 World Series, the Rangers have proven to be a ball club with heart. Their team roster has included some of the top players in baseball, with Hall of Famers like Harold Baines, Iván "Pudge" Rodríguez, and Nolan Ryan, to name just a few. The Rangers worked to mend their former reputation as chronic strugglers, moving away from the joke about the old Senators that had been revived for the new Senators: "Washington—first in war, first in peace, still last in the American League."

The team's debut came about in a circuitous fashion. MLB was in a tizzy in 1961, when the original Washington Senators moved to Minnesota and became the Twins. MLB was already planning an expansion, so they moved it up a year. In part this was to halt the formation of the new Continent League, as well as to prevent the loss of baseball's exemption from the Sherman Antitrust Act. Two teams were created that year: the Los Angeles Angels and a new version of the Senators. The team played their first season at aging Griffith Stadium, then the following year moved to the new District of Columbia Stadium (RFK Stadium) under a 10-year lease. In 1972, after their move to Texas, they played in Arlington Stadium, then in 1993 they made the switch to the Ballpark in Arlington, later known as Globe Life Park.

But by 2016, things were not rosy at Globe—the ballpark could turn beastly hot under the Texas sun, and many fans stayed away from day games. And still the heat and frequent rain continued to take their toll on the structure. That year the Rangers announced their plans to build a new air-conditioned field with a retractable roof. Happily, Arlington residents approved the construction with a 60 percent favorable vote. Although Globe Life Field was meant to open in March 2020, the COVID-19 pandemic delayed the start of baseball that year. The first MLB game was actually played on July 24.

BALLPARK STATS

ADDRESS
734 Stadium Drive, Arlington, TX 76011

OWNER/OPERATOR
Texas Rangers

ARCHITECT
HKS, Inc.; VLK Architects, Inc.

CAPACITY
40,300

RECORD BASEBALL ATTENDANCE
42,472 on 10/27/2023 (World Series, Game 1)

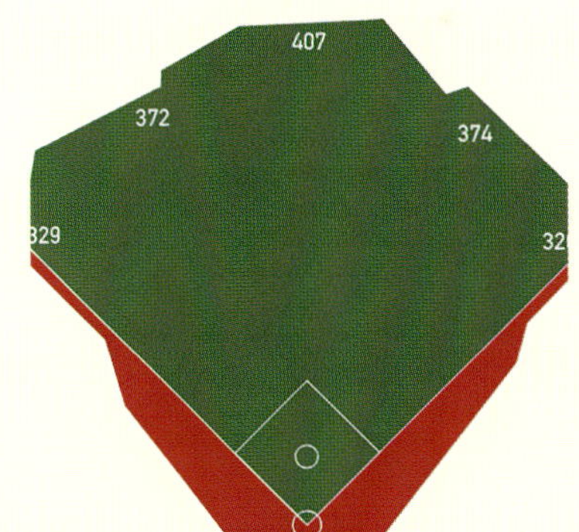

FIELD SIZE

- **Left field** 329 feet (100 m)
- **Left center** 372 feet (113 m)
- **Center field** 407 feet (124 m)
- **Right center** 374 feet (114 m)
- **Right field** 326 feet (99 m)
- **Backstop** 42 feet (13 m)

SURFACE
Shaw Sports B1K

TEAM MASCOT
The Captain

The Captain, the team's mascot, is a palomino horse dressed in a team uniform. He was introduced in 2002 and wears the number 72 in honor of the year the Rangers relocated to Dallas–Forth Worth. Here he encourages fans to get loud. A relatively rare and recent development are the cheerleaders flanking him. The Six Shooters Squad is an all-female interactive group that performs at Rangers' home games and home playoff games.

GLOBE LIFE FIELD FIRSTS

FIRST MLB GAME: 7/24/2020, Rangers over Colorado Rockies, 1–0

FIRST HOME RUN: 7/26/2020, Joey Gallo vs. Colorado Rockies

FIRST NO-HITTER: 4/9/2021, Joe Musgrave (San Diego Padres)

FIRST ALL-STAR GAME: 2024

FIRST PLAYOFF GAME: 10/10/2015, Rangers over Baltimore Orioles, 7–1

FIRST WORLD SERIES GAME: 10/27/2023, Rangers over Arizona D-backs, 6–5 in Game 1

DESIGN AND CONSTRUCTION

The architects involved in the build include architect of record H.K.S., Inc., as well as David M. Schwartz Architectural Services, Inc. The total cost of construction came to $1.2 billion, making this the second-most-expensive MLB ballpark ever built after the new Yankee Stadium.

Outside, the facade of Globe Life Field primarily consists of glass, brick, and steel. Other materials in the build include curtain wall systems, precast walls, limestone, granite, and masonry veneer. One of the most distinctive architectural features are the brick arches that run along the ballpark's north facade, which are reminiscent of the exterior of Globe Life Park.

The 5.5-acre (2.23 ha) retractable roof, the largest single-panel operable roof in the world, provides shade and a comfortable environment throughout the year, with temperatures averaging at 72°F (22°C). When the roof is retracted, it is docked behind the third base grandstand. It weighs in at 24 million pounds (10.88 million kg) and is composed of a white rubber membrane on the north and south sloped planes, while the flat center is covered with 223 clear panels made of ETFE (ethylene tetrafluoroethylene), a transparent plastic polymer-type material. The roof support structure consists of five steel trusses and tie-in steel between each truss and required 19,000 tons of steel. Astonishingly, the roof can open in roughly 12 minutes.

To facilitate viewing, transparent building materials were installed throughout Globe Life Field, creating wide-open views and letting in natural light. In addition to the translucent panels, glass can be found on all four sides of the exterior. Even the clear panels in the roof allow natural daylight into the ballpark when it is closed.

Within the stadium are found ample concession spaces, plenty of gathering spots, and unobstructed views from the seats. Meanwhile, the stadium lies at one end of Texas Live!—an upbeat dining, entertainment, and hospitality complex that includes sports bars, restaurants, and a 300-room hotel. The NFL Cowboy's AT&T Stadium is positioned at the other end.

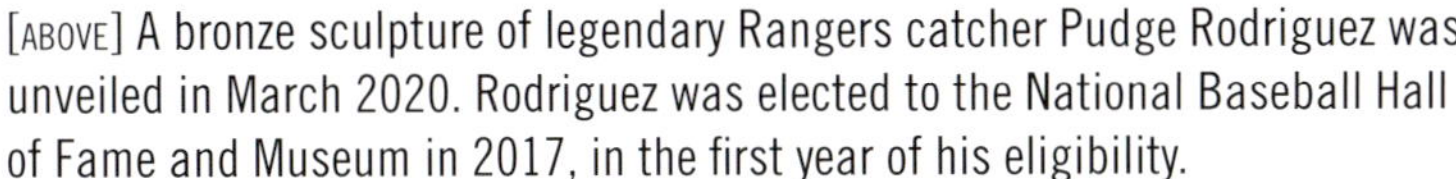

[ABOVE] A bronze sculpture of legendary Rangers catcher Pudge Rodriguez was unveiled in March 2020. Rodriguez was elected to the National Baseball Hall of Fame and Museum in 2017, in the first year of his eligibility.

[TOP RIGHT] Captured in bronze by Antonio Tobias Mendoza, Hall of Fame great Nolan Ryan stands outside the entrance to the ballpark.

[BOTTOM RIGHT] A bronze baseball glove pronounces that Globe Life Field is the "Home of the Texas Rangers."

PUBLIC REACTIONS

The reviews of the new stadium were for the most part quite glowing. Many writers and fans considered it a huge improvement over the "old" Globe Life—from the seats to the concourses, from the concessions to the viewing areas. They concurred that the stadium, complete with its movable roof, was designed to impress. They appreciated the wide-open concourse areas for fans to take in the entire field, and how seats seem to have a great view of the field. They even noted the all-you-can-eat seats in the outfield for budget-conscious families and all the fun things for kids to do.

On the other hand, some reviewers complained that the venue's exterior was boxy and not impressive. There were also criticisms of the industrial look of the interior, with its exposed wires and pipes.

RANGERS ACHIEVEMENTS

WORLD SERIES CHAMPIONSHIPS: 1 (2023)

AL PENNANTS: 3 (2010, 2011, 2023)

AL WEST DIVISION TITLES: 7 (1996, 1998, 1999, 2010, 2011, 2015, 2016)

WILD CARD BERTHS: 2 (2012, 2023)

PLAYOFF APPEARANCES: 9 (1996, 1998, 1999, 2010, 2011, 2012, 2015, 2016, 2023)

WORST SEASON RECORD: 2011, 96–66 (.593)

BEST SEASON RECORD: 1963, 106–56 (.345)*

* as Washington Senators

A few critics have panned the industrial look of the Globe Life Field interior, but whatever its style shortcomings, the artwork that decorates its concourses is worth a look.

[TOP] A colorful, energetic mural shows iconic ball players, including Nolan Ryan, Alex Rodriguez, Michael Young, Pudge Rodriquez, Adrian Beltre, and many other famous players who have donned a Texas Rangers uniform during their careers.

[LEFT] A mixed media panel by Ray Phillips is entitled *Triple Play*.

[BELOW] The *All Y'All Can Eat* mural depicts beloved ball game food, like hot dogs, pizza, popcorn, french fries, cold drinks, ice cream, peanuts, pretzels, and hamburgers.

[OPPOSITE PAGE] A fascinating collage of baseballs forms a pitcher surrounded by bats, both broken and whole.

FEATURES AND AMENITIES

Globe Life is in Arlington, which means there is a lot to do. Other fun and fascinating places to visit in the area include the Bureau of Engraving and Printing, the Grapevine Village Railroad, and Fossil Rim Wildlife Center. There are also two theme parks—Six Flags Over Texas and Six Flags Hurricane Harbor water park.

STADIUM TOURS Tours of the stadium are a must for fans young and old. There's nothing quite like going behind the scenes to view Chuck Morgan's PA Booth or the private suites, luxury lounges, and more. Clubhouse tours are 60 minutes long and include a trip down to the Texas Ranger's clubhouse and locker room. Premium tours run 90 minutes and include 30 minutes on the field to take it all in from the players' viewpoint. Ballpark tours take place when the field is unavailable, and include a 60-minute tour of the state-of-the-art ballpark, including the history of the Rangers. Private group tours can also be arranged.

TEXAS LIVE! Just beyond the stadium lies Texas Live!, an entertainment complex developed by the Cordish Companies that was constructed in three phases. The first phase, dubbed Rangers Republic, includes a two-level venue with multiple restaurants and offering interactive games and team memorabilia; the second phase is the Live! Arena, a multi-level venue with restaurants, a performance stage for concerts, and an outdoor beer garden. Arlington Backyard, the third phase, is a large, covered venue that hosts concerts, charitable functions, and community events.

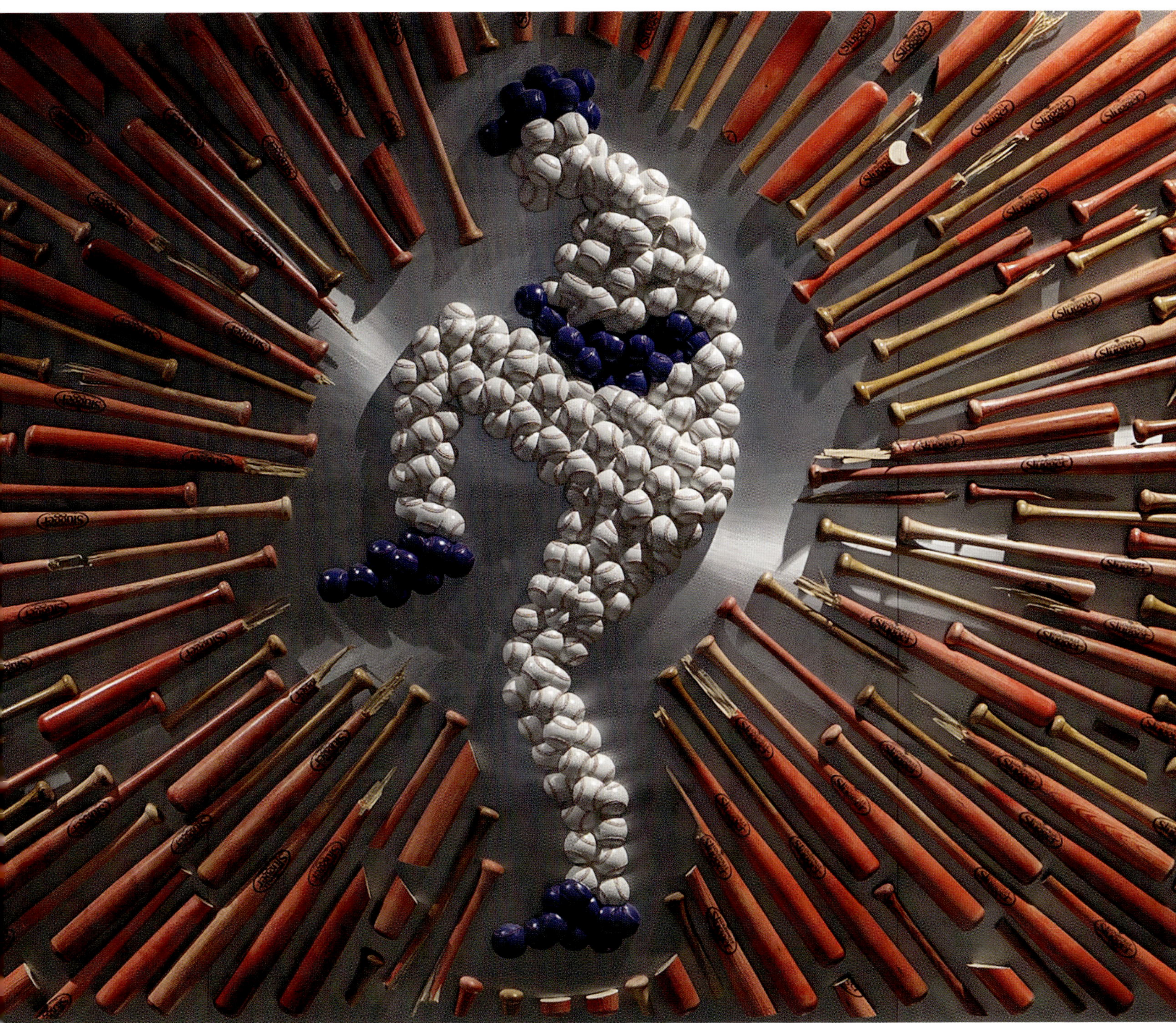

ARLINGTON STADIUM
1972–1993

In 1965, Arlington Stadium went up as a rather small minor league ballpark. Originally called Turnpike Stadium (after nearby Dallas–Fort Worth Turnpike, now a part of Interstate 30 known as the Tom Landry Highway), it initially seated 10,000, then expanded to 20,500 seats in 1970. It had been built to be expandable up to 50,000 seats and upgradeable to MLB standards of the era—little major work would be necessary for it to be ready for a Major League team. In 1971, after the second incarnation of the Washington Senators announced their new home would be the Dallas–Fort Worth area and their new name would be the Texas Rangers, the stadium was expanded to seat over 35,700 fans and was renamed Arlington Stadium. The stadium had been built with MLB hopes in mind, but it still had a jerry-built, minor league feel—although it still could boast that with its bowl configuration, there were few bad seats to be had there. Its greatest drawback was its lack of roof, which earned it the label of hottest stadium in the Majors.

By 1989, it was clear that aging Arlington did not offer the amenities that brought in the level of revenue MLB franchises required. That lack made it hard for the Rangers to afford quality players. The club was then owned by an investment group headed by George W. Bush, and it threatened to move the team from Arlington if public money could not be found to build a new ballpark. In January 1991, after an advertising campaign rallied residents, more than 65 percent of voters approved the new ballpark. A citywide sales tax would go up by half a cent to help pay for its construction.

GLOBE LIFE PARK
1994–2019

Arlington Stadium's replacement, Globe Life Park, opened in April 1994 as the Ballpark in Arlington. The venue was designed by H.K.S., Inc., and Driehaus Prize winner David M. Schwartz of Washington, DC. The team opted for a retro-style ballpark, one that would incorporate features of the classic Jewel Box parks from decades earlier. The roofed home run porch harken to Tiger Stadium, and the white steel frieze surrounding the upper deck was inspired by the original Yankee Stadium. They even built the out-of-town scoreboard into the left field wall, an homage to Fenway Park (it was later replaced with a video board). They copied the nooks and crannies found in the outfield from Ebbets Field and the arched windows from Comiskey Park. Still, there were elements of

[LEFT] April 1991: Then President George H. W. Bush (*left*) chats with baseball broadcaster Joe Morgan in the Rangers locker room along with son George W. Bush. "Dubya" was at that time part-owner and managing general partner of the team and had been part of the effort to secure funding for Globe Life Park. He left this position when he was elected governor of Texas in 1994, then sold his stake in the team in 1998 before his own terms as US president.

[BELOW] An aerial view of the stadium. On September 29, 2019, after the Rangers' final home game, played against the New York Yankees, home plate was removed and transferred to Globe Life Field.

the Lone Star State—Texas-style carvings found throughout the space. The exterior facades were composed of brick and Texas Sunset Red granite, while friezes re-created scenes from both the history of Texas and of baseball. A novel seating arrangement placed plenty of high-dollar seats close to the infield, which boosted sales.

Mortgage lender Ameriquest bought the naming rights to the field in 2004, and it became Ameriquest Field in Arlington. When the Rangers severed their ties with Ameriquest in March 2007, they announced a new name—Rangers Ballpark in Arlington. Another change occurred when insurance company Globe Life bought the naming rights on February 5, 2014, and renamed the facility Globe Life Park in Arlington.

In 2019, after 15 years spent at the "stadium of many names," the Rangers departed for their new home. At this time, city officials announced they would not be demolishing the structure—as is so often the fate of older stadiums. In 2020, Globe Life Park was retrofitted as a football and soccer venue, and it became home to the Dallas Jackals of Major League Rugby, North Texas SC of MLS Next Pro, and the Arlington Renegades of the XLF. To accommodate these sports, many of the park's lower sections were removed to make room for a rectangular field, which sits horizontally when viewed from behind the home plate. New seats were added to the ballpark's former outfield. And the stadium received yet another name when Choctaw Casinos & Resorts bought the naming rights on August 25, 2021.

While Globe Life Field was still under construction, *Going to the Show* by sculptor Harry Weber was unveiled in front. It captures Bengie Molina and Neftali Feliz celebrating the victory over the Yankees in Game 6 of the American League Championship Series on October 22nd, 2010, in Arlington, which earned the Texas Rangers their first trip to the World Series. In the background is the teams' former home, Globe Life Park.

2000–PRESENT

DAIKIN PARK

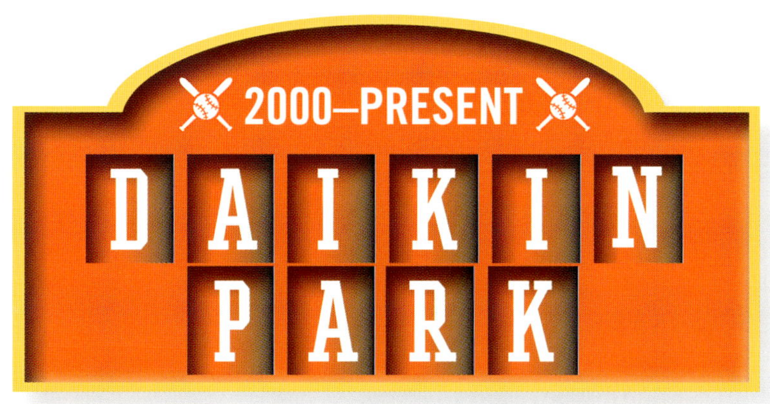

HOME OF THE HOUSTON ASTROS

AMERICAN LEAGUE (2013–PRESENT)

FROM 1888 UNTIL 1961, *the city of Houston's lone professional baseball club was the minor league Houston Buffaloes. It took an expansion by MLB to bestow the Astros on Bayou City in 1962, where they would soon be playing in the world's first domed sports stadium. The year 2000 saw them moving to a new stadium with a retractable roof, a venue affectionately known as "the Juice Box."*

Daikin Park is currently home to the Houston Astros, one of baseball's earliest expansion teams, which appeared the same year as the Mets, in 1962. First known as the Houston Colt .45s, they played in a temporary structure called Colt Stadium. Three years later they were renamed the Astros, in recognition of Houston's role as the home of the Johnson Space Center, and that same year

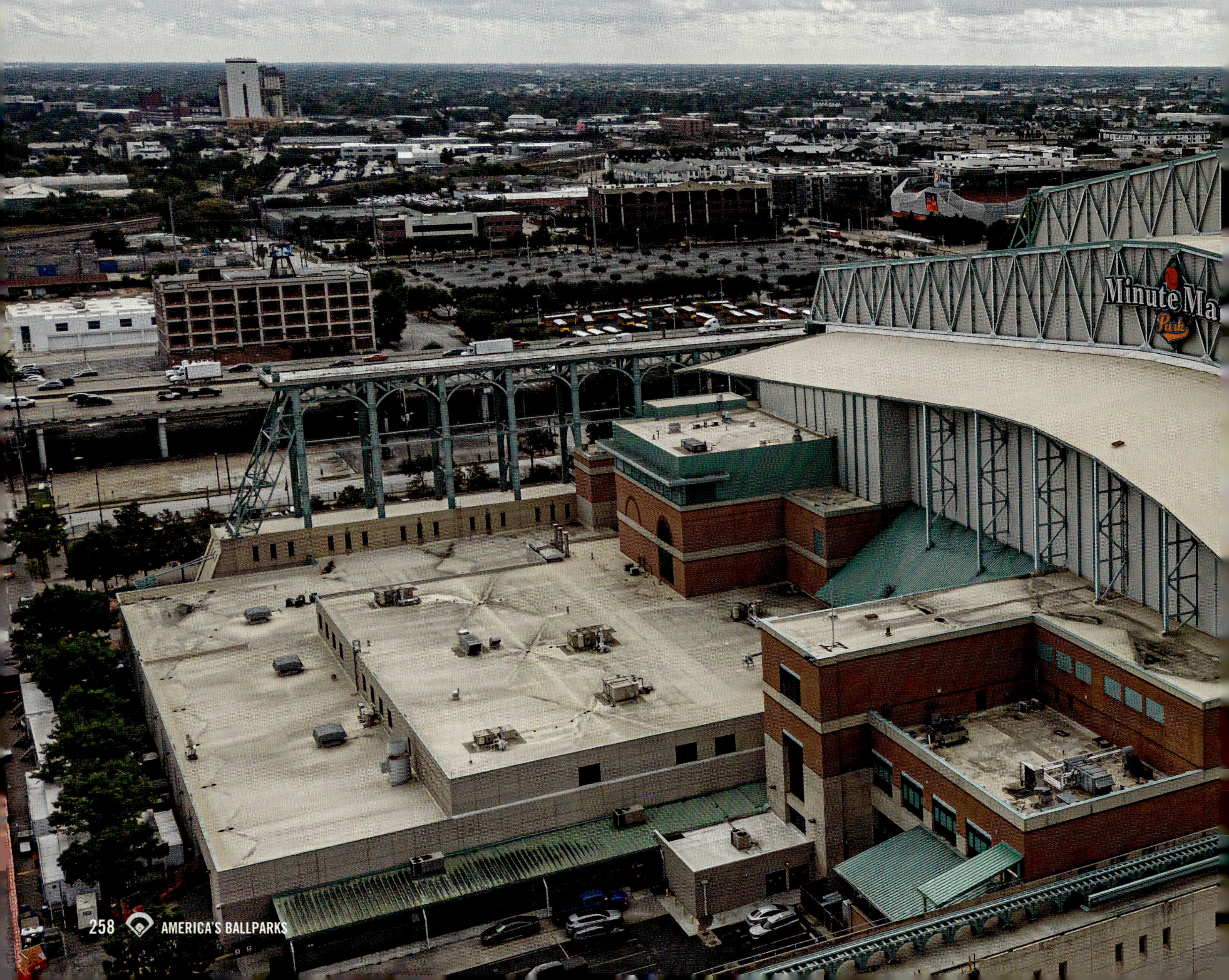

[RIGHT] The Home Plate entrance to the ballpark

they moved into the Astrodome, the world's first domed sports arena. The team played in the National League for 51 seasons, as part of the NL West Division from 1969 to 1993, then in the NL Central Division from 1994 to 2012. In 2013 the team was switched to the American League as part of an MLB realignment. They now play in the AL West Division.

The team saw their first winning record in 1972, made the playoffs in 1980, and earned three division titles during that decade. Aided by the potent bats of the "Killer B's," a group of talented hitters led by the team's only Hall of Famers, Craig Biggio and Jeff Bagwell, the Astros became a potent threat in the late 1990s and early 2000s. They earned four more division titles, made two Wild Card appearances, and in 2005 played the White Sox in the World Series, where they were, unfortunately, swept.

A slump over the next eight years was followed by a blossoming under new owner Jim Crane. The Astros began applying sabermetrics to their performance, as well as other analytic technologies, and with their switch to the American League they transformed themselves into one of baseball's most dynamic and successful clubs. They've won more than 100 games in four

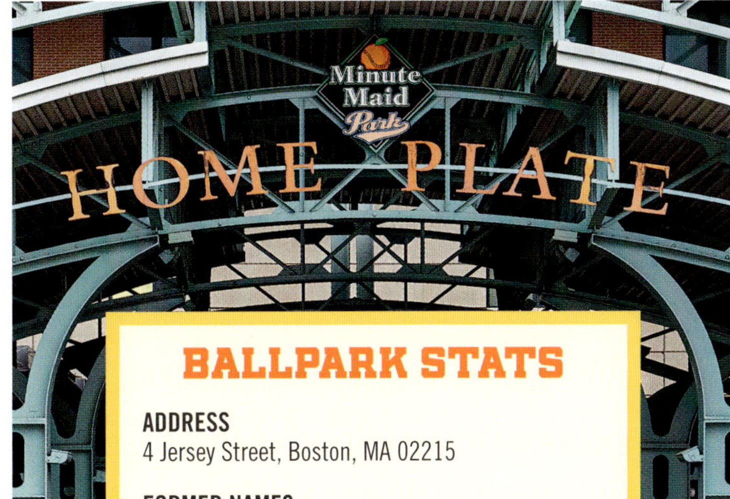

BALLPARK STATS

ADDRESS
4 Jersey Street, Boston, MA 02215

FORMER NAMES
The Ballpark at Union Station (2000)
Enron Field (2000–2002)
Astros Field (February–July 2002)

OWNER/OPERATOR
Harris County-Houston Sports Authority

ARCHITECT
HOK Sport (now Populous); Molina & Associates

CAPACITY
41,168

RECORD BASEBALL ATTENDANCE
44,203, on 9/26/2001 (vs. St. Louis Cardinals)

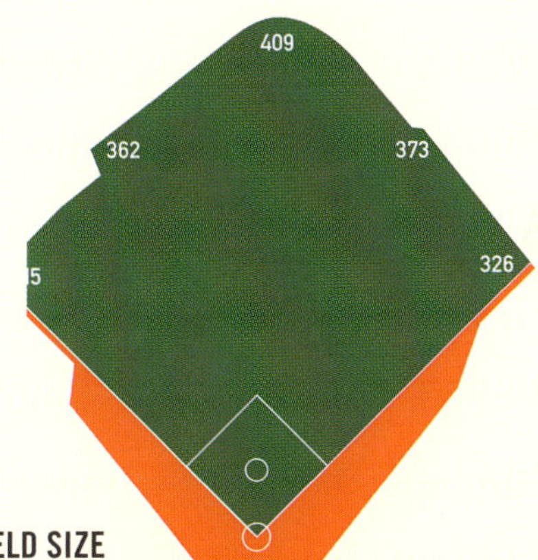

FIELD SIZE

- **Left field** 3315 feet (96.0 m)
- **Left-center** 366 feet (111.6 m)
- **Left-center (deep)** 399 feet (121.6 m)
- **Center field** 409 feet (124.7 m)
- **Right-center (deep)** 408 feet (124.4 m)
- **Right-center** 370 feet (112.8 m)
- **Right field** 326 feet (99.4 m)
- **Backstop** 49 feet (15 m)

SURFACE
Platinum TE Paspalum

TEAM MASCOT
Orbit

seasons, broke a record by appearing in six consecutive American League Championship Series, and won four American League pennants. In 2017 they also won their first World Series, beating the formidable Los Angeles Dodgers.

The Astros played in the Astrodome for 34 years before it became clear they needed a new venue. After a lot of political to-ing and fro-ing, an agreement was reached between the owners and Houston, whereby the franchise would be able to build behind the city's historic Union Station. This brick edifice dated to 1911 and was listed on the National Register of Historic Places. The plan was to incorporate the station into the ballpark plans, co-opting Union Station's lobby while reutilizing the building for a clubhouse, cafe, team store, and office space. In addition, a large model train was included within the park as an homage to the station.

As a result of its location, the Astros' future home was first referred to as the Ballpark at Union Station. Then Enron, the utility giant, purchased the naming rights. In early 2002, after Enron declared bankruptcy due to fraudulent practices, the ball club was able to take back the naming rights. The venue was called Astros Field until July 2002, when the team sold the naming rights to the locally based Coca-Cola subsidiary Minute Maid.

DESIGN AND CONSTRUCTION

The stadium was designed by HOK Sport, now known as Populous, and Molina and Associates. In late 1997 it was announced that local company Brown & Root Services would manage construction of the stadium, while electrification of the retractable roof was developed by VAHLE, Inc. Astros president Tal Smith suggested the location of the center-field flagpole and asked for a traditional "keyhole," a dirt path from home plate to the pitcher's mound. The dirt path never materialized, but the flagpole became known as Tal's Hill. The finished structure presented an interesting dialogue between the stately red-brick station and the soaring aqua girders and curved white roof of the stadium it adjoins.

[LEFT] Union Station, 1913

[BELOW] The exterior of Daikin Park at the intersection of Crawford Street and Texas Avenue shows how the former train station was incorporated into the design of the ballpark.

THE SIGN-STEALING SCANDAL

In a detailed 2019 report from *The Athletic* magazine, the Astros were accused of "sign stealing" during the two previous seasons. This term refers to videotaping other teams during games and analyzing the signs sent to pitchers from the catcher. The players in the Astros' dugout purportedly viewed the video feed, figured out the signs, then let the batter know what kind of pitch was coming; for instance, by banging a trash can lid. As a result of the investigation, MLB decided on inflicting the maximum punishment, levying a $5 million fine and stripping the team of it first- and second-round picks in the 2020 and 2021 draft. Certain members of the management staff were suspended or fired by the ball club.

[ABOVE] Astro Evan Gattis at bat during a 2018 game at Minute Maid between Houston and the Boston Red Sox.

[LEFT] An aerial view shows a rare sighting of the ballpark with its roof open. It's been noted that the Juice Box's roof policy favors a closed-roofed game. For example, a total of two open-roofed games were played in the 2023 season.

DAIKIN PARK FIRSTS

FIRST MLB GAME: 3/30/2000, Astros over NY Yankees, 6–5 (exhibition game)*

FIRST HOME RUN: 3/30/2000, Ricky Ledee (NY Yankees)*

FIRST NO-HITTER: 8/21/2015, Mike Fiers vs. Dodgers

FIRST ALL-STAR GAME: Scheduled for 2024

FIRST PLAYOFF GAME: 10/9/2001, Atlanta Braves over Astros, 7–5*

FIRST WORLD SERIES GAME: 10/25/2005, Chicago White Sox over Astros, 7–5 in Game 3

* as Enron Field

PUBLIC REACTION

Many fans and critics found the new park overly gimmicky; other grumblers disliked the hill in center field with a flagpole, the hokey train, and Enron for the unpopular name. One architectural critic had had enough and vented thus: "Nostalgia just for the sake of cuteness without context is artificial. These faux retro parks are an abomination."

But ultimately, Minute Maid Park (now Daikin) won over a number of its critics simply because when the gimmicks and other irritants were set aside, it proved to be an architecturally brilliant park. By incorporating Union Station's framework into the design, even to the point of using its roof to inspire the stadium's roof, the facility maintained a consistent design ethic seen in few new sports arenas. Subtle cues taken from the train motif are represented throughout the interior—in graphic displays, in the retractable roof tracks that resemble train tracks, and in the elegant stone arches in left field influenced by the station's facade—serving to link the two structures together.

Other notable features include the retractable three-panel roof with its 50,000-square-foot (4,645 m^2) sliding glass door which allows a view of the Houston city skyline; unusual interior intimacy for a roofed venue; coherent exterior design, Crawford boxes; one of the last hand-operated out-of-town scoreboards; a main concourse with great visual access to the field; terrific standing-room areas, including a balcony that juts over the field; social spaces in center field; and dining that includes regional cuisine. Finally, the local scene surrounding the stadium continues to develop, showing real potential for the future.

Ongoing concerns include the lack of a kids' area, an excess of team stores—including one in Union Station—crowding and bottlenecks on the Main Concourse, social spaces that are reserved only for groups, and a lack of tables, chairs, and other types of seating on all concourses. Also the retractable roof is open only during 16 percent of the games, even when outside temperatures are mild.

[ABOVE] The Crawford Boxes are a section of seating in Daikin Park running parallel to Crawford Street. As a tribute to the old Union Station, the left-field side of the stadium features a railway track and train. The train chugs along an 800-foot (240 m) track on top of the exterior wall when the Astros first take the field, when an Astros player hits a home run, and when the Astros win a game. The train is an upscaled replica of the *General* 4-4-0 and is moved by a cable that is operated by the driver. The model train's hopper originally held logs, but during the Minute Maid naming agreement, it held oranges.

[LEFT] Union Station Lobby, which served as a concourse to Houston's original Union Station, is the main entrance to the baseball park. Decked out in Astros pennants, it still retains the grandeur of the original 1911 structure.

SEATING CHART

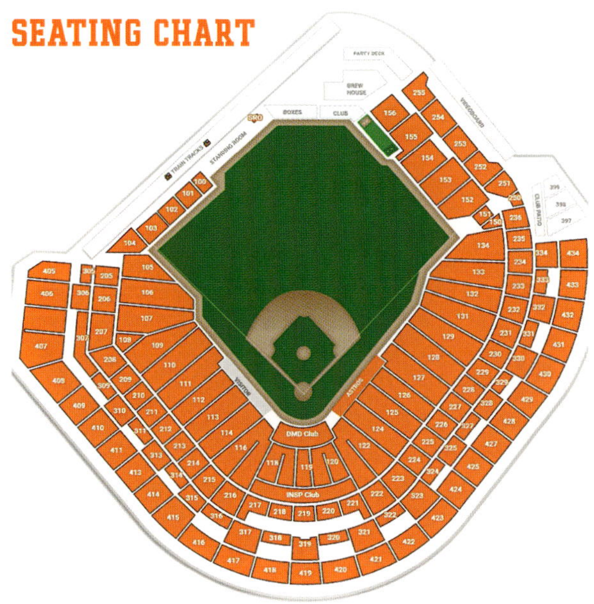

FEATURES AND AMENITIES

The field was renovated in 2010 during the offseason and again in 2017 during the offseason. It currently has a seating capacity of 41,168, which includes 5,197 club seats and 63 luxury suites.

ASTROS HALL OF FAME The Astros Hall of Fame walkway, which opened in 2019, is located on the Left Field Concourse in the former Home Run Alley and directly behind the Crawford Boxes. The accomplishments of the 26 inductees—including players, executives, and broadcasters—are highlighted with signage, photos, and displays containing artifacts from their careers.

HONORED PLAYERS Statues of Astros players Jeff Bagwell and Craig Biggio are located in the exterior space known as the Plaza at Daikin Park. The Plaza also displays pennants for the Astros' division and league championships, as well as two World Series titles, while several plaques commemorate notable Astros and their achievements.

ASTROS ACHIEVEMENTS

WORLD SERIES CHAMPIONSHIPS: 2 (2017, 2022)

NL PENNANTS: 1 (2005)

AL PENNANTS: 4 (2017, 2019, 2021, 2022)

NL WEST DIVISION TITLES: 3 (1980, 1981, 1986)

NL CENTRAL DIVISION TITLES: 4 (1997, 1998, 1999, 2001)

AL WEST DIVISION TITLES: 6 (2017, 2018, 2019, 2021, 2022, 2023)

WILD CARD BERTHS: 4 (2004, 2005, 2015, 2020)

PLAYOFF APPEARANCES: 17 (1980, 1981, 1986, 1997, 1998, 1999, 2001, 2004, 2005, 2015, 2017, 2018, 2019, 2020, 2021, 2022, 2023)

WORST SEASON RECORD: 2013, 51–111 (.315)

BEST SEASON RECORD: 2019, 107–55 (.660)

CHICK-FIL-A COWS In 2006 the Chick-fil-A cows debuted at the fair poles wearing Astro caps and saying, "Eat More Fowl." If an Astros player hits the pole, all fans in attendance get a coupon for a free chicken sandwich from Chick-fil-A.

PHILLIPS66 The "Phillips66 Home Run Porch" is located in left-center field above the field of play. It features an oversized classic gasoline pump that displays the total number of Astros home runs hit since the park opened. The exclusive Phillips66 Diamond Club offers first-class gourmet dining and is an elegant spot to watch the game, or hold business conferences or private parties.

FOOD AND DRINK There are plenty of food options at the stadium. Along with the typical concession fare of burgers, hot dogs, pizza, and nachos, there are more unusual favorites like the 18-hour smoked brisket and catfish po'boy with Cajun fries.

The Phillips66 gas pump keeps a running tally of homers hit at the park.

Orbit, the Houston Astros' mascot, is a lime-green space alien wearing an Astros jersey and with antennae jutting from his ball cap that extend into baseballs. The anthropomorphic alien was introduced in 1990.

OTHER HOMES OF THE ASTROS

ASTRODOME

1965–1999

Houston's Astrodome was the world's first multipurpose, domed sports stadium. It was financed and assisted in development by Roy Hofheinz, the mayor of Houston and a man known for pioneering modern stadiums. Construction on the venue began in 1963, and it officially opened in 1965. It housed the Houston Astros from 1965 to 2000, and the NFL Houston Oilers from 1968 to 1996. It was a part-time venue of the NBA Houston Rockets and home to the Houston Livestock Show and Rodeo from 1966 until 2002. At its opening in 1965, it was dubbed the "Eighth Wonder of the World."

The Astrodome was designed by a number of architectural firms, including Herman Lloyd & W. B. Morgan; Wilson, Morris, Crain & Anderson; and Praeger-Kavanagh-Waterbury, along with structural engineer Walter P. Moore. A number of engineering changes were necessitated, including the modest flattening of the supposed "hemispherical roof" and the use of a new paving process called "lime stabilization" to cope with changes in the chemistry of the soil. As a multipurpose stadium intended for both baseball and football, the facility was nearly circular and used lower seating areas that move. It launched the era of fully domed stadiums, including Caesars Superdome in New Orleans, the now-demolished Pontiac Silverdome near Detroit, Atlanta's Georgia Dome, the Hubert H. Humphrey Metrodome in Minneapolis, the RCA Dome in Indianapolis, and the Kingdome in Seattle.

[BELOW] The Astrodome, with a rich history filled with both ups and downs, was listed on the National Register of Historic Places in 2014 for its architectural and cultural significance.

> **"You and the people of Houston and Harris County have shown the world what men can accomplish when imagination, energy and sheer determination are combined in one tremendous project. The Astrodome will stand as a deserved tribute to the genius of its planners."**
>
> —PRESIDENT LYNDON B. JOHNSON SAID UPON THE ASTRODOME'S COMPLETION IN 1965

The Oilers departed the venue in 1996 to become the Tennessee Titans, followed by the Astros in 1999, who moved to Enron Field. After the construction of the retractable-roofed Reliant Stadium—built to house Houston's new NFL franchise, the Texans—the Houston Livestock Show and Rodeo chose to move there as well, leaving the Astrodome without any major tenants.

On August 31, 2005, after the massive destruction of Hurricane Katrina, Harris County and the State of Louisiana agreed to allow at least 25,000 evacuees from New Orleans to take shelter in the Astrodome until they could return home. The evacuation began on September 1, 2005, and all scheduled events at the Astrodome for the final four months of 2005 were canceled.

In 2008 the Astrodome was declared noncompliant with fire code, and parts of it were demolished in 2013. On November 5, 2013, Houston voters nixed a $213 million referendum to renovate and convert the Astrodome into a state-of-the-art convention center and exhibition space. Another plan to turn it into a covered, semi-climate-controlled park for festivals and concerts fell through. Discussions to convert it to an underground parking facility were put on hold in 2019. The venue is still standing, but no future plans for the stadium have been announced.

[ABOVE] The Astrodome in its heyday projected a thoroughly modern, even futuristic vibe, proclaiming to the rest of the world that Houston truly was "Space City."

[BELOW] Cots fill the floor under the dome. A total of about 25,000 Hurricane Katrina evacuees found shelter in the Astrodome in 2005.

COLT STADIUM

The Astros' first home field, Colt Stadium, had always been a temporary solution and was even once described in print as "a barn-like thing." It consisted of a single-deck grandstand with two outfield bleachers where fans were plagued by heat and mosquitoes . . . factors that led to the building of a domed replacement. After the team left, the structure was dismantled and moved to Mexico, where it was used by two different cities.

1968–PRESENT

OAKLAND-ALAMEDA COUNTY COLISEUM

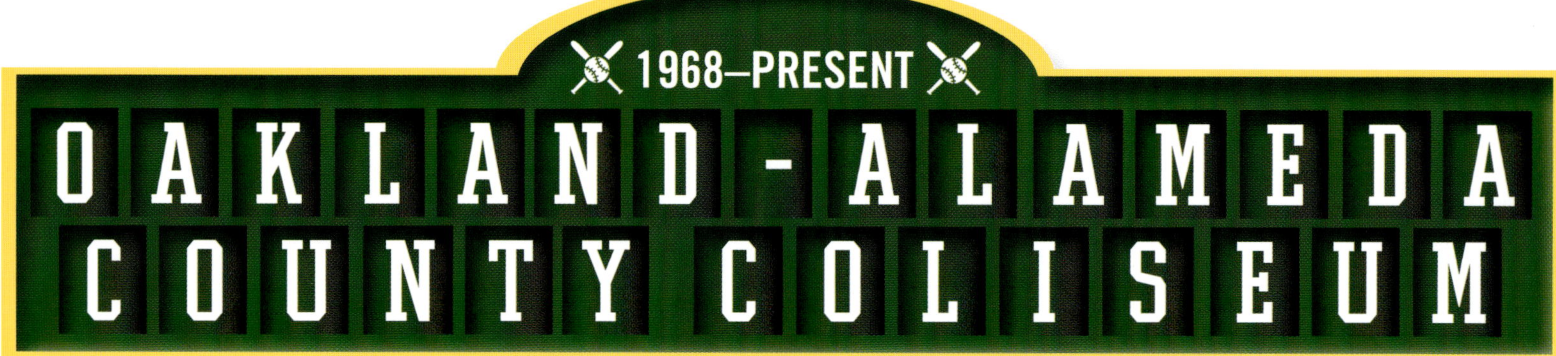

FORMER HOME OF THE OAKLAND ATHLETICS

AMERICAN LEAGUE (1901–PRESENT)

THIS MERCURIAL TEAM, *which has played out of Philadelphia; Kansas City, Missouri; Oakland's Coliseum; and now Las Vegas, has at times been formidable. Their impressive record of 9 World Series championships, 15 pennants, and 17 division titles is the second-highest in the American League after the New York Yankees. Their record-setting 20 consecutive wins during the 2002 season would go on to stimulate an interest in the application of sabermetrics for improving on-field performance.*

The Philadelphia Athletics, founded in 1901, would become one of the American League's eight charter clubs. Making their mark within their first decade, they won three World Series in 1910, 1911, and 1913, followed by back-to-back titles in 1929 and 1930. Much of the team's success was due to shrewd owner/manager Connie Mack. He managed the club for 50 years and holds the record as the longest-serving manager in the Majors. During his tenure, Mack's team won nine pennants and appeared in eight World Series. Those early

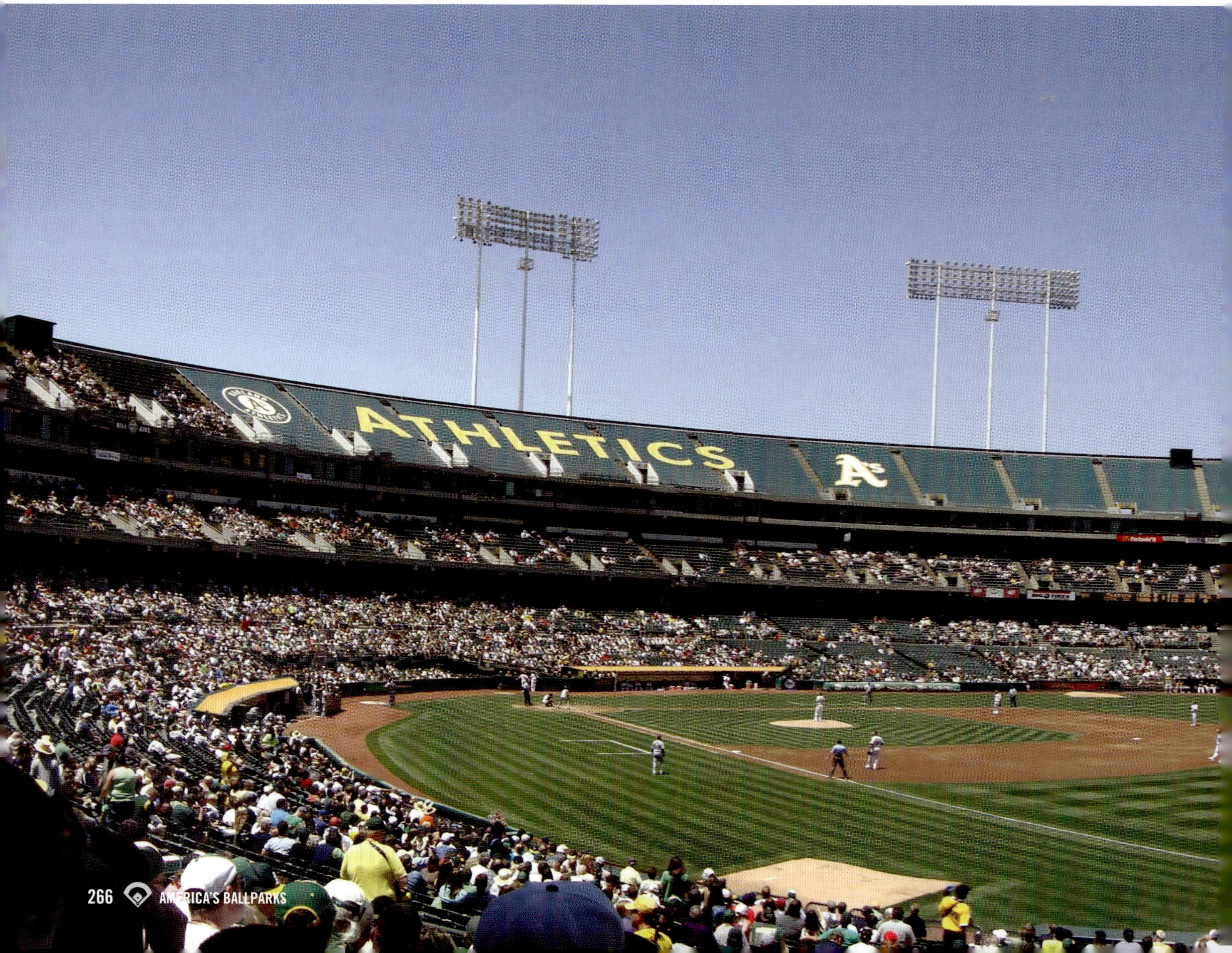

teams were supported by Hall of Famers like Chief Bender, Frank "Home Run" Baker, Jimmie Fox, and Lefty Grove. After relocating to Kansas City in 1955, the franchise faced declining attendance and, subsequently, a growing desire to move into the expanding West Coast sports market.

In 1968 the A's departed for Oakland, California, where a new stadium awaited them. The West Coast certainly agreed with the team—they won consecutive World Series in 1972, 1973, and 1974, inspired by players like Vida Blue, Catfish Hunter, Reggie Jackson, Rollie Fingers, and puckish owner Charlie O. Finley. Another streak followed after they were sold to Walter A. Haas—three consecutive pennant wins and a World Series win in 1989. This time the key players included Jose Canseco and Mark McGwire, a.k.a the "Bash Brothers," as well as Dennis Eckersley, Rickey Henderson, and manager Tony LaRussa.

Prior to the A's arrival in California, during the 1950s and 1960s the business and political leaders of Oakland regularly found themselves competing with nearby San Francisco. They desired recognition for their city as a thriving metropolitan area with its own identity and culture—apart from its proximity to San Francisco. The acquisition of a professional sports franchise was one way to cement this distinction. Civic leaders got a boost when Oakland was awarded the football Raiders, the eighth AFL franchise, on January 30, 1960, but they still had no stadium fit for AFL football or Major League Baseball. To oversee the financing and development of a multi-use facility, the city formed a nonprofit corporation made up of prominent Oakland businessmen. This group, including real estate developer Robert T. Nahas, former senator William Knowland, and Edgar F. Kaiser, would eventually became the stadium's governing board.

BALLPARK STATS

ADDRESS
7000 South Coliseum Way, Oakland, CA 94621

FORMER NAMES
Oakland–Alameda County Coliseum (1966–1998, 2008–2011, 2016–2019, 2020, 2023–present)
Network Associates Coliseum (1998–2004)
McAfee Coliseum (2004–2008)
Overstock.com Coliseum (2011)
O.co Coliseum (2011–2016)
RingCentral Coliseum (2019–2020, 2020–2023)

OWNER
Oakland–Alameda County Coliseum Authority

OPERATOR
AEG

ARCHITECT
Skidmore, Owings & Merrill; NTB

CAPACITY
46,847

RECORD BASEBALL ATTENDANCE
56,310 on 7/21/2018 (vs. SF Giants)

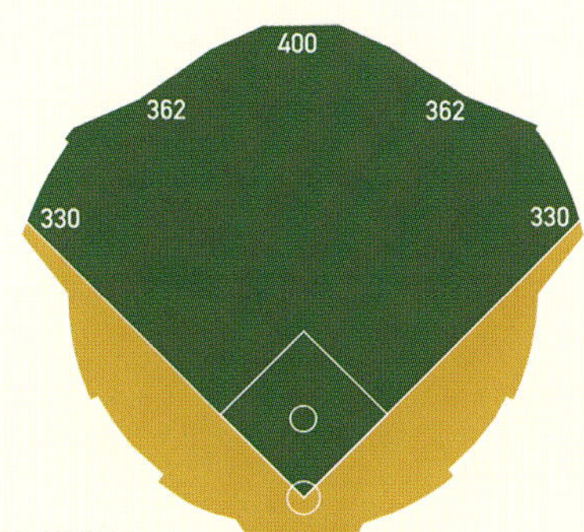

FIELD SIZE
- **Left field** 330 feet (101 m)
- **Left center** 388 feet (118 m)
- **Center field** 400 feet (122 m)
- **Right center** 388 feet (118 m)
- **Right field** 330 feet (101 m)
- **Backstop** 60 feet (18 m)

SURFACE
Tifway II Bermuda grass

TEAM MASCOT
Stomper

> “In its sheer scale and its gritty, utilitarian aesthetic, it is both a landmark and an emblem of Oakland. It has played an important role in the evolution of Oakland as a place.”
>
> —DAN MOORE, *THE OAKLANDSIDE*, 2021

A pedestrian bridge connects a BART stop with the Oakland Coliseum complex. BART is the rapid transit system serving the San Francisco Bay Area.

ATHLETICS ACHIEVEMENTS

WORLD SERIES CHAMPIONSHIPS: 9 (1910*, 1911*, 1913*, 1929*, 1930*, 1972, 1973, 1974, 1989)

AL PENNANTS: 15 (1902*, 1905*, 1910*, 1911*, 1913*, 1914*, 1929,* 1930*, 1931*, 1972, 1973, 1974, 1988, 1989, 1990)

AL WEST DIVISION TITLES: 17 (1971, 1971, 1972, 1973, 1974, 1975, 1981, 1988, 1989, 1990, 1992, 2000, 2002, 2003, 2006, 2012, 2013, 2020)

WILD CARD BERTHS: 4 (2001, 2014, 2018, 2019)

PLAYOFF APPEARANCES: 29 (1905*, 1910*, 1911*, 1913*, 1914*, 1929*, 1930*, 1931*, 1971, 1972, 1973, 1974, 1975, 1981, 1988, 1989, 1990, 1992, 2000, 2001, 2002, 2003, 2006, 2012, 2013, 2014, 2018, 2019, 2020)

WORST SEASON RECORD: 1916, 36–117 (.235)

BEST SEASON RECORD: 2002, 103–59 (.636)

* as Philadelphia Athletics

In November 1960, an East Oakland site was chosen alongside the new Nimitz Freeway. The Port of Oakland was instrumental in this choice—a parcel at the head of San Leandro Bay had been given to the East Bay Regional Park District in exchange for 105 acres (42 ha) of parkland on the other side of the freeway, which the port then donated to the city. Once $25 million in financing was arranged, in 1962 construction began—without a pro baseball team in sight. In 1965 there was talk the Cleveland Indians were considering a move to the West Coast, but they never acted on it. Meanwhile, Charlie Finley was dissatisfied in Kansas City, and when he expressed his admiration for Oakland's new facility, Robert Nahas helped persuade him to bring his team west.

The NFL Raiders moved to the stadium in 1966, while the Athletics did not arrive there until two years later. And as was often the case with multi-use stadiums, the design served neither sport particularly well. Ten years after their debut at the Coliseum, the A's were already looking to leave—officials from the Louisiana Superdome negotiated with team management regarding a possible move to their venue in New Orleans. But the team was unable to break their lease with the Coliseum. After the Raiders departed for Los Angeles in 1982, many baseball-specific improvements were made. Yet, the stadium tried to lure the Raiders to come back, agreeing to add 20,000 extra seats. When the Raiders returned to Oakland 13 years later, the seating had expanded to a capacity of 63,026, but the inspiring view of the Oakland foothills was now obscured by an outfield grandstand. The fans called it Mount Davis, after Raiders owner, Al Davis. In 2006 the A's began placing a tarp over this top-tier seating during games, creating the lowest-capacity stadium in the Major Leagues. The A's were the last MLB team to share a stadium full-time with an NFL team, an arrangement that ended in 2020, when the Raiders moved to Las Vegas.

The deep bowl of the structure has a playing field that is actually below sea level. The 1994 comedy *Angels in the Outfield* was filmed in part at Oakland–Alameda County Coliseum, which was standing in for Anaheim Stadium.

DESIGN AND CONSTRUCTION

Designed by Skidmore, Owings & Merrill and HNTB, with Myron Goldsmith acting as principal design architect and Guy F. Atkinson Company as general contractor, the Coliseum was built at a cost of $25.5 million. The complex consisted of an outdoor stadium, an enclosed arena, and a connecting exhibit hall, whose roof acted as the central pedestrian plaza. At its completion the Oakland-Alameda County Coliseum looked unlike any other American sports venue. It utilized an "underground" design—the playing field is not only below ground level, it is actually 21 feet (6.4 m) below sea level. As a result, fans entering the stadium walk on to the main concourse at the top of the first level of seats. This, combined with the hill that was built up around the stadium to create the upper concourse, means that only the third deck can be seen from outside the park.

The designers may have had faith in their novel approach to the "sunken" stadium, but fans and critics were not always kind after it opened. "The exterior looks like a concrete parking garage and is not very attractive," one fan wrote, then added, "The Coliseum has the narrowest main concourse we've been in and was quite crowded." On the plus side, visitors often lauded the ambiance in the stands and praised the helpfulness of the staff.

OAKLAND-ALAMEDA COUNTY COLISEUM FIRSTS

FIRST MLB GAME: 4/17/1968, Baltimore Orioles over A's, 4–1

FIRST HOME RUN: 4/17/1968, Powell (Baltimore Orioles)

FIRST NO-HITTER: 5/8/1968, Jim "Catfish" Hunter vs. Minnesota Twins

FIRST ALL-STAR GAME: 7/14/1987, NL defeats AL, 2–0

FIRST PLAYOFF GAME: 10/5/1971, Baltimore Orioles over A's, 5–3

FIRST WORLD SERIES GAME: 10/18/1972, Cincinnati Reds over A's, 1–0 in Game 3

FEATURES AND AMENITIES

The Coliseum ultimately did serve the purpose the town fathers intended, becoming a multi-sports hub that enhanced the Oakland experience both for residents and visitors. Features and amenities included the following.

THE TREEHOUSE This area sits above the left field bleachers and is accessed with a Treehouse Pass. The 10,000-square-foot (929 m^2) area consists of the Don Julio Deck, with a bar and lounge seating; the Bulleit Bar, an urban treehouse with a bar, living wall, ping-pong, pool, and foosball tables, and numerous seating options; and a standing-room, terraced deck with drink rails and views of the field.

[ABOVE] The Oakland Athletics mascot, Stomper, poses for a photo with sailors assigned to the amphibious assault ship USS *Bonhomme Richard* during San Francisco Fleet Week, 2018.

[LEFT] The team insignia—the familiar letter "A"—is one of the oldest sports logos still in use. An image in *Harper's Weekly* of the team with their rivals, the Brooklyn Atlantics, shows the "A" appearing on their uniforms as early as 1866.

SHIBE PARK TAVERN This pub offers a nostalgic look at Athletics' history in Philadelphia with an actual brick from Shibe Park; it features an updated bar, new seating, and a pool table.

THE STOMPING GROUND This area near the right-field flagpoles is a fun and interactive space where children can enjoy themselves while adults watch the field. It features a stage and video wall for interactive events, a digital experience where youngsters race against their favorite A's players or Stomper, a replica A's dugout, a simulated hitting and pitching machine, foosball, and a photo booth.

FOOD AND DRINK There is the usual assortment of "stadium" food at the concessions, but fans looking for interesting local fare can sample the offerings of the food trucks on Championship Plaza.

SEATING CHART

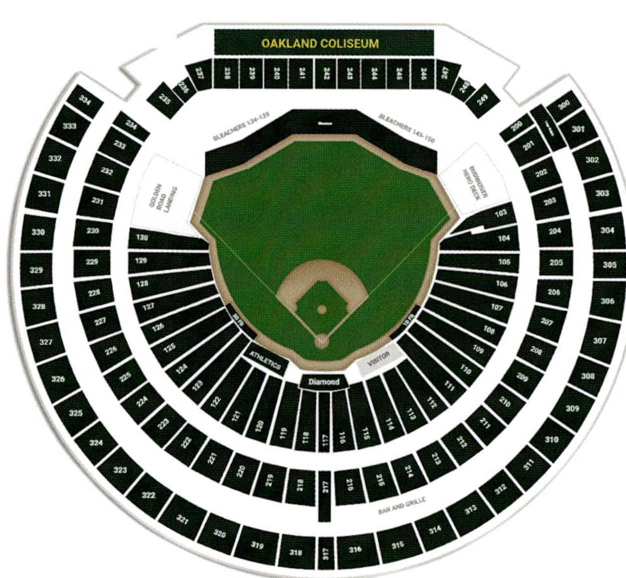

MOVING TO LAS VEGAS

By 2020, the A's found themselves the only major sports team left in Oakland. The NHL California Golden Seals relocated to Cleveland in 1976, the NBA Golden State Warriors moved across the Bay to San Francisco in 2019, and the NFL Oakland Raiders moved to Las Vegas in 2020. Meanwhile, the Coliseum was widely criticized for being poorly maintained and out of date. Along with Tropicana Field, it is typically rated one of the worst ballparks in Major League Baseball. Yet, when the A's ownership sought government assistance for constructing a new park, the negotiations proved fruitless.

Then on April 20, 2023, the team revealed they had entered a land purchase agreement with the Red Rock Resort in Paradise, Las Vegas. On May 9, 2023, the Athletics announced their future location will now be the site of Tropicana Las Vegas, a hotel/casino that will be demolished to make room for a $1.5 billion project—a 33,000-seat ballpark with a retractable roof and a 1,500-room hotel and casino. Nevada governor Joe Lombardo signed a $380 million stadium funding bill into law on June 15, 2023, and on November 16, 2023, MLB owners unanimously approved the Athletics' move to the Las Vegas area. Heartbroken A's fans have held protests against the move, but the die, so to speak, has been cast.

[BOTTOM] Oakland A's fans hang a sign protesting the owners' desire to move the team out of Oakland, August 16, 2010. In 2009, the City of San Jose had attempted to open negotiations with the team regarding a move to the city. That move never came to be.

[BELOW] Déjà vu all over again. After news of the latest plans to move the A's an advertising campaign called "Rooted in Oakland" was launched to emphasize the club's apparent commitment to building a ballpark in its longtime home city prior to shifting their focus to Las Vegas. Those hopes were dashed when plans were announced for a retractable roof ballpark that would be built in Paradise, Nevada, to house the team. Slated to open for the 2028 MLB season, this new ballpark will be the first in the franchise's history to be solely theirs without a companion sports team tenant since the completion of Philadelphia's Shibe Park in 1909.

> "I've been an A's fan as long as I can remember, I've seen every single home game since I was a little boy; they belong in Oakland and thrive in this city, maybe someday we can be champions again, but we shouldn't give up and move to Vegas like the Raiders, keep fighting for your team Oakland!"
>
> —GEORGE WALKER, A'S FAN, ROOTEDINOAKLAND.ORG

OTHER HOMES OF THE ATHLETICS
EARLY BALLPARKS
1901–1954

The early Philadelphia Athletics, an MLB ball club that played in Philadelphia from 1901 to 1954, first played in Columbia Park at 29th and Columbia in North Philadelphia, which became their venue for two games in the 1905 World Series. In April 1909 the team moved to Shibe Park at 21st and Lehigh Avenues, in a section of North Philadelphia called Swampoodle. They remained there until 1954. The park was the first concrete-and-steel stadium in the Major League and was named for Ben Shibe, an Athletics stockholder and baseball manufacturer. The team prospered here over the next few decades, but in the 1930s it went into a 30-year decline that endured through three cities. (See Philadelphia Phillies, Shibe Park/ Connie Mack Stadium page 31.)

Athletics Jimmie Foxx and Al Simmons flank Yankees' legends Babe Ruth and Lou Gehrig, circa 1925–1932, when the A's were based in their original home of Philly. The team moved to Kansas City in 1954, but after more than 10 lean years, they moved to Oakland in 1967.

ORIGINS OF THE NAME

The team's name derived from the term "athletic club" used for local gentlemen's clubs—and it dates to 1860, when an amateur team, the Athletic Club of Philadelphia, was created. The team turned professional in 1875 and became a charter member of the National League in 1876 but were expelled after one season. A later version of the Athletics played for the American Association from 1882 to 1891. Current club nicknames include the A's, the Swingin' A's, Green Elephants, the Elephants, and the Green and Gold.

[LEFT AND BELOW] What began as a gibe aimed at Benjamin Shibe for spending too much on the Athletics became a part of the team's identity. Beginning in 1903 the "white elephant" began appearing on all sorts of A's merchandise, such as pennants, banners, score books, and buttons.

THE STORIED ELEPHANT MASCOT

At the turn of the 20th century, New York Giants manager John McGraw told reporters that Philadelphia manufacturer Benjamin Shibe had a "white elephant on his hands" after he gained controlling interest in the Athletics. Athletics manager Connie Mack one-upped him by adopting a white elephant as the team mascot. He even presented McGraw with a toy stuffed elephant at the 1905 World Series. The A's were wearing an elephant logo on their sweaters by 1909, and by 1918 it turned up on their uniform jerseys. During 1963, after the team relocated to Kansas City, owner Charlie Finley changed the mascot to a mule—named Charlie O—perhaps to appeal to Midwestern farmers, or perhaps to attract the local Democrats, whose party symbol was another long-ear, a donkey. Since 1988 the A's have worn an elephant illustration on their left sleeve, and starting in the mid-1980s a costumed elephant appeared on the field. Originally named Harry Elephante, he became Stomper in 1997.

MUNICIPAL STADIUM
1955–1967

This Kansas City sports fixture was designed by Osborn Engineering and opened July 3, 1923. It has three earlier names: Muehlebach Field (1923–1937), Ruppert Stadium (1937–1943), and Blues Stadium (1943–1954). When it opened in 1923 its capacity was 17,476, then it increased to 35,561 in 1971. It was built for the minor league Kansas City Blues of the American Association by owner and businessman George E. Muehlebach. He moved his team there as a replacement for their previous home, Association Park, after its railroad company owner ran tracks through the outfield in 1922. The stadium also hosted the Kansas City Monarchs, the longest-running team in the Negro Leagues, from 1923 to 1955. Three of the first Colored World Series games were held here in 1924, and the Negro Leagues Baseball Museum, founded in 1990, is just blocks away from its former site.

The stadium consisted of a single-deck, covered grandstand, running from the right-field foul pole down and around most of the left-field line. When the New York Yankees bought the Blues as its top farm team in 1937, the stadium was renamed Ruppert Stadium to honor Yankees' owner, Col. Jacob Ruppert. After his death the venue became Blues Stadium in 1943.

Fans watch a game between the K.C. Monarchs and the Indianapolis Clowns in 1953. Beginning in 1923 the Monarchs called this ballpark home, under both its Muehlebach Field and Ruppert Stadium names.

In 1953, Chicago real estate tycoon Arnold Johnson bought both Blues Stadium and Yankee Stadium. After purchasing the Philadelphia Athletics from Connie Mack in 1954, he relocated them to Kansas City. He sold Blues Stadium to Kansas City, which renamed it Municipal Stadium and leased it back to Johnson for the A's.

Prior to the 1955 season the facility underwent an almost complete remodeling. On opening day, former President Harry S. Truman, a Missouri man himself, threw out the ceremonial first pitch. The Athletics remained at Municipal until 1967; other Kansas City teams it hosted include the MLB Royals from 1969 to 1972, the AFL/NFL Chiefs from 1963 to 1971, and the NASL Spurs from 1968 to 1969. In 1971, during the stadium's final football game, it became the site of the longest game in NFL history, a Christmas Day playoff match between the Chiefs and the Miami Dolphins, with the double-overtime playoff contest lasting 82 minutes and 40 seconds. Municipal Stadium was finally demolished in 1976, replaced by a municipal garden. Today the site is being redeveloped with single-family homes.

Former President Harry S. Truman (*center*) tossed out the first ball at the Kansas City Athletics opening game at the newly renovated Municipal Stadium on April 12, 1955. Athletics manager Lou Boudreau is at left; Detroit Tigers manager Stanley "Bucky" Harris is at right. A's owner, Arnold Johnson, is standing behind Bucky Harris.

HOME OF THE SAN FRANCISCO GIANTS

NATIONAL LEAGUE (1883–PRESENT)

LIKE THE BROOKLYN DODGERS IN THE MID-1950S, *the New York Giants were also baseball pioneers of the West Coast. They settled in San Francisco, and the city took them into its heart. Although they may not always play like the "old" team from the Polo Grounds, the Giants of Oracle Park still have the power to attract loyal, lifelong fans.*

The Giants were a mainstay of New York sports for decades before they upped stakes and headed to California. Founded in 1883 as the New York Gothams, they then took the name Giants starting in 1885. One of the oldest clubs in professional baseball, they evolved into a truly formidable franchise that accumulated more wins than any other major American sports team.

The early Giants played in an Upper Manhattan field called the Polo Grounds, where they remained for 75 years. Then in 1957, team owner Horace Stoneham was convinced to follow their archrivals, the Dodgers, to California by none other than Dodgers owner Walter O'Malley. The Giants and their rivals were the first MLB teams to play on the West Coast, making baseball a sport that now spanned the nation. Eventually some established teams followed them west, while others were created as western expansion franchises.

San Francisco welcomed the Giants, who played two seasons in Seals Stadium, home to the PCL's San Francisco Seals from 1931 to 1957, before moving to newly completed Candlestick Park in 1960. This multi-use stadium was also home to the NFL San Francisco 49ers starting in 1971.

In spite of achieving winning seasons during their first 14 years in San Francisco, the team had an erratic record over their first five decades, making only nine playoff appearances and winning a mere three pennants. They returned to form in the early 2000s, when outfielder Barry Bonds hit 73 home runs, breaking the record for most homers in a season. Then, in 2007, Bonds would surpass Hank Aaron's career record of 755 home runs (Bonds ended his career with a record 762 home runs, 586 hit with the Giants). The team also won the World Series in 2010, 2012, and 2014, reestablishing much of their former luster. The fans noticed—from October 1, 2010, through June 16, 2017, the Giants set a National League record with 530 consecutive sellouts.

In 1992, San Francisco businessman Peter Magowan, an avid Giants fan, found enough local investors to buy the team. Construction on a new stadium began in 1997, and roughly three years later—and after an outlay of $357 million—Pacific Bell Park opened on April 11, 2000. Three years later it briefly became SBC Park during the 2004–2005 season. Then, from 2006 to 2018, the stadium was called AT&T Park until the naming rights went to computer software company Oracle, whose naming rights deal is for 20 years. In addition to the Giants, the ballfield has also been home to the San Francisco Demons of the XLF (2001), the NCAA Kraft Hunger Bowl (2002–2013), the California Redwoods of the UFL (2009), and the California Golden Bears, NCAA (2011).

DESIGN AND CONSTRUCTION

Considered one of the most beautiful and best-situated ballparks in the Majors, the venue was designed by esteemed architect firm HOK Sport (now Populous). The chosen site was an industrial waterfront section of downtown San Francisco called China Basin, in the up-and-coming neighborhoods of South Beach and Mission Bay. The field was situated on the edge of an inlet of San Francisco Bay, which the team renamed McCovey Cove in 2000 in honor of the team's Hall of Fame batter Willie McCovey. To avoid the chilling wind that plagued Candlestick Park, a team of engineers studied the problem and were able to greatly reduce the gusting. The park's harborside location means that damp fog and cool temperatures during summer games are still a possibility.

BALLPARK STATS

ADDRESS
24 Willie Mays Plaza, San Francisco, CA 94107

FORMER NAMES
Pacific Bell Park (2000–2003)
SBC Park (2004–2005)
AT&T Park (2006–2018)

OWNER
Port of San Francisco

OPERATOR
San Francisco Baseball Associates LP

ARCHITECT
HOK Sport (now Populous)

CAPACITY
41,915

RECORD BASEBALL ATTENDANCE
44,046 on 10/8/2010 (NLDS Game 2)

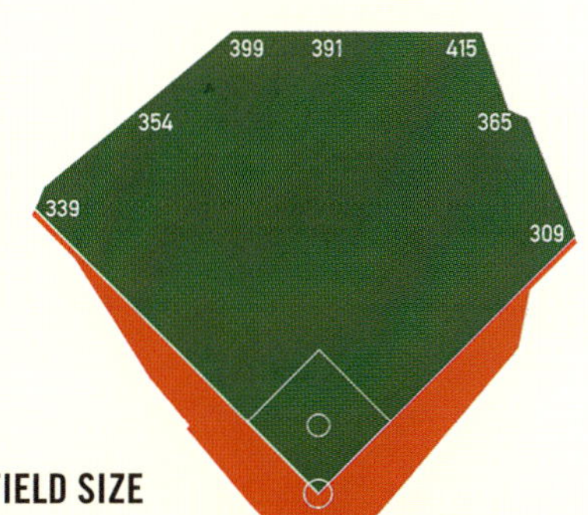

FIELD SIZE

Left field line 339 feet (103 m)
Left field 354 feet (108 m)
Left-center field 399 feet (122 m)
Center field 391 feet (119 m)
Right-center field 415 feet (126 m)
Right field 365 feet (111 m)
Right field line 309 feet (94 m)
Backstop 48 feet (15 m)

SURFACE
Tifway 419 Bermuda grass

TEAM MASCOT
Lou Seal

[ABOVE] A neon sign lights up the stadium's name at the Willie Mays Gate, and palm trees line the courtyard that features a statue of "the Say Hey Kid."

The stadium, which opened on April 11, 2000, cost $357 million to construct and was the first ballpark built without public funding since Dodger Stadium in 1962. The original seating capacity of 40,800 was increased over time. The stadium now offers 68 luxury suites, 5,200 club seats on the club level, and an additional 1,500 club seats at field level behind home plate. Oracle is considered a pitcher's park—easily the most pitcher-friendly park in the National League—because the depth of the outfield limits home runs. In 2010, Oracle Park became the first ballpark in the Majors to receive the LEED Silver Certification for Existing Buildings, Operations, and Maintenance.

PUBLIC REACTIONS

When it opened, Oracle Park was universally praised for its classic design, cozy atmosphere, and clear views of the playing field, as well as its location in one of the most fascinating cities in the United States. It stunned those early game-goers with its spectacular views of the water, the famous Frisco skyline, and the Bay Bridge, and it continues to be rated one of the most attractive and welcoming stadiums in the country.

FEATURES AND AMENITIES

The lively spirit that permeates the park makes it a favorite for regular fans and new guests alike. There are historical displays, fun traditions, a wide range of food and drink choices, a mini-version of the ball field for kids, and even an educational garden.

WALL OF FAME The Giants' Wall of Fame debuted on September 2008, at the King Street side of the ballpark. As part of the 50th

A sculpture of Willie McCovey overlooks McCovey Cove and the bay.

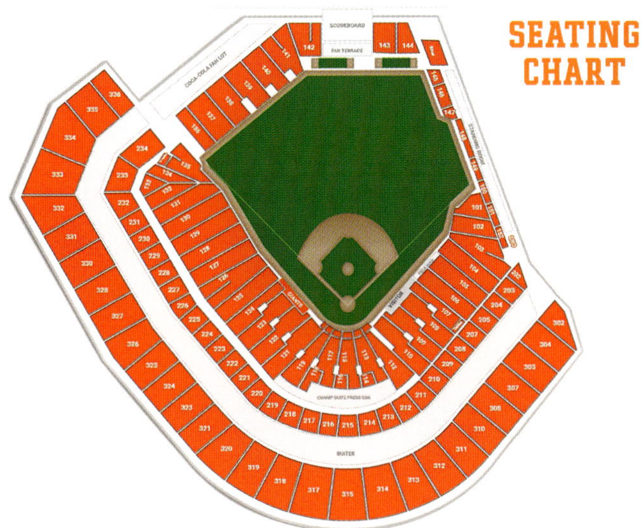

anniversary celebration of the Giants' move to San Francisco, 48 retired team members were inducted, on the basis of longevity and achievement.

FAMILY-FRIENDLY FEATURES On the Promenade Level above the left field bleachers sits the Fan Lot, an interactive area for children and adults that includes a miniature replica of the stadium. Above the field looms an 80-foot-long (24 m) Coca Cola bottle with playground slides that light up for every Giants' home run. To the bottle's right is the giant 1927 Old-Time Four-Fingered Baseball Glove, a behemoth made of steel and fiberglass.

GARDEN AT ORACLE PARK The Garden at Oracle Park is a living, learning classroom that, through hands-on activities, encourages

[ABOVE RIGHT] Fans rise from their seats for the national anthem in the bleacher section below the Coca-Cola bottle slide and steel-and-fiberglass "Giant 1927 Old-Time Four-Fingered Baseball Glove."

[BELOW RIGHT] Players with the San Francisco Giants watch the baseball game from the dugout at Oracle Park.

[BELOW] Lou Seal, a marine mammal dressed in a Giants jersey, has served as team mascot since 1996. He was christened after a naming contest, and the six people who suggested Lou Seal got to watch a game from a luxury box.

GIANTS ACHIEVEMENTS

WORLD SERIES CHAMPIONSHIPS: 8 (1905*, 1921*, 1922*, 1933*, 1954*, 2010, 2012, 2014)

NL PENNANTS: 23 (1888*, 1889*, 1904*, 1905*, 1911*, 1912*, 1913*, 1917*, 1921*, 1922*, 1923*, 1924*, 1933*, 1936*, 1937*, 1951*, 1954*, 1962, 1989, 2002, 2010, 2012, 2014)

NL WEST DIVISION TITLES: 9 (1971, 1987, 1989, 1997, 2000, 2003, 2010, 2012, 2021)

WILD CARD BERTHS: 3 (2002, 2014, 2016)

PLAYOFF APPEARANCES: 27 (1905*, 1911*, 1912*, 1913*, 1917*, 1921*, 1922*, 1923*, 1924*, 1933*, 1936*, 1937*, 1951*, 1954*, 1962, 1971, 1987, 1989, 1997, 2000, 2002, 2003, 2010, 2012, 2014, 2016, 2021)

WORST SEASON RECORD: 1902, 48–88 (.353)*

BEST SEASON RECORD: 1904, 106–47 (.693)*

* as NY Giants

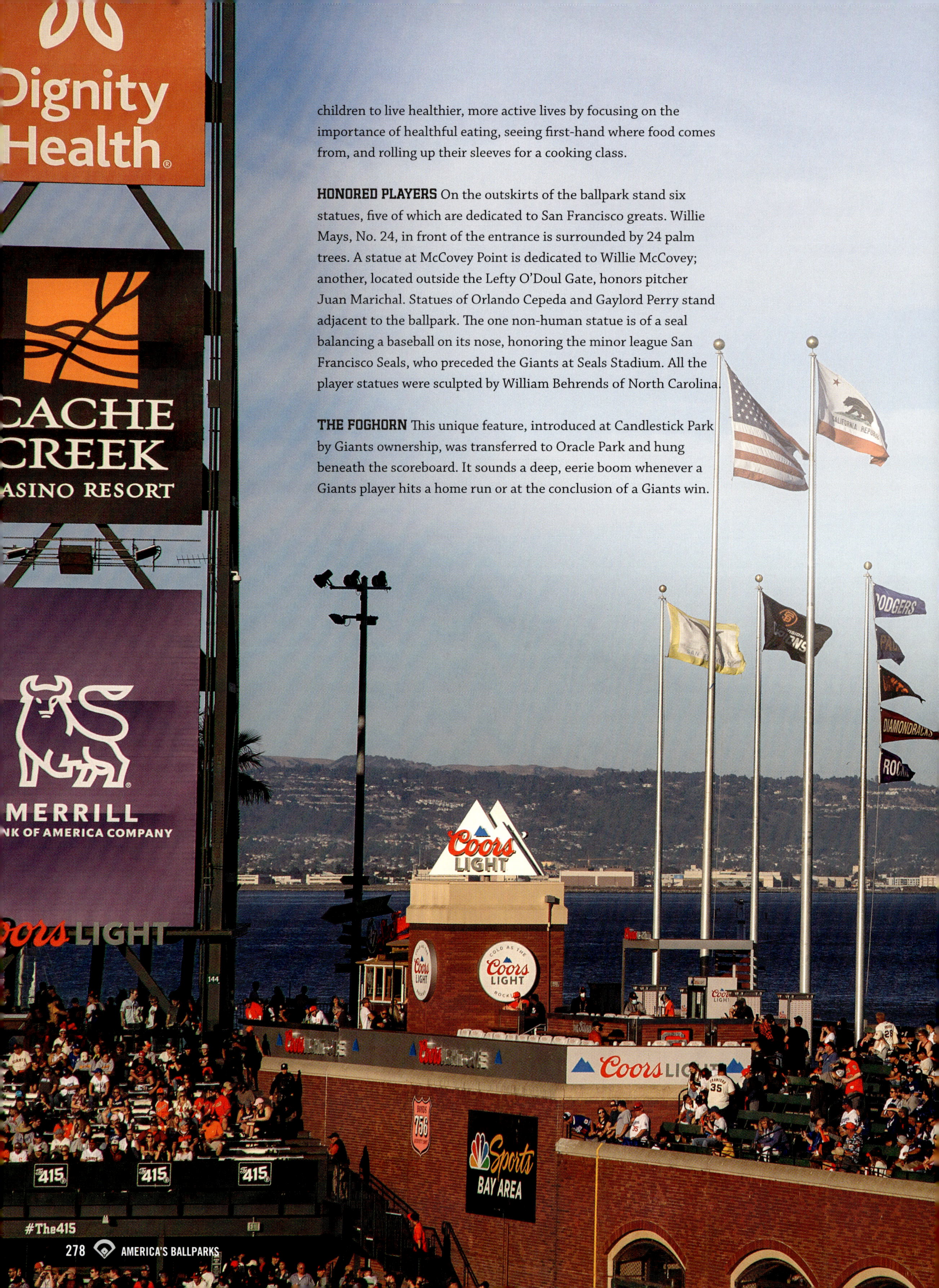

children to live healthier, more active lives by focusing on the importance of healthful eating, seeing first-hand where food comes from, and rolling up their sleeves for a cooking class.

HONORED PLAYERS On the outskirts of the ballpark stand six statues, five of which are dedicated to San Francisco greats. Willie Mays, No. 24, in front of the entrance is surrounded by 24 palm trees. A statue at McCovey Point is dedicated to Willie McCovey; another, located outside the Lefty O'Doul Gate, honors pitcher Juan Marichal. Statues of Orlando Cepeda and Gaylord Perry stand adjacent to the ballpark. The one non-human statue is of a seal balancing a baseball on its nose, honoring the minor league San Francisco Seals, who preceded the Giants at Seals Stadium. All the player statues were sculpted by William Behrends of North Carolina.

THE FOGHORN This unique feature, introduced at Candlestick Park by Giants ownership, was transferred to Oracle Park and hung beneath the scoreboard. It sounds a deep, eerie boom whenever a Giants player hits a home run or at the conclusion of a Giants win.

FOOD AND DRINK The @Café, a social media café, opened in 2013 and features large screens showing fans' social media posts from Facebook, X, and Instagram. Food concessions offer classic ballpark fare, like hot dogs and nachos, but more adventurous fans can try Mission tacos, lumpia (fried spring rolls), porchetta sandwiches, Gilroy garlic or Dungeness crab fries, or a poke bowl.

WATER DOGS PLAY FETCH

Oracle Park's right-field fence is built on the edge of the water, and home runs hit over the right field bleachers and into the drink are called "splashdown homers." During games, fans often congregate on the creek in small boats, hoping to catch one. When the ballpark first opened, the Giants had a team of trained Portuguese water dogs, known as BARK (Baseball's Aquatic Retrieval Korps), to retrieve balls that fell into the water. These balls were then auctioned off to benefit animal shelters.

ORACLE PARK FIRSTS

FIRST MLB GAME: 4/11/2000, LA Dodgers over Giants, 6–5*

FIRST HOME RUN: 4/11/2000, Kevin Elster (LA Dodgers)*

FIRST NO-HITTER: 7/10/2009, Jonathan Sánchez vs Padres†

FIRST ALL-STAR GAME: 7/10/2007, AL over NL, 5–4†

FIRST PLAYOFF GAME: 10/4/2000, Giants over NY Mets, 5–1*

FIRST WORLD SERIES GAME: 10/27/2010, Giants over Texas Rangers, 11–7 in Game 1†

* as Pacific Bell Park

† as AT&T Park

[ABOVE] A lively and festive view of McCovey Cove shows it filled with fans in boats, kayaks, rafts, and other watercraft wearing Giants gear while holding signs and gloves, hoping to catch a splashdown home run ball.

[RIGHT] Oracle Park logo on one of the entrance gates

[BACKGROUND] The San Francisco Bay lies directly beyond the right-field wall at Oracle Park. The right-field wall, designed to resemble the one at the Polo Grounds, includes Levi's Landing and the "Splash Hit" counter, which keeps a tally of hits knocked into the water by Giants players since the park opened. As of June 2, 2023, the count was 100—35 hit by Barry Bonds, the only player to record two splash hits in a single game so far.

OTHER HOMES OF THE GIANTS

POLO GROUNDS
1891–1957

Two years later the Gothams-turned-Giants moved to Coogan's Hollow in Harlem, where they played in several stadiums called the Polo Grounds: Polo II located at 155th and 157th Streets along 8th Avenue, and Polo III along 157th and 159th Streets (formerly Brotherhood Park), which had a seating capacity of 16,000. Here, the main double-decked grandstand arched around home plate and down the baselines, with bleachers located in dead center field. By 1911, the venue had the largest seating capacity in baseball. Built mainly of wood, the ballpark was, as so many others were, swept by a fire on April 14, 1911. All that remained were the outfield bleachers.

The next iteration of the Polo Grounds was a modern steel-and-concrete stadium designed by architect Henry Beaumont Herts at a cost $500,000. Polo IV had a seating capacity of 16,000, but it was only partially completed when the New York

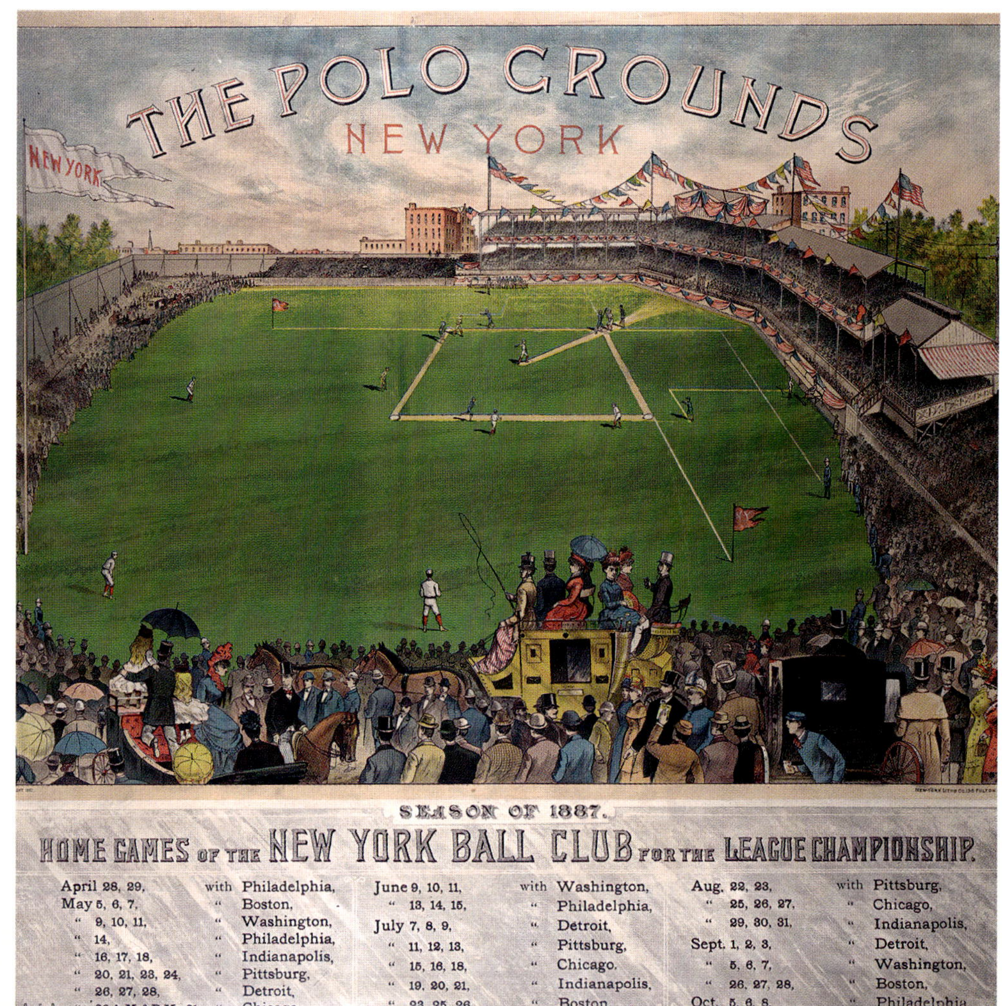

[ABOVE] Calendar for the 1887 season at the Polo Grounds. The original Polo Grounds was home to the New York Metropolitans from 1880 through 1885, and the New York Giants from 1883 through 1888. By 1889, when the grid extension plan of uptown Manhattan began to impact the playing field, the Giants were forced to begin their 1889 season at Oakland Park in Jersey City, New Jersey.

[ABOVE] The New York Gothams in 1883. The team name would change to the Giants two years later.

[ABOVE RIGHT] Ticket for the 1922 World Series (then known as the World's Championship Series). Every game of this 19th edition of the Series was played at the Polo Grounds because both the National League champion New York Giants and the American League champion New York Yankees called the ballpark home. The home team designation alternated with each game.

[RIGHT] Fans crowd the stands to watch Game 1 of the 1922 World Series, October 4. The Giants beat the Yankees in five games in the first Series with a permanent best-of-seven format.

Giants first played there on June 28, 1911. The grandstand received a second deck, and seating was expanded to nearly 55,000 in 1922. In later decades the stadium occasionally saw play by the New York Yankees and New York Mets.

Very few alterations were made to the facility during the following decades as the Giants continued to post winning seasons one after another. One of baseball's most iconic moments took place at this field, a walk-off home run on October 3, 1951, that ended the intense National League pennant playoffs between the Giants and their archrivals, the Brooklyn Dodgers. After the Giants' victory, sportswriters called it "the shot heard round the world."

Yet, by the 1950s the Giants were no longer filling seats. The ballpark needed major updating, and the neighborhood around it, now full of tenements, was changing. Support from the city for a new stadium was not on the table, so in 1957 owner Horace Stoneham relocated his team to San Francisco and the promise of a new ball field. Polo Grounds was demolished on April 10, 1964, making way for several 30-story housing projects. A plaque now marks where the venerable ballpark once stood.

[ABOVE] The 1937 World Series again saw the Giants and Yankees in competition. The buildings lining Edgecombe Avenue on Coogan's Bluff form a backdrop for the park.

[BELOW] A 1913 postcard shows the newly rebuilt Polo Grounds after fire destroyed the original.

CANDLESTICK PARK
1960–1999

Perhaps best known to pop music fans as the site of the very last Beatles concert, Candlestick Park served as the former home of the San Francisco Giants from 1960 to 1999. It was also home to the NFL 49ers until 2013, when they relocated to new Levi's Stadium in Santa Clara. Through no fault of its own, Candlestick Park was loathed by many fans for the cold, wet, gusty winds that buffeted the stands and the field even on mild summer days. Critics also grumbled over its unorthodox shape, something like a warped Cheerio. Still, plenty of fans came out to "the Stick" for the action on the field, especially to see future Hall of Famers like Willie Mays, Willie McCovey, and Barry Bonds run the bases.

Stories vary, but the field was possibly named after Candlestick Point, a rock quarry, where in the early 1900s a pinnacle of rocks could be seen jutting up across the bay. Another explanation claims it was named for the long-billed "candlestick" birds that lived along the shore. Corporate naming rights were sold to 3Com Corporation in 1995, then Monster Cable in 2004. *Sports Illustrated*'s Peter King once wryly referred to the park as "Candle3Monsterstick." After the 49ers moved to Levi's Stadium, the park had no permanent tenant. The last music act to perform there was returning Beatle Paul McCartney, who again took the stage on August 14, 2014. Demolition of the ballpark was begun in November of that year and completed in September 2015.

[ABOVE] In 1957, San Francisco Giants staff gather in a field to promote where Candlestick Park, the new home of the Giants, will be built.

[BOTTOM] The Giants play a game at the ballpark in the 1990s, when it was known as 3Com Stadium.

[ABOVE] A postcard of Candlestick Park shows its position on the western shore of San Francisco Bay. As beautiful as the site was, it resulted in some miserable weather conditions for players and fans.

[TOP RIGHT] Minutes after the 6.9 Loma Prieta earthquake rolled through the area, an SFPD squad car occupies the playing field of Candlestick Park, interrupting the 1989 "Bay Bridge" World Series, when the Giants were playing their neighbors, the Oakland A's, on October 17, 1989. The quake struck at 5:04 pm,
about 30 minutes before the first pitch was to be thrown. The Series was postponed for 10 days, and when it resumed the A's swept the Giants.

[MIDDLE RIGHT, TOP] Willie Mays, No. 24 of the San Francisco Giants, steals second base as Eddie Kasko of the Cincinnati Reds catches the throw during an MLB game on May 30, 1961, at Candlestick Park.

[MIDDLE RIGHT, BOTTOM] Will Clark on base with bat, circa 1986–1993. Known as "Will the Thrill," Clark homered in his first home game at Candlestick.

[BOTTOM] An overgrown path leads to the abandoned park before its demolition.

"GIANT" RECORDS

The Giant's achievements on the field have often been superlative—they have won more games than any other team and have the second-highest winning percentage. They competed in the World Series 20 times and won it 8 times, making them fifth in line behind their old rivals, the Yankees. They won a record 23rd National League pennant in 2014—but were surpassed by their other rivals, the Dodgers, in 2022, with 24 crowns. The Giants can boast 66 members in the National Hall of Fame; 55 players and 11 managers, more than any other franchise. These include earlier icons like Christy Mathewson, Willie Mays, Mel Ott, and Carl Hubbel.

HOME OF THE SAN DIEGO PADRES

NATIONAL LEAGUE (1969–PRESENT)

LOCATED IN BEAUTIFUL, BALMY DOWNTOWN SAN DIEGO, *versatile Petco Park is home to the Padres ball club, but is also utilized for football, concerts, soccer, rugby, tennis, motor sports, and golf. Often rated one of the greatest venues in baseball, Petco Park is renowned for its many fan-friendly attractions and a grandstand that offers peerless sight lines combined with an intimate setting.*

The San Diego Padres were one of four expansion teams formed by MLB in 1969, along with the Montreal Expos (currently the Washington Nationals), the Kansas City Royals, and the Seattle Pilots (now the Milwaukee Brewers). The franchise took its name from a Pacific Coast League team that came to San Diego in 1936 and won the PCL title in 1937. That team's secret weapon was an 18-year-old San Diego resident named Ted Williams, a future Hall of Famer who played his entire career with the Red Sox.

The name *Padres* is significant for San Diego because in Spanish it means "fathers," and it represents the Franciscan friars who founded the city in 1769. Current nicknames include the Pads, the Friars, Slam Diego Padres, and

Slam Diego. The latter two were coined after August 20, 2020, when the team became the first in MLB history to hit a grand slam in four consecutive games.

The fledgling ball club floundered during their early years, finishing in last place for its first six seasons in the NL West. One of the team's saving graces was first baseman Nate Colbert, drafted from the Astros, who would become the Padres' career leader in home runs. In the 1980s things perked up—the team won five NL West titles and played in the World Series in 1984 and 1998. During these years the team's "It Guy"—or perhaps "Hit Guy"—was Hall of Famer Tony Gwynn, the winner of eight batting titles.

After 35 years at San Diego Stadium, the team relocated to Petco Park. Erected at the intersection of three downtown neighborhoods, the facility is technically in the East Village. It sits at the edge of the historic Gaslamp Quarter, close to San Diego Bay, and offers lively "downtown" experiences before or after the game, including entertainment, dining, and nightlife. This choice of location was intended to revitalize a flagging neighborhood, with the new stadium part of a larger project that designated 26 blocks of East Village as a "Ballpark District." As such, the Padres and their development partners were required to commit to at least $311 million in new construction within the district. As promised, a vital community of shops, eateries, and other enterprises began to flourish on the west and north sides of the ballpark—areas that were formerly home to rundown buildings and vacant lots—and the partnership's investment has approached $600 million. The neighborhood will continue to improve, but visitors already find it an appealing destination.

DESIGN AND CONSTRUCTION

The talented firms behind the new facility included style trendsetters Populous (then HOK Sport), Antoine Predock (design), Spurlock Poirier (landscape), ROMA (urban planning), Thornton Tomasetti (structural engineering), and Heritage Architecture & Planning (historic preservation). Their concept for the stadium would result in a ballpark

BALLPARK STATS

ADDRESS
19 Tony Gwynn Drive, San Diego, CA 92101

OWNER
City of San Diego/San Diego Padres

OPERATOR
Padres LP

ARCHITECT
HOK Sport (now Populous)

CAPACITY
40,209

RECORD BASEBALL ATTENDANCE
45,567 on 3/30/2014 (Opening Day vs. LA Dodgers)

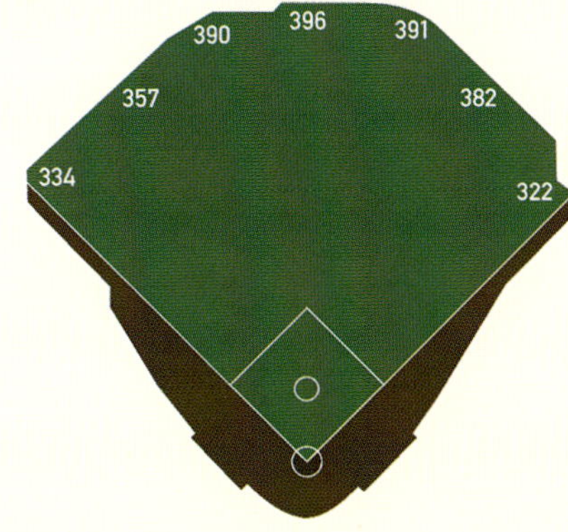

FIELD SIZE

- **Left field line** 334 feet (102 m)
- **Left field** 357 feet (109 m)
- **Left field alley** 390 feet (119 m)
- **Center field** 396 feet (121 m)
- **Right field alley** 391 feet (119 m)
- **Right field** 382 feet (116 m)
- **Right field line** 322 feet (98 m)

SURFACE
BullsEye Bermuda (grass)

TEAM MASCOT
The Swinging Friar

that is unique in presentation and feel. At Petco Park, even the two four-story structures, called Garden Buildings, that provide access to the upper levels are beautiful. They contain planters, water features, long escalators, and access bridges. The stadium's exterior is made of stucco and natural sandstone imported from India. The deeper gold tones, which are complemented by a pale cream color, were influenced by the bluffs at nearby Torry Pines, and the soaring, exposed steel girders have a white marine finish that evokes the city's nautical history.

The stadium was meant to open in 2002, but several delays occurred during construction—one was due to a court decision that nullified a passed proposition approving the city's portion of stadium financing, requiring a second vote; the other was concern over a historic landmark at the site, the Western Metal Supply Company warehouse. The team finally agreed to renovate the building in accordance with the secretary of the interior's standards and, in an example of adaptive use, incorporated it into the stadium design. During the delay the Padres played at Qualcomm Stadium. The park finally opened on April 8, 2004, with the cost for land, construction, and infrastructure coming to $450 million.

PUBLIC REACTIONS

Reviewers couldn't find enough superlatives to describe this ballpark. "Spectacular" and "magnificent" were applied to the design, the city views, and the way the facility managed to reference the sea, the sky, the Southern California landscape, the beauty of nature, and the spirit and cultural diversity of San Diego. It was also commended for its state-of-the-art technology and fan-friendly amenities.

Another plus was how the venue's central location made it easy to reach by public transport. The main entrance, behind home plate, faces the San Diego Trolley station at 12th and Imperial Transit Center. The park is also roughly 1 mile (1.6 km) away from Santa Fe Depot station, which is served by Amtrak and Coaster.

The designers and builders surely must have done something right in 2004—in 2023 their soaring arena was voted best MLB stadium by *USA Today*, who called it the "perfect" ballpark and cited the stadium's stunning view of the city skyline, the pleasures of Gallagher Square, and the range of delicious food.

PETCO PARK FIRSTS

FIRST MLB GAME: 4/8/2004, Padres over SF Giants, 4–3

FIRST HOME RUN: 4/8/2004, Marquis Grissom (SF Giants)

FIRST NO-HITTER: 7/13/2013, Tim Lincecum (SF Giants)

FIRST ALL-STAR GAME: 7/12/2016, AL over NL, 4–2

FIRST PLAYOFF GAME: 10/8/2005, St. Louis Cardinals over Padres, 7–4

[BELOW] Petco Park, with its SoCal vibe, is often lauded as the prettiest park in MLB.

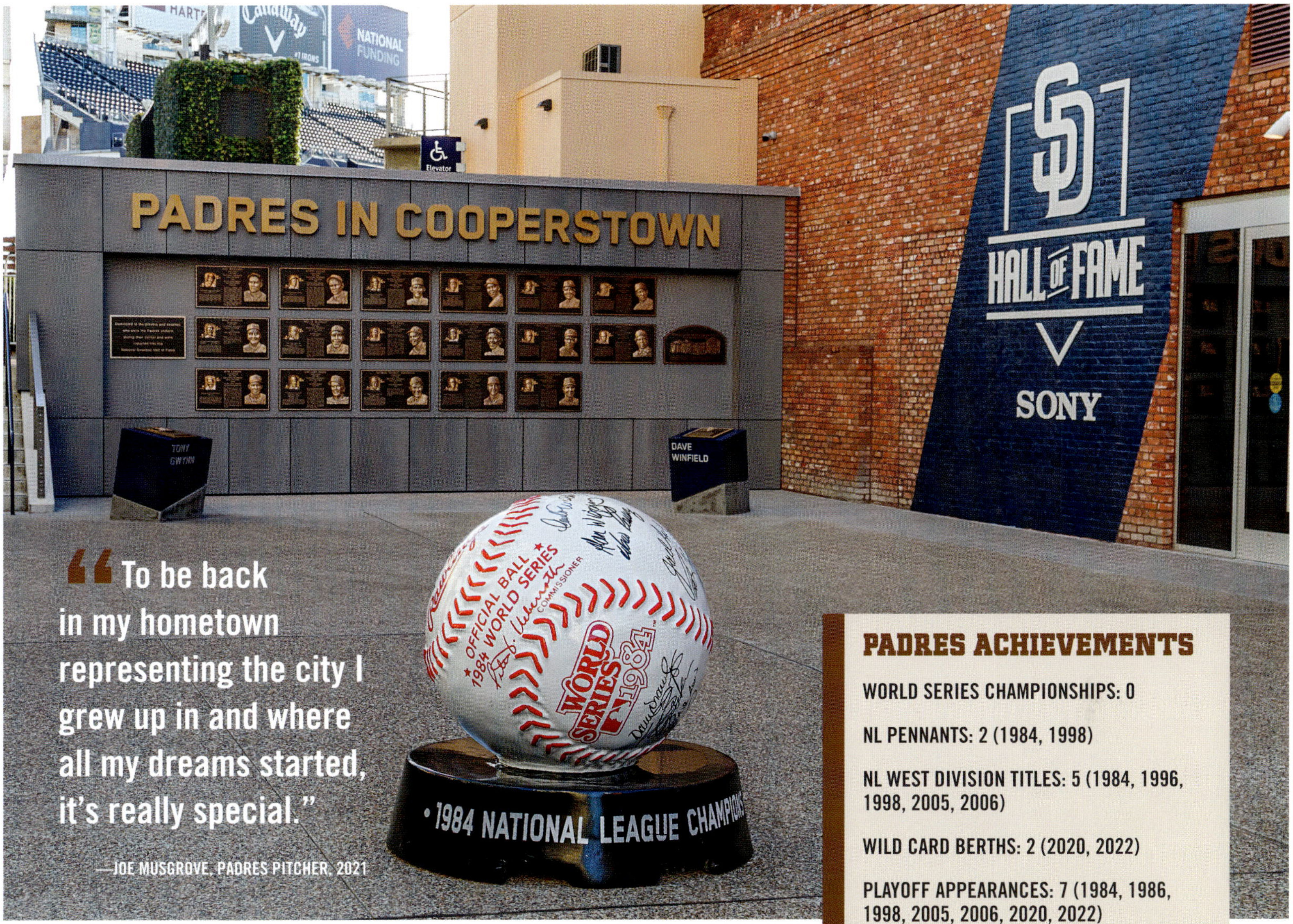

> "To be back in my hometown representing the city I grew up in and where all my dreams started, it's really special."
>
> —JOE MUSGROVE, PADRES PITCHER, 2021

PADRES ACHIEVEMENTS

WORLD SERIES CHAMPIONSHIPS: 0

NL PENNANTS: 2 (1984, 1998)

NL WEST DIVISION TITLES: 5 (1984, 1996, 1998, 2005, 2006)

WILD CARD BERTHS: 2 (2020, 2022)

PLAYOFF APPEARANCES: 7 (1984, 1986, 1998, 2005, 2006, 2020, 2022)

WORST SEASON RECORD: 1969, 52–110 (.321)

BEST SEASON RECORD: 2020, 37–23 (.617)

[ABOVE] Hall of Fame Plaza features the "Padres in Cooperstown" wall.

FEATURES AND AMENITIES

The many attractions, historical displays, and eateries at this ballpark are sure to please the fans who flock here for more than a ball game.

HONORED PLAYERS Petco Park honors Padres players and the history of San Diego baseball in multiple ways. The Hall of Fame Plaza, located behind the left field stands, prominently features plaques on the wall of Padres players who went on to be inducted into Cooperstown's Major League Baseball Hall of Fame, including such luminaries as Ted Williams, Sparky Anderson, Goose Gossage, Roberto Alomar, Greg Maddux, Mike Piazza, and many others. The plaques for Dave Winfield and Tony Gwynn, who were inducted to the MLB Hall of Fame as San Diego Padres, in a Padres uniform, are mounted on special pedestals. Other displays honor members inducted in the San Diego Padres Hall of Fame. The Padres Hall of Fame also includes historical video and multimedia content. There are also three statues at Petco Park, as well as retired numbers on display at Home Plate Plaza and in the Ring of Honor, on the upper deck above the press box behind home plate. Along with Padres players, athletes who are San Diegans or have excelled athletically in San Diego are honored at the Breitbard Hall of Fame, located on the wall of the Western Metal Supply building inside the main concourse.

A statue of right fielder Tony Gwynn stands in Gallagher Square. Drafted in 1981, Gwynn spent 20 years in a San Diego uniform—his entire MLB career—earning himself the nickname "Mr. Padre."

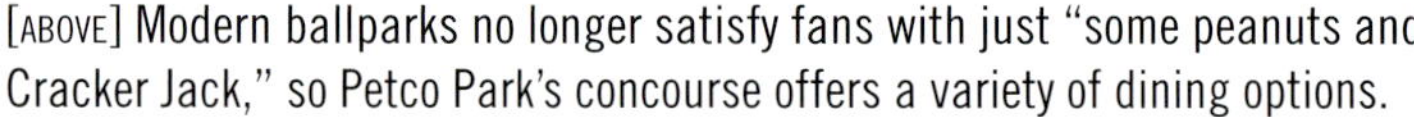

[ABOVE] Modern ballparks no longer satisfy fans with just "some peanuts and Cracker Jack," so Petco Park's concourse offers a variety of dining options.

[BELOW RIGHT] An aerial shot shows the ballpark, with its back to San Diego Bay, and the surrounding Gaslamp District neighborhood.

GALLAGHER SQUARE Also called the Park in the Park, Gallagher Square is a grassy area of approximately 2.8 acres (1.1 ha) located outside the outfield wall but inside the Petco gates. This small park contains a mini little league infield diamond and a play area for kids, shady trees, a statue of Padres icon Tony Gwynn, and lots of space to sprawl on the grass.

WESTERN METAL SUPPLY CO. WAREHOUSE The rustic brick Western Metal Supply Company warehouse, the historic landmark incorporated into the ballpark's left-field design, is now home to the largest souvenir shop, a number of party suites, and the capacious Hall of Fame Bar and Grill, and displays the lockers of Hall of Famers like Tony Gwynn, Dave Winfield, and Randy Jones. The rooftop is available for parties, and there are even bleachers overlooking the field. Also on the left-field corner of the stands is a picnic area that features a Mission Bell, which is rung whenever the Padres win a game.

PALM COURT PLAZA The main entrance to the stadium from the Gaslamp District, Palm Court Plaza, is composed of commemorative bricks purchased by more than 10,000 fans who participated in the SD Ballpark Brick Program. Memorial bricks can also be ordered from the Padres Legacy Brick Program, which is part of their 20th anniversary celebration for 2024. These bricks will be placed in Tony Gwynn Plaza near his statue.

LEXUS CLUB This is a private space on Field Level near third base; fine dining is provided by a private chef and Brandt Beef/Ranch 45. The Blue Shield Club Restaurant & Lounge is a private club with an all-you-can-eat buffet.

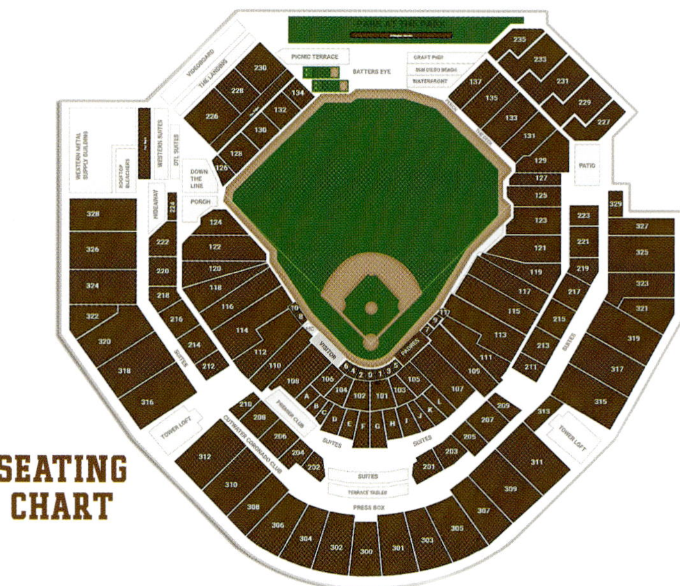

FOOD AND DRINK The park concessions prepare a wide variety of snacks and munchies, including burgers, hot dogs, pizza, street corn, chicken burgers, and fresh seafood. Specialty offerings from Taste of San Diego include Barrio Dog, Carnitas Snack Shack, Din Tai Fung, Bluewater Sea Food, Grand Ole BBQ, Gaglione Brothers, Negihama Sushi, Ranch 45 and Brandt Beef, and Puesto.

[ABOVE] The Western Metal Supply Co.'s warehouse, designed in 1909, is an integral part of the Petco Park aesthetic. Its balcony seating, called "The Rail," is said to be this ballpark's version of Fenway Park's Green Monster seating.

[LEFT] The Swinging Friar mascot honors the contributions of the Franciscan friars who helped to establish San Diego.

PETCO SUPPORTS PET CARE

San Diego based pet supplies retailer Petco, which originally bought naming rights to the stadium in 2004 for $60 million over 22 years, signed a new deal in 2021 that ensured the stadium would bear their name at least through 2027. Petco's new logo appears on digital signage throughout the park. The company has also enlisted the team to support initiatives for improved pet care and recently developed a strategic partnership with players Manny Machado and Fernando Tatis Jr., who will promote the well-being of pets. Petco will also address pet health by collaborating with players on social and other digital media.

OTHER HOMES OF THE PADRES

SAN DIEGO STADIUM
1969–2003

This multipurpose stadium, home to two pro sports franchise—the Padres and the NFL Chargers—was in Mission Valley on the outskirts of the city. The massive four-tier facility broke ground in 1965 and opened for football on April 19, 1967, as San Diego Stadium. It became known as Jack Murphy Stadium in 1981, named for a local sportswriter who had drummed up support for this sports venue in the 1960s. Fans called it "The Murph." In 1997, San Diego-based telecom equipment company Qualcomm bought the naming rights , a deal that lasted until 2017. When these expired, they were purchased by San Diego County Credit Union, and "The Q" became SDCCU Stadium. In 2020 it reverted to San Diego Stadium.

The Padres made their home there from the time of their formation through 2004. The Chargers played there from 1967 to 2016. The venue was updated several times, perhaps the most substantial change taking place in 1997, when it was completely enclosed except for the scoreboard. It remained home to the San Diego State Aztecs through the 2019 football season and was demolished from December 2020 to March 2021. Afterward the Aztecs built a smaller college facility, Snapdragon Stadium, in part of the parking lot.

[ABOVE] San Diego Stadium was known for its stunning interior space, especially the grandstand seating in a range of earth tones. It did have the disadvantage of seats far from any field action.

[LEFT] An image of Jack Murphy hung near the east end zone on the field at SDCCU Stadium.

[BELOW] The stadium in 2014, then known as Qualcomm Stadium. The building was the first in the "octorad" style of multi-use venues, with a square-circle footprint that—theoretically—was better for hosting both football and baseball games.

HONORING THE MILITARY

In 1996, the Padres were proud to become the first national sports team to have an annual military appreciation event. In 2000 the team began wearing a camouflage jersey to honor members of the military. Then in 2008 the players began wearing camouflage jerseys at Sunday home games. They also wear them on Memorial Day, Independence Day, and Labor Day. Since 1995, large numbers of Marine recruits from the nearby Marine Corps Recruit Depot visit the field during Military Appreciation Day, and the team recognizes them with a Fourth Inning Stretch while the Marine Hymn is played on the organ. The team's outreach also includes mailing game tapes to US Navy ships in the Pacific Fleet, many of which are homeported in San Diego.

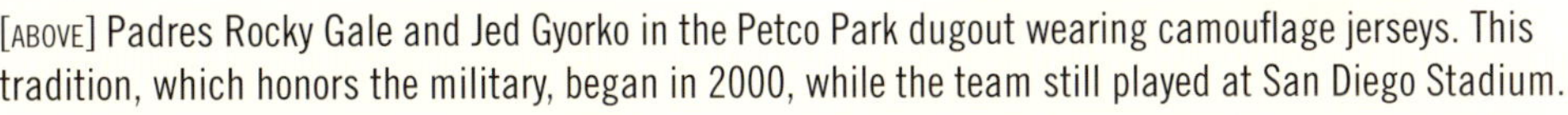

[ABOVE] Padres Rocky Gale and Jed Gyorko in the Petco Park dugout wearing camouflage jerseys. This tradition, which honors the military, began in 2000, while the team still played at San Diego Stadium.

[BELOW] The demolition of San Diego Stadium, previously named SDCCU, Qualcomm, and Jack Murphy Stadium, began in February 2021.

HOME OF THE SEATTLE MARINERS

AMERICAN LEAGUE (1977–PRESENT)

CONSIDERED ONE OF THE PREMIER BASEBALL STADIUMS *in the Majors, T-Mobile Park contains five main levels and two sets of bleachers, plus a real grass field, a unique retractable roof, and all the modern amenities. The resident Mariners are a team with a mission, eager to replicate their past glory—like setting the AL record in 2001 for most games won in a season—and their loyal followers always remain supportive.*

T-Mobile Park is home to the American League Mariners, an expansion team in the West Division. They are actually the second expansion team to play in Seattle, and therein lies a story . . .

It started with an MLB expansion team called the Seattle Pilots, a benighted club that lasted only one year in the Emerald City before heading off to Milwaukee as the Brewers in 1970. In part the Pilots left because their home field, city-owned Sick Stadium, was in a serious state of deterioration. There was not even a working scoreboard when they moved in. Also, fan attendance was abysmal. Then plans to build them a new stadium were put on hold by opponents of the measure. When the Pilots' owners declared bankruptcy, the Major Leagues finally took control of the team and approved their sale and relocation to the Midwest.

The incensed Seattle city fathers then sued Major League Baseball for breach of contract. Meanwhile, King County started work on the Kingdome, confident that pro baseball would return within a year or two. In 1976, the league agreed to award Seattle another franchise if they dropped the suit. A new team, called the Mariners, would begin play in 1997, and a group of investors led by entertainer Danny Kaye would oversee their finances this time. The Mariners started playing at the Kingdome on April 6, 1977, and remained there until 1999.

The team name relates to the maritime culture of Seattle, which is on Puget Sound. As the city expanded from a rough pioneer settlement to a major urban center, a number of maritime industries sprang up to serve its businesses and citizens. Among these enterprises were a commercial fishing fleet, marinas geared to pleasure craft, and the family diving business of Henry "King of the Divers" Finch, which salvaged shipwrecks in the early 1900s. Today the Port of Seattle is one of the country's major container ports and a key gateway for international trade.

A SERIOUS DROUGHT

In spite of a supportive fan base, the M's did not produce a winning team until 1991, and after that happy "glitch" their luck did not return until the mid-1990s. This era witnessed their most successful period, aided by Hall of Famers Edgar Martinez, Ken Griffey Jr., and "the Big Unit"—6-foot, 10-inch power pitcher Randy Johnson. They earned their first playoff berth in 1995 with their first division championship, then defeated the Yankees in the American League Division series. The momentum from this win helped to keep baseball alive in Seattle and would become an iconic moment in team history. They went on to win another Division Series title in 1997. In 2001 they astonished MLB by setting an American League record for the most wins in a season—116—and tying the 1906 season of the National League Cubs. Then followed the longest postseason drought in all four major North American sports; the team did not make the playoffs again until 2022. As of 2023, the Mariners

BALLPARK STATS

ADDRESS
1250 First Avenue South, Seattle, WA 98134

FORMER NAME
Safeco Field (1999–2018)

OWNER/OPERATOR
Washington State Major League Baseball Stadium Public Facilities District

ARCHITECT
NBBJ; 360 Architecture

CAPACITY
47,929

RECORD BASEBALL ATTENDANCE
57,816 on 3/31/1998 (vs. Cleveland Guardians)

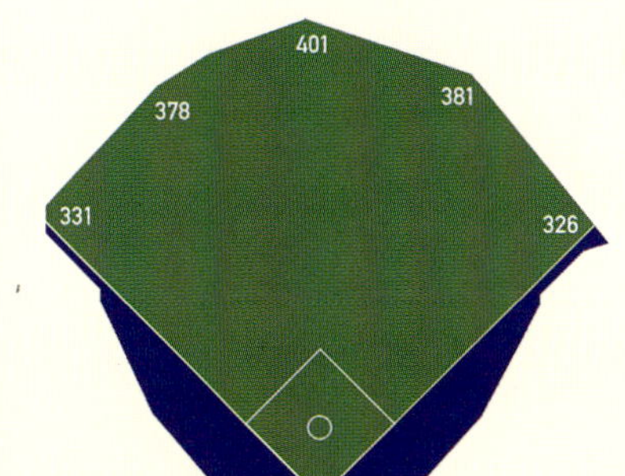

FIELD SIZE

- **Left field** 331 feet (101 m)
- **Left-center** 378 feet (115 m)
- **Center field** 401 feet (122 m)
- **Right-center** 381 feet (116 m)
- **Right field** 326 feet (99 m)
- **Backstop** 69 feet (21 m)

SURFACE
Kentucky bluegrass–perennial ryegrass blend

TEAM MASCOT
The Mariner Moose

are the only active ball club that has not appeared in the World Series. But hope burns eternal . . .

By 1994 the team was actively seeking a new venue. A task force was appointed to assess the situation, while the community feared the team would leave Seattle if a new stadium was not approved. After funding for the new facility was voted down by a tiny margin, the state legislature came up with a different package that would include a food and beverage tax, a car rental surcharge, and ballpark admission tax, among other surcharges. The King County council approved the package, and construction began in 1997 at a site near the Kingdome in an industrial area south of downtown.

The new facility—named Safeco Stadium after the team accepted a 20-year, $40 million deal with the Seattle-based insurance company—opened on July 15, 1999. In 2018 the Safeco sign was taken down and the new T-Mobile sign went up, based this time on an $87.5 million deal for 25 years.

Safeco Field had been considered a pitcher's park since its opening day, so the Mariners moved the fences closer to home plate before the 2013 season, "to create an environment that is fair for both hitters and pitchers," according to General Manager Jack Zduriencik.

In 2023, attendance at T-Mobile Park grew 9.10 percent over the year for an average of 29,295 patrons per game, and the team now ranked in the top 10 for stadium attendance.

DESIGN AND CONSTRUCTION

NBBJ and 360 Architecture were the designers of the stadium, which ended up costing $517 million, including $126 million contributed by the Seattle Mariners. T-Mobile Park is considered a "retro-modern" ballpark, meaning it resembles stadiums from previous

[BELOW] Located in the industrial SoDo district of Seattle, the brick-faced T-Mobile Park evokes the feel of old-style urban ballparks.

eras, yet still provides fans with plenty of technological innovation, as well as local flavor. The brick facade harken back to classical urban architecture, while both the entry rotunda and the concourses have an "old timey" feel, especially the latter with their exposed steel beams overhead.

The five main levels to the stadium are: Field (or Street), Main Concourse (100 level), Club Level (200 level), Suite Level, and Upper Concourse (300 level). Two bleacher sections sit above left field and below the center-field scoreboard. The field is approximately at street level, so most gates require visitors to ascend by using stairs, elevators, or escalators to access the main concourse.

A favorite with visitors is the ballpark's one-of-a-kind retractable roof. When closed, it acts like an umbrella, covering but not enclosing the ballpark, thus preserving an open-air environment but keeping out the elements. The structure covers nearly 9 acres (3.6 ha), weighs 22 million pounds (9,979,000 kg), and contains enough steel to build a skyscraper 55 stories tall; its three movable roof panels glide on 128 steel wheels powered by 96 10-horsepower electric motors. As a precaution the roof is designed to withstand 6 to 7 feet (1.8–2.1 m) of snow and sustained winds of up to 70 miles per hour (113 kph). The field features one of the most comprehensive scoreboard systems in Major League Baseball, including 11 electronic displays, but there is also an old-fashioned hand-operated scoreboard in left field.

SEATING CHART

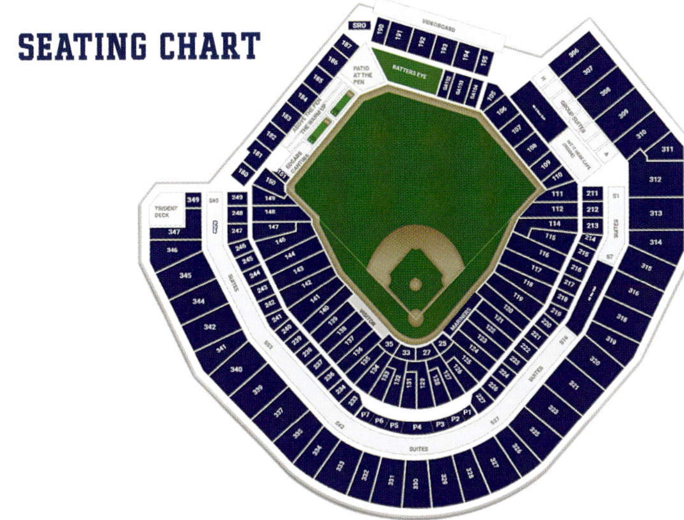

PUBLIC REACTIONS

The Mariners offered the public a chance to tour their new stadium before it opened at an event called "Intro Day." The response to Safeco Field was very positive, and there was a perceptible level

[ABOVE RIGHT] An overhead shot of the ballpark shows its innovative retractable roof. One of the field's former idiosyncrasies resulted from the roof's open position, when it overhung the BNSF Railway tracks that bound the stadium to the east on one side and the other side hung over the right-field stands. An echo was created from the whistles of passing trains, and train horns once blared inside the stadium. An overpass built for the street that bounds the stadium to the north has alleviated most of this noise.

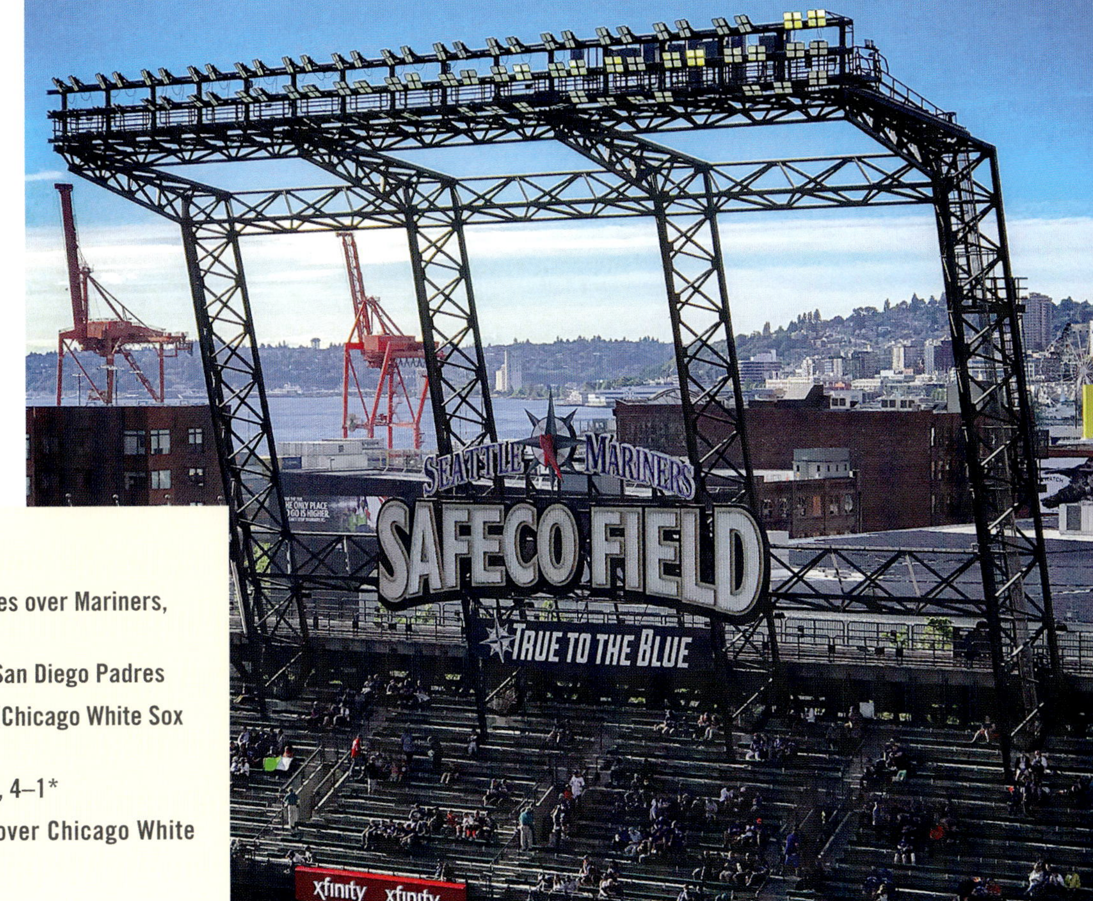

[RIGHT] The ballpark opened in 1999 as Safeco Field, a name it was known as until 2018. The "True to the Blue" team slogan hangs below the field name.

T-MOBILE PARK FIRSTS

FIRST MLB GAME: 7/15/1999, San Diego Padres over Mariners, 3–2*

FIRST HOME RUN: 7/15/1999, Russ Davis vs. San Diego Padres

FIRST NO-HITTER: 4/21/2012, Philip Humber (Chicago White Sox—perfect game)*

FIRST ALL-STAR GAME: 7/10/2001, AL over NL, 4–1*

FIRST PLAYOFF GAME: 10/6/2000, Mariners over Chicago White Sox, 2–1

* as Safeco Field

of excitement as the crowd of thousands moved throughout the venue. After the stadium opened, fans noted the pleasure of viewing players on natural grass, as well as the great views of the city. And everyone seems to have appreciated the retractable roof. With its nods to baseball's past, as well as an acknowledgment of modern technology, Safeco was considered a refreshing change from the Kingdome, which had been labeled sterile and boring, and not great at hosting any sport.

Current online postings congratulate the ball club for doing such a good job over the years with renovations and maintenance at T-Mobile Park. Optimism was expressed that the team would have no need to seek out a new stadium in the near future.

FEATURES AND AMENITIES

This 19.59-acre (8 ha) outdoor ballpark offers plenty of attractions to entertain and satisfy fans before, during, and after games.

[ABOVE] Among the outstanding pieces of public art installed throughout the stadium is *The Tempest,* a unique and eye-catching chandelier made of white resin baseball bats that hangs in the entrance lobby.

[RIGHT] Located at the Baseball Museum of the Pacific Northwest in T-Mobile Park, the Mariners Hall of Fame honors players who have been retired from baseball for two seasons and who wore the Mariners' uniform for at least five seasons. Inductees as of 2023 include Jay Buhner, Alvin Davis, Ken Griffey Jr., Félix Hernández, Randy Johnson, Edgar Martínez, Jamie Moyer, Dave Niehaus, Lou Piniella, Ichiro Suzuki, and Dan Wilson.

MARINERS ACHIEVEMENTS

WORLD SERIES CHAMPIONSHIPS: 0

AL PENNANTS: 0

AL WEST DIVISION TITLES: 3 (1995, 1997, 2001)

WILD CARD BERTHS: 2 (2000, 2022)

PLAYOFF APPEARANCES: 5 (1995, 1997, 2000, 2001, 2022)

WORST SEASON: 1978, 56–104 (.350)

BEST SEASON Record: 2001, 116–46 (.716)

PUBLIC ART

During the venue's construction, the Ballpark PFD board approved a budget of $1.31 million for public art. Noteworthy examples include *The Tempest,* an intriguing chandelier made of 1,000 resin baseball bats that hangs above the home plate entry. A 27-foot-diameter (8.3 m) compass rose mosaic in the Home Plate Rotunda captures a number of elements from the history of baseball and reflects the team's insignia. Both were created by the artists' group Stable. A wall mural by Thom Ross commemorating the 1995 ALDS playoffs' iconic Game 5 shows Ken Griffey Jr. sliding into home plate, surrounded by other players. A sculpture of Dave Neihaus seated at his broadcast desk honors the Mariners' play-by-play announcer, who worked with them for more than 30 years. This was by Lou Cella, who also sculpted the Ken Griffey Jr. statue outside the Home Plate Gate. Seattle artist Ross Palmer Beecher created two large "quilts" constructed from pieces of found metal and stitched together with red wire that create the logos of all Major League Baseball teams. Other artists featured here include Donald Fels, Tina Hoggat, Helen Lessick, Ries Niemi, Gerard Tsutakawa, and Gu Xiong.

HALL OF FAME

The Mariners Hall of Fame revisits and honors the careers of the greatest Seattle players and team affiliates.

FAN-FRIENDLY AND KIDS' AREAS

"The Pen" is a fenced-in area beside the bull pens that allows fans to get up close with players as they prepare to take the field. Nearby is the Patio at the Pen, where fans can congregate, drink, and watch the

[ABOVE] Stadium-goers begin to fill seats during the Mariners' pre-game batting practice. Fans at the ballpark always seem deeply engaged with the action on the field or the stadium's celebratory effects for outstanding plays.

[RIGHT] The Mariner Moose, the team's antlered, anthropomorphic mascot, was first introduced on April 13, 1990. A moose was chosen after a contest was held for children 14 and under to suggest a mascot. Moose are also symbols of the Pacific Northwest, where Seattle is located.

game. Meanwhile, the Kids' Corner offers a free timed run, pitching and hitting challenges, and more for kids 14 and under. The Kid's Clubhouse team store is geared to younger fans, carrying apparel and Mariner Moose items.

FOOD AND DRINK

Even during the team's off seasons fans have always found tempting treats to eat and drink at the stadium's concessions. Popular new offerings include "designer" pizzas, calzones, luau plates, quesadillas, and smoked beef short rib sandwiches. Major venues that are sure to please include Din Tai Fung Chinese dumplings, Lil Woody's Royal Ranch grass-fed beef burgers, Way Back Crab Shack, Pure Acai acai bowls, and Hit It Here Cafe, a sit-down restaurant. The ballpark provides a wide range of craft beers, including brands from Washington State producers like Bale Breaker Brewing, Georgetown Brewing, gluten-free Ghostfish Brewing, Reuben's Brews, and more. There are also batch cocktails at Scotty's Juice and a large selection of fine wines at the Chateau by Chateau Ste. Michelle Wine Bar.

BUHNER BUZZ CUT NIGHT

In the mid-1990s, Mariners slugger Jay Buhner was a popular player, whose signature look was a bald head. The Mariners took advantage of this popularity by creating a marketing promotion called Buhner Buzz Cut Night. From 1994 to 2001, fans at both the Kingdome and then Safeco Field received free admission if they were bald or had their heads shaved before the game. Buhner himself would sometimes help out with the clippers. More than 22,000 Mariners supporters got free tickets, including a number of women.

OTHER HOMES OF THE MARINERS

KINGDOME

1977–1999

The Kingdome once occupied a significant place in the Seattle skyline near Pioneer Square, a looming concrete saucer adorned with spokes that had an interior volume of 67 million cubic feet (1,897, 230 m^3) and weighed 130,000 tons. It is not hard to imagine the shocking gap it left when it was finally imploded.

The idea of constructing a covered stadium in Seattle to attract a professional football or baseball team was proposed in 1959. After several rejected measures, King County voters finally approved the project in 1968 with the issuing of $40 million in municipal bonds. Construction began in 1972, and the Kingdome opened in 1976. The following year the Mariners moved into the new stadium. No Sick Park woes for them. They would share the venue with the NFL Seattle Seahawks. It was also home to the NBA Seattle SuperSonics from 1978 to 1985, and additionally served as the venue for the NASL Seattle Sounders.

Inside, the Kingdome measured 660 feet (200 m) across, with the largest concrete roof in the world—7.85 acres (3.2 ha). The Mariners soon discovered their home field was leaning more toward a football stadium than a multipurpose stadium, so it had serious issues as a ballpark. Foul territory was overly large, and seats in the

The Kingdome was the site of the 50th Major League All-Star Game, held on Tuesday, July 17, 1979.

[ABOVE] With its position overlooking Puget Sound, the Kingdome was an impressive sight in its heyday and was considered an iconic feature of the Seattle skyline for close to a quarter century.

[BELOW] The Kingdome dissolves in a cloud of debris as it is imploded in March 2000.

upper deck could be 617 feet (188 m) from home plate. Most fans in the outfield seats on the 300 level were unable to view areas of right and center field.

The critics and the public were not kind to the covered stadium, unhappy with its design and its hulking presence. Some sports writers and fans called it "the Tomb"—because of its gray concrete and lack of noise—or "Puget Puke." It was also maligned for altering the character of historic neighborhoods like the International District and Pioneer Square, especially when sports bars and T-shirt shops began popping up as fans surged through on game days.

During the 1990s the Seahawks' and Mariners' ownership expressed their dissatisfaction—in part due to loss of revenue—to the city and began threatening to relocate unless they received new, publicly funded stadiums. Another critical issue was the integrity of the stadium's roof—ceiling tiles actually collapsed onto the seating area before a Mariners' game in 1994. Public funding packages for new, purpose-built stadiums for the baseball and football franchises were approved in 1995 and 1997, respectively.

The Mariners moved to Safeco Field—now T-Mobile Park—midway through the 1999 season, and the Seahawks temporarily moved to Husky Stadium. On March 26, 2000, the Kingdome was demolished by implosion. The empty site became the home of the Seahawks' new stadium, Lumen Field, which opened in 2002. In 2015, King County finally paid off the bonds used to build and repair the Kingdome, 15 years after its demolition.

"It wasn't perfect—but it was ours."

—SEATTLE MARINERS, ON X

WHERE ARE THEY?

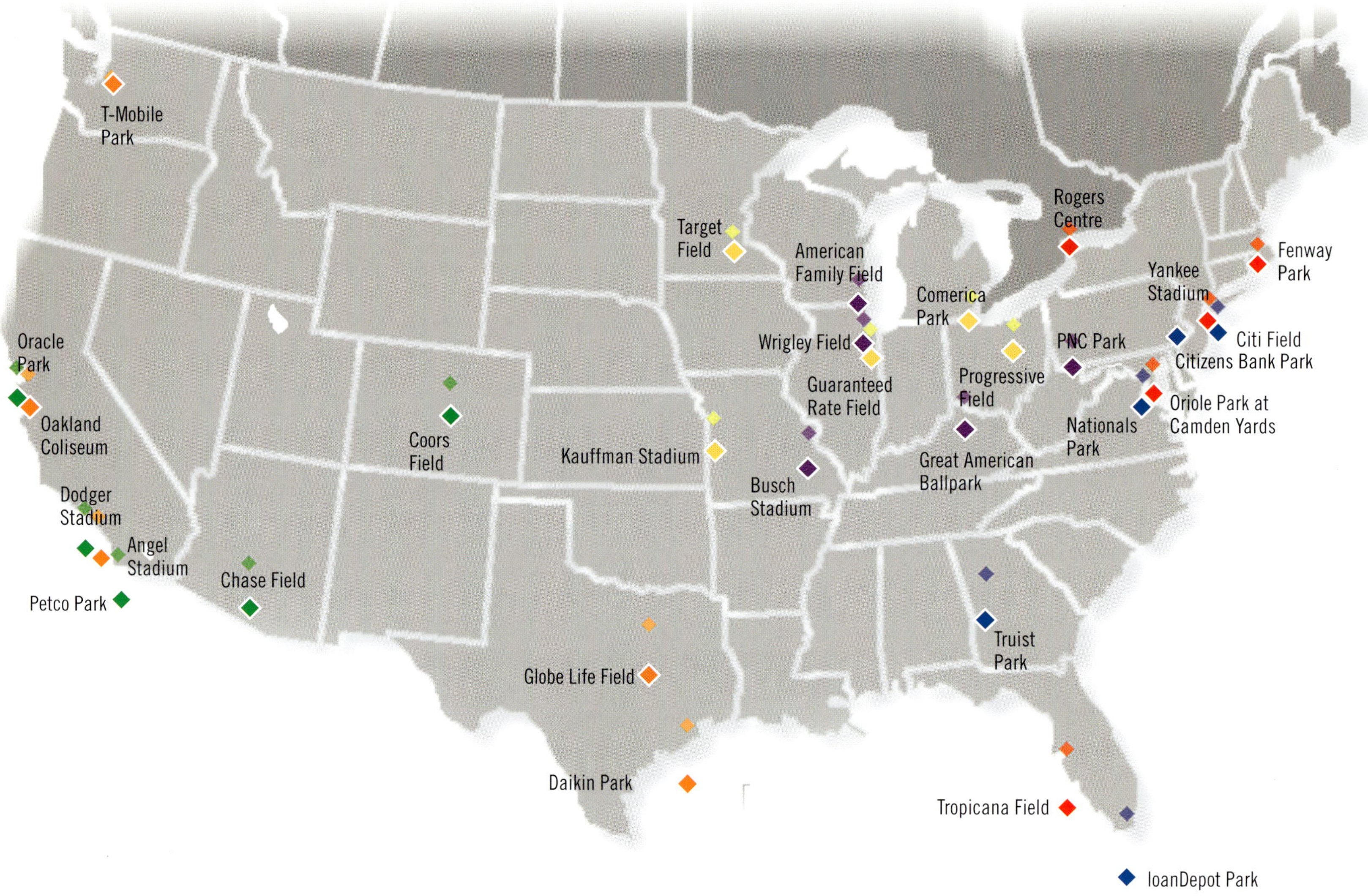

T-Mobile Park
Oracle Park
Oakland Coliseum
Dodger Stadium
Angel Stadium
Petco Park
Chase Field
Coors Field
Target Field
Kauffman Stadium
Globe Life Field
Daikin Park
American Family Field
Wrigley Field
Guaranteed Rate Field
Busch Stadium
Comerica Park
Progressive Field
Great American Ballpark
Rogers Centre
PNC Park
Nationals Park
Truist Park
Tropicana Field
loanDepot Park
Yankee Stadium
Fenway Park
Citi Field
Citizens Bank Park
Oriole Park at Camden Yards

DIVISION	AL	NL
East	◆ (red)	◆ (blue)
Central	◆ (yellow)	◆ (purple)
West	◆ (orange)	◆ (dark green)

NATIONAL LEAGUE (NL)

NL EAST
- Atlanta Braves
- Miami Marlins
- New York Mets
- Philadelphia Phillies
- Washington Nationals

NL CENTRAL
- Chicago Cubs
- Cincinnati Reds
- Milwaukee Brewers
- Pittsburgh Pirates
- St. Louis Cardinals

NL WEST
- Arizona Diamondbacks
- Colorado Rockies
- Los Angeles Dodgers
- San Diego Padres
- San Francisco Giants

AMERICAN LEAGUE (NL)

AL EAST
- Baltimore Orioles
- Boston Red Sox
- New York Yankees
- Tampa Bay Rays
- Toronto Blue Jays

AL CENTRAL
- Chicago White Sox
- Cleveland Guardians
- Detroit Tigers
- Kansas City Royals
- Minnesota Twins

AL WEST
- Houston Astros
- Los Angeles Angels
- Oakland Athletics
- Seattle Mariners
- Texas Rangers

INDEX OF BALLPARKS

ABOUT THE AUTHOR

Nancy J. Hajeski is a lifelong baseball fan, as well as the author of the biography of a sports legend— *Ali: The Official Story of the Greatest of All Time.* She has also written historical fiction for Penguin-Putnam, four Jane Austen graphic novel adaptations for Marvel Entertainment, gardening and natural health guides for National Geographic, yoga manuals, guides to true crime and astrology, and an award-winning coffee table book on the Fab Four called *The Beatles: Here, There and Everywhere.*

ACKNOWLEDGMENTS

Many thanks to Atsuko Sasaki and Marc X. Grigoroff for their invaluable help with the Japanese Stadiums feature.

PHOTOGRAPHY & ART CREDITS

KEY

DT = Dreamstime.com SS = Shutterstock.com
AL = Alamy Stock Photo PD = Public domain
LOC = Library of Congress
CC = Creative Commons

t = top m = middle b = bottom
l = left r = right
bg = background image

Front cover: logo: Enterlinedesign/DT; tl Pictures Now/AL; tr PD; b Americanspirit/DT

Back cover: t Rockymtnphoto/DT; tm PD; bm Julio35/DT; b Everett Collection Inc/AL

Title page: Brodogg1313/DT

Introduction: 6t LOC; 6b Hawaii State Archives; 7 Ffooter/DT; 8 North Wind Picture Archives/AL; 9 Kirkikisphoto/DT

Banner baseball bats: Maksim Rybak/DT

Ballfield schematics: XrysD/CC BY-SA 4.0

Close-up feature background: Enterlinedesign/DT

Vintage photo frame: Silverv/DT

EAST DIVISION

10l Gerrymphotos/DT; 10r Americanspirit/DT; 10ml Babar760/DT; 10mr Kmiragaya/DT; 10bl Wickedgood/DT; 10br Wickedgood/DT; 11tl Lohrtom/DT; 11tr Dreammediapeel/DT; 11bl Marcusjones2000/DT; 11br Marpit/DT; 12–13 bk Wickedgood/DT; 12–13 Nckprz15/DT; 14 Ffooter/DT; 15t Malrite/CC BY-SA 3.0; 15b Gordon Donovan/SS; 16t Ffooter/DT; 16b 4kclips/DT; 17t Ffooter/DT; 17b Debby Wong/SS; 18t RLFE Pix/AL; 18b Ffooter/DT; 19t Wickedgood/DT; 9box t Keystone Press/AL; 19box m lightworks; 20l RLFE Pix/AL; 20t PD; 20r Brooklynboy321/DT; 21t Stadium08; 21b Mishella/DT; 22–23 Brickwall9487/DT; 23 Philadelphia Phillies; 24 Groovysoup/DT; 25t Bkushner/DT; 25b Mfschramm/DT; 26 Ffooter/DT; 27t Swa1959/DT; 27b minimoniotaku/CC BY 2.0; 28t Ffooter/DT; 4kclips/DT; 29box NASA; 29b Mfschramm/DT; 30tr PD; 30bl PD; 30br Pennsylvania Historical and Museum Commission; 31tl AL; 31m Glasshouse Images/AL; 31b ClassicStock/AL; 32t piemags/DCM/AL; 32–33 Americanspirit/DT; 33t UPI/AL; 33m Hum Historical/AL; 34box Jnickert/DT; 35l Walleyelj/DT; 35tr dpa picture alliance/AL; 35br Steveheap/DT; 36t Brodogg1313/DT; 36 Walleyelj/DT; 36–37 baseball diamond Stojkovicsrdjan/DT; 36–37 ball player silhouettes Ednal1/DT; 37t Brodogg1313/DT; 37b Conor P. Fitzgerald/SS; 38–30 Wickedgood/DT; 38–39bg PD; 40t Wickedgood/DT; 40b Wickedgood/DT; 41t PD; 41m Wickedgood/DT; 41b Zoke/CC BY-SA 4.0; 42tl Mbastos /DT; 42mr LOC; 42b Wickedgood/DT; 43tr Maurice Savage/AL; 43mr Wickedgood/DT; 43b Actionsports/DT; 44b Wickedgood/DT; 44–45 Wenling01/DT; 46tr J0yce/DT; 46mr Felixcasio/DT; 46b LOC; 47tl Wickedgood/DT; 47tm Wickedgood/DT; 47tr Wickedgood/DT; 47ml Boston Public Library; 47mr Wickedgood/DT; 47b Boston Public Library; 48 Kmiragaya/DT; 49t Marcusjones2000/DT; 49m Miami Marlins; 50t Felixcasio/DT; 50 box 2018 Felix Mizioznikov/SS; 51 Korzeniewski/DT; 52 Kmiragaya/DT; 53t Felixcasio/DT; 53b Lohrtom/DT; 54t Scenic Florida; 54 Enchanteddrmzceo/ CC BY-SA 3.0; 55t PD; 55m Aneese/DT; 55b Yaras1/DT; 56–57 Wickedgood/DT; 58 Kirkikisphoto/DT; 59l LOC; 59r Wickedgood/DT; 60–61 UPI/AL; 61t Foolishproductionsphotography/DT; 61m Foolishproductionsphotography/DT; 61b Foolishproductionsphotography/DT; 62t PD; 62b Glasshouse Images/AL; 63box Rodrigolab/DT;63b UPI/AL; 64–65 Americanspirit/DT; 66l United States Fish and Wildlife Service; 66r Maurice Savage/AL; 67t Jackienix/DT; 67b UPI/AL; 68t Defmusik/DT; 68–69 Panoramic Images/AL; 69tl Theroff97/DT; 69tr Chuck Franklin/AL; 70t Traub Co.; 70b The Protected Art Archive/AL; 71tl Wasted Time R/CC BY 3.0; 71tr Baltimore Sun; 71bl Picaryl; 71br Phil Romans/CC BY-NC-ND 2.0; 72b Em2017/DT; 72bg Kitleong/DT; 73 Mohammedsoliman4/DT; 74–75 Rabbit75/DT; 75m Adwo/DT; 75b Lagron49/DT; 76 Rosevite2000/DT; 77t Macleoddesigns/DT; 77b Dgareri/DT; 78t Toronto Star; 78b Robert Taylor/ CC BY 2.0; 79t Jerry Reuss/CC BY-SA 2.0; 79b TorontoGuy79/CC BY-SA 4.0; 80–81 Felix Mizioznikov/SS; 82 Dreammediapeel/DT; 83 DomCritelli/SS; 84t ZUMA Press Inc/AL; 84bl Tbintb/DT; 84m Kirby Lee/AL; 85t Tbintb/DT; 85box PD; 86 Mr. Lando/SS; 87 Rajeshpandit1/DT; 88–89 Marcusjones2000/DT; 89 University of College/SS; 90t LOC; 90b Marcusjones2000/DT; 91t 2020 Rob Hainer/SS; 91bl Marcusjones2000/DT; 91br WorldTraveler_1/SS; 92tr Atlanta Fulton County Recreation Authority; 92tl Jack Miller/CC BY-SA 2.0; 92ml MediaPunch Inc/AL; 92bl Brooklynboy321/DT; 93tl Guynamedjames/DT; 93tr Walleyelj/DT; 93tmr Dreammediapeel/DT; 93bmr NARA; 93br RyanW20.01/CC BY-SA 4.0; 94tl Currier & Ives; 94tr PD; 94br Scukrov/DT; 95t Gado Images/AL; 95m Luke Durda/AL; 96tl PD; 96tr LOC; 97tr Chronicle/AL; 97mr PD; 97bl Chronicle/AL; 98ml David Wilson/CC BY 2.0; 98mr William Alden III/ CC BY-SA 2.0; 98bl Wickedgood/DT; 98br piemags/DCM/AL; 99tl fair use; 99tr Mr.schultz/CC BY-SA 3.0; 100–101 Eddtoro35/DT; 102–103 Vlafuente83/DT; 104t Eddtoro35/DT; 104br Littleny/DT; 105 Szgergely/DT; 106t Dleindec/DT; 106br UPI/AL; 107m UPI/AL; 107box Chris Ptacek/CC BY 2.0; 108t PD; 108–109 Julio35/DT; 109tl Chronicle/AL; 110tl Robcorbett/DT; 110tr Science History Images/AL; 109tr National Museum of American History; 110m Robcorbett/DT; 110–111 Wickedgood/DT; 111 Julio35/DT

CENTRAL DIVISION

112tl Ffooter/DT; 112tr Ginosphotos/DT; 112ml Brian1000/DT; 112mr redlegsfan21/CC BY-SA 2.0; 112bl Ffooter/DT; 112br Ffooter/DT; 113tl Ffooter/DT;113bl Ffooter/DT; 113tr Stechouse/DT; 113br Ffooter/DT; 114–115 Balloonguy/DT; 114–115bg Balloonguy/DT; 115 Aaron of L.A. Photography/SS; 116–117 Stacy Revere; 117 Ken Mattison/CC-BY-NC-ND-2.0; 118tr daveynin/CC BY 2.0; 18bl ZUMA Press, Inc./AL; 119 Wisconsinart/DT; 120t Milwaukee County Stadium; 120m grandfather of Robert Jahnke/CC BY-SA 2.0; 120–121 ZUMA Press, Inc./AL; 121m Jwhouk; 121t Wickedgood/DT; 122–123 Carlosphotos/DT; 124–125 Andreykr/DT; 125 Leighleo/DT; 126 Adamwineke/DT; 127tl Todd Awbrey/CC BY-NC-ND 2.0; 127tr Ginosphotos/DT; 127br Ffooter/DT; 128t PD; 128m PD; 128bl DELAYWAVE/CC BY-SA 3.0; 129tr Wickedgood/DT; 129mr Rdikeman/CC BY-SA 3.0; 129br Johnmaxmena; 130 Walleyelj/DT; 131tl slgckgc/CC BY 2.0; 131ml Frutman/DT; 131bl Lagron49/DT; 131mr Walleyelj/DT; 131br Brodogg1313/DT; 132–133 Garry Shear-gshear93/CC0 1.0; 132–133bg Bmosh99/DT; 134t Actionsports/DT; 134b Gepapix/DT; 135 Gina Rodgers/AL; 136box James R. Martin/SS; 136ml Bmosh99/DT; 136b Anderm/DT; 137t Gepapix/DT; 137ml Jim West/AL; 137bl Nyker1/DT; 137br Cal Sport Media/AL; 1385 PD; 138ml LOC; 138mr PD; 138–139 Historic Collection/AL; 139t Chronicle/AL; 140–141 Wickedgood/DT; 141tl Jerryb8/DT; 141tr Jerryb8/DT; 142–143 Antony-022/CC BY-SA 4.0; 143 Alexeys/DT; 144 Alexeys/DT; 145 Ffooter/DT; 146tl Zuma Press, Inc./AL; 146tr Bill Florence/SS; 147t Nathan/CC BY-SA 4.0; 147b Fernando Garcia Esteban/SS; 148t PD; 148bl PD; 148br PD; 149t Cincinnati Reds; 149b Hum Images/AL; 150m Riverfront Stadium; 150b Brent and MariLynn/CC BY 2.0; 150–151 Americanspirit/DT; 151ml Gerald R. Ford Presidential Library; 151br Shelby Bell; 152–153 Joseph Sohm/SS; 152–153 bg PD; 154 Bret Habura/SS; 155bl Mohammedsoliman4/DT; 155br Jenny Solomon/SS; 156 Ken Lund/CC BY-SA 2.0; 157t Jhendrickson3/DT; 157mr Roberto Galan/SS; 157bl Frank Romeo/SS; 158t PD; 158m Glasshouse Images/AL; 159t Chicago History Museum/AL; 159tmr Comiskey Park; 159bmr LOC; 159box Sandrafoyt/DT; 160

Mwkruse/CC BY-SA 3.0; 161 PD; 161b Stephen Reeves/SS; 162tl PD; 162mr UNC Libraries; 162–163 Vintagerie Ephemera Collection/ AL; 163tr RLPM Collection/AL; 163tl Jim West/ AL; 164t RLPM Collection/AL; 164ml Science History Images/AL; 164br Heritage Image Partnership Ltd /AL; 164box PD; 165tr TSN Archives; 165ml PD; 165mr Chuck Franklin/ AL; 165 Parkerjh/CC BY-SA 4.0; 166–167 Clewisleake/DT; 167 Lephotography/DT; 168 UPI/AL; 169 Ffooter/DT; 170 Chrislabasco/DT; 171t Jcsteck7/DT; 171bl Wirestock/DT; 171br Tribune Content Agency LLC/AL; 172–173 Woodsnorthphotography/DT; 172bg PD; 174 Sepavo/DT; 175 Robert Pernell/SS; 176t Zuma Press, Inc./AL; 176b Woodsnorthphotography/ DT; 177t Wally Gobetz/CC BY-NC-ND 2.0; 177b Paul McKinnon/SS; 178t PD; 178b PD; 179t PD; 179b Marc Rockland/CC BY-SA 4.0; 80t PD; 180b PD; 181t Sandrafoyt/DT; 181m Smithsonian; 181b piemags/DCM/AL; 182–183 Karenfoleyphotography/DT; 182–183bg Maniacalv/DT; 183 Cleveland Guardians; 184 Erik Drost/CC BY 2.0; 185t Stechouse/DT; 185m Stechouse/DT; 185b Erik Drost/CC BY 2.0; 186 Droopydogajna/DT; 186–187 Maniacalv/ DT; 188tr PD; 188tl Whitestar666/CC BY-SA 4.0; 188m PD; 188bl Mark Kanning/AL; 188bt LOC; 189t Chronicle/AL; 189m Wasted Time R/ CC BY 3.0; 189b PD; 190–191 Krainiac/DT; 192l Kirkikisphoto/DT; 192–193 Ffooter/DT; 193b Kirkikisphoto/DT; 94t Rwhphoto/DT; 194b Images-USA/AL; 195t Kirkikisphoto/DT; 195b Frank Romeo/SS; 196tl PD; 196tr Fiskness/DT; 196tl PD; 196m Steven R. Swanson/CC BY-SA 4.0; 197t PD; 197m Imdan/DT; 197b Bobak Ha'Eri; 198–199 Walleyelj/DT; 199 Jetcityimage/ DT; 200t 4kclips/DT; 200m RLPM Collection/ AL; 200bl NBL; 200br Boscophotos1/DT; 201tr Ffooter/DT; 201b Americanspirit/DT; 202tl Heaslet/DT; 202tr Wickedgood/DT; 202br Ernitz/ DT; 203 Gnagel/DT; 204 Kirkikisphoto/DT; 205tr Carlosstudios/DT; 205ml Carlosstudios/DT; 205box PD

WEST DIVISION

206tl Ffooter/DT; 206tr Neilld/DT; 206ml Trevg/DT; 206mr Ffooter/DT; 06bl Ffooter/ DT; 206br Tom Haymes/CC BY-NC-SA 2.0; 207tl Splosh/DT; 207tr Chris6d/CC BY-SA 4.0; 207bl redlegsfan21CC BY-SA 2.0; 207br Amy Roswurm/SS; 208–209 mikeledray/SS; 209tl Pictorial Press Ltd/AL; 210 Orange County Archives; 211tl Ken Lund/ CC BY-SA 2.0; 211tr Courtesy Angels; 211bl mikeledray/SS; 211br Ben Olender, Los Angeles Times/digital. library.ucla.edu/CC BY 4.0; 212tr Scukrov/DT; 212–213 CrispyCream27/ CC BY-SA 4.0; 213t Aijohn784/DT; 214t Lohrtom/DT; 215 Usataro/ DT; 216–217 Imdan/DT; 217t Aksitaykut/DT; 218t Harold Stiver/SS; 219box Imdan/DT; 219b Timrobertsaerial/DT; 220t Joseph Hendrickson/ SS; 220b Wickedgood/DT; 221tr Eutoch/DT;221b Ecurb/CC BY-SA 3.0; 222mt LOC; 222mb LOC; 222t The Metropolitan Museum of Art; 222b RLFE Pix/AL; 223t LOC; 223b The Protected Art Archive/AL; 224tl Busch Stadium; 24tr Mikericci/DT; 224ml Actionsports/DT; 225box Library of Congress via Picryl.com; 25b Littleny/ DT; 226–227 Lohrtom/DT; 227t Goldnelk/DT; 228 Rockymtnphoto/DT; 229m Jim West/AL; 230tl Jim West/AL; 229b Wellesenterprises/DT; 230bl Bdingman/DT; 30br Cecouchman/DT; 231t Ffooter/DT; 231b Bdingman/DT; 232 Knapp. keith/CC BY-SA 3.0; 233t Candyceherman/DT; 233b James Kirkikis/SS; 234–235 Wirestock/ DT; 235tr Miune/SS; 236 Wellesenterprises/DT; 237tr Underwatermaui/DT; 237b Ffooter/DT; 237m PD; 238tl Vita1068/DT; 238b Kitleong/DT; 239tl Ffooter/DT; 239tr Wickedgood/DT; 239b Visions of America, LLC/AL; 240tl Lohrtom/DT; 240tr Robert Landau/AL; 240box Peregrine/AL; 241tr Vita1068/DT; 241bl ZUMA Press, Inc./AL; 241br RLFE Pix/AL; 242tl Niday Picture Library/ AL; 242tr PD; 242m Ebbets Field; 242bl Brooklyn Dodgers; 242br PF-(bygone1)/AL; 243tr NY Daily News; 243b Pictures Now/AL; 44tl Picryl.com; 244tr Vita1068/DT; 244ml RCA; 244ml Science History Images/AL; 244bl PD; 245t Walter Cicchetti/SS; 245m trekandshoot/SS; 245b The Sporting News Archives; 246tr RLPM Collection/ AL; 246m Nicescene/SS; 246bl Aspnn/DT; 247t Osugi/SS; 247b Jaruncha/DT; 248t Kampwit/ DT; 248b Juncel1/DT; 249t Sepavo/DT; 249mr tkyszk/SS; 249br Juanalbertocasado/DT; 250–251 4kclips/DT; 251t Luca Marella/DT; 252 Djpillow/DT; 253tl Djpillow/DT; 253tr Djpillow/ DT; 253b Djpillow/DT; 254t Djpillow/DT; 254m Djpillow/DT; 254b Djpillow/DT; 255 Djpillow/ DT; 256t AW Distributors; 256b Clewisleake/DT; 257tl George H.W. Bush Presidential Library and Museum; 257mr Felixcasio/DT; 257b Djpillow/ DT; 258–259 4kclips/DT; 259tr Jhendrickson3/ DT; 260tl PD; 260b Brian Reading/CC BY-SA 3.0; 261t Dgmate/DT; 261b Actionsports/ DT; 262tr Gabbro/AL; 262b Brian Reading/CC BY-SA 3.0; 263mr Brian Reading/CC BY-SA 3.0; 263br mikkaelaraya2012 on DeviantArt; 264 Astrodome; 264b Ed Schipul/CC BY-SA 2.0; 265t Everett Collection Inc/AL; 265b Abaca Press/AL; 266–267 Brodogg1313/DT; 268 Andreistanescu/DT; 269 trekandshoot/SS; 270t David Wa/AL; 270ml Oakland Athletics; 271tr Quintin Soloviev/CC BY-SA 4.0; 271b Eric Broder Van Dyke/SS; 272t PD; 272m PD; 272b Oakland Athletics; 273tr PD; 273b Harry Barth/Harry S. Truman Library; 274–275 Nicholasj309/DT; 276t Nicholasj309/DT; 276br Ffooter/DT; 277tr Brodogg1313/DT; 277bl Conor P. Fitzgerald/SS; 277br Elliottcowand/DT; 278–279 Photobulb/ DT; 279m Elliottcowand/DT; 279tr Brodogg1313/ DT; 280t Hum Images/AL; 280ml PD; 280mr PD; 280b PD; 281tr Everett Collection Historical/AL; 281 ml Morris–Jumel Mansion; 281b Chronicle/ AL;

282t Underwood Archives, Inc/AL; 282–283 Americanspirit/DT; 283tl Heritage Image Partnership Ltd /AL; 283tr Jon Leonoudakis/AL; 283mtr Alon Alexander/ AL; 283mbr Americanspirit/DT; 284–285 Shengyinglin/DT; 286 Shengyinglin/DT; 287t Sherryvsmith/DT; 287b Pradoeddy/DT; 288tl WoodsnorthPhotography/AL; 288br Aerial Archives/AL; 289t Alancrosthwaite/DT; 289bl Keeton Gale/SS; 289box Maximiliankrebs/DT; 290t Wickedgood/DT; 290ml ZUMA Press Inc/AL; 290–291 Wellesenterprises/DT; 291t Keeton10/ DT; 291b ZUMA Press Inc/AL; 292–293 Actionsports/DT; 293 Seattle Mariners; 294 landewarphotography/DT; 295mr Actionsports/ DT; 295b Mickem/DT; 296l Brodogg1313/ DT; 296br Brodogg1313/DT; 297t Ffooter/DT; 297ml Afagundes/DT; 297b clare_and_ben/ CC BY-NC-ND 2.0; 298t Smith Western Co.; 298bWickedgood/DT; 299 Kingdome; 299b agefotostock /AL; 299tl Dave Pattison/AL; 300 Tele52/DT

“If the people don’t want to come out to the ballpark, nobody’s going to stop them.”

——YOGI BERRA, YANKEE CATCHER